MW00794886

John Stark
M. G.

MEMOIR

AND

OFFICIAL CORRESPONDENCE

OF

GEN. JOHN STARK,

WITH NOTICES OF SEVERAL OTHER

OFFICERS OF THE REVOLUTION.

ALSO, A BIOGRAPHY OF

CAPT. PHINEHAS STEVENS,

AND OF

COL. ROBERT ROGERS,

WITH AN ACCOUNT OF HIS

SERVICES IN AMERICA DURING THE "SEVEN YEARS' WAR."

BY CALEB STARK.

CONCORD:
PUBLISHED BY EDSON C. EASTMAN.
1877.

(Cover illustration from *A Revolutionary Pilgrimage* by Ernest Peixotto)

- Notice -

The foxing, or discoloration with age, characteristic of old books, may show through to some extent in reprints such as this, especially when the foxing is very severe in the original book. We feel that the contents of this book warrant its reissue despite these blemishes, and hope you will agree and read it with pleasure.

A Facsimile Reprint
Published 1999 by

HERITAGE BOOKS, INC.
1540E Pointer Ridge Place
Bowie, Maryland 20716
1-800-398-7709
www.heritagebooks.com

ISBN 0-7884-1088-1

TO OUR READERS.

MUCH of the information contained in this volume was obtained from individuals well acquainted with and even related to officers of the "Seven Years' War," and who afterward served with them in the war of the Revolution, to the principal events of which they were eye witnesses. Their narratives of what they had performed and seen have been familiar to us from childhood.

While contemplating the character of the heroes of the Revolution, the scenes in which an important portion of their lives was engaged, and their entire devotion to the cause of their native land, the heart is chilled with the reflection that, of those war-worn veterans—the pioneers of American Independence—a few only now remain, tottering on the verge of the grave, to witness the result of their unparalleled sufferings and victorious toils.

Although the ingratitute of the nation to which their valor gave birth, in neglecting to perform what had solemnly been promised to her officers and soldiers in the hour of that nation's direst peril, caused the suns of many of them to go down in clouds of misfortune, it is imperatively incumbent upon those of the present generation to bestow appropriate honors upon their memory.

It is to be hoped that their posterity, cheered by the perusal of the annals of the past, and inspired with a due sense of gratitude for their national prosperity, will never become objects deserving the insulting taunt that the spirit of the Revolution, which, like an adamantine rock, withstood the angry billows that dashed against it, has become extinct, with the departure of the heroic souls it once animated.

If, in this feeble attempt to throw light upon that desperate and long doubtful struggle, which, under Heaven's favor, founded this now potent nation, it shall be our fortune to rescue from oblivion traits of character and examples of devoted patriotism worthy of imitation, we shall consider our humble labors compensated.

We acknowledge obligations to several gentlemen for information and documents furnished: among whom we name with pleasure, Colonel Henry Stevens, of Burlington, Vermont, President of the Historical and Antiquarian Societies of that State; Charles C. Sheafe, Esq., of Boston; I. S. Hunt, Esq., of Sudbury, Massachusetts; and William F. Goodwin, Esq., of Concord, New-Hampshire; to the authors of the Histories of Concord and Manchester; and J. D. Butler, Esq., author of the address before the Legislature of Vermont, October 20, 1848.

Our production, such as it is, we offer to the consideration of the independent freemen of the United States, who will, we hope, receive it with candid indulgence, and cast the mantle of charity over its errors.

A people who inherit the enviable privilege of occupying the vast domains of this mighty and only Republic on earth, will, we confidently trust, through future ages, continue to be, what their progenitors of the iron days of '76 were—the undaunted champions and guardians of Liberty.

Firm as her hills, may freedom's spirit stand,
Repelling despots from her heaven-blest land;
And never be her glorious standard furled,
Till the dread power who made, shall crush the world.

CONTENTS.

INDEX OF GENERAL STARK'S CORRESPONDENCE.

NOTICE.

A reference has been made in note (page 322) to a portrait intended for this volume. Since the work was printed, a new engraving has been prepared for the frontispiece.

ERRATA.

Page 41, line 14, read one hundred and *fifty* yards.

Page 61, note, for *continental* read *continual.*

Page 333, last paragraph, *current* read *currant.*

MEMOIR OF JOHN STARK.

Archibald Stark was born at Glasgow, Scotland, in 1697, and received his education at the University of that city. At an early age he removed, with his father and family, to Londonderry, Ireland, where he married Eleanor Nichols, the daughter of a Scottish emigrant.

In 1720 he embarked with a company of adventurers for New-Hampshire, whither a considerable party of his countrymen had previously proceeded, to form a settlement.

After a tedious voyage, during which all his children died, the emigrants arrived at Boston late in autumn. As many of them were ill with the small-pox they were not permitted to land, and were, in consequence, compelled to depart for the wilds of Maine. At a place called Sheepscot, near the site of the present town of Wiscasset, they endured their first trial of the horrors of a northern winter in the forests of New-England.

In the course of the year following, after encountering and enduring many severe hardships and privations, they joined their Scottish friends, who had preceded them, at Nutfield, (now Londonderry, N. H.) then a wilderness, rendered hideous by the frequent incursions of hostile savages, who, at that period, and for many succeeding years, harrassed the frontiers. His house in Londonderry having been burned in 1736, he, in consequence, removed to that portion of land on Merrimack river, then known as Harrytown, and settled upon a lot, which had been granted to Samuel Thaxter by the government of Massachusetts, a short distance above the Falls of Amoskeag.

There several of his friends soon afterward followed him, and the new location received the name of Derryfield. Several sons and daughters were born to him, after his arrival in America, to whom, at his fireside, he gave the best education his own acquirements and the circumstances of the times would permit. "His education fitted him for the walks of civil life, yet," says the Historian of Manchester, "we find him a volunteer for the protection of the frontier against the ravages of the Indians in 1745; and for the protection of the people in his immediate neighborhood, a fort was built at the outlet of Swager's, or Fort brook, which, in compliment to his enterprise in erecting and garrisoning the same, was called *Stark's Fort.*"

His sons were William, John, Samuel, and Archibald, who all held commissions in the British service during the "seven years'" or "French war," and were distinguished for good conduct, coolness and bravery. William, the eldest, served with reputation on the northern frontiers, and, under General Wolfe, in the expeditions to Louisburgh and Quebec, where his courage and address rendered signal services. He afterward tarnished his well earned fame by joining the British army at New-York. In 1776 he obtained the rank of colonel of dragoons, but was soon afterward killed by a fall from his horse.

A stone, in the old burial ground at Manchester, bears this inscription:

Here Lyes The Body of Mr.

ARCHIBALD STARK. HE

Departed This Life June 25th,

1758, Aged 61 Years.

At this period hunting was the most agreeable and profitable occupation of the young men of New-Hampshire. They were accustomed, at certain seasons, to dwell in forest camps, at great distances from home, and thus became inured to hardships, and were early taught lessons of self-dependence. They were often, in the pursuit of their vocation, brought in contact with the native savages, from whom they obtained a knowledge of their language and customs, and became excellent marksmen.

Their occupation as hunters, in the wild forest, was admirably adapted to prepare these hardy woodsmen for the arduous services they were soon afterward called upon to render their country, in a war which engaged all the thoughts, fears and energies of New-England.

John Stark, the subject of this memoir, was born at Londonderry, in New-Hampshire, August 28th, 1728. He resided with his father until March, 1752, when, in company with his brother William, David Stinson, and Amos Eastman, he proceeded on a hunting expedition to Baker's river, in the township of Rumney, (now so called) but then a forest, without an inhabitant or name.

They constructed a camp in the woods of hemlock boughs and bark, in which they deposited the supplies of provision, ammunition, traps and necessaries which had been drawn hither on their Indian sleds, and commenced their operations. The game was abundant, and prior to the 28th day of April they had collected furs of the value of five hundred and sixty pounds sterling.

On that day they were interrupted by a scout of ten St. Francis Indians, commanded by a chief named Francis Titigaw. Signs of the enemy had been observed on the previous day, and the party had concluded to leave the hunting ground. John Stark, being the youngest of the party, was directed to collect the traps, and while thus engaged, at sunset, fell into the enemy's hands. While stooping to the water to take up a trap, the Indians suddenly sprang from their ambuscade. A sharp hissing sound, as of a snake, accompanied the movement. He looked up and found himself a prisoner, surrounded by savages, with guns pointed toward him, rendering escape impossible.

When interrogated by his captors in regard to his companions, he pointed in a contrary direction to the true position of their camp, and thus induced them to travel two miles out of their way. His friends, alarmed at his long absence, discharged several guns which discovered their position to the savages, who, proceeding a distance down the river, turned their encampment and formed an ambush to intercept their canoe.

The hunters suspecting what had taken place, were proceeding down the river—William Stark and Stinson in the canoe, and Eastman on the shore. Soon after day break, on the 29th of April, the latter fell into the ambuscade and was taken. The Indians then directed John to hail the boat, and bid the occupants to come on shore. He called to them, stated his own and Eastman's situation, and urged them to escape to the opposite shore.

Perceiving the boat turned from its course, a portion of the Indians rose and fired into it. At this critical instant, Stark had the daring temerity to strike up their guns; and when the remainder were about to fire, struck all the guns he could reach. One ball, however, pierced the canoe paddle in the hands of William Stark, and another killed Stinson. John then shouted to his brother to escape, as they had fired all their guns. He profited by the advice and made good his retreat.*

* After the return of William Stark to the settlements, a party from Rumford (now Concord, N. H.) started for the scene of the disaster. They found the body of Stinson stripped and scalped, which they buried in the woods, near the place where he fell; and returned in safety, bringing home the paddle of the canoe pierced with a ball.

Baker's river is a small stream flowing into the *Pemigewasset*, and is so called from Captain Thomas Baker, of North-Hampton, Mass., who, in 1720, with a scouting party of thirty-four men, passed up Connecticut river, and crossed the heights of land to the Pemigewasset; where, at the junction of that river with the small stream above named, he destroyed a party of Indians, killing their chief, Wattanummon, with his own hand, himself and the sachem firing at each other at the same moment.

Exasperated by this conduct of their prisoner, the Indians beat him severely; made prize of all the furs collected by the party, and proceeded to the place now occupied by the town of Haverhill, upon Connecticut river, where two of their party had been stationed to obtain and prepare provisions for the returning scout. There they tarried one night, and continued their route to the Upper Coös. From thence they dispatched three of their party, with Eastman, to St. Francis. The remainder of the Indians employed themselves, for some time, in hunting upon a small stream called John's river.

The prisoner was liberated during the day, but confined at night. While there, they allowed him to try his luck as a hunter. He succeeded in trapping one beaver, and shooting another; and received their skins as a present in compliment to his skill.

The Indians, with their captive, arrived at St. Francis on the 9th of June following, where he remained nearly five weeks. He was well treated by the tribe, and obtained a knowledge of their language and modes of warfare, which proved of great service to him in his subsequent military career. In July, Mr. Wheelwright, of Boston, and Captain Stevens, of Charlestown, N. H., who were the agents employed by Massachusetts to redeem her captives, arrived at Montreal. Not finding the prisoners they expected to find, belonging to Massachusetts, they redeemed Stark and Eastman; and, returning by way of Albany, arrived at Derryfield in August following. The ransom of Stark was one hundred and three dollars, and that of his friend Eastman sixty dollars.† These sums

He destroyed their wigwams, and the party, loading themselves with as much of the fur, collected by the enemy, as they could carry home, burned the remainder.—*Farmer's Hist. Coll.*

A considerable branch flows into Baker's river, from Stinson's pond, and is called Stinson's brook. The pond is four hundred rods long, and two hundred and eighty rods wide. Its name is probably derived from the circumstance that David Stinson was killed in its vicinity by the savages, April 29th, 1752.*—*Hayward's Gaz.*

* On a journey to the White Mountains we last year visited the place.

† Eastman was sold to a Frenchman.

were *never repaid by the State.* Massachusetts, pursuing a more liberal policy, redeemed all her captives.

It may here be remarked, as a singular fact, that the scout which captured these prisoners accompanied the returning party to Albany, and there disposed of the furs taken from them without molestation.

When the prisoners arrived at St. Francis, they were compelled to undergo the ceremony of running the gantlet. The young warriors of the tribe arranged themselves in two lines, each armed with a rod or club to strike the captive, as he passed them, singing some ditty which had been taught him for the occasion, and bearing in his hands a pole six or eight feet long, with the skin of some bird or animal attached to one end of it.

Eastman advanced first, singing words which meant, "I'll beat all your young men." The latter, considering themselves insulted, beat him so severely with their rods that he fell exhausted as soon as he had passed the lines.*

Stark followed, singing the words, "I'll kiss all your women," his pole being ornamented with a loon skin. After receiving a blow or two, he turned his pole right and left, dealing a blow at each turn, and made his way without much injury, his enemies making way for him to avoid the sweeping blows dealt by his pole.

This feat pleased the old Indians, who enjoyed the sport at their young men's expense.

The principal portion of the labor and menial drudgery of Indians is performed by squaws and captives. They directed Stark to hoe corn. He at first carefully *hoed* the weeds, and *cut up* the corn; but finding his purpose of freeing himself from the labor not answered by this process, he boldly threw his hoe into the river, declaring that "it was the business of squaws, and not warriors, to hoe corn."

* Stark stated that the first one who struck him was a youth, whom he knocked down; and that he did not see him again while he remained at the village.

Instead of being enraged at this action, the Indians were pleased with his boldness, released him from his task, and called him "young chief." He was adopted by the sachem, and treated with kindness while he remained at the village. In the latter days of his life he often related, with much humor, the incidents of his captivity, observing that he had experienced more genuine kindness from the savages of St. Francis, than he ever knew prisoners of war to receive from more civilized nations.

Not daunted by this unfortunate enterprise, our adventurer repaired the next season to the river Androscoggin to pursue his vocation, and *raise means to discharge his redemption debt.* Upon this occasion he was very successful, and returned with a valuable lot of fur.

The reports of these prisoners, concerning the *Coös Territory*, induced the authorities of the province to dispatch a party to explore this hitherto unknown region. Colonel Lovewell, Major Talford and Captain Page were ordered to enlist a company for that service. They engaged Mr. Stark as their guide, and under his direction, on the 10th of March, 1753, their journey was commenced.

In seven days they reached Connecticut river at Piermont. There they passed one night; and, having made such observations as their time would allow, returned, reaching Concord on the thirteenth day from the time of their departure. An account of the proceedings of this surveying party, with the names of the company, is to be found in the History of Manchester.

In 1754 a report was current that the French were erecting a fort at the Upper Coös; and Captain Powers was dispatched by Governor Wentworth with thirty men and a flag of truce, to demand their authority for so doing. He applied to Mr. Stark to accompany him, who conducted the party to the Upper Coös, by way of the Little Ox-Bow, by the same route he had traveled two years before, as a captive to the Indians. Finding no French garrison there, the company returned, being, we believe, the first party of English adventurers who explored the Coös intervals, where are now located the flourishing towns of Haverhill and Newbury.

Mr. Stark had acquired so much reputation by these expeditions, that, upon the breaking out of the "seven years' war," he was commissioned by the Governor as second lieutenant of Rogers' company of rangers, attached to Blanchard's regiment. Captain Rogers, possessing a bold and adventurous spirit, soon mustered a band of rugged foresters, every man of whom, as a hunter, could hit the size of a dollar at a hundred yards' distance; could follow the trail of man or beast; endure the fatigues of long marches, the pangs of hunger, and the cold of winter nights, often passed without fire, shelter, or covering, other than their common clothing, a blanket, perhaps a bearskin, and the boughs of the pine or hemlock.

Their knowledge of Indian character, customs and manners, was accurate. They were principally recruited in the vicinity of Amoskeag Falls; where Rogers was accustomed to meet them at the annual fishing season; whom he knew to be accustomed to traveling in forests, and hunting, and upon whose courage and fidelity implicit confidence could be placed. They were men who could face, with equal resolution, the savage animals of their native woods, the mountain tempests, or engage in the combat of heroes.

In the summer of 1755, Rogers, with his command, was ordered to Coös to burn the intervals, preparatory to the erection of a fort. Before reaching their place of destination, a new order directed them to join their regiment, at Fort Edward, by way of Number Four. They reached headquarters in August, a short time before the provincial army, under the command of General Johnson, was attacked by the French and Indians, at the south end of Lake George, near Bloody pond, so named from the slaughter on this occasion.

The French were defeated with the loss of one thousand killed, wounded and prisoners, with all their baggage. Their general, the Baron Dieskau, was wounded and taken prisoner. General Johnson was created a baronet; but the honors bestowed upon him were earned and deserved by General Lyman, who was the real hero of the battle of Lake George.

After the enemy gave way, he urged a pursuit; but Johnson, having received a slight wound, became alarmed, and would not allow of it. In fact, he never commenced the erection of the fort, afterward called William Henry, until the rangers returned from a reconnoitering scout, with the information that the French were building a fortress at Ticonderoga. The campaign passed without any other occurrence worthy of notice. In autumn the regiment was discharged, and Lieutenant Stark returned home.

In the winter of 1756 the British commander at Fort Edward resolved to establish a permanent corps of rangers, to counteract the operations of the French and Indian scouts, which harassed the frontiers, and hung upon the wings of the army. Rogers was appointed to enlist and command the corps. He selected Stark again for his second lieutenant, (his own brother, Richard, being his first lieutenant) raised a company, and in April following reported himself and soldiers at Fort Edward.

Although no important military operations were attempted during this campaign, the rangers were constantly on foot, watching the motions of the enemy at Crown Point and Ticonderoga, cutting off their convoys of supplies, and often making prisoners of sentinels at their posts. One of their parties brought in the scalp of a French sentinel, killed near the gate of Crown Point. The rangers sometimes used the scalping knife, in retaliation for the cruelties of the French and their savage allies.

"On one of our expeditions," says Rogers, "my lord Howe did me the honor to accompany me, being desirous, as he expressed himself, of learning our method of marching, ambushing, retreating, &c.; and on our return expressed his opinion of us very generously." George, Lord Viscount Howe, was at this time second in command of the British forces in the north.

In the autumn of 1756 the corps of rangers was reinforced by two companies from Halifax, which raised it to the force of three hundred, strong. These hardy woodsmen were familiar with all the practices of the French and Indian partisans, and, in many a fierce conflict, evinced their ability to contend with and defeat them upon their own terms, either of force or stratagem.

In January, 1757, a detachment of rangers marched from Fort William Henry to intercept supplies passing between Crown Point and Ticonderoga. They passed over Lake George, and turned the latter fortress, without being observed. They captured several sleds, and destroyed their loading. One sled, however, escaped, and was driven back to the fort.

Knowing that the garrison would immediately be notified of their presence in the vicinity, the party commenced their retreat homeward; when, at the distance of three miles from Ticonderoga, they were, in the afternoon of January 21st, suddenly attacked by a force of French and Indians, springing from concealment in their front. The strength of the enemy was in numbers more than double that of their own, and a sanguinary action ensued. According to the numbers engaged, a more desperate and bloody encounter did not occur during the war. Rogers was twice wounded, Captain Spikeman killed, and the command devolved upon Lieutenant Stark, as senior officer; who, by his prudence and firmness, secured the wounded, and drew off the detachment in such order as to keep the enemy at bay. By marching all night, they reached Lake George at eight o'clock next morning. The wounded, who, during the night march, had kept up their spirits, were by that time so overcome with cold, fatigue, and loss of blood, that they could march no farther. It became, therefore, necessary to forward a notice to the fort, that sleighs might be sent for them. Lieutenant Stark volunteered for this purpose, and, by undergoing extraordinary fatigues, reached Fort William Henry, distant forty miles, the next evening.* Sleighs were immediately dispatched to bring in the wounded, who arrived at the fort on the evening of the 23d of January.

General Stark stated, in after times, that he was never conscious of taking the life of an individual except in this action. While the rangers were defending their position on the crest of the hill, he observed that several balls struck near him from a certain direction. In a moment afterward he discovered an Indian stretched at full length upon a rock, behind a large tree. His gun was soon ready, and he saw the Indian rising for another shot at him. His fusee was instantly leveled, discharged, and the savage rolled from the rock into the snow, pierced by the bullet through the head. †

Rogers, after he received his second wound, advised a retreat; but Stark, now having the command, and being almost the only officer fit for duty, declared that he had a good position, and would fight the enemy until dark, and then retreat; that in such a course consisted their only safety; and that he would shoot the first man who fled. While speaking thus, a ball broke the lock of his gun; and, at the same moment, observing a Frenchman fall, he sprang forward, seized his gun, returned to his place, and continued the action. His decision, prudence and courage no doubt saved the party in the present instance, and afterward contributed much toward the attainment of that success and celebrity which distinguished the career of the rangers in the campaigns of the "seven years' war." So said many of his veteran comrades.

In the reorganization of the corps, he was promoted to fill the vacancy occasioned by the death of Captain Spikeman.

* The snow was at this time four feet deep upon a level, and the journey was performed on snow-shoes.

† He was at this period twenty-eight years of age. He had been an expert and successful hunter, and was well known to be one of the best marksmen of his time; and the most savage animals of his native forests—the catamounts, bears, wolves and wildcats—in numerous instances, felt the effects of his unerring aim.

In March, 1757, while commander of the rangers stationed at Fort William Henry, one of his eccentricities saved the garrison from surprise and capture.

At this time Fort Edward, on the Hudson, and Fort William Henry, at the south end of Lake George, were the two most northerly frontier posts of the British dominions in North America. They were situated fifteen miles apart. The latter fort was at this period occupied by an Irish regiment, and about one hundred and fifty rangers. The nearest French post was Ticonderoga, forty miles northward.

With the exception of the uneasiness occasioned by the small-pox, then among them, the garrison at Fort William Henry rested in confident security on the night of March 17, 1757.

While going his rounds, on the evening of the 16th, Captain Stark overheard a squad of his men, who were of the Scotch-Irish race, planning a celebration in honor of St. Patrick, for the next night. He afterward said he had then no presentiment of approaching danger, but disliked these wild Irish demonstrations. He therefore called for the ranger sutler, Samuel Blodget, and gave him directions to deliver the rangers their regular rations of grog until the evening of the 17th; and after that, no more, without a written order from himself. On that evening he retired to his quarters, directing his orderly sergeant to say to all applicants for written orders that he was confined to his bunk with a lame right hand, and would not be disturbed. The Irish troops received an extra supply of rum on the night of the 16th, and commenced their carousal, which they carried on with unabated vigor through the night and during the ensuing day, in honor of St. Patrick, and his wife Shelah. They drank so freely that the officer of the day could find none of them fit for duty as sentinels; and the rangers, who were sober, supplied their places. The rangers, seeing the Irish thus enjoying themselves, desired the same privilege. The sutler informed them of his orders, and the captain's quarters were beset to obtain a written order. The orderly refused to disturb his officer, as he was confined with a painfully lame right hand, and could not write. The soldiers felt somewhat cross, but bore their disappointment like philosophers.

At two o'clock on the morning of the 18th, a ranger sentinel on the ramparts observed a light upon the lake, and soon afterward became aware that a large force was advancing in the direction of the fortress.

Notice was instantly conveyed to the ranger captain. The lame hand was instantly restored to health, and he was among his soldiers. The commander of the post was quietly notified, and the rangers silently mustered upon the walls. The French army, of more than twenty-five hundred men, with a large force of Indians in their rear, commanded by General, the Marquis Vaudreuil, advanced and halted within about thirty rods of the fort. A detachment of five hundred men immediately came forward with scaling ladders, thinking to carry the place by surprise.

They planted their ladders, and mounted; but as the foremost men were about placing their feet upon the ramparts, a deep, stern voice gave the word "fire." A volley of musketry was instantly poured, with fatal effect, upon the assailants, while the guns of the fortress opened with grape and canister upon the columns in the rear. The enemy were repulsed, and fell back, confused and mortified.

The expedition had been concerted with the hope of carrying the fort by surprise, in consequence of the excesses which the French general knew would be committed by the adorers of St. Patrick, upon the anniversary of that worthy saint's birth. The roar of the guns dissipated the fumes of alcohol from the brains of the regulars; and the garrison was soon in condition for a vigorous defence.

At day light the French general sent a flag of truce by his lieutenant general of artillery, (he brought, however, no artillery on this occasion) and formally summoned the garrison to surrender. He stated that "they occupied territory belonging to his most christian majesty, the King of France. He offered them their lives, and the officers were to be allowed to retain their baggage and side arms; the troops were to march out with the honors of war. He suggested, however, that it would be well for them to bestow some presents upon the Indians, to keep them quiet; that if these terms were not accepted, a general assault would be made by their whole army, and if the fort was taken, no quarter would be given."

The messenger had been brought in blind-fold, and after delivering his message was conducted to another apartment, while the council of war considered their answer. It was gallantly and unanimously resolved, by the officers, to bury themselves in its ruins, rather than surrender the fortress. The disastrous defeat of General Braddock, two years previously, was fresh in the memory of the soldiers. They crowded around the commander's quarters, anxiously awaiting the council's decision. "Monongahela and revenge," were the words shouted by the men. The French officer was again brought before the council, where the colonel commanding gave him their answer, allowing him twenty minutes to regain the French army.

In the course of the day a general attack was made upon the fort, with great obstinacy and perseverance, upon four different points, but was, at every position assailed, gallantly repulsed by its heroic defenders.

The enemy then burned a vessel on the stocks, set fire to the wood-piles and the rangers' summer huts, outside of the walls, and after a siege of five days retreated, carrying away most of their wounded. They concealed their loss in killed by cutting holes in the ice and throwing into the lake the bodies of the slain, after having, as report says, scalped them, to obtain the bounty then offered by both governments for the scalps of their enemies. Several wounded prisoners, who were brought in after the French had retreated, reported that their orders were, if the place was carried, to put every man, woman and child in it to death.

On the part of the garrison not a man was killed, and but few wounded. Captain Stark was struck by a spent ball, which produced a slight contusion, but drew no blood. It was not a wound, but was the only injury he ever received from an enemy's weapon during the whole course of his military career.

Some time after this affair, a few gentlemen from Nantucket, strangers to him, presented Captain Stark with a cane, made from the bone of a whale, headed with ivory, as a token of their admiration of his conduct in the defence of Fort William Henry. The cane is still in the possession of his family.

Thus terminated the first siege of Fort William Henry, in March, 1757. In the month of August following, it was surrendered to the Marquis de Montcalm, after a siege of nine days, and entirely destroyed.

The cause of its capture was as follows: In 1757 the Earl of Loudoun was appointed commander-in-chief of the British forces in North America. He came to America with the hope of reaping a harvest of laurels, but gained none.

He drew off most of the forces from the north to Nova Scotia, threatened Louisburgh and Quebec, but effected nothing except a waste of time and treasure. He left a garrison of 4,000 men at Fort Edward, under the command of General Webb, an inefficient and imbecile officer, who suffered Fort William Henry to be besieged and reduced by the French, without making the slightest effort for its relief. General Wolfe, in his position, would have acted a bolder part, and no doubt have compelled the enemy to retreat. Sir William Johnson came to Fort Edward and urged General Webb to make a movement for the relief of the besieged fort. The troops were once paraded for that purpose; but Webb's courage failing him, they were ordered back to their quarters, and a message dispatched to Colonel Monroe, advising him to capitulate on the best terms he could obtain.

Captain Stark proceeded to New-York to join the eastern expedition, but was there attacked with the small-pox, and compelled to remain until the return of the armament. After his recovery he rejoined the army at Albany, in October, and passed the winter at Fort Edward.

In March, 1758, Lord Loudoun returned to England, having added nothing to his military reputation by his American campaign.

The command of the British forces now devolved upon Major-General James Abercrombie, who resolved to attempt the reduction of Ticonderoga. Preparations were accordingly commenced to assemble for that purpose the most powerful armament ever mustered in America. In addition to a large force of disciplined regulars, numerous detachments of provincials were called out, and every preparation made to insure success. Of this army, Lord Viscount Howe was second in command.

"On the morning of July 5th the whole army (of 16,000 men) embarked in bateaux for Ticonderoga (on the waters of Lake George.) The order of march afforded a splendid military show. The regular troops occupied the centre, and the provincials formed the wings. For the advanced guard, the light infantry flanked the right, and the rangers the left, of Bradstreet's bateau men."

The services of Captain Stark had long before this period attracted the notice of Lord Howe, by whom he had been treated with great kindness and respect. His lordship had accompanied the rangers on a scout; and had, on that occasion, been conducted to the summit of Mount Defiance, a mountain eight hundred feet in height, overlooking and commanding the works of Ticonderoga. He perceived, at that time, the advantage which a few pieces of heavy artillery, placed there in battery, would afford a besieging army over the garrison. But General Abercrombie, supposing his force of sufficient strength to carry the place by assault, brought no artillery with his army.

On the evening before the attack, Captain Stark had a long conversation with Lord Howe in his tent, seated with him upon the bear-skins which composed his lordship's camp-bed, respecting the mode of attack, and the position of the fort. They supped together, and orders were given him for the rangers to carry the bridge, between Lake George and the plains of Ticonderoga, at an early hour in the morning.

On the morning of July 6th, they advanced at day-light; but on approaching the bridge, Rogers, who was with the front column, perceiving a body of French and Indians prepared to dispute the passage, halted a few moments, which caused the rear guard, which was advancing rapidly, to press upon the front. Stark, who led the rear column, not knowing the cause of the delay and confusion consequent upon the halting of the front column, rushed forward, exclaiming, "It is no time for delay;" and calling on the troops to follow, pushed boldly on to the bridge, where, after a contest of a few minutes, the enemy broke and fled, leaving a clear passage for the army.

The attacks upon the French lines were made on the 6th, 7th and 8th of July, and proved unsuccessful, partly through the overweening confidence of the commander-in-chief, in neglecting to bring up his artillery with the army, at the expense of 1,608 regulars, and 334 provincials killed, wounded and prisoners. The French force under Montcalm scarcely amounted to 3000 men, Indians included.

Of those who fell, none was more regretted than Lord Howe, who was mortally wounded in the action with the enemy's advanced guard. He had driven them in, but following up his success too closely, received a fatal wound. His fall checked the advance of the army, and paralyzed their efforts. Other attacks were made, but without success. On the evening of the 8th, the General ordered a retreat, directing the "corps of rangers to cover his rear." In general orders next day, he thanked the army for their good behavior—a compliment which his troops could not bestow upon their general.

The following extract relates to transactions of the afternoon and evening of the 7th of July, 1758.

"Major Rogers held the position with 450 men, while Captain Stark, with the remainder of the rangers, (250) went with Captain Abercrombie and Colonel Clerk to reconnoitre the enemy's works. They returned in the evening, Colonel Clerk reporting that the enemy's works were of little importance.

Captain Stark, however, was of a different opinion; and did not hesitate to say that the French had formidable preparations for defence. Stark was but a provincial woodsman, and Clerk a British engineer. The opinion of the former was unheeded, while, most unfortunately, the advice of the latter was followed.

Early on the morning of the 8th, Abercrombie, relying upon the report of his engineer, as to the flimsy nature of the French defences, determined to commence the attack without bringing up his artillery." *

The regret of Captain Stark for the fate of the gallant Lord Howe, who thus fell at the age of thirty-three, lasted his lifetime. He often remarked, however, during the Revolution, that he became more reconciled to his fate, since his talents, had he lived, might have been employed against the United States. He considered him the ablest commander under whom he ever served. To his military services and private virtues the General Court of Massachusetts paid an honorable tribute, by causing a monument to be erected to his memory, in Westmister Abbey.

Until the close of the campaign the rangers were constantly employed in excursions to the French forts, and in pursuit of their flying parties.

Returning home on furlough, Captain Stark was, on the 20th of August, 1758, married to Elizabeth, daughter of Captain Caleb Page, one of the original proprietors of Dunbarton, N. H.

* History of Manchester.

In the spring of 1759, having enlisted a new company, he returned to Fort Edward, and was present under General Amherst, at the reduction of Ticonderoga and Crown Point. After the surrender of the latter fort, he was ordered by that general, with a force of two hundred rangers, to construct a road through the wilderness from Crown Point to Number Four, on Connecticut river.

The capitulation of Canada put an end, for the time, to military operations in America. This circumstance, together with the jealousies of the British officers, induced him to leave the service. General Amherst assured him, by an official letter, of his protection; and that, if he should be inclined to reënter the service, he should not lose his rank by retiring.

In the campaign of 1759, the name of Captain Stark is mentioned several times in general orders, as follows:

June 13, 1759. "Captain Stark, with his company of rangers, will join the detachment from the 'four mile post.'"

June 27. "Captain Stark will have a red flag in his bateau; and every bateau must be near enough to call to each other, and ready to follow Captain Stark immediately, as he knows where the covering party is posted, and will row in at a proper time. The fishermen will take their arms, which Captain Loring will deliver; and great care must be taken that they are not too much crowded. Captain Stark will receive his orders when the whole is to return from Major Campbell."

According to the above order, a large detachment of rangers and other troops were sent out in bateaux, covered by a strong force on shore, that fresh-fish might be procured for the use of the army, one bateau being allowed to each battalion.

October 10. "Captain Stark is to man three whale boats, with seven men each, and to attend such directions as he shall receive from Captain Loring."

After the conquest of Canada had been completed, Captain Stark returned home, and directed his attention to the cultivation of a large farm, to the care of his mills, and the settlement of a new township, first called Starkstown, and afterwards Dunbarton, from the town and castle in Scotland, from the vicinity of which his ancestors emigrated; himself, his brother William, and Captain Caleb Page being the principal proprietors of the new township. From the time he left the army, until 1774, he uniformly espoused the cause of his countrymen; and from his military services and respectable standing, was a person around whom could rally the people of his vicinity, and exchange ideas upon the then critical situation of the provinces.

He was appointed one of the committee of safety, and discharged the difficult duties devolving upon him with firmness and moderation, endeavoring, to the utmost of his abilities, to promote union of sentiment and preparation for action, should that become necessary.

The transactions of April 19, 1775, rendered no longer doubtful the course to be pursued by patriots and friends of the land that gave them birth.

The cry of blood from Lexington and Concord had sounded the tocsin of alarm, and roused a nation to arms. "The sword had been drawn and the scabbard thrown away!"

Captain Stark received the report of these events while occupied in his saw-mill. He immediately returned to his house—a mile distant—changed his dress, mounted a horse, and proceeded toward the theatre of action. Being well known along the route, he encouraged the people to volunteer, telling them that the time had arrived when a blow should be struck for the liberties of their country, and recommended Medford as a place of rendezvous. Thither he was followed by many of his old soldiers, and hundreds of citizens, who thus answered his appeal to their patriotism.

His important public services, and uniform attachment to the cause of equal rights, were potent inducements in the minds of his countrymen who, at his call, had appeared in arms, to elect him their colonel by an unanimous vote. Isaac Wyman was chosen lieutenant colonel, and Andrew McClary major of the regiment.

The late venerable Jonathan Eastman, senior, informed the writer that the election took place at the hall of a tavern, in Medford, afterward called the New-Hampshire Hall; that it was a hand vote, and he held up his hand for his friend John Stark.

A regiment containing thirteen full companies was soon organized, and reduced to a tolerable state of discipline. As the colonel had left home at ten minutes' notice, he returned to arrange his affairs. Having accomplished this object, he joined the army for the campaign.

While examining Noddle's island with a party of officers, by request of General Ward, with a view to erect batteries against the British shipping, their object having been accomplished, on their return, they discovered a British party upon the same errand. The latter attempted to cut off their retreat by seizing their boat, which, after exchanging a few shots, they reached, and returned to camp.

At the battle of Bunker's hill the New-Hampshire regiments constituted the left wing of the American line, and the attacks of the enemy were repulsed in a manner worthy of the brightest days of chivalry.

The regiment opposed to the New-Hampshire line was the Welsh fusileers, which had been distinguished at the battle of Minden, and was considered the finest light infantry regiment in the British army.

"The troops advanced, and displayed in front of our line," (said an eye witness) "with the coolness and precision of troops upon parade. Not a shot was fired until they came within eighty yards of our line, when a fire opened upon them so rapid and deadly that in a few moments they broke and fled in confusion. They were immediately rallied, reinforced, again led to the attack, and once more gave way before the fatal fire of the New-Hampshire marksmen. A third attempt was made to turn our left, which was repulsed with great slaughter.

No farther attempts were made to turn our flank. Our men were brought into action with the utmost coolness, and without being fatigued. Colonel Stark observed to Captain Henry Dearborn, who suggested the propriety of hastening the march over Charlestown neck, which was enfiladed by the guns of the frigate Lively on one side, and two floating batteries on the other, that "one fresh man in action was worth ten tired ones."

The Welsh fusileers came into the field more than 700 strong, and mustered but 83 on parade next morning. In the heat of the action some one reported to Colonel Stark that his son, a youth under sixteen years of age, who had followed him to the field, had just been killed. "If he is," said the veteran, "it is no time to talk of private affairs while the enemy are advancing in our front. Back to your post!" The report proved groundless; the son referred to was unhurt; was a staff officer throughout the war, and was the youngest survivor of the action who was present when the corner stone of the Bunker hill monument was laid in 1825.*

The position occupied by the New-Hampshire troops was at the rail fence, about forty yards in the rear of the redoubt, toward Mystic river. The hay had been recently mown, and lay in windrows and cocks upon the field. Two fences, forming a lane, ran parallel to each other along their front. The rails of one were taken up and passed through those of the other, while the hay, suspended from top to bottom, gave the whole line the appearance of a breast-work. This arrangement, hastily prepared, served to deceive the enemy, and give confidence to the men, although it was in reality no defencive cover.

When the redoubt was carried, and retreat became unavoidable, Colonel Stark drew off his troops in such order as not to be pursued. The men were unwilling to quit their position, having repulsed the enemy so often as to consider themselves completely victorious. While the

* See Memoir of Major Caleb Stark, contained in this volume.

British were storming the redoubt, these troops could hardly be prevented from leaving their lines and attacking the enemy's rear. Their commander had witnessed such scenes before. He foresaw the fate of the redoubt; knew that his men had but few bayonets, and but one or two rounds of ammunition remaining. He therefore considered any attempt to succor the right of the line would be an act of madness.

General Gage, surveying the scene of action from the cupola of the Province House, just before the attack, remarked to one of his staff, who inquired whether he thought the rebels would await the assault of the royal troops, "that if one John Stark was with them, they would fight; for he was a brave fellow and had served under him, in 1758–9, at Lake George."

The late General Winslow, of Boston, was on the ground at 10 o'clock, the day after the action. (Sunday.) Before a wall hastily thrown upon the beach of Mystic river, he counted 96 men dead; he saw no officers among them, as they had probably been removed. The company of Captain John Moore was posted behind the stone-wall at that place.*

* A merchant of Boston, writes to his brother in Scotland, June 24, 1775: "To the great satisfaction of all good men, Doctor Warren was slain, who was one of their first and greatest leaders."

"Early next morning I went over and saw the field of battle, before any of the dead were buried, which was the first thing of the sort I ever saw; and I pray God I may never have the opportunity of seeing the like again. The rebels are employed since that day fortifying all the hills and passes within four miles, to prevent the troops from advancing into the country. We hourly expect the troops to make a movement against them; but they are too few in numbers, not less than 20,000 being equal to the task. I cannot help mentioning one thing which serves to show the hellish disposition of the accursed rebels: by parcels of ammunition left on the field, their balls were all found to be poisoned!" About as rational as were the British officers, who, mistrusting the buzzing of large flying bugs in the evening for something different, wrote to England that the rebels fired at them with air guns!

It was the intention of the enemy to have occupied Dorchester heights. The dispositions for that purpose were made, and the 18th of June was the day appointed to carry the design into effect. Fortunately the appearance of the Americans on Breed's hill, on the morning of the 17th, disconcerted the plan; and the losses sustained in the action of that day so weakened the British forces, that the expedition to Dorchester heights was postponed, and in due time the position was occupied by the Americans. Its battery expelled the British from Boston.

It is a singular coincidence that the battle of Bunker's hill, in 1775, and that of Bennington, in 1777, were fought on Saturday, commencing at nearly the same hour.

The British official report admitted a loss of 1,064 killed and wounded; while that of the provincials was about 334. The ground along the whole line of the rail fence was thickly strewn with dead and wounded.

We may truly consider that the memorable stand made on the heights of Charlestown, by a small force of undisciplined and ill-armed yeomanry, was, in its moral influence, to the American revolution, what the defence at the pass of Thermopylæ was to the campaign of Xerxes.

It partially convinced the arrogant invaders of our soil, that to conquer American rebels on the floor of parliament was a less formidable task than to subdue them while with arms in their hands, defending the fair fields of their country, their homes, their fire-sides, and the tombs of their forefathers.

Immediately after the retreat, intrenchments were formed by the New-Hampshire line at Winter hill; and the campaign passed away in a few abortive projects for settling the rank of general and field officers, and in reënlisting the troops.

We have often heard the following incident related, which, although no conflict ensued, exhibited traits of character of the men who fought at Breed's hill, and who composed a portion of the force which held the British army for nearly a year in a state of seige at Boston.

After the batteries on Dorchester heights had opened their fire upon the town, Admiral Graves called upon General Sir William Howe, and stated that unless the rebels were dislodged from those heights, he could not keep a ship in the harbor. Orders were immediately issued for a strong force to embark in boats at night, and proceed to storm the heights. The troops were accordingly embarked, but a furious tempest suddenly arising, placed the detachment in extreme peril, and compelled the abandonment of the enterprise.

A flag of truce was soon afterward sent to the American lines, proposing that if the cannonade was discontinued, the British army would evacuate Boston on or before a specified day in March, (ten days being the limit of the truce.) The terms were accepted by General Washington, and the firing ceased.

The proposed time expired, and no notice was received from the enemy to signify that they intended to comply with the terms of the truce. Washington, supposing he had been made a dupe of British treachery and falsehood, determined to attack and carry the town by assault. He ordered a strong force to enter the town by way of Roxbury neck, while at the same time a force, under the command of Colonel Stark, was directed to pass over on rafts and carry the battery on Copp's hill.

The wife of Colonel Stark was at this time in the camp on a visit; and was directed by him to mount on horseback, after the embarkation of the troops, and remain in sight to watch the result. If the party were fired upon, she was directed to ride into the country, spread the alarm, and arouse the people.

The troops effected their passage over the river unmolested. She observed them land, advance up the height and take possession of the battery. The enemy's rear guard were then embarking at the end of Long wharf.

The troops, on entering the works, found the guns loaded, and lighted matches lying beside them, indicating that mischief had been intended; but, for some reason, the design had not been carried out.

General Washington entered by way of the neck, and the Americans obtained possesion of a ravaged town, the inhabitants of which could hardly realize the fact that they were free from the merciless exactions and despotic sway of British tyranny.

The wife of General Stark has often related this incident.

After the evacuation of Boston, Colonel Stark was ordered, with two regiments—the fifth and twenty-fifth—under his command, to proceed to New-York and assist in arranging the defences of that city, where he remained until May, 1776, when his regiment, with five others, was ordered to march by way of Albany to Canada.

He joined the army at St. John's, and advanced to the mouth of the Sorelle. There he met the army retreating from Quebec, commanded by General Thomas. While there, the latter died of the small-pox, and the command devolved upon General Arnold, who employed himself in plundering the merchants of Montreal, for his private emolument, making use of his official station to cover his exactions. He boldly seized upon property as he pleased, threatening and sometimes using force. A large amount of goods was conveyed to Albany, and sold for his benefit.*

He was soon, however, superseded in his command by General Sullivan. The latter was persuaded to detach an expedition against Trois Rivières. This movement was strongly opposed by Colonel Stark, as being imprudent and hazardous. It was formed in the face of the enemy, and on the opposite side of the St. Lawrence, or Lake St. Pierre, nearly ten miles broad, at a time when the enemy had a strong naval force on the river, and the Americans none. The expedition proved a failure, as Stark had predicted, and its commander, General Thompson, was made prisoner.

Upon their return, the remains of this ill-fated enterprise suffered severe losses by the small-pox, which quickly spread through the army. A retreat now became necessary. It was ably conducted by General Sullivan, before the close pursuit of a superior force, which continued until the troops reached St. John's. Not a boat or piece of artillery was lost. The troops, after setting fire to all the public buildings and barracks at St. John's, embarked in boats for the Isle aux Noix. Colonel Stark, with his staff, was in the last boat that left the shore. They were in

* Eor farther particulars, see Wilkinson's Memoirs.

sight when the advanced guard of the enemy arrived among the smoking ruins. On the 18th of June the army encamped upon the Isle aux Noix, and before the enemy could prepare boats to pursue, they had again embarked, and safely landed at Crown Point.

Colonel Stark's regiment was quartered at Chimney Point, directly opposite Crown Point, on the eastern shore of Lake Champlain, at that place about a hundred and sixteen rods wide. The army remained in this position until ordered to evacuate Crown Point, and fall back upon Ticonderoga.

Against this removal Colonel Stark and other field officers presented a remonstrance to General Schuyler, then in command, showing that their present position ought not to be abandoned, as it commanded the lake, and could be rendered more capable of defence than Ticonderoga. General Schuyler being of a different opinion, the removal took place. After events proved that the memorialists were correct. (See the answer of General Schuyler, and General Washington's letter to Congress upon the subject, in another part of this work.)

On the 6th and 7th of July the army reached Ticonderoga, and, on the morning following, the Declaration of Independence was read to the army. It was received with shouts of applause. Powder was too precious an article to be afforded upon the occasion.

General Gates, soon after this, assumed the command; and assigned to Colonel Stark the command of a brigade, with orders to clear and fortify Mount Independence, (so named on the above occasion) and then a wilderness—in clearing which the soldiers destroyed a large number of rattle-snakes.

In the autumn of this year Congress promoted several junior colonels to the rank of brigadiers; against which Colonel Stark protested, on the ground of insecurity of rank, and that such proceedings would plant the seeds of discord among the officers of the army.

When it was ascertained that the British army, under Sir Guy Carleton,* had retired to winter quarters in Canada, Colonel Stark's regiment, with several others, were detached from the northern army to reinforce General Washington at Newtown, Penn., where he arrived a few days before the battle of Trenton, where, leading the van of Sullivan's division, he contributed his share in that bloodless and fortunate *coup-de-main.*

* The following anecdote furnished to the writer by the late Captain Jonathan Eastman, (senior) refers to the late General Badger, of Gilmanton, N. H.

While the American army, after the retreat from Canada in 1776, lay at Crown Point, the British forces being at St. John's, the American general was desirous of obtaining information relative to their anticipated movements.

Lieutenant Badger volunteered for the purpose. He selected three men who had been rangers in the French war, and who knew the country well, for his companions. They embarked in a boat and landed near St. John's at dark.

On that night a ball was given by the British officers, of which they obtained information from a Canadian, whom they made a prisoner.

Leaving him at the boat in charge of two of his men, Badger proceeded with the other into the town, intending to make prisoner, an officer.

His attendant was well acquainted with the locality, and while in the dark watching near a house occupied for officers quarters, they observed a young officer come out in full ball-dress. They sprang upon him ere he was aware of their presence, and with presented pistols, compelled him to go with them in silence.

When they reached the boat, a new and bolder idea was conceived by Badger; being of the same size of his prisoner, he ordered the latter to change dresses with him, determined, under the mask of a British uniform, to attend the ball, and gather what information he could from the conversation of those present.

The circumstance that many of the officers who were present had lately arrived, and were strangers to each other, favored his enterprise.

He obtained from their conversation such intelligence as he desired; the most important item of which was that Sir Guy Carleton did not intend to advance toward Crown Point the present season, but intended to retire to winter quarters in Canada.

Lieutenant Badger danced as long as he pleased, and when tired of that amusement, returned to his boat, released the Canadian, and with his military prisoner returned to camp. This news thus acquired, enabled the general of the northern army to detach several regiments to reinforce General Washington at Newtown, Penn., and contributed their aid at Trenton and Princeton.

The officer thus captured would give no information; but Badger had learned sufficient for all purposes. When the captive army of Burgoyne marched for Cambridge, Mass., Lieut Badger was attached to the troops who acted as their escort. On the second day's march, Badger came accidentally in the vicinity of his former prisoner; the latter having previously seen none but hostile faces in the ranks of the escort, embraced Badger with the affection of a brother.

If the invasion of Canada in 1775–6 had concluded with no result commensurate with the losses incurred, the attempt to defend Long Island and New-York with inadequate forces, and without a fleet, against a superior veteran force, supported by a powerful naval armament, was still more unfortunate.

The Americans were driven from one breast-work to another, leaving at each retreat prisoners to fill the British hulks—there to perish by thousands—until a considerable army was reduced to scarcely more than a brigadier's command. It then retreated through New-Jersey to New-town, Penn., and there waited until reinforcements could be spared from the northern army to aid in retrieving its fortunes.

The timely arrival of several half-filled regiments from Ticonderoga, who had marched more than 200 miles, ill-supplied, ill-clothed, and so poorly shod that their march could be traced by their tracks in blood, mainly contributed toward gaining two victories, which revived the desponding hopes of the country. Had these last efforts failed, who can not anticipate the melancholy result?

In the council of war, preceding the affair at Trenton, in giving his opinion, Stark observed to General Washington: "Your men have too long been accustomed to place their dependence for safety upon spades and pick-axes. If you ever effect to establish the independence of these States, you must teach them to place dependence upon their fire-arms and their courage."

Here it may be proper to introduce a circumstance, the particulars of which were related at the funeral of General Stark, by a veteran comrade in arms there present. Previous to the important action of Trenton, the American army was upon the point of being broken up by suffering, desertion, and the expiration of the term of enlistment of a great portion of the troops. A few days previous the term of the New-Hampshire regiments expired. The most gloomy period of the war had arrived. Every hope of the country was concentrated in the action of the ill-supplied, ill-clothed, ill-shod, and unpaid troops, then assembled under the orders of Washington, on the banks of the Delaware. Their only chance of striking a blow was at some of the detached posts of the enemy by surprise. Trenton was the nearest practicable point of attack, and Princeton, twelve miles distant, the next. An army of British veterans, (4,000 strong) well supplied, commanded by Earl Cornwallis, was approaching to crush this "forlorn hope" of America. Had these last efforts failed, heaven only knows the result.

In this trying emergency, while officers of other lines did the same, Colonel Stark, aware that the fate of the country depended upon the retention of the troops then in the field, appealed to the patriotism of the men of the Granite hills, who composed the New-Hampshire regiments. He told them that if they left the army all was lost; reminded them of their deeds at Bunker's hill, and other occasions in the Canada campaign; assured them that if Congress did not pay their arrears, his own private property should make it up to them. He proposed a re-enlistment for six weeks; and such was his influence and popularity, that not a man refused. Thus two half-filled, but veteran regiments, of tried valor and fidelity, were retained for the approaching crisis, and nobly they sustained the efforts of their leader.

The Hessians were attacked, at opposite points of the town, by the division of Sullivan, and that led by Washington, in person. Colonel Stark led Sullivan's advanced guard, and General Greene that of Washington.

"General Sullivan's division halted near Howell's ferry, to enable the division led by General Washington to make a circuit to attack the enemy in an opposite direction. Here it was discovered by Captain John Glover, of the Marblehead regiment, that the best secured arms of the officers and men were wet, and not in firing condition. The communication was made to General Sullivan, in presence of General St. Clair. Sullivan cast a look at St. Clair, and observed, 'What is to be done?' who instantly replied, 'You have nothing for it but to push on and charge.'

We soon marched (Colonel Stark in command of the advanced guard) the troops, with orders to clear their muskets as they moved on, in the best manner in their power, which occasioned a good deal of squibbing. In the meantime an officer was dispatched to apprise the General (W.) of the state of our arms, who returned for answer, by his aid-de-camp, Colonel Samuel Webb, that 'we must advance and charge.'

It was now broad day, and the storm beat violently in our faces. The attack had commenced on the left, and was immediately answered by Colonel Stark in front, who forced the enemy's picket, and pressed it into the town, our column being close at his heels. The enemy made a momentary show of resistance, by a wild and ill-directed fire from the windows of their quarters, which they abandoned as we advanced; and made an attempt to form in the main street, which might have succeeded, but for a six-gun battery opened by Captain T. Forest, under the immediate orders of General Washington, at the head of King street, which annoyed the enemy in various directions; and the decision of Captain William Washington, who, seconded by Lieutenant James Monroe, * led the advanced guard of the left column, per-

* James Monroe was afterward President of the United States. Colonel William Washington was the gallant commander of the cavalry at the route of Tarleton's legion, in Morgan's battle at the Cowpens, which action was in effect, as regards the fate of Lord Cornwallis and his army, in 1781, what the victory of Bennington, in 1777, was to the invading army of General Burgoyne.

After the defeat at Cowpens, Colonel Tarleton retreated in the rear of his flying troops, pursued by the dragoons of Colonel Washington. He faced about once, and confronted the leader of the dragoons. A blow from the sabre of the latter wounded two of his fingers. The goodness of his horse prevented his capture. Afterward, speaking to a patriotic southern lady of Colonel Washington, he remarked that he had understood the "fellow was so illiterate that he could not write his name, and he should like to see his face." The lady replied, "he can make his mark; and you might, by facing about on your retreat from the Cowpens, have seen his face."

It is but justice to say of the gallant General Tarleton, (a brave man he undoubtedly was) that in after days, in the British parliament, he deceiving that the enemy were about to form a battery, rushed forward, drove the artillerists from their guns, and took two pieces in the act of firing.

These officers were both wounded: the captain in the wrist, and the lieutenant through the fleshy part of the shoulder. These particular acts of gallantry have never been noticed, and yet they could not have been too highly appreciated; for, if the enemy had got his artillery into operation in a narrow street, it might have checked our movement and given him time to reflect; and if he had retired across the bridge in his rear, and taken post, he would have placed a defile between us, which, in our half-naked and half-frozen condition, he ought to have defended against our utmost efforts; and we, in turn, might have been compelled to retreat, which would have been fatal to us. But while I render justice to the services of Forest, Washington, and Monroe, I must not withhold due praise to the 'dauntless Stark, who dealt death wherever he found resistance, and broke down all opposition before him.'

The 2d of January was a critical day for the American cause. Their advanced guard had been driven across the Assampink by Lord Cornwallis; and had he followed up his success and crossed the river, thirty minutes would have brought on an engagement, and thirty more would have decided the contest; and then, covered with woe, Columbia might have wept the loss of her beloved chief, and most valorous sons.

In this awful moment, the guardian genius of our country admonished Lord Cornwallis that his troops were

fended the character of the Americans for courage and conduct, saying to a certain non-fighting member who, in a tirading speech, was denouncing the cowardly yankees, "if you had fought with them as often as I have, you would perhaps entertain a different opinion."

Colonel Ackland, who commanded the grenadiers under General Burgoyne, at hearing the courage of the Americans defamed at a public dinner in London, contradicted the assertion in unequivocal terms. A duel ensued, in which the gallant colonel was slain.

His widow, Lady Harriet, afterward married a chaplain, Mr. Brudenel, who had accompanied the expedition of General Burgoyne in America.

fatigued, and that the Americans were without retreat. Under this impression, he addressed his general officers: 'The men had been under arms all day; they were languid and required rest; he had the enemy safe enough, and could dispose of them next morning. For these reasons, he proposed that the troops should make fires, refresh themselves, and take repose.'

General Grant, his second, acquiesced, and others followed; but Sir William Erskine exclaimed, 'My lord, if you trust those people to-night, you will see nothing of them in the morning.'

This admonition was not regarded; the enemy made their fires and went to supper, as we did also, our advanced sentries being posted within one hundred and yards of each other.

The American guards at the watch-fires were doubled, the neighboring fences supplying fuel. The army, in detachments, was so noiselessly drawn off as to escape the notice of the enemy. The night was cold and dark; the guards kept up the watch-fires until nearly day-light, when the remaining fuel was thrown upon them, and the men followed the army's track.

Next morning Lord Cornwallis, with chagrin and disappointment at having lost what he supposed an opportunity of finishing the war, discovered that the enemy had retired; and soon after, the roar of artillery at Princeton indicated the direction of his march.

On the 5th of January, soon after the action, an aid-de-camp of Washington bore a flag of truce to Brunswick. The British officers spoke freely of the trick Washington had played them, and the race they had run; having made a forced march from Trenton to Brunswick, being alarmed for the safety of their magazines.

The aid-de-camp, Colonel Fitzgerald, conveyed to General Leslie the information of the fall of his son, Captain Leslie. The veteran was much affected by the recital of the respect which had been shown to his remains, and retiring to a window shed tears. When Colonel Fitzgerald returned, he sent his acknowledgments to General Washington."*

Colonel Stark was with Washington when he re-crossed the Delaware, was engaged at Princeton, and remained with him until his winter quarters were established on the heights of Morristown. The term of his men's enlistment having then expired, he returned to New-Hampshire to recruit another regiment.

In March, 1777, the new regiment was completed, and he repaired to Exeter to receive instructions for the campaign. There he was informed that a new list of promotions had been made out by Congress, and his name omitted. The cause of this flagrant injustice was easily traced to the malignant influence of several officers of high rank, and members of Congress, who were displeased with his unbending character.

He waited upon Generals Sullivan and Poor, wished them all possible success, and resigned his commission. They endeavored to dissuade him from this course; but he replied, "that an officer who would not maintain his rank, was unworthy to serve his country." He warned them of the dangerous situation of the army at Ticonderoga, and the necessity of immediate relief. He declared his readiness again to take the field, whenever his country required his services, and retired to his estate. His letter of resignation is as follows:

"*To the Honorable the Council and House of Representatives for the State of New-Hampshire, in General Court assembled:*

GENTLEMEN—

Ever since hostilities commenced, I have, so far as in me lay, endeavored to prevent my country from being ravaged and enslaved by our cruel and unnatural enemy. I have undergone the hardships and fatigues of two campaigns with cheerfulness and alacrity, ever enjoying the pleasing satisfaction that I was doing my God and country the greatest service my abilities would admit of; and it was with the utmost gratitude that I accepted the important command to which this State appointed me. I should have served with the greatest pleasure, more especially at this

* Wilkinson's Memoir.

important crisis, when our country calls for the utmost exertions of every American; but am extremely grieved that I am in honor bound to leave the service, Congress having thought proper to promote junior officers over my head: so that, lest I should show myself unworthy of the honor conferred on me, and a want of that spirit which ought to glow in the breast of every officer appointed by this Honorable House, in not suitably resenting an indignity, I must (though grieved to leave the service of my country) beg leave to resign my commission; hoping that you will make choice of some gentleman, who may honor the cause and his country, to succeed

Your most obliged, humble servant,

JOHN STARK."

His zeal for the cause continuing as ardent as ever, he fitted out all his family and servants, capable of bearing arms, and dispatched them to the army.

Upon receiving his letter of resignation, the council and house of delegates of New-Hampshire, on the 21st of March, 1777, passed the following resolve:

"*Voted*, That the thanks of both Houses, in convention, be given to Colonel Stark, for his good services in the present war; and that, from his early and steadfast attachment to the cause of his country, they make not the least doubt that his future conduct, in whatever state of life providence may place him, will manifest the same noble disposition of mind."

"Thereupon the thanks of both Houses were presented to Colonel Stark by the honorable president." Colonel Stark was called before the assembly, and received their thanks.

The cause of American Independence was never exposed to a more doubtful crisis than in the eventful campaign of 1777.

That of the preceding year had been extremely disastrous; but when the affairs of the States appeared to be irretrievably ruined, two brilliant actions, toward its close, threw a sudden ray of light upon the surrounding gloom.

The winter was passed in raising men and means for another and more desperate struggle. The edicts of royal indignation had gone forth, denouncing vengeance on the devoted heads of the leaders of this unnatural rebellion; and new armies of veteran troops were organizing to execute their mandates.

Ticonderoga was at this period occupied by the whole force of the United States' army in the north. It was the key stone of that region, and deemed of sufficient strength to oppose an effectual barrier to any advance of the enemy from Canada. The victorious career of the invader soon dispelled the delusion. He made himself master of the heights of Mount Defiance with the utmost secrecy, and drew up several pieces of heavy ordnance. These being placed in battery, and discharged at a vessel on the lake, gave notice to the American general that his post was no longer tenable.

Nothing now could save the army but a precipitate retreat, and preparations were immediately commenced for that purpose. The baggage was embarked in boats, and the retreat commenced on the night of the 5th of July. On the same night the stores in the fortress and those on Mount Independence were improvidently set on fire, the light of which informed the enemy of the movement.*

The retreating army was immediately pursued by Frazer's light infantry brigade and Reidesel's Yagers, on land and water, with such diligence that the rear guard of 1000 men, under Colonel Warner, was overtaken next day at Hubbardton, and brought to action.

* Which of our historians might not profitably copy the following account of the evacuation of Ticonderoga, albeit it fell from the lips of a negro? "About 11 o'clock on Saturday night, orders were given by our colonel to parade. We immediately obeyed. He then ordered our tents to be struck and carried to the battery. On doing this, the orders were to take up our packs and march, which we also did; passed the general's house on fire; marched twenty miles without a halt, and then had a brush with the enemy."—*Butler*.

Near the scene of a bloody hand-to-hand contest, during the attacks upon Ticonderoga in 1758, is a fine spring. We were informed by a veteran soldier of the first New-Hampshire regiment, Mr. William Beard, of Dunbarton, N. H., that the soldiers found a skull near it, which they cleansed and used for a drinking-cup, and that one of his comrades said he intended to carry it home. In the haste of the retreat on the night of July 5, it was left behind.

The contest was well fought, if we may rely upon Anbury's statement, that Earl Balcarras, second in command of the light infantry, received nearly thirty balls through his jacket and trowsers, only one of which wounded him slightly in the hip. The assailants would have been repulsed by Warner, but Reidesel's Germans came up in season to save them; and the gallant Warner, after performing all that an intelligent and fearless soldier could do, was compelled to give way before superior numbers. Colonel Francis, a brave and valuable officer, (father of the late eminent financier of Boston) with others of less note, fell upon this occasion.

One of the most unfortunate results of this affair was felt by the Americans in the loss of all their baggage, few of the officers and men having any clothing except that upon their persons.

The army continued its disorderly retreat toward the Hudson, breaking down bridges, and blocking up the streams with timber-trees.

The news of the fall of Ticonderoga * spread rapidly through the country, giving rise to the most fearful forebodings. The people in general appeared to be paralyzed with terror and astonishment. All was considered as lost. But there were men whose nerves had not been unstrung by the misfortunes of two disastrous campaigns; whose warrior spirits arose with the dangers that surrounded them; who could look upon this dreary night of disaster as the harbinger of a more glorious day; who could foresee that the invader, notwithstanding his hitherto triumphant advance, would not be able to retrace his steps, should he be so inclined. Around such men the hopes and strength of the country gathered.

* Five days after the evacuation of Ticonderoga, in a letter from Stockbridge, Mass., it was written: "We are greatly burdened with people who have fled from the 'Hampshire Grants.'" It was feared that Manchester must be abandoned. In a letter dated there, July 15, it is said: "We learn that a large scout of the enemy are disposed to take a tour to this post. The inhabitants, with their families, can not be quieted without the assurance of the arrival of troops directly."

The people of New-Hampshire had performed all that it was supposed they could do. Public credit was at a low ebb; and the ability to support a single extra regiment was doubted, even if one could be raised.

The State council had been notified, by the authorities of Vermont, that unless speedy assistance was sent them, they must yield to circumstances, and accept the protection of the enemy, which would leave New-Hampshire a frontier State.* In this emergency shone forth the spirit and patriotism of that man of his country, John Langdon. Ever honored be his memory!

He was then presiding officer of the assembly and, upon the receipt of the news from the north, thus addressed that body:

"I have three thousand dollars in hard money; my plate I will pledge for as much more. I have seventy hogsheads of Tobago rum, which shall be sold for the most they will bring. These are at the service of the State. If we succeed, I shall be remunerated; if not, they will be of no use to me. We can raise a brigade; and our friend Stark, who so nobly sustained the honor of our arms at Bunker's hill, may safely be entrusted with the command, and we will check Burgoyne." †

* See letter of Ira Allen, Secretary of Vermont.

† The following anecdote is a sample of many others which might be cited, to exhibit the zeal manifested in consequence of Mr. Langdon's proposition, to furnish means for the Bennington enterprise.

As soon as it was decided to raise volunteer companies, and place them under the command of General Stark, Colonel Gordon Hutchins (member of the assembly from Concord) mounted his horse, and traveling all night with all possible haste, reached Concord on the Sabbath afternoon, before the close of public service.

Dismounting at the meeting-house door, he walked up the aisle of the old North Church, while Mr. Walker was preaching. Mr. Walker paused in his sermon, and said: "Colonel Hutchins, are you the bearer of any message?" "Yes," replied the colonel, "General Burgoyne with his army is on his march to Albany. General Stark has offered to take the command of the New-Hampshire men, and if we all turn out we can cut off Burgoyne's march." Whereupon, the Rev. Mr. Walker said: "My hearers, those of you who are willing to go, had better leave at once." At which all the men in the meeting-house rose and went out; many immediately enlisted. The whole night was spent in preparation, and a company was ready to march next day. Phinehas Eastman said, "I can't go,

This noble proposal infused new life into the assembly, and arrangements were immediately commenced for carrying it out.

A messenger was dispatched to Colonel Stark, who, stung with the injustice of Congress in promoting junior officers over him, had resigned his commission, and retired to private life. He had left the army three months before, and was now living upon his estate on the banks of the Merrimack.

He returned with the messenger, and waited upon the council. He listened to their proposal. They assured him that his former patriotic services were duly remembered and appreciated, and urged him to forget the past, and assume the command of their troops.

He informed them that he had no confidence in the commander of the northern army; but if they would organize a brigade to be by him commanded, to hang upon the left wing and rear of the enemy, with full authority to direct their operations according to his own judgment, without responsibility to any other authority than their own body, he would again take the field. The council closed with the terms, and issued a commission, investing him with as ample powers as he could have desired.

Recruiting officers were immediately employed under his orders, in beating up for volunteers. His popularity, military reputation and previous successes (for he had seen more actual service than most of the continental officers) were strong inducements with the yeomanry of New-Hampshire to volunteer under his command.

More men than his orders called for were soon engaged, and marched to Charlestown, on Connecticut river, as a place of general rendezvous. From thence they were

for I have no shoes," to which Samuel Thompson, a shoe-maker, replied, "Don't be troubled about that, for you shall have a pair before morning," which was done. The late Jonathan Eastman, senior, esq., was in similar want of shoes, and a new pair was also made for him before morning. *Rev. N. Bouton's History of Concord.*

ordered to Bennington, Vt., as fast as they could be equipped with arms, ammunition and supplies.

On the 30th of July the General wrote from Charlestown to the New-Hampshire Council: "I am informed that the enemy have left Castleton, with an intent to march to Bennington. We are detained by the want of bullet molds. There is but one pair in town, and the few balls sent by the council go but little way."

One pair of bullet molds for an army! In many other particulars the troops were equally deficient. The address of J. D. Butler, Esq., before the Legislature of Vermont, on the reception of the Bennington cannon, contains many interesting particulars in regard to the expedition.

General Stark crossed the mountains to Manchester, in Vermont, where, after reinforcing and consulting with Colonel Warner, he proceeded to assume the command of his brigade, then mustering at Bennington, where he arrived on the 9th of August.

Soon afterward an officer of the northern army arrived, with instructions to conduct the New-Hampshire levies to the main army, then at Stillwater. To these orders General Stark declined to submit, declaring himself to be only responsible to the authorities of New-Hampshire, who had invested him with an independent command, and promptly refused to permit the troops to march to join the army commanded by General Schuyler. *

The officer reported the result of his mission to head quarters, and General Schuyler complained to Congress, urging the necessity of reinforcements of men and supplies.

Congress resolved "That the council of New-Hamp-

* To the remark of the officer, that he was assuming a fearful responsibility, he replied, that he had "often assumed responsibilities for the good of his country, and should do so again."

It may here be observed that the New-Hampshire brigade mustered on Thursday, the 14th; although nominally consisting of 1,332 privates, it was, in real strength, but little more than half that number, as one company had been left at Number Four, two on the mountains, and others elsewhere, or weakened by sickness and desertion. The strength of Stark's force was, by General Schuyler, estimated at 700 or 800 men. He was joined by Captain Robinson, with the Bennington militia, and by many volunteers in the vicinity.

shire be informed that the instructions which General Stark says he has received from them, are destructive of military subordination, and highly prejudicial to the common cause at this crisis; and that, therefore, they be desired to instruct General Stark to conform himself to the same rules which other general officers of the militia are subject to, whenever they are called out at the expense of the United States."

This vote of censure neither the council nor their general considered of much account. He knew no other authority than the State council; and had he submitted to the demand of General Schuyler, the campaign would have terminated with the ruin of the northern army; and General Burgoyne would have reached Albany, from whence he could coöperate with Howe and Clinton, and find the task an easy one to crush the other American armies.

General Stark now proceeded with all diligence to organize and discipline his forces, collect supplies, and prepare for active duty as soon as occasion should require. The commander of the northern army soon opened a correspondence with him, and he detailed to him his plan of operations; which was to intercept and cut off the enemy's supplies, remove beyond his reach all the cattle and stores of the country, harrass his rear, and attack any of his detachments which should afford him an opportunity. The plan was approved by General Schuyler, and while arrangements were making to carry it out, General Burgoyne himself furnished the desired opportunity.

That general had heard of the arrival of the militia at Bennington. He also knew that large magazines of flour and other supplies were to be found in the vicinity; and while waiting to hear of the success of Colonel St. Leger, who had been ordered to march by a different route from that pursued by his main army, and reduce Fort Stanwix on his way, he resolved to detach a force sufficient, as he supposed, to look down all opposition, to disperse the enemy on his left, and secure the stores of provisions collected in the vicinity, which the necessities of his army already required.

The force consisted of 500 German regulars, a detachment of British light infantry and dismounted dragoons, a party of tories, 200 Indians, with two pieces of light brass field artillery, commanded by Lieut. Colonel Baum, a brave and intelligent officer, who was attended by the veteran Colonel Philip Skene, who well knew the country and the inhabitants, as an assistant and adviser.

Another detachment of 600 Germans, with a similar accompanying force of tories and Indians, with two heavier brass field pieces, were also ordered to be in readiness to march at a moment's warning to support Colonel Baum, if he had occasion to call for assistance.

While encamped at Battenkill, awaiting orders, Colonel Baum addressed the following note to General Burgoyne:

"BATTENKILL, 12 August, 1777.

Sir—I had the honor of acquainting your Excellency, by a man sent yesterday by Col. Skene, to head quarters, of the several corps under my command being encamped at Saratoga, as well as my intention to proceed next morning at five o'clock. The corps moved at that time, and marched a mile, when I received a letter from Brig. Gen. Frazer, signifying your Excellency's order to post the corps advantageously on Battenkill, until I should receive fresh instructions. The corps is now encamped at that place, and waits your order.

I will not trouble you with the various reports, which are spread, as they seem rather to be founded on the different feelings of the people who occasion them.

I have the honor to be, &c.,

F. BAUM.

The reinforcement of fifty chasseurs, which your Excellency was pleased to order, joined me last night."

INSTRUCTIONS FOR LIEUT. COL. BAUM, ON A SECRET EXPEDITION TO CONNECTICUT RIVER.

"The object of your expedition is to try the affections of the country, to disconcert the councils of the enemy, to mount Reidesel's dragoons, to complete Peters' corps, and to obtain large supplies of cattle, horses and carriages.

The several corps of which the inclosed is a list, are to be under your command. The troops must take no tents; and what little baggage is carried by officers, must be on their own bat-horses.

You are to proceed by the route from Battenkill to Arlington, and take post there, so as to secure the pass to Manchester. You are to remain at Arlington until the detachment of provincials, under Capt. Sherwood, shall join you from the southward.

You are then to proceed to Manchester, where you will take post, so as to secure the pass of the mountains, on the road from Manchester to Rockingham; from thence you will detach the Indians and light troops to the northward, toward Otter creek. On their return, and also receiving intelligence that no enemy is in force in the neighborhood of Rockingham, (on Connecticut river) you will proceed by the road over the mountains to Rockingham, where you will take post. This will be the most distant point of the expedition; and must be proceeded upon with caution, as you will have the defile of the mountains behind you, which might make a return difficult. You must therefore endeavor to be well informed of the force of the enemy's militia in the neighboring country.

You are to remain there as long as may be necessary to fulfill the intention of the expedition from thence, while the Indians and light troops are detached up the river; and you are afterward to descend by the Connecticut river to Brattleborough; and from that place, by the quickest march, you are to return by the great road to Albany.

During your whole progress, your detachments are to have orders to bring in all horses fit to mount the dragoons, under your command, or to serve as bat-horses to the troops, together with as many saddles and bridles as can be found. The number of horses requisite, besides those necessary for mounting the regiment of dragoons, ought to be thirteen hundred. If you can bring more for the army, it will be better.

Your parties are likewise to bring in wagons and other convenient carriages, with as many draft oxen as will be necessary to draw them, and all cattle fit for slaughter, (milch cows excepted) which are to be left for the use of the inhabitants. Regular receipts, in the form hereto subjoined, are to be given in all places where any of the above named articles are taken, to such persons as have remained in their habitations, and otherwise complied with the terms of General Burgoyne's manifesto; but no receipts are to be given to such as are known to be acting in the service of the rebels.

As you will have with you persons perfectly acquainted with the abilities of the country, it may, perhaps, be advisable to tax the several districts with their portion of the articles, and limit the hours for their delivery; should you find it necessary to move before such delivery can be made, hostages of the most respectable people should be taken to secure their following you the next day. All possible means are to be used to prevent plundering.

As it is probable Capt. Sherwood, who is already to the southward, and will join you at Arlington, will drive in a considerable quantity of horses and cattle to you; you will therefore send in the cattle to the army with a proper detachment from Peters' corps, to cover them, in order to disincumber yourself. You must always keep the regiment of dragoons compact.

The dragoons themselves must ride and take care of the horses of the regiment. Those horses which are destined for the use of the army, should be tied together in strings of ten each, so that one man may lead ten horses. You will give directions to the unarmed men of Peters' corps to conduct them, and inhabitants whom you can trust. You must always take your camps in good positions; but at the same time where there is pasture. You must have a chain of sentinels around your cattle and horses while grazing.

Col. Skene will be with you as much as possible, in order to assist you with his advice; to help you distinguish the good subjects from the bad; to procure the best intelligence of the enemy; and to choose those people who are to bring the accounts of your progress and success.

When you find it necessary to halt for a day or two, you must always entrench the camp of the regiment of dragoons, in order never to risk an attack or affront from the enemy. As you will return with the regiment of dragoons, mounted, you must always have a detachment of Capt. Frazer's or Peters' corps in front of the column, and the same in the rear, to prevent your falling into an ambuscade when you march through the woods.

You will use all possible means to make the country believe that you are the advanced corps of the army, and that it is intended to pass the Connecticut river on the route to Boston. You will likewise insinuate that the main army from Albany will be joined at Springfield by a corps of troops from Rhode-Island. You will send off, occasionally, cattle or carriages to prevent being too much incumbered; and give me as frequent intelligence of your situation as possible.

It is highly probable that the corps under Mr. Warner, now supposed to be at Manchester, will retreat before you; but should they, contrary to expectation, be able to collect in great force, and post themselves advantageously, it is left to your discretion to attack them or not, always bearing in mind that your corps is too valuable to let any considerable loss be hazarded on this occasion.

Should any corps be moved from Mr. Arnold's main army in order to intercept your retreat, you are to take as strong a post as the country will afford, and send the quickest intelligence to me; and you may depend on my making such a movement as shall put the enemy between two fires, or otherwise effectually sustain you. It is imagined the progress of the whole of the expedition can be effected in about a fortnight; but every movement of it must depend upon your success in obtaining such a supply of provisions as will enable you to subsist for your return to the army, in case you get no more; and should not the army reach Albany before your expedition should be completed, I will find means to send you notice of it, and give your route another direction. All persons acting in committees, or any officers acting under the direction of Congress, either civil or military, are to be made prisoners.

J. BURGOYNE."

The above instructions, and the following letters, are copied from Burgoyne's defence before Parliament.

INSTRUCTIONS OF COL. SKENE, UPON THE EXPEDITION TO BENNINGTON.

"SIR—I request the favor of you to proceed with Lieut. Col. Baum upon an expedition of which he has the command, and which will march this evening or to-morrow morning. The object of his orders is to try the affections of the country to disconcert the councils of the enemy, to mount the regiment of Reidesel's dragoons, to complete Lieut. Col. Peters' corps (tories,) and to procure a large supply of horses for the use of the troops, together with cattle and carriages.

The route marked out for this expedition is to Arlington and Manchester; and in case it should be found that the enemy is not in too great force upon the Connecticut, it is intended to pass the mountains to Rockingham, and descend the river from thence to Brattleborough. Some hours before the corps march for Arlington, Colonel Peters, with all his men, is to set forward for Bennington, and afterward are to join you at Arlington.

Receipts are to be given for all horses and cattle taken from the country. Lieut. Col. Baum is directed to communicate the rest of his instructions, and to consult with you upon all matters of intelligence, negotiation with the inhabitants, roads and other means, depending upon a knowledge of the country, for carrying his instructions into execution.

I rely upon your zeal and activity for the fullest assistance, particularly in having it understood in all the country through which you pass, that the corps of Colonel Baum is the first detachment of the advanced guard; and that the whole army is proceeding to Boston, expecting to be joined on the route by the army from Rhode-Island.

I need not recommend to you to continue the requisites of the service with every principle of humanity in the mode of obtaining them; and it may be proper to inform the country that the means to prevent their cattle and horses being taken for the future, will be to resist the enemy when they shall presume to force them, and drive them voluntarily to my camp.

I have the honor to be, &c.,

J. BURGOYNE.

The following letters of Colonel Baum give an account of his progress up to the 14th of August, 1777, at 9 o'clock P. M.

CAMBRIDGE, 13 August, 1777.

Sir—In consequence of your Excellency's order, I moved this morning at 4 o'clock with the corps under my command; and after a march of sixteen miles, arrived at Cambridge at four in the evening. On the road I received intelligence of forty or fifty rebels being left to guard some cattle. I ordered thirty provincials and fifty savages to quicken their march in hopes to surprise them. They took five prisoners in arms, who declared themselves to be in the service of Congress; yet the enemy received advice of our approach, and abandoned the house in which they were posted. The provincials and savages continued their march about a mile, when they fell in with a party of fifteen men, who fired upon our people and took to the woods with great precipitation. The fire was quick on our side, but I can not learn if the enemy sustained any loss. A private of Captain Sherwood's company was the only one who was slightly wounded in the thigh.

From the many people who came from Bennington, they agree that the number of the enemy amounted to 1,800. I will be particularly careful, on my approach to that place, to be fully informed of their strength and situation, and take the precaution necessary to fulfill both the orders and instructions of your Excellency.

I cannot ascertain the number of cattle, carts and wagons taken here, as they have not as yet been collected. A few horses have been also brought in; but I am sorry to acquaint you that the savages either destroy or drive away what is not paid for with ready money. If your Excellency would allow me to purchase the horses, stipulating the price, I think they might be procured cheap; otherwise, they ruin all they meet with. Your Excellency may depend on hearing how I proceed at Bennington, and of my success there.

Paying my respectful compliments to General Reidesel,

I am, &c.,

F. BAUM.*

P. S. The names of the men taken in arms are George Duncan, David Starrow, Samuel Bell and Matthew Bell. Hugh Moore, a noted rebel, surrendered himself yesterday evening.

The express left Cambridge at 4 o'clock on the morning of the 14th of August.

* Frederick Baum.

SANCOICK, 14 *August*, 9 o'clock P. M.

Sir :—I have the honor to inform your Excellency that I arrived here at eight in the morning, having had intelligence of a party of the enemy being in possession of a mill, which they abandoned at our approach, but in their usual way, fired from the bushes; and, took their road to Bennington; a savage was slightly wounded. They broke down a bridge which has retarded our march above an hour. They left in the mill about seventy-eight barrels of fine flour, one thousand bushels of wheat, twenty bushels of salt, and about one thousand dollars' worth of pearl and potashes.

I have ordered twenty provincials and an officer to guard the provisions and pass of the bridge. By the five prisoners taken here, they agree that from 1,500 to 1,800 men are in Bennington, but are supposed to leave at our approach. I will proceed so far to-day as to fall on the enemy to-morrow early, and make such disposition as I think necessary from the intelligence I may receive. People are flocking in hourly, but want to be armed; the savages can not be ruled. They ruin, and take everything they please.

I am, &c., F. BAUM.

I beg your Excellency to pardon the hurry of this letter, it is wrote on the head of a barrel."*

On perceiving the brigade, the enemy halted; selected an advantageous position upon elevated ground, and commenced intrenching their camp, by felling timber-trees and forming log breast-works for their several corps; for, according to the British plan of their works which, together with the orders of General Burgoyne, fell into the hands of General Stark, several redoubts were thrown up. In fact, the enemy tore down all the houses of hewn timber in the vicinity, and used the materials thus obtained for that purpose.

* Burgoyne's Defence.

As the ground was not suitable for a general and immediate action, the American commander concluded to fall back one mile, and prepare his troops for battle.

The whole day of the 15th proving stormy, nothing farther took place than a skirmish on the enemy's front. A chosen body of men, several of whom had served in the ranger corps of the "seven years' war," were ordered to try the enemy's temper, and harass their operations while forming intrenchments. In this expedition thirty of the enemy were killed and wounded; among them two Indian chiefs were slain, whose silver ornaments were brought to camp by the victorious rangers, who returned without losing a man, or one of the scout receiving a wound. This success was hailed by the troops in camp as an omen of farther good fortune. The rain poured down in torrents during the whole night; and the situation of the Americans, in their bush huts, and the enemy in their intrenchments, was uncomfortable.

At one o'clock on the morning of August 16th, the camp was aroused by the arrival of the Berkshire volunteers, led by Colonel Symonds—those from Pittsfield being conducted and commanded by their pastor, Rev. Thomas Allen. This worthy, patriotic and exemplary descendant of one of Cromwell's Ironsides, proceeded at once to the general's quarters, (a log house) and addressed him in substance, as follows:

"The people of Berkshire have often turned out to fight the enemy, but have not been permitted to do so. We have resolved that if you do not let us fight now, never to come again." "Would you go now," observed the general, "in this dark and rainy night? No; go to your people; tell them to take rest if they can; and if God sends us sunshine to-morrow, and I do not give you fighting enough, I will never call upon you to come again."

The storm continued until nearly noon on Saturday, the 16th of August. When the rain ceased, the clouds suddenly broke away, and the sun came out in full splendor.

We have reason to believe its appearance was welcome and cheering to the martial husbandmen who had assembled in arms for the defence of their soil and firesides, and that they obeyed the order to march to battle with alacrity, and the spirits of men resolved to "live free or die."

An order had been dispatched to Colonel Warner, who was at Manchester with one hundred and fifty continental troops, to hasten his march to the scene of action, which order he promptly obeyed.

During the retreat from Ticonderoga, Hale's regiment surrendered to a force of British and tories, who, not being able to carry away their arms, had left them stacked in the woods. General Stark being apprised of this fact had, a short time previously, directed Colonel Warner to secure them for the use of his corps. He had just returned, when the order to march arrived. He reached Bennington in season to use them, in the second action, with glorious effect.

Colonel Baum took advantgage of the delay occasioned by the storm of the 15th, to inform General Burgoyne of his situation, and call for Colonel Breyman's corps, who immediately marched to his support.

Their preparations being completed, the Americans left their camp and marched in quest of the enemy. They were found in the position they had fortified, with their artillery properly posted, and prepared to receive the assailants.

The German commander harangued his men, stating that the countrymen opposed to them were the owners of the soil, and would probably fight well to defend it; but that they could have no chance of success against their superior discipline and favorable position, surrounded by breast-works and supported by artillery, of which their opponents possessed not a single piece; and the arrival of Colonel Breyman, with a reinforcement superior to their present force, with two heavier pieces of artillery, was hourly expected.

Common report has attributed a brief address to the American general, such as: "There, my boys, are your enemies, the red-coats and tories; you must beat them, or my wife sleeps a widow to-night." We will here, however, introduce the address, with a quotation from the graphic pen of New-York's talented bard, Fitz-Greene Halleck. Speaking of the traits of New-England character, he writes:

"And minds have there been nurtured whose control
Is felt e'en in their nation's destiny;—
Men who swayed senates with a statesman's soul,
And looked on armies with a leader's eye;
Names which adorn and dignify the scroll
Whose leaves contain their country's history;
And tales of love and war—now list to one,
Of the White Mountaineer—the STARK of Bennington.

When on that field his band the Hessians fought,
Briefly he spoke before the fight began:
'Soldiers, those German gentlemen were bought
For four pounds eight and seven pence, per man,
By England's King: a bargain, it is thought.
Are we worth more? let's prove it while we can:
For we must beat them, boys, ere set of sun,
Or my wife sleeps a widow.'—*It was done.*"*

* "The tories, who had joined the king's troops, confident that in these last days the time of recompense for all their maltreatment had come, were intrenched in front of the German battery. They braved the battle fire, that they might, if by any means possible, turn their castle in the air into a castle on the earth.

On the other hand, the assailants saw before them a band of mercenaries, bought at thirty crowns a head, and of whose speech they could not understand a syllable. They saw a horde whose orders were to make spoil of every horse, every ox, every wheel-carriage, every saddle, every bridle, leaving only milch cows as special clemency; to carry off all provisions, to tax every village as much as it could pay—tories being judges; to take hostages for payment of the tax, to let loose Indians and tories to do what they pleased with the refractory vanquished. They knew that they were the last hope of New-England; that if they were repelled, there was no reserve to fall back on; that the dragoons, now dismounted before them, on the morrow would be cavalry, a winged army pouncing upon the fugitives in every valley, while Indians would set fire to every hill-side hamlet and scalp its inmates. Stark was full of high disdain from a sense of injured merit; rivals had been promoted over his head, and he left a subaltern.

"Men
That never set a squadron in the field,
Nor the division of a battle knew,
More than a spinster, except the bookish theorick."

The enemy occupied elevated ground, with a gradual slope on the north and west. At some short distance on his right flowed the river Hoosac, and along his front the little river Walloomsac to its junction with the former river.

His position was reconnoitered at a mile's distance, and the plan of attack arranged. Two detachments were ordered to diverge to the right and left, passing through the woods and corn-fields, and by circuitous routes turn the enemy's flanks, unite their force, and attack his rear. Colonel Nichols, on their left, and Colonel Herrick, on their right, had the command of these attacks. Herrick's force was three hundred, that of Nichols two hundred; but a reinforcement of one hundred men was sent him, at his own demand, before his attack commenced.

Colonels Hubbard and Stickney, with two hundred men, were posted on the enemy's right, to attack the tory breast-work; and one hundred men were stationed in front to attract the enemy's attention to that quarter.

The General took his position with the reserve. The attack on the flanks and rear of the enemy was to be the signal for a general assault.

Colonel Baum with his glass observed the movements of the flanking parties, and supposed they were running away.*

He had insisted upon having a separate command and independent authority. Had he taken his position only to expose his weakness, like one who plunges into deep water though he can not swim? He was tried; and to be found wanting, or not wanting? It was for him in these moments a fearful question. Was he to prove a mere partizan, a scout, or was he to prove a general?

> "expert
> When to advance, or stand, or turn the sway
> Of battle: open when, and when to close
> The ridges of grim war."

He heard the warwhoop of the savages, who had captivated him in his youth, and forced him to run the gauntlet. Is it any wonder his words to his men were: "There are your enemies, the red-coats and tories; we must have them in half an hour, or this night my wife sleeps a widow!" No wonder the engagement was the hottest he had ever witnessed, resembling a continental clap of thunder."—*Butler's Address.*

* So said his servant and waiter, Henry Archelaus, who died at Weare, N. H., many years ago.

The flanking parties were soon concealed from his view by the woods. In the meantime the reserve slowly advanced. The General ordered frequent halts, and was observed often to look at his watch, saying to himself, "It is time they were there."

The artillery of the enemy soon commenced playing upon the reserve, which advanced slowly as at first. At three o'clock in the afternoon, Colonel Nichols opened his fire upon their left, which was immediately answered by Colonel Herrick on their right. The troops in front pressed forward, and the action became general.

The enemy were, after a sharp contest, forced from their works,* and driven upon the reserve, which soon decided the action. The Indians in the enemy's rear fired on the right and left, and fled on the appearance of the flanking detachments, as they approached each other to form a junction.

The prisoners were speedily collected, and hurried from the field, escorted by a force sufficient to secure them. The remainder of these undisciplined volunteers, exulting in their success, could not be prevented from dispersing in quest of refreshment and plunder, not anticipating more fighting that day.

The drums and bugles of the German reinforcement, under the orders of Colonel Breyman, were, in the space of an hour, heard in the distance, announcing to the victors that another and more desperate conflict was at hand.

Colonel Warner's drums at the same time gave notice of his approach in an opposite direction. The men of the New-Hampshire brigade who were near were rallied, and a second action commenced.

* In regard to the attack of the redoubts, Butler says: "On a sudden a solitary wagon, containing all the Germans' spare ammunition, exploded in the midst of the redoubt. You would have thought that explosion to have been an order given for every American to charge with railroad speed; for the redoubt was instantly stormed, and carried on every side."—*Butler's Address.*

Colonel Warner was directed to divide his force, and attack the right and left flanks of the enemy; which service he performed with his accustomed gallantry, and succeeded in checking the Germans until the scattered troops of New-Hampshire could be again formed, and brought up to his support.

The action continued, and was obstinately fought on both sides until dark, the enemy fighting on a retreat for two miles. They then gave way at all points. They were pursued some distance, and many more prisoners taken. The remainder escaped under cover of the night, while the conquerors, worn down by the fatigues of the day, returned to camp. With one hour more of daylight, the whole detachment would have been captured.

The fruits of this signal and almost unexpected victory, thus obtained by raw militia over European veterans, tories and savages, were four pieces of brass artillery, eight brass-barreled drums, eight loads of baggage, one thousand stand of arms, many Hessian dragoon swords, and seven hundred and fifty prisoners; two hundred and seven of the enemy fell upon the field of battle. The loss of the Americans was about thirty killed and forty wounded. But the most important result of this victory was the restoration of confidence to the desponding armies of America, while it gave a death blow to the hopes of the invader.

Lieut. Colonel Baum, who was mortally wounded, died soon after the action, and was buried with military honors.

The Hessians and English were treated as prisoners of war, and marched from the field in their ranks; but the tories,* 152 in number, were tied in pairs; to each pair a

* The most unique punishment to which they (the tories and spies) were subjected, was decreed by the Council of Bennington, in January, 1778, after this fashion:

"Let the overseer of the tories detach ten of them, with proper officers to take the charge, and march them in two distinct files from this place through the Green Mountains, for breaking a path through the snow. Let each man be provided with three days' provisions; let them march and tread the snow in said road of suitable width for a sleigh and span of horses; order them to return, marching in the same manner, with all convenient speed. Let them march at 6 o'clock to-morrow morning." Early rising.—*Butler's Address before the Vermont Antiquarian Society.*

horse was attached by traces with, in some cases, a negro for his rider; they were led away amid the jeers and scoffs of the victors—the good house-wives of Bennington taking down beds to furnish cords for the occasion. Many of their neighbors had gone over to the enemy the day before the battle. Collections of trophies of this victory were presented to the States of New-Hampshire, Massachusetts and Vermont.

"This success," says an eloquent writer, "was the first link in the chain of events, which opened a new scene to America. It raised her from the depths of despair to the summit of hope, and added unfading laurels to the brow of the veteran who commanded."

The question of American Independence was no longer considered doubtful. France, in due time, engaged in the contest with zeal and vigor, joyously embracing the opportunity thus afforded of humbling her most ancient and most hated foe.

Immediately after the action at Bennington, troops were detached, under the command of active officers, in every direction, to secure all cattle and stores of provisions within the enemy's reach, and to disconcert his foraging parties. The march of General Burgoyne's army was in consequence checked for nearly a month, during which period the Americans found time to muster a force sufficient to put an end to his progress. Madam Reidesel, in her memoir, speaking of the Bennington expedition, says "This unfortunate event paralyzed at once all our operations."

A Hessian officer's journal describes the combat in the intrenchment, occupied by the Germans, as follows:

"Then for a few moments, the bayonet, the butt of the rifle, the sabre and the pike were in full play, and men fell, as they rarely have fallen in modern warfare, under the

Symsbury mines furnished a subterranean prison for a portion of the spies and tories condemned by the Council of Bennington; others were held in duress, under the supervision of overseers who, in the above described instance, employed them for the benefit of the traveling public.

direct blows of their adversaries. Colonel Baum, sword in hand, led the remainder of his men, but soon sank mortally wounded; and save a few, who darted here and there between the surrounding assailants, his whole corps, with the loyalists who had joined them, were disabled or taken prisoners."

Butler's discourse before the Vermont Legislature, on the reception of the Bennington cannon, contains the following passages:

If Burgoyne was thunderstruck when an antagonist, he had never heard of, 'came cranking in and cut him from the best of his troops, a huge half-moon, a monstrous cantleout,' what would he have thought had he known that antagonist's history? How twenty-five years before Stark had been led along as a ransomed captive, over the very ground where the British army lay encamped? How he had been given up by his savage masters for one Indian pony? I copy the following from the original journal of the officer who redeemed the captive:

"July 12, 1752.

This day John Stark was brought to Montreal by his Indian master. He was taken a hunting this spring. He is given up for an Indian pony, for which we paid five hundred and fifteen livres ($103). The boy, sold for a French horse, in little more than a score of years had become a man, more precious than the wedges of Ophir." Mr. Butler continues: Ascertaining that a veteran of Bennington was still living, (1848) some eight miles from my house at Wells River, I paid him a visit about a week ago. His name is Thomas Mellen, and though upward of ninety-two years of age, he is so far from being bald or bowed down, that you would think him in the Indian summer of life. His dress was all of gray homespun, and he sat on a couch, the covering of which was sheep-skins, with the wool on. I will repeat his statements so far as possible, in his own words:

"I enlisted," said he, "at Francestown, N. H., in Colonel Stickney's regiment and Captain Clark's company, as soon as I learned that Stark would accept the command of the State troops; six or seven others from the same town joined the army at the same time. We marched forthwith to Number Four, and stayed there a week. Meantime I received a horn of powder and run two or three hundred bullets; I had brought my own gun. Then my company went on to Manchester; soon after I went, with a hundred others, under Colonel Emerson, down the valley of Otter Creek; on this excursion we lived like lords, on pigs and chickens, in the houses of tories who had fled. When we returned to Manchester, bringing two hogsheads of West India rum, we heard that the Hessians were on their way to invade Vermont. Late in the afternoon of rainy Friday, we were ordered off for Bennington in spite of rain, mud and darkness. We pushed on all night, making the best progress we could; about day-break I, with Lieut. Miltimore, came near Bennington, and slept a little while on a hay-mow, when the barn-yard fowls waked us; we went for bread and milk to the sign of the 'wolf,' and then hurried three miles west to Stark's main body.

Stark and * * * * * * rode up near the enemy to reconnoitre; were fired at by the cannon, and came galloping back. Stark rode with shoulders bent forward, and cried out to his men: 'Those rascals know that I am an officer; don't you see they honor me with a big gun as a salute.' We were marched round and round a circular hill till we were tired. Stark said it was to amuse the Germans. All the while a cannonade was kept up upon us from their breast-works; it hurt no body, and it lessened our fear of the great guns. After a while I was sent, with twelve others, to lie in ambush, on a knoll a little north, and watch for tories on their way to join Baum. Presently we saw six coming toward us who, mistrusting us for tories, came too near us to escape. We disarmed and sent them, under a guard of three, to Stark. While I sat on the hillock, I espied one Indian whom I thought

I could kill, and more than once cocked my gun, but the orders were not to fire. He was cooking his dinner, and now and then shot at some of our people.

Between two and three o'clock the battle began. The Germans fired by platoons, and were soon hidden by the smoke. Our men fired each on his own hook, aiming wherever he saw a flash; few on our side had either bayonets or cartridges. At last I stole away from my post and ran down to the battle. The first time I fired I put three balls in my gun; before I had time to fire many rounds our men rushed over the breast-works, but I and many others chased straggling Hessians in the woods; we pursued until we met Breyman with 800 fresh troops and larger cannon, which opened a fire of grape shot; some of the grape shot riddled a Virginia fence near me; one shot struck a small white oak behind which I stood; though it hit higher than my head I fled from the tree, thinking it might be aimed at again. We skirmishers ran back till we met a large body of Stark's men and then faced about. I soon started for a brook I saw a few rods behind, for I had drank nothing all day, and should have died of thirst if I had not chewed a bullet all the time. I had not gone a rod when I was stopped by an officer, sword in hand, ready to cut me down as a runaway, who, on my complaining of thirst, handed me his canteen, which was full of rum; I drank and forgot my thirst. But the enemy outflanked us, and I said to a comrade, 'we must run, or they will have us.' He said: 'I will have one fire first.' At that moment, a major, on a black horse, rode along behind us, shouting 'fight on boys, reinforcements close by.' While he was yet speaking, a grape shot went through his horse's head; it bled a good deal, but the major kept his seat, and rode on to encourage others. In a few minutes we saw Warner's men hurrying to help us; they opened right and left of us, and one half of them attacked each flank of the enemy, and beat back those who were just closing round us. Stark's men now took heart and stood their ground. My gun barrel was at this time too hot to hold, so I seized the musket of a dead Hessian, in which my bullets went down easier than in my own. Right in front were the cannon, and seeing an officer on horse-back waving his sword to the artillery, I fired at him twice; his horse fell; he cut the traces of an artillery horse, mounted him and rode off. I afterward heard that the officer was Major Skene. Soon the Germans ran, and we followed; many of them threw down their guns on the ground, or offered them to us, or kneeled, some in puddles of water. One said to me, 'Wir sind ein bruder!' I pushed him behind me and rushed on. The enemy beat a parley, minded to give up, but our men did not understand it. I came to one wounded man flat on the ground, crying water or quarter. I snatched the sword out of his scabbard, and while I ran on and fired, carried it in my mouth, thinking I might need it. The Germans fled by the road and in a wood each side of it; many of their scabbards caught in the brush and held the fugitives till we seized them. We chased them till dark; Colonel Johnston, of Haverhill, wanted to chase them all night. We might have mastered them all, as they stopped within three miles of the battle field; but Stark, saying 'he would run no risk of spoiling a good day's work,' ordered a halt, and return to quarters.

I was coming back, when I was ordered by Stark himself, who knew me, as I had been one of his body guards in Canada, to help draw off a field-piece. I told him 'I was worn out.' His answer was, 'don't seem to disobey; take hold, and if you can't hold out, slip away in the dark.' Before we had dragged the gun far, Warner rode near us. Some one pointing to a dead man by the road-side, said, 'Your brother is killed,' 'Is it Jesse?' asked Warner. And when the answer was 'yes,' he jumped off his horse, stooped and gazed in the dead man's face, and then rode away without saying a word. On my way back I got the belt of the Hessian whose sword I had taken in the pursuit. I also found a barber's pack, but was obliged to give up all my findings till the booty was divided. To the best of my remembrance, my share was four dollars and some odd cents. One tory, with his left eye shot out, was led in, mounted on a horse, who had also lost his left eye. It seems to me cruel now—it did not then.

My company lay down and slept in a corn-field, near where we had fought—each man having a hill of corn for a pillow. When I waked next morning, I was so beaten out that I could not get up till I had rolled about a good while.

After breakfast I went to see them bury the dead. I saw thirteen tories, mostly shot through the head, buried in one hole. Not more than a rod from where I fought, we found Captain McClary dead and stripped naked. We scraped a hole with sticks, and just covered him with earth. We saw many of the wounded who had lain out all night. Afterward we went to Bennington, and saw the prisoners paraded. They were drawn up in one long line; the British foremost, then the Waldeckers, next the Indians, and hindmost the tories.

A letter is still preserved, written by Secretary Fay, of Bennington, at six o'clock on the afternoon of the battle, and sent hither and thither as a circular. It says: 'Stark is now in an action which has been for some time very severe. The enemy were driven; but, being reinforced, made a second stand, and still continue the conflict. But we have taken their cannon; and prisoners, said to number four or five hundred, are now arriving.'

When the smoke cleared away, those who had vanquished the tories beheld, among the captives, among the wounded, among the killed, their neighbors, and in some cases their kinsmen. My own mother's father was in the battle under Stark. My step-mother's father, but for an accident, might have fought in the same engagement under Baum; and these, my 'two grand-fathers, were cousins.'"

The following incident, resting upon good authority, we have never seen published.

All the men of Bennington, capable of bearing arms, were acting as volunteers in the American battalions, leaving in the town old men, and the wives, daughters, and sisters of the brave men who had advanced to repel the British, German and Indian force, which had invaded their soil.

A runaway from the field, who fled at the first fire, circulated a rumor in the town that General Stark was killed, and his forces routed, which spread consternation through the place.

One lady, the wife of an opulent inhabitant, then with his command engaged in the action—a lady who had not even been accustomed to perform household labor—went alone to the barn-yard, yoked a pair of oxen, attached them to a hay-cart; with her own hands, unaided, loaded the cart with her most valuable articles, and drove the team into the woods, where she sunk down exhausted with her uncommon exertions.

When the victors returned, search was made for her, and by lantern-light she was found by her friends, instead of the savages of whose approach a false rumor had given notice.

"Who of us can figure to himself the tortures of suspense by which the women and helpless ones all around about Bennington were excruciated during the hour of battle? In my boyhood, my grand-mother often related to me how, on that day she, with many other women of Williamstown, and their minister, resorted to the meeting-house and continued in prayer for their kinsmen who were on the field of blood, till late at night, when a courier came, announcing glad tidings. She could never refrain from tears when she spoke of hearing the cannon peals again and again booming over the hills, and knew not but each peal spoke defeat and death to those she held most dear, and threatened her home with outrage, pillage and flames."

* * * * * * *

"One more such stroke," said Washington, on learning the tidings, "and we shall have no great cause for anxiety as to the future designs of Britain." *

In the second engagement, after the arrival of Colonel Warner with one hundred and fifty men, the advance of the enemy was checked. Mr. Butler says: "Stark's battalion, you would have said, arose out of the earth at a stamp of his foot. He ordered a hogshead of rum, and it was ready for distribution among his men; but they, refusing to taste while the victory was doubtful, and flushed with success an hour before, rushed to meet the fresh troops of Breyman. The field pieces which we to-night 'begin to possess, were turned against those who came to Baum's rescue. Breyman's cannon, of large calibre, were taken and retaken more than twice; but at last remained in the hands of Americans. The cannon were an emblem of victory on that eventful day.'

* * * * * * *

'But what could overcome the men who fought for their fire-sides and freedom, and who,' in the words of Stark, 'had every man been an Alexander, or a Charles of Sweden, they could not have behaved more gallantly.'

'One of the soldiers who went into battle bare-foot, or nearly so, seeing a good pair of shoes on one of the slain, transferred them to his own feet, but found the dead man's shoes a fleeting inheritance—being killed in the course of the action.'

'The whole expense of Stark's brigade, for mustering, mileage, rations, wages, and contingent charges, was £16,492 12*s.* 10*d.* of continental money, which was paid by the United States, according to such a scale of depreciation that every single dollar of hard money paid for thirty-three dollars of the account. So that £491 and 1*d*, or less than $2,000, paid for the two-fold and ever memorable victory.'"

* * * * * * *

* The retreat of St. Leger from Fort Stanwix, and the surrender of Burgoyne, amply supplied the "one more stroke" hoped for by Washington.

It is the testimony of cotemporary journals that we read of the victories at Bennington as "sowing the seed of all the laurels that Gates reaped during the campaign."

Soon after the battle of Bennington, General Burgoyne wrote to Lord George Germaine: "The Hampshire grants in particular, unpeopled and almost unknown in the last war, now abound with the most active and rebellious race upon the continent; and hang like a gathering storm upon my left. In all parts, their industry and management in driving cattle and removing corn are indefatigible, and it becomes impracticable to move without a portable magazine.

Another most embarrassing circumstance is the want of communication with Sir William Howe. Of the messengers I have sent, I know of two being hanged, and am ignorant whether any of the rest arrived. The same fate has probably attended those dispatched by Sir William, for only one letter has come to hand, informing me that his intention is for Pennsylvania; that Washington has detached Sullivan with 2,500 men to Albany, and that Putnam is in the highlands with 4,000 men. No operation has yet been undertaken in my favor."

The situation of General Burgoyne became every day more critical and desperate. The defeat of Baum and Breyman, and the failure of Colonel St. Leger's expedition, came upon him in rapid succession. Colonel St. Leger had defeated General Herkimer, (slain in the action) and invested Fort Stanwix on the second of August. The fort was bravely defended by Colonel Peter Ganesvoort, of the New-York line, until August 22, when the siege was raised by a forced march of General Arnold. The enemy heard of his approach, which was the signal for the Indians, of whom Colonel St. Leger had a large party, to desert. He therefore raised the seige and retreated to Canada, while Arnold was thirty miles distant from the fort.

General Burgoyne was thus deprived of the support of 1,500 good troops. By these several disasters he lost the support of more than 2,500 men; and as the scouts of the victorious Americans carried beyond his reach all the supplies of the country, and disturbed his foraging parties, he was obliged to obtain his subsistance from Canada. As he had invaded the country with so much of the "pomp and circumstance of war," and sounding proclamations, declaring that "Britons never retrograde," his British pride prompted him to try his fortune in an engagement with an army of nearly twice his numbers, more than half of which had volunteered since the victory of Bennington. But for that, to him, fatal expedition, he would probably have reached Albany and effected a junction with Sir Henry Clinton, who advanced some distance up Hudson river for that purpose. Happily, for the cause of American liberty, that junction never took place.

The affairs consequent upon the battle of Bennington having been arranged, General Stark, with his volunteers, approached the main army, and entered the camp on the 18th of September.

General Gates, sensible that an engagement must soon take place, was desirous of adding these victorious troops to his army. They were drawn up and addressed by him; but to no purpose. "Their time had expired, they had performed their part, and must return to their farms, as their harvests now waited for them." Thus they reasoned among themselves, and commenced their route homeward.

Their general being then without a command, proceeded to New-Hampshire to make his report to the council. His return was a triumphal march. He was waited upon by committees of congratulation wherever he came, and was received with the warmest demonstration of the people's gratitude. His triumph over his enemies in and out of Congress was complete. Their malignant acts of injustice had given him an independent command; and his good fortune had confounded their machinations, by a victory which had turned in its favor the doubtful tide upon which floated the forlorn hope of American independence.

General Stark was soon afterward at the head of a more formidable command of New-Hampshire volunteers, and again advanced, by order of the council of that State, to the theatre of action.*

After capturing Fort Edward, and securing the garrison left at that post by General Burgoyne, and leaving there a detachment of his own troops, he descended the Hudson river and disposed of his forces in such a manner as to enable him to check any attempt of General Burgoyne to retreat.

After his defeat, on the 7th of October, that general concluded to abandon his artillery, his wounded men, and heavy baggage, and with his remaining troops, lightly equipped, cross the Hudson, force his way back to Fort Edward, and retreat from thence to Canada.

He was not then aware that the garrison he had stationed at Fort Edward were prisoners, and that General Stark, with a force of 2,500 men, had arrived in the evening, and then occupied the opposite shore of the river fronting his camp. †

* In this second expedition of New-Hampshire troops, impressed with the certainty that Burgoyne must be captured, volunteers flocked to his standard from all quarters, mustering nearly 3,000 men.

The militia turned out with the understanding that they were to serve under General Stark. This argument induced the men to march and the general to remain on the field.—*Farmer's Ed. Belknap.*

† By this movement Burgoyne became completely surrounded; and General Stark earnestly advised General Gates to attack his camp and thus compel an unconditional surrender. A capitulation, however, was the most prudent, and perhaps equally advantageous mode of ending the military career of Lieutenant General Burgoyne. He never afterward commanded an army. He in later days made no ordinary figure as a member of parliament, and was distinguished as an elegant miscellaneous writer. General Burgoyne was the natural son of Lord Bingly. His wife, clandestinely married, was the Lady Charlotte Stanley, daughter of the Earl of Derby, who died at Kensington palace, during his absence in America, in 1776. Her memory was embalmed in the fond regrets of the general, in the following verses:

"Encompassed in an angel's frame,
An angel's virtues lay;
Too soon did heaven assert its claim,
And call its own away.

My Anna's worth, my Anna's charms,
Must never more return—
What now can fill these widowed arms;
Ah me! my Anna's urn."

In the course of the night he ordered a sergeant, with a party, to cross the river and ascertain whether the passage was practicable. He returned with a report that an army occupied the opposite shore, and had watch-fires burning. Disbelieving this report, the general dispatched one of his staff to ascertain the truth. His boat was hailed, and, no answer being returned, was fired upon by the American sentinel.

Soon afterward a flag of truce was dispatched to the head quarters of General Gates, which caused a cessation of hostilities, and eventually resulted in the surrender of the British army at Saratoga.

Thus ended with glory the campaign of 1777 in the north, which had so inauspiciously commenced with the retreat from Ticonderoga.

Colonel Breyman was killed, when the British lines were stormed, on the 7th of October, 1777 ; and General Frazer, one of Burgoyne's ablest officers, fell on the same day. In a small house, near the battle ground, he died. We visited the house a few years ago, and were shown the stain made by the hero's life-blood upon the floor. His last words, says Baroness de Reidesel, who was by his side, were: "Oh fatal ambition ! Poor General Burgoyne ! Oh my poor wife ! "

Speaking of the heroes of Bennington, General Stark stated, in his official dispatch to the New-Hampshire council, "Too much honor can not be given to our brave officers and soldiers, for their gallant behavior in advancing through fire and smoke, and mounting breastworks supported by cannon. Had every man been an Alexander, or a Charles XII., they could not have behaved more gallantly. I can not particularize any officer, as they all behaved with the greatest spirit.

Colonels Warner and Herrick, by their superior intelligence and experience, were of great service to me. I desire they may be recommended to Congress."

The general was an enthusiastic admirer of Charles XII., king of Sweden.

Five days after the battle of Bennington, a resolution was offered in Congress, censuring General Stark for not submitting to the army regulations.

"Thereupon a member from New-Hampshire rose and said 'that he had not the least doubt but the first battle they heard of from the north would be fought by Stark and the troops under his command, notwithstanding some gentlemen, in their warmth, had spoken disrespectfully of them; and that he should not be afraid to risk his honor or his life on a wager, that Stark's men would do as much as any equal number of troops toward the defence of the country.'"

In a letter home, that speaker says: "Judge my feelings, when the very next day I had a confirmation of all I had asserted, by an express, from General Schuyler, detailing the defeats of Baum and Breyman."*

Upon the receipt of this news, Congress, on motion of Mr. Bland, of Virginia, *Resolved*, that the thanks of Congress be presented to General Stark, of the New-Hampshire militia, and the officers and troops under his command, for their brave and successful attack upon, and signal victory over the enemy in their lines at Bennington; and that Brigadier Stark be appointed a brigadier in the army of the United States.

By order of Congress—

JOHN HANCOCK, *President*."

One member of Congress voted against the passage of the foregoing resolution, who, as Mr. Everett states in his biography of Stark, was Hon. Samuel Chase, of Maryland.

The war being now over in the north, the general returned to New-Hampshire to obtain recruits and supplies. In December he received orders from Congress to repair to Albany, and prepare for a winter expedition to Canada, according to the following resolves:

* Butler's Address.

"IN CONGRESS, Dec. 3d, 1777.

Whereas, the surprise and destroying of the enemy's shipping at St. John's and elsewhere, on Lake Champlain, during the winter, is an expedition of the utmost importance, and of which there is the greatest prrospect of success, provided it can be conducted with prudence, resolution and secrecy—

Resolved, That the Hon'ble James Duane, Esq., be authorized and directed, in a personal conference, to communicate the enterprise to Brigadier General Stark, who is appointed to the command, and to consider with him the best and most practicable means for its accomplishment;

That Brig'r Gen. Stark be authorized, with the utmost secrecy, to select or raise a competent number of volunteers for this service, and to receive, from the commanding officer of the northern department, a sufficient quantity of military stores, carriages and provision (or, if more convenient, to hire carriages and purchase provisions); and that the sum of five thousand dollars, for those and other contingent expenses be advanced, out of the military chest in the said department, to him or his order, for the expenditure whereof he is to be accountable;

That, if the expedition should be successful, the sum of $20,000 shall be paid to the said Gen. Stark and his officers and men, to be divided among them in proportion as the pay of continental officers and privates bears to each other, as a reward for their service, and in full satisfaction of all wages and claims, or in such proportion, more advantageous to the privates, as the general and his officers shall ascertain.

But, if stipulated wages should be preferred to the chance of such reward, the general shall be at liberty to retain the officers and men, at double continental pay and rations, during the expedition, in consequence of the inclemency of the season and the importance of the service;

That General Stark be enjoined to keep secret the said enterprise, and not to communicate it until the nature of the operation shall render it necessary;

That a warrant, in the words following and subscribed by the president, shall be transmitted to Gen. Stark:

'*In Congress*, York Town, 3d Dec., 1777.

Whereas, Brigadier General Stark is appointed to command and direct a secret expedition during the winter season, you are therefore directed and required, upon his order, to supply him with such sum of money, not exceeding five thousand dollars, and such carriages, military stores and provisions as he may require, taking his vouchers for the same, and for which he will be accountable.

By order of Congress—

HENRY LAURENS, *President*.

To the Commanding Officer, Pay Master General, Quarter Master General, and Commissioner of Stores and Provisions in the Northern Department:

That if, from any unforeseen accident, General Stark should be unable or unwilling to engage in the said enterprise, the commanding officer in the northern department be in such case directed and authorized to appoint some other brave and diligent officer to the said command; and that the officer so commanding shall have the same rewards and pay as before proposed;

That all officers in the service of the United States, and all civil officers and others, be requested to give every aid and assistance in their power for forwarding and securing the success of the said enterprise.*

CHAS. THOMPSON, *Secretary*.

* Extract from the Minutes.

MANOUR LIVINGSTON, 16th Dec., 1777.

Sir—Congress, from a high sense of your patriotism, activity and valor, have conferred upon you the chief command of an important enterprise, which they have very much at heart, as, under divine providence, its success entirely depends upon expedition and secrecy.

I am enjoined by Congress to meet you, as soon as possible, at Albany, and there deliver your commission and instructions; and, in a personal conference, fully explain their views. The time you will be pleased to fix; and you may be assured, if health permits, of my punctual attendance. When you are apprised that not a moment is to be lost, and that the security of the United States, and your own in particular, now call for your exertions, I am persuaded all farther arguments must be unnecessary.

I left your friend, General Folsom, in good health and spirits, the 5th instant. He desired me to present you with his respectful compliments.

It is with singular pleasure I congratulate you and your brave militia on the honor which you have acquired at the important battle of Bennington. I feel it the more gratefully, as it has eminently contributed to rescue this devoted State (New-York) from the dangers with which it was surrounded.

Waiting for your speedy answer, by the return of the express, whom you will order to take the shortest route to this place,

I have the honor to be, &c.,

JAMES DUANE.

BRIGADIER GENERAL STARK.

ALBANY, 14th Jan'y, 1778.

Sir—This evening I had the honor of your favor of yesterday, by the express, and shall communicate its contents to Congress, as soon as an opportunity offers on which I can securely rely. Indeed, without the most urgent necessity, I would not commit any thing on this important subject to paper, well knowing that, by declaring it unseasonably, the enterprise must in all probability be blasted. I observe that you make your election of the wages, instead of the bounty. I have no doubt but that you may safely trust to the liberality of Congress in case of success. But this you will be pleased to consider as the opinion of an individual having no authority beyond the instructions I communicated to you at the conference. With a high sense of your merit, and the greatest personal regard,

I am, sir, &c., &c.,

JAMES DUANE.*

BRIGADIER GENERAL STARK.'"

In consequence of this order of Congress, preparations were made for carrying it into execution, with every prospect of success. Had the undertaking been crowned with good fortune, it would have contributed much to insure the safety of the northern frontiers during the remainder of the war. Supplies were obtained of provisions, snow-shoes, conveyances, and every thing required for a winter campaign. The troops were engaged, equipped and ready to march, and their leader was confident of a successful issue —when Congress thought proper to abandon the design.

Early in 1778 he was ordered to assume the command of the northern department at Albany. For this service he had very few reliable troops, and was obliged to depend for support, at times, upon the militia. He had two large frontier rivers to guard, and was surrounded by tories, spies, peculators, and public defaulters. In regulating these abuses, he succeeded like most reformers. Those detected cursed him, while their friends complained; and in November he gladly received notice from General Washington that General Gates desired his assistance in

* James Duane was a member from New-York, of the first congress, in 1774, and the first mayor of New-York, after the evacuation of that city by the British army. He was appointed United States district judge, for the district of New-York, in October, 1789, and died at Albany in 1797.—*Allen's Biographical Dictionary.*

Rhode-Island, with orders to proceed thither. General Hand succeeded him at Albany, but shortly afterward left the command with equal pleasure.

On joining General Gates at Providence, he was directed to take post at East Greenwich, on account of his popularity with the militia, and with a view to ascertain and counteract the designs of the enemy from Rhode-Island. When the season for action was over he returned, by way of Boston, to New-Hampshire, to urge the necessity of recruits and supplies.

In the spring of 1779 he joined the army at Providence, and, by direction of General Gates, examined the coast from Providence to Point Judith, as well as the east side of the bay, as far as Mount Hope. Few troops were employed on this station; and more than ordinary vigilance was required to prevent inroads, and establish a regular system of espionage. In autumn, indications of a descent from the enemy being discovered, he removed his head quarters to Point Judith, seldom resting more than one night in a place.

Late in October the enemy were in motion, and his command were for some days upon constant duty. About the 10th of November the British army decamped from Rhode-Island, and at day light next morning General Stark took possession of Newport, and placed guards in the streets to prevent plunder, and preserve order.

At this time General Washington, fearful that on the arrival of the Newport reinforcement at New-York, an attack might be made upon his army, ordered Generals Gates and Stark, with the troops who had blockaded Newport, excepting a small garrison, to join him in New-Jersey, whence, soon afterward, he directed the latter to proceed to New-Hampshire to make requisitions of troops and supplies.

Having performed this service, he returned to the army at Morristown in May, 1780, and was present at the battle of Springfield, on Short hills, in June following. The affair at Springfield appears to have been as follows:

General Knyphausen, with a force of 5,000 Hessians, made a marauding incursion into New-Jersey, and advanced to Springfield June 23, 1780. The American army was ordered under arms, to oppose them. Maxwell's brigade engaged their advanced guard, but was forced to fall back before superior numbers, until reinforced by Stark's brigade, when a stand was made on high ground near Springfield. While this contest continued, a detachment of the British forced the bridge, after a gallant defence of forty minutes, and burned the village. The enemy then drew off his forces, and commenced his retreat, in which, by order of General Greene, Stark's and Maxwell's brigades closely pursued, and harrassed him for several miles. The pursuers brought back several prisoners, and a quantity of baggage abandoned by the enemy.

Immediately after this General Stark was dispatched to New-England, with orders to collect a body of militia and volunteers, and conduct them to West-Point. He arrived with the troops at West-Point while General Washington was absent to meet Count de Rochambeau at Hartford, Connecticut, shortly before Arnold's desertion. Upon delivering up the reinforcement, he joined his division at Liberty Pole, New-Jersey.

In September he was ordered to relieve the Pennsylvania line, under General St. Clair, which had occupied West-Point after Arnold's treason. General St. Clair marched next day to Liberty Pole.

While at West-Point he was called upon to participate in the melancholy duty of deciding the fate of Major Andrè.* He was one of the thirteen generals who com-

*JUDGMENT OF THE BOARD OF GENERAL OFFICERS, IN THE CASE OF MAJOR JOHN ANDRE.

The Board, having considered the letter of His Excellency, General Washington, respecting Major Andrè, adjutant general to the British army, the confession of Major Andrè, and the papers produced to them:

REPORT, to His Excellency, the commander-in-chief, the following facts which appear to them relative to Major Andrè:

First.—That he came on shore from the Vulture, sloop-of-war, in the night of the 21st of September instant, on an interview with General Arnold, in a private and secret manner.

posed the military tribunal. He was duly sensible of the hardship of the case; but, with his brother officers, was also aware that the liberty of his country was at stake, and that the safety of her army depended upon the example. Their decision, stern and unfeeling as it has since been termed by those who have lived in less dangerous times, had undoubtedly an effect, throughout the war, of preventing a recurrence of the same necessity. An almost universal distrust of each other, at this time, prevailed in the army. Indeed, to such an extent did this feeling increase, that it was deemed unsafe to trust the custody of the prisoner to the guard of soldiers alone. Officers* were present, relieving each other by turns; and, by every attention in their power, they endeavored to alleviate the painful

Secondly.—That he changed his dress within our lines, and, under a feigned name, and in disguised habit, passed our works at Stoney and Verplank's Points, on the evening of the twenty-second of September instant, and was taken the morning of the twenty-third of September instant, at Tarry Town, in a disguised habit, being then on his way to New-York; and when taken, he had in his possession several papers which contained intelligence for the enemy.

The Board, having maturely considered these facts, DO ALSO REPORT to His Excellency, General Washington, That Major Andrè, adjutant general to the British army, ought to be considered as a spy from the enemy; and that, agreeably to the law and usage of nations, it is their opinion he ought to suffer death.

NATH. GREENE, M. Gen'l., President.
STERLING, M. G.
AR. ST. CLAIR, M. G.
LA. FAYETTE, M. G.
R. HOWE, M. G.
STEUBEN, M. G.
SAMUEL H. PARSONS, B. Gen'l.
JAMES CLINTON, B. Gen'l.
H. KNOX, Brigr. Gen'l. Artillery.
JNO. GLOVER, B. Gen'l.
JOHN PATTERSON, B. Gen'l.
EDWARD HAND, B. Gen'l.
J. HUNTINGTON, B. Gen'l.
JOHN STARK, B. Gen'l.
JOHN LAWRENCE, J. A. Genl.

In regard to the execution of Major Andrè, six members were in favor of his being shot; six others were of opinion that he ought to be hung as a spy. General Greene, the president, decided the question in favor of the latter.

* The late Major C. Stark, and his brother, Lieutenant Archibald Stark, were among those who were frequently in his place of confinement, and were present at his execution.

situation of a high-minded soldier who, in an evil hour, became the dupe of a traitor whose name has gone down to posterity with scarcely a ray of honor to lighten the darkness of his memory.

At this time General Washington formed the design of surprising Staten island. To mask his intention, General Stark was detached, with 2,500 of the best troops of the army, with a suitable proportion of cavalry and field artillery, accompanied by a large train of wagons, teamsters, and cattle-drivers, with orders to advance near Manhattan island; bring away all the cattle, grain and forage to be found, and hover about the vicinity of New-York until farther orders; if attacked by the enemy, to collect his force upon advantageous ground, and trust to his own conduct and the goodness of his troops for the result. The enemy, suspecting some design from another quarter, suffered this detachment to pillage the country, (principally peopled by the disaffected) as far as Morrisania and King's bridge, for several days, and then quietly return with their booty. Colonel Humphreys, aid-de-camp to General Washington, crossed the Hudson on a stormy night, informed that the Staten island project was abandoned, and directed the foragers to retire. The army soon afterward went into winter quarters at West-Point, New Windsor and Fishkill. General Stark was there visited with a severe illness, and returned home on furlough, with the standing order for men and supplies.

In the spring of 1781 he was ordered once more to assume the command of the northern department, and fix his head quarters at Saratoga. Some feeble detachments of militia from New-York, Massachussetts and New-Hampshire constituted all the disposable force for the protection of this extensive frontier. If the country was in a sad condition in 1778, it was ten fold more so in 1781. It was overrun with spies and traitors. Robberies were frequent, and many inhabitants (non-combatants) carried prisoners to Canada.

General Schuyler's house, at Albany, was robbed, and two of his servants carried away. The general saved himself by retreating to his chamber, barricading the door, and firing through it upon the marauders. The reports of his pistols roused the city military; but the plunderers escaped.

Soon after the establishment of the military post at Saratoga, a party of these brigands was discovered within the lines, unarmed, and a British commission found upon their leader, a refugee from the States. A board of officers examined the case, pronounced him a spy, and condemned him to be hanged; which sentence was executed on the next day.*

One of the prisoners, upon promise of quarter, informed that he belonged to a party of fifteen, who had come down from Canada as spies; that his companions were then variously disguised and scattered through the country to ascertain its defensive condition, for the benefit of the British officers in Canada, who were planning an inroad; and that their boats had been concealed on the shore of Lake George. A lieutenant, with a sufficient force, with the prisoner for a guide, was dispatched to the place, with

* DEATH WARRANT OF THOMAS LOVELACE. *By John Stark, Esq., Brigadier General in the army of the United States, and Commander of the Northern Department, &c.*

At a general court-martial, held at Saratoga, October second, 1781, whereof Colonel Weissenfels was president, Thomas Lovelace, of the tory forces in the British army, was brought before the court, charged with being a spy; and the court, after hearing the examinations, and other testimony, have pronounced their opinion that he was a spy, and, by the usages of war, he be hanged by the neck until he be dead; which sentence being approved by me, you will remove him from the main guard to-morrow, the 8th instant, at half past ten o'clock A. M., and exactly at eleven o'clock cause him him to be hanged by the neck until he be dead—for which this is your sufficient warrant.

Given under my hand and seal, at my head quarters, at Saratoga, this 7th day of October, in the year of our Lord one thousand seven hundred and eighty-one.

By the General's command—

JOHN STARK,
Brig. General Commanding. [L. S.]

CALEB STARK, *Brigade Major.*
To the Adjutant of the day.

orders "to wait five days for the return of the party." He found the boats, and remained there one day. The prisoner escaped in the night, and, becoming alarmed for his safety, he disobeyed his orders and returned to Saratoga.

.Ten days would have elapsed before a force could have been brought against him from the information of the escaped spy, and soon after the officer's retreat, the facts were ascertained that the tories returned to their boats two days afterward, and escaped. The officer was censured for not capturing the whole party, as he might and ought to have done. The relatives of the spy, residing in the vicinity, complained to the commander-in-chief, and said much about retaliation. General Washington demanded a copy of the proceedings, which were forwarded to him; and no farther notice was taken of the matter. The cure of the body politic was radical. No other parties * of a similar character appeared in the northern department during the war.

After the surrender of Earl Cornwallis, and the apprehension of inroads from Canada had disappeared, General Stark dismissed the militia, with thanks for their good conduct; and, after securing the public stores, was ordered to retire, by way of Albany, to New-England, to recruit men and collect supplies for the next campaign.

During the year of 1782 he was afflicted with rheumatism, and did not return to the army until ordered to head quarters by General Washington, in April, 1783. He was there present at the appointed time, and received the warm and hearty thanks of the commander-in-chief for his punctuality.

* A party of the same character was captured at Bennington, soon after General Stark assumed the command of the troops there concentrated. On this occasion all his address was necessarily employed to prevent the sovereign people from exercising summary justice upon the culprits. They were sentenced to Symmsbury mines. Lynch law was often the most potent authority in those days.

During the years 1778 and 1781, many such persons, arrested as spies or traitors to the continent, were condemned by courts-martial, ordered by General Stark, and sentenced to be confined in prison, or be compelled to serve on board public American ships for the remainder of the war.

The celebrated Newburg letters* were then operating upon the minds of the officers as well as soldiers. His influence was exerted, with that of other general officers, in allaying the feelings of distrust and discontent then manifested, and to induce the troops to disband without confusion, or suffering their victorious laurels to be tarnished by acts of hostile violence against their country.

Several officers at this time retained a partiality for orders of aristocracy. The establishment of the Cincinnati Society was the result. He made several objections to the formation of this order: one of which was that its principles had no affinity with the character and conduct of the illustrious Roman general, whose name had been adopted.

"To imitate that great man," he observed, "we should return to the occupations we have temporarily abandoned, without ostentation, holding ourselves ever in readiness to obey the call of our country." This course he strictly observed during the remainder of his life.

The independence of the United States having been acknowledged by England, her army, on the 25th of November, 1783, evacuated New-York. During the following month most of the continental troops returned to their homes, many of them having a journey, on foot, of six hundred miles to perform, bearing in their arms, "as presents," their muskets and bayonets, with their certificate of service, their honorable discharges, and a few "caricatures" of money, in the shape of depreciated continental paper, in their pockets.†

* The Newburg letters were written by General John Armstrong, who, in 1813, was chief of the war department. The predictions contained in those letters, in regard to the officers and soldiers of the revolution, and the neglect of the United States government to satisfy the just demands promised to secure their fidelity and valor in the hour of trial, have since been more than verified.

† One soldier informed the writer that during his journey home (two hundred miles) he called at a farm house for a drink of milk, for which he offered to pay "silver money." The good housewife was indignant; said "he was either an Englishman or a tory," for no honest, true American could have "silver money."

After this concluding scene of the revolutionary drama, General Stark, bidding adieu to his friends of the army, and to the cares of public life, retired to his estate. He there devoted the remainder of his days to the various duties incumbent upon a patriot—an extensive agriculturist, and the father of a numerous family.

His long, useful, and active career terminated on the 8th day of May, 1822, in the ninety-fourth year of his age. His funeral was attended by a numerous concourse of his countrymen, at his late residence on the banks of the Merrimack; the Rev. Dr. Dana, of Londonderry, officiating as chaplain. His remains were interred with military honors in a cemetery upon his own estate, which had been inclosed, by his order, several years previous to his decease. The well disciplined company of light infantry, from Goffstown, performed, in satisfactory manner, the duties of military escort, and fired three volleys over the grave of the last American general of the revolutionary army, who surrendered his arms to his God.

The cemetery occupies elevated ground, and may be seen for a considerable distance up and down the river. On the 16th of August, 1829, (the anniversary of Bennington victory) a block of granite, emblematic of his republican firmness of character, hewn in the form of an obelisk, upon which his name was inscribed, was, by his family, erected to his memory.

Such is an imperfect outline of the life and services of a soldier of New-Hampshire, who was a bold and firm defender of his country's rights in the "times that tried men's souls;" and who contributed as much as any other individual toward the successful result of the long and

Having, by the exhibition of his honorable discharge, convinced her of his true character, he was made welcome to a lodging, and the best refreshments the house afforded. In the morning a substantial breakfast was furnished him, after partaking of which, the good people placed a plentiful luncheon in his knapsack; and having thanked his kind entertainers, the veteran went on his way rejoicing.

hard-fought contest which established the independence of the United States of America.

In the path of duty no man was more stern and unbending; yet no one better knew how to win the affections of his soldiers. Fearless, cool and intrepid in the midst of danger, his manner and presence inspired courage and confidence in those he commanded.

When visited by the writer, in 1819, he was the *last* survivor of the American revolutionary generals—the only relic of that glorious band of patriots who were his compeers, to read the history of their sufferings and triumphs. He was then more than 91 years of age.

> As the proud oak that braves the pelting storm,
> Unbroke, unbent, tho' lightnings play sublime;
> Tho' ninety years have marked thy war-worn form,
> Thou stand 'st alone amid the march of Time.
>
> First in the lists where warring champions stood,
> Whose free born spirits brooked no sceptered lord;
> Thy deeds of fame were writ in tyrant's blood,
> And freedom blessed thy ever conquering sword.

Although broken down with age and infirmities, his memory was clear and distinct, in regard to the military events of the French war, particularly as to the actions of Lord Howe, and several others under whom he served.

The events of the revolution, being of later date, had mostly escaped him. To a question respecting Bunker's hill action, he answered, "all I know about it is, that we gained the victory."

The events of the war of 1812 were regarded by him with attention and great interest. When he learned that the Bennington cannon had been surrendered at Detroit, he was highly incensed at the loss of "his guns," as he termed them, and regretted that the weakness, incident to old age, prevented him from again taking the field for his country.

The pieces surrendered were inscribed, "taken at Bennington, August 16, 1777." An officer of Hull's army mentioned the following incident respecting them:

He was standing near the field artillery, when the British officer of the day directed the evening salutes to be fired from the captured cannon; at the same time observing the inscription, he said he would cause another line to be added to the verse; "retaken at Detroit, August 15, 1812."

The guns were recovered at the capture of Fort George, and transferred to Sackett's Harbor; and with them, said our informant, we fired salutes in honor of the victory gained over General Proctor and Tecumseh in 1813, at the river Thames, U. C. The two lightest pieces were presented by Congress to the State of Vermont a few years since.

One of the heavier pieces, marked with many sword cuts, is supposed to be in the possession of the company of New-Boston artillery belonging to the ninth regiment of N. H. Militia.

Tradition reports that the gun was presented to that regiment by General Stark; as such it is still regarded and retained, although the legislature of New-Hampshire, a few years ago, passed a resolve that it should be placed in the State Capitol, at Concord.

Of the trophies presented to New-Hampshire, by General Stark, the brass barreled drum, and a Hessian ammunition bag, have found their way to the State Capitol. The musket, sword and grenadier's cap are yet missing.

The cannon granted to Vermont might long ago have adorned the State House of New-Hampshire, had her legislature ever considered them worthy of an application to Congress. They could easily have been obtained while our State was represented in the national councils by a Woodbury, an Atherton, a Hubbard, or a Pierce, to support her claim.

We will not, however, complain; they are in good hands. The highlanders of Vermont were ever true to the cause of liberty; and the achievements of their Allen, Warner, Herrick, Baker, and others, during the war of independence, entitle their names to be handed down with undying honors to future ages.

May these trophies be preserved, by our Vermont friends, as lasting mementos of the patriotism and bravery of the White and Green mountaineers in the trial days of 1777.

It may here be remarked, that while Congress liberally bestowed upon other distinguished actors, in the great drama of the revolution, swords and medals, in approbation of their services, the total defeat of a veteran enemy, the capture or destruction of one thousand men, and a death blow dealt to the invader's hopes, was complimented by a generous vote of thanks bestowed upon General Stark and his brave officers and soldiers.

The general received from Congress the following compliment in 1786:

"In pursuance of an act of Congress, of the thirtieth day of September, A. D. 1783,

JOHN STARK, Esquire, is to rank as Major General by Brevet, in the army of the United States of America.

Given under my hand, at New-York, the ninth day of June, 1786.

[L. S.] NATHANIEL GORHAM, *President.*

Entered in the war office—

Henry Knox, *Secretary of War.**

The writer was informed by an old lady in Kentucky, formerly a resident of Boston, and intimately acquainted with General Stark and Dr. Belknap, that in May, 1798, she bore a message from the general to the doctor, inviting him to come to his residence and spend a fortnight, to receive from him an account of the campaign in Canada in 1776, as no correct history of it had then appeared. She delivered the message, and the historian was preparing to accept the invitation, when a sudden paralytic attack put an end to his life, June 20, 1798. Thus the opportunity of

* Copied from the original commission.

obtaining information upon the subject, from a living, intelligent, and prominent actor in the scene, was lost.

His character was as unexceptionable in his private as in his public life. His manners were frank and open. He spake his thoughts boldly, and without concealment of his meaning, on all occasions. He was a man of kindness and hospitality, which, through life, he extended to all his comrades in arms, and others who sought his assistance. He ever sustained a reputation for honor and integrity—friendly to the industrious and enterprising, but severe to the idle and unworthy.

Society may venerate his memory as that of an honest and useful citizen; while his conduct, as an intrepid and faithful soldier, occupies a distinguished and honorable position in the history of his country.

He lived about forty-five years after the battle of Bennington, and proved the Nestor of the revolution, for he survived all his comrades in arms, of equal rank, in America.

He lived to see the fruits of his toils endured, and dangers braved, in the establishment of his nation's independence, the prosperity of her institutions, and the happiness of his countrymen.

On the eighth day of May, 1822, he received marching orders from the only Power he ever feared, and "took up his line of march" for the Soldier's Home.

Beside his native silvery stream,
The hero's relics low are laid;
Of battle's deeds no more he'll dream,
Fame claims no more—her debt is paid;
But o'er him still her laurels bloom,
And crown with brightest wreaths his tomb.

In person, the General was of middle stature, well proportioned for strength and activity. Constant exercise prevented his ever becoming corpulent. He always traveled on horseback, even if accompanied by his family in a carriage; and at an advanced age, mounted his horse with ease, without other aid than the stirrup.

His features were bold and prominent; the nose was well formed; the eyes, light-blue, keen and piercing, deeply sunk under projecting brows. His lips were generally closely compressed. He was not bald; but his hair became white, and covered his head. His whole appearance indicated courage, coolness, activity, and confidence in himself, whether called upon to perform the duties of an enterprising partizan, or a calculating and considerate general.

At a public dinner, given at Concord, N. H., in honor of Hon. Richard M. Johnson, a gentleman present gave the following sentiment:

Colonel Richard M. Johnson—From the shoulders up, the image of General John Stark!

The general's children were eleven in number: five sons and six daughters, and all, excepting one, reached the age of maturity. Three of his sons were officers of the United States army. A notice of Caleb, the eldest, is contained in this volume.

Archibald attended his father during his command of the northern department in 1778, and during the campaign in Rhode-Island. As a lieutenant, he accompanied General Sullivan's expedition against the Six Nations. He was present at their defeat, and witnessed the destruction of their settlements as far as the Gennessee river. He served through the war. He died September 11, 1791.

Benjamin Franklin was commissioned as a lieutenant in 1799, when, during the administration of President John Adams, war * was declared against the French Republic. He died July 25, 1806.

[Copied from one of General Stark's memorandum books.]

John Stark, son of Archibald Stark, was born August 28, 1728.

Elizabeth Page, *alias* Elizabeth Stark, daughter of Caleb and Elizabeth Page, was born February 16, 1737–8. Died 29th June, 1814.

Married August 20, 1758.

Caleb Stark, born December 3, 1759. Died August 26, 1838.

Archibald Stark, born May 28, 1761. Died September 11, 1791.

John Stark, born April 17, 1763. Deceased.

Eleanor Stark, born May 4, 1765. Died August 20, 1767.

Eleanor Stark, Jun'r, born June 30, 1767. Deceased.

Sarah Stark, born June 11, 1769. Died January 29, 1801.

Elizabeth Stark, born August 10, 1771. Died May 14, 1813.

Mary Stark, born September 19, 1773. Deceased.

Charles Stark, born December 2, 1775. (He sailed from Boston in the brig Sipsburgh, Benjamin Wheelwright, Master, November, 1776, and was heard of no more.†

Benjamin Franklin Stark, born January 16, 1777. Died July 25, 1806.

Sophia Stark, born January 21, 1782.

The above and foregoing children were born of the above Elizabeth Stark.

The Stark family is supposed to have originated in Germany. Tradition reports that persons of that name came to Scotland, with a body of Germans, sent over by the Duchess of Burgundy, (widow of Charles the Bold) under the orders of General Martin Swart, to support the claim of Perkin Warbeck (the pretended son of Edward IV) to the crown of England, in the reign of Henry VII. They

* The only events of this war, worthy of notice, were the two brilliant victories obtained by the United States frigate Constellation, rated at 36 guns, over the French frigates Insurgente, (February 9, 1799) and Vengeance (February 1, 1800). The French frigates mounted fifty or more guns each. For the capture of the former, the merchants of Lloyd's coffee-house presented Commodore Truxtun a silver pitcher, with an appropriate inscription; and Congress voted him a gold medal for his triumph over the Vengeance. The pitcher we have seen in the possession of his daughter, Mrs. Sarah Benbridge, of Cincinnati, Ohio.

† The vessel was owned by Major Stark. His brother-in-law, Thomas McKinstry, and one of his clerks, Mr. Heath, were also lost in her.

were defeated on the plain of Stoke, and the fugitives escaped to Scotland.

The book of heraldry contains a legend that one of the name saved the life of a king of Scotland, by slaying a wild bull, which attacked his majesty while hunting. For this exploit he was created a baronet. The following is copied from the book.

> "Stark—Scotland and America;
> A bull's head erased, ar,
> (distilling blood, p. p. r.)
> Fortiorum fortia facta."

In 1840 a communication was received by the secretary of State, at Washington, from the government of Hesse Cassel, requesting inquiries to be made to ascertain the fact "whether or not the officer who commanded the Americans, at the battle of Bennington, was born in Germany; stating that, upon the answer of that question, depended the decision of a law suit which had been for several years pending, in which a large estate was involved. Inquiry was also to be made as to his heirs, and if any were dead, who were their representatives." The answers were furnished, by the writer, to Honorable John Forsyth, then Secretary of State, and nothing farther has been received upon the subject.

ROLL OF CAPTAIN JOHN STARK'S COMPANY OF RANGERS ENLISTED FOR THE YEAR 1759, AND TO THE END OF THE WAR.

John Allen,
Richard Aspinwall,
Daniel Abbot,
Reuben Allen,
Jasper Bagley,
Tristram Barnard,
George Berry,
James Broderick,
Andrew Boynton,
Daniel Blair,
James Bannerty,
John Babson,
James Colbey,
James Chase,
James Crayton,
Jacob Colbey,
James Cratston,
Jedediah Crain,
Caleb Dalton,
Abner Dane,
Samuel Doherty,
Adam Dickey,
Robert Dickey,
John Evans,
Joseph Farwell,
James Fling,
John Fram,
William Gamble,
Joseph George,
William Garrals,
Andrew Gilman,
Edward Gordon,
John George,
James McGlachan,
Jonathan Hobbs,
Ezra Heath,
John Hall,
Joseph Hall,
Thomas Hall,
Elisha Hutchins,
Robert Hurd,
James Humphrey,
Robert Humphrey,
Jonathan Hobbs,
Sargent Jewell,
Richard Kinneston,
William Kinneston,
Lt. Joshua Martin,
Nath'l Martin,
John Martin,
James McMullen,
Josiah Molan,
Jasper Needham,
Samuel Mackers,
Alexander McNeil,
Nehemiah McNeil,
Daniel McNeil,
Daniel Newell,
James Peters,
William Peters,
James Kimmbey,
Bimsley Pottle,
John Peney,
John Robinson,
Layers Rowe,
James Roose,
James Russ,
Joseph Sewall,
Robert Stuart,
Robert Starret,
Isibule Sterling,
Josiah Swett,
Edward Webber,
George Whalley.

The general orders in 1759 required the ranger companies to consist of one hundred privates each. Where a full company could not be obtained by enlistment, the number deficient was made up by volunteers, or men drafted from the provincial regiments then in the royal service.

These hardy soldiers, with their veteran comrades of the "seven years' war," constituted the nucleus around which, in 1775, assembled the army of the revolution.

NAMES OF PERSONS DISCHARGED FROM COLONEL JOHN STARK'S REGIMENT, WHOSE ARMS AND ACCOUTERMENTS WERE RETAINED.

	Company.		Company.
James Nesmith,	Reid.	James Stone,	Kinsman.
Samuel Thompson,	"	Solomon Call,	"
Eben McIlvain,	"	John Palmer,	"
Hugh Alexander,	"	William Perkins,	"
John Nesmith,	"	Stephen Flanders,	"
Hugh Connel,	"	John Burns,	"
Nehemiah Lockhart,	"	Abiel Austin,	"
Eben'r Eastman,	Kinsman.	John Folsom,	"
John McPhersen,	"	Jonathan Bell,	"
Stilman Corser,	Reid.	William Gamble,	"
John Young,	"	Stephen Dudley,	"
James Orr,	"	Capt. Henry Dearborn,	"
Richard Straw,	"	Robert McDonnel,	Moore.
Simeon Mudget,	Kinsman.	Andrew Robinson,	"
Thomas Morril,	Reid.	William Frazer,	"
Hugh Campbell,	"	Josiah Bachelder,	"
John Peterson,	"	David Abbot,	"
Samuel Morris,	"	Daniel Ladd,	"
James Caldwell,	"	William Graves,	"
Joseph Harris,	"	John Page,	"
James Folsom,	Kinsman.	Samuel Lakeman,	"
Wells Davis,	"	Robert Page,	"
James Colamer,	"	James Colamer,	"
John Little,	"	James Noyes,	"
Peter Butterfield,	"	Andrew Silkens,	"
James Wier,	"	Jonathan Robey,	"
Robert Adams,	"		

Amount of appraised articles, £78, 17*s*., 10*d*.

Winter Hill, January 11, 1776. A true return of the guns and cartouch boxes * delivered in camp, from the soldiers discharged from Colonel Stark's regiment, being the sixth, agreeably to general orders, appraised by us, the subscribers, appointed by Brig'r Gen'l Sullivan for that purpose.

JOSEPH CILLEY, Major.
EZRA FOLSOM, Captain.
AMOS MORRIL, Lieut.

* The arms, &c., and their value, are, in the original return, placed against each name.

All or the larger portion of the men before named were in the action at Bunker's hill.

We copy, from the "Siege of Boston," a list of the officers of the New-Hampshire regiments who were in the action at Bunker's hill.

STARK'S REGIMENT.

CAPTAINS.	LIEUTENANTS.	ENSIGNS.
Isaac Baldwin,	John Hale,	Stephen Hoyt.
Elisha Woodbury,	Thomas Hardy,	Jona. Corliss.
Samuel Richards,	Moses Little,	Jesse Carr.
John Moore,	Jonas McLaughlin,	Nath'l Boyd.
Joshua Abbot,	Samuel Atkinson,	Abiel Chandler.
Gordon Hutchins,	Joseph Soper,	Daniel Livermore.
Aaron Kinsman,	Ebenezer Eastman,	Samuel Dearborn.
Henry Dearborn,	Amos Morril,	Michael McClary.
Daniel Moore,	Ebenezer Frye,	John Moore.
George Reid,	Abraham Reid,	James Anderson.

The regiment contained thirteen companies; and but ten captains, lieutenants and ensigns, are named in the above list. An old manuscript contains charges, by Colonel Stark, to his officers, for advances. We find as captains, charged with sundries, Captain Chandler, November 19, 1775; Captain James McCurdy, June 1776; Captain Morril, March 14, 1776; Captain Walker, March 14, 1776; Captain Noah Cook, November 20, 1775; Dr. Obadiah Williams, June 10, 1775; Lieutenant Amos Morril, November 20, 1775.

REED'S REGIMENT.*

CAPTAINS.	LIEUTENANTS.	ENSIGNS.
John Marcy,	Isaac Farwell,	James Taggart, 48.
Benjamin Mann,	Benjamin Brewer,	Samuel Pettengill, 49.
Josiah Crosby,	Daniel Wilkins,	Thomas Maxwell, 44.
William Walker,	James Brown,	William Roby, 46.
Philip Thomas,	John Harper,	Ezekiel Rand, 46.
Ezra Towne,	Josiah Brown,	John Hackness, 52.
Jona. Whitcomb,	Elijah Clayes,	Stephen Carter, 59.
Jacob Hinds,	Isaac Stone,	George Aldrich, 54.
Levi Spaulding,	Joseph Bradford,	Thomas Buff, 44.
Hezekiah Hutchins,	Amos Emerson,	John Marsh, 44.

* Colonel James Reed was not in the action. He was struck with blindness, and left the service in 1776.

ITEMS FROM COLONEL STARK'S ACCOUNT BOOK.

Camp on Isle aux Noix, June 20, 1776.

	£	s.	d.
Lieutenant Carr, to cash lent, lawful money,	0	18	0
Chimney Point.			
Jonathan Carr, to cash lent, lawful money,	0	4	0

Paid August 20, 1776.

Mess bill. Cash laid out by Colonel Stark.

	£	s.	d.
To ½ case gin, bought at Crown Point,	1	13	9
To 1 case gin, bought of Mr. Tucker,	3	12	9
To 1 do. bought of Mr. Avery,	3	9	9
To cash paid for brewing a barrel of beer,	0	2	0

Extract from the speech of Colonel Potter, at the anniversary dinner of the Amoskeag Veterans, February 22, 1859:

"Stark, at Lake George, when a shot from the enemy broke the lock of his gun, deliberately running over to the enemy's line, and seizing the gun of a prostrate Frenchman, to use instead of his own, shew his individualism.

It was the same quality that, at the news of Lexington battle, led him to throw down his crow-bar, shut down the gate of his saw-mill, seize his arms, mount his horse, and ride to the post of danger. It was his striking individualism that induced fourteen full companies to flock to his standard in less than as many days.

It was individualism that stamped the heights of Bunker's hill with the impress of American valor. Each battalion seemed to be actuated by individualism. The battle was fought by individualism. Each commander of a battalion or regiment, seemed to fight in his own way, and 'on his own hook.'

Prescott fought at his redoubt; Warren, with a major general's commission in his pocket, fought as a volunteer. Stark came up to the rail fence breast-work, (itself an individualism) continued it down to the beach, and, in a a moment as it were, built a wall to the water's edge of the stones upon the beach. Then was displayed that individualism so often spoken of by Washington, to his honor.

Taking a stake in his hand, he deliberately walked in front of his line, the distance of thirty or forty yards, where, setting up the stake in the ground, he shouted: 'Boys, the red coats are coming up the hill. If one of you fire a gun till they reach that stake, I'll shoot him.'

It was the same individualism that, at Bennington, dictated the memorable speech: 'There are the enemy, boys, the red coats and tories; you must beat them, or Betty Stark sleeps a widow to-night.'"

The speaker obtained the anecdote of the stake from George W. Park Custis, who said he had often heard General Washington relate it, to show the cool courage of General Stark. In his speech, at the tomb of Washington, before the Amoskeag Veterans, General Custis alluded to the fact of the stake, and stated his authority.

The following relates to statements contained in Powers' History of Coös:

In Stark's Memoir, page 15, the exploring expeditions to Coös are noticed.

Mr. Powers disbelieves that any party, acting under the orders of government, did in reality visit that region in 1752, or prior to 1754.

Belknap (vol. 2, p. 215) states that a "party was sent up in the spring of 1752, to view the meadows and lay out the townships."

Stark and Eastman passed, in 1752, as captives to the Indians, through the Coös country. The former, as pilot, attended the expedition of Colonel Lovewell, in 1753, and in 1754, in the same capacity, that conducted by Captain Peter Powers.

The following extract, from the History of Manchester, (p. 279—281) relates to the subject:

"About the time Stark was taken, Sebattis and Plausawa, Indians living at St. Francis, but who had formerly lived in the Merrimack valley, came to Canterbury, and having been kindly treated by Messrs. Miles and Lindsay, with whom they had formerly been acquainted, they left the place, having seized upon and captured two negroes, belonging to the men who had treated them with so much hospitality. One of the negroes escaped and informed of his captors, while the other was sold at Crown Point.

This conduct of the Indians produced the greatest consternation and alarm, and the project of taking armed possession of the Coös country was prosecuted with renewed vigor.

The assembly of New-Hampshire, in answer to the memorial of those engaged in the project, so far complied with the wishes of the memorialists as to assume the expense of cutting and making a road from the settlements upon the Merrimack, to the 'Coös meadows;' and appointed a committee to survey and mark the road. This active preparation to seize their lands did not escape the notice of the Indians; and in January, 1753, they sent six Indians, with a flag of truce, to the fort at Number Four, to remonstrate against the proceedings of the English. They took strong grounds upon the subject, and it is highly propable that the whole procedure was at the instance and under the direction of the French.

They told Captain Stevens that they were displeased 'at our people going to take a view of the Coös meadows *last spring*' (spring of 1752); 'and that for the English to settle *Cowos* was what they could not agree to; and as the English had no need of that land, but had enough without it, they must think the English had a mind for war if they would go there, and that they should have a strong war.' *

Meantime, about the 10th of March, 1753, the committee, appointed by the assembly to survey and *mark* the road to Coös, commenced the performance of their duty. The committee consisted of Zacheus Lovewell, of Duns-

* The Rev. Mr. Powers, in his History of the Coös Country, undertakes to show that Dr. Belknap has misconstrued this extract from Colonel Williams' letter, and that no such persons visited the Coös country in the spring of 1752. But in this matter Dr. Belknap is *right* and Mr. Powers *wrong*. Mr. Powers does not quote the extract correctly. As given above (from the original letter of Colonel Williams, of March 19, 1753) no one can doubt, were other proofs wanting, that our people went into the Coös country in the spring of 1752.

table, John Talford, of Chester, and Caleb Page of Starkstown. They hired sixteen men at Amoskeag and Pennacook to assist in the expedition; and John Stark, of Derryfield, as pilot, he having passed through the Coös country, as a captive, the spring previous. Caleb Page was the surveyor.

The committee performed the duties assigned them in twenty days, returning to Concord on the 31st of March. As most of the men engaged in this expedition were from Amoskeag, the following account is added, giving the names, time, and capacity in which each one was employed.

March, 1753. Messrs. ZACHEUS LOVEWELL, JOHN TALFORD, and CALEB PAGE, charge ye Prôvince of New-Hamp'r, *Dr.* For themselves and men, here named, hired to survey and make the road to Coös, in March, curr't:

				£	s.	d.
Zacheus Lovewell,	22	days, a	35s.	38	10	0
John Talford,	22	"	35	38	10	0
Caleb Page,	22	"	35	38	10	0
Nath'l Smith,	19½	"	30	29	5	0
John Eveny,	19½	"	30	29	5	0
Reuben Kimball,	19½	"	30	29	5	0
Benj. Laikin,	19½	"	30	29	5	0
Enoch Webster,	19½	"	30	29	5	0
Eben. Copp,	19½	"	30	29	5	0
Jona. Burbank,	19½	"	30	29	5	0
John Johnson,	19½	"	30	29	5	0
Benj. Eastman,	19½	"	30	29	5	0
Peter Bowen,	19½	"	30	29	5	0
Nath'l Ingalls,	22	"	30	33	0	0
Robert Rogers,	19½	"	30	29	5	0
John Combs,	22	"	30	33	0	0
Wm. McCluer,	22	"	30	33	0	0
John Stark, pilot,	21	"	35	36	15	0
Abraham Perry,	22	"	30	33	0	0
Caleb Page, surveyor,	22	"	60	66	0	0
Zach. Lovewell, John Talford, Caleb Page, each one day attendance to appoint• the day's and prepare for ye march,				5	5	0
Caleb Page, jurney to Rumford, to hire men, four days,			35	7	0	0
Old tenor,				684	5	0

Dated 31st of March, 1753.

ZACHEUS LOVEWELL,
JOHN TALFORD,
CALEB PAGE, } *Committee.**

*See files in Secretary's office.

The author of the History of Manchester has collected other information in regard to the expeditions to Coös, which will probably appear in the edition of Belknap's History of New-Hampshire, which he is now preparing for publication. We have a recollection of seeing, in boyhood, a journal of the above survey, written by our ancestor, Captain Caleb Page, surveyor of the expedition, but thought no more of it, until a letter was received from John Farmer, Esq., making inquiries concerning such a paper. He was then preparing his edition of Belknap's History. Search was made for the manuscript, but without success.

THE BATTLE OF BENNINGTON, August 16, 1777.

BY REV. THOMAS P. RODMAN.

Copied from the Rhode-Island Book.

Up through a cloudy sky, the sun
  Was buffeting his way
On such a morn as ushers in
  A sultry August day.
Hot was the air—and hotter yet,
  Men's thoughts within them grew;
They, *Britons*, *Hessians*, *Tories*, saw,
  They saw their homesteads too!

They thought of all their country's wrongs;
  They thought of noble lives,
Poured out in battle with their foes;—
  They thought upon their wives,
Their children and their aged sires,
  Their firesides, churches, God!
And these deep thoughts made hallowed ground
  Each foot of soil they trod.

Their leader was a veteran man—
  A man of earnest will;—
His very presence was a host;
  He'd fought at Bunker's hill!
A *living monument* he stood,
  Of stirring deeds of fame;
Of deeds that shed a fadeless light
  On his own deathless name!

Of Charlestown's flames, of Warren's blood,
  His presence told the tale;
It made each patriot's heart beat quick,
  Though lip and cheek grew pale;
It spoke of Princeton, Morristown;—
  Told Trenton's thrilling story;
It lit futurity with hope,
  And on the past shed glory.

Who were those men? their leader, who?
  Where stood they on that morn?
The men were northern yeomanry,—
  Brave men as e'er were born;
Who, in the reaper's merry row,
  Or warrior's rank could stand;
Right worthy such a noble troop—
  John Stark led on the band.

Walloomsac wanders by the spot
  Where *they*, that morning, stood;
Then rolled the war-cloud o'er the stream,
  The waves were tinged with blood;
And the near hills that dark cloud girt,
  And fires like lightning flashed;
And shrieks and groans, like howling blasts,
  Rose as the bayonets clashed.

The night before, the yankee host
  Came gathering from afar,
And in each belted bosom glowed
  The spirit of the war!
All full of fight, through rainy storm,
  Night cloudy, starless, dark—
They came, and gathered as they came,
  Around the valiant Stark!

There was a Berkshire Parson—he
  And all his flock were there,
And like true *churchmen* militant,
  The arm of flesh made bare.
Out spoke the Dominie, and said:—
  "For battle have we come,
"These many times; and after this,
  "We mean to stay at home,

"If now we come in vain." Said Stark:—
  "What! would you go to-night,
"To battle it with yonder troops?
  "God send us morning light,
"And we will give you work enough;
  Let but the morning come,
"And if ye hear no voice of war,
  "Go back and stay at home."

The morning came—there stood the foe;—
  Stark eyed them as they stood;
Few words he spoke—'twas not a time
  For moralizing mood;
"See there, the *enemy*, my boys—
  Now, strong in valor's might,
"*Beat them*, or Betty * Stark will sleep
  "In widowhood to-night!"

Each soldier there had left at home,
  A sweetheart, wife or mother;
A blooming sister, or perchance,
  A fair-haired, blue-eyed brother;
Each from a fireside came, and thoughts
  These simple words awoke,
That nerved up every warrior's arm,
  And guided every stroke.

Fireside and woman!—mighty words!
  How wond'rous is the spell
They work upon the manly heart,
  Who knoweth not full well?
And than the *women* of this land,
  That never land hath known
A truer, nobler-hearted race,
  Each yankee boy must own.

*** General Stark's wife's name was *Elizabeth Page*.**

Brief eloquence was Stark's—nor vain;
  Scarce uttered he the words,
When burst the musket's rattling peal;—
  Out leaped the flashing swords;—
And when brave Stark in after time,
  Told the proud tale of wonder,
He said "the battle din was one
  Continual clap of thunder."

Two hours they strove, when victory crowned
  The valiant yankee boys;
Nought but the memory of the dead
  Bedimmed their glorious joys!
Aye—there's the rub; the hour of strife,
  Though follow years of fame,
Is still in mournful memory linked
  With some death-hallowed name.

The cypress with the laurel twines—
  The PÆAN sounds a knell—
The trophied column marks the spot
  Where friends and brothers fell!
Fame's mantle, a funeral pall
  Seems to the grief-dimmed eye;
For ever where the bravest fall,
  The best-beloved die!

THE TOMB OF GENERAL STARK.

BY HERRICK.

No trappings of State their bright honors unfolding,
  No gorgeous display mark the place of thy rest;
Yet the granite points out where thy relics lie mould'ring,
  And the wild rose is shedding its sweets o'er thy breast.

The zephyrs of evening shall sport with the willow,
  And play through the grass where the sweet flow'rets creep,
Where the thoughts of the brave as they bend o'er thy pillow,
  Shall hallow the spot of the hero's last sleep.

As from glory and honor to death thou descendedst,
  It was mete thou shouldst lie by the Merrimack's wave;
It was well thou shouldst sleep 'mongst the hills thou defendedst
  And take thy last rest in so simple a grave.

There for ever thou 'lt sleep, and tho' ages roll o'er thee,
  And crumble the stone o'er thine ashes to earth,
The sons of the free shall with reverence adore thee—
  The pride of the mountains that gave thee thy birth.

CORRESPONDENCE.

In regard to the following correspondence, we will here state that the letters from General Stark are copies of the original draughts, a few of which are in his own hand writing; all subsequent to the campaign of 1777 were written by his brigade major, and aid-de-camp. The letters addressed to him are copied from the originals now in the possession of the writer of the foregoing memoir.

Copy of a Petition to the Government of New-Hampshire, in 1754, as on file in the office of the Secretary of State.

Amos Eastman, of Pennacook (Concord), and John Stark, of Starkstown (Dunbarton), both in the province of New-Hampshire, of lawful age, testify and say "that on the 28th day of April, 1752, they were in company with William Stark, of Starkstown, and David Stinson, of Londonderry, on one of the branches of the Permigwasset river, about eighteen miles from Stevenstown (Salisbury); that on the same day, toward night, the Indians captivated the said John, and the next morning, soon after day break, captivated the said Amos; and fired upon David Stinson and William Stark; they killed and scalped the said David (the said William made his escape), and carried the deponents both to Canada;

That the stuff the Indians took from the deponents and their company was of the value of five hundred and sixty pounds at least, old tenor, for which they have no restitution;

That the said Amos was sold to the French, and for his redemption paid sixty dollars to his master, besides all his expenses of getting home; that the said John purchased his redemption of the Indians, for which he paid one hundred and three dollars, besides his expenses in getting home; that there were ten Indians in the company who captivated the deponents, and lived at St. Francis. They often told the deponents it was not peace. One Francis Titigaw was the chief of the scout. There was in the scout one named Peer, a young sagamore, who belonged to St. Francis.

The deponents made oath to the preceding, May 23, 1754, before Joseph Blanchard, one of his majesty's justices of the peace.

In a memorial presented by John and William Stark to Governor Wentworth, in 1754, they say that they gave no offence to the Indians; that they had it in their power to destroy them, or defeat their enterprise; but esteeming it a time of peace with all the Indians who own themselves subjects of the French king, free from any expectation of any hostilities to be committed against them, they peaceably applied themselves to their own business, till ambushed by the Indians. They killed, scalped and stripped David Stinson, one of their company, captivated the aforesaid John and Amos, and shot at the said William, who escaped; that they carried the said captives to Canada, and, at the same time, took the goods and effects of your memorialists and said David Stinson, in company, of the value of five hundred and sixty pounds at least, old tenor."

The government never refunded any portion of the above. In this respect Massachusetts adopted a more liberal policy, and redeemed all her captives from the Indians.

Medford, May 18, 1775.

Gentlemen—About the 29th of April last, a committee, sent from the provincial Congress of the province of New-Hampshire, to the provincial Congress of the Prov. of Mass. Bay, having discretionary instructions from said Congress, advised to raise a regiment from the province of New-Hampshire as soon as possible, under the constitution or establishment of the Massachusetts Bay, but to be deemed as part of the quota of men from the province of New-Hampshire, and that the New-Hampshire Congress would establish said measures. In consequence of which a number of officers from the province of New-Hampshire convened and made choice of their field officers for said regiment, who have raised the same—584 of whom are now present at Medford, exclusive of drummers and fifers, and the remainder are hereby expected. And, as a great number of those already here (who expected, when they enlisted, to draw arms from the provincial stock) are destitute of the same, and can not be furnished (as no arms are to be procured here, at present), must inevitably return from whence they came, unless they are supplied from some quarter speedily, I humbly pray that you would maturely consider our defenceless situation, and adopt some measure or measures whereby they may be equipped. In confidence of your immediate compliance with the above request,

I am, in the country's common cause,

Your most obedient, humble serv't,

JOHN STARK.

N. B. The gentlemen who present this to the convention can give you particular information as to our present situation.*

Superscribed "the Chairman of Prov'l Congress, for the province of New-Hampshire, now sitting at Exeter."

* Vol. 1, State papers, p. 149.

To the Hon. Council of New-Hampshire.

Medford, May 29, 1775.

Gentlemen—Yours of the 20th inst. I have received, and note the contents; and as to fire-arms for the regiment under my command, the greater part who were destitute when I wrote you, are since furnished; and I am informed from the officers of the several companies, that the remainder will be equipped very shortly, so that I flatter myself this difficulty will be speedily removed as to my regiment; but as to the manner of procuring them, whether by the respective towns to which they belong, or by individuals, I can not at present inform you, as no account thereof has as yet come to hand. But I would beg leave still to entreat you to take a little farther notice of us; and, in the first place, consider that a considerable part of the regiment are destitute of blankets (and can not be supplied by their towns), and are very much exposed; some of whom, for want thereof, by reason of colds, are very much indisposed, and thereby rendered unfit for duty; and, secondly, that we are in great want of money; and that neither the officers or soldiers can subsist without it, much longer, by any means. And this I am well assured of from daily complaints which are made to me, that unless you, by some means or other, advance some money to the army directly (as there is no room in my mind to doubt but there is a very considerable sum in the province, belonging thereto), their courage will fail, and they will return; and by that means, we shall work our own destruction. Again, I would recommend a sutler or supplier for the army; and if it should be necessary that there should be a sutler or sutlers, and you can not find one in that province who will undertake it on reasonable terms, I know of a gentleman in this province who will, if applied to. I would likewise be glad if a chest of medicine might be procured for the use of the regiment, and tools for the armorer to repair arms with. According to your request, I have inclosed and transmitted to the committee of safety a return of the men who have enlisted in the service of the province of New-Hampshire (now under my command), and who expect to be paid therefrom. Your speedy compliance with the above will greatly oblige

Yours, in the common cause,

JOHN STARK.

The Congress of the Colony of New-Hampshire,

To John Stark, Esq., Greeting.

We, reposing especial trust and confidence in your courage and good conduct, do, by these presents, constitute and appoint you, the said John Stark, to be colonel of the first regiment of foot, raised by the Congress aforesaid, for the defence of the American colonies.

You are, therefore, carefully and diligently to discharge the duty of a colonel, in leading, ordering, and exercising the said regiment in arms, both inferior officers and soldiers, and to keep them in good order and discipline. And they are hereby commanded to obey you as their colonel; and you are yourself to observe and follow such orders and instructions as you shall, from time to time, receive from the general and commander-in-chief of the forces raised in the colony, aforesaid, or any other your superior officers, according to such military rules and discipline of war as have been, or hereafter shall be, ordered by the Congress of said colony, in pursuance of the trust reposed in you.

By order of the Congress—

MATTHEW THORNTON, *President.*

Exeter, the third day of June, A. D. 1775.

E. THOMPSON, *Secretary.*

Colonel Stark to Hon. Matthew Thornton, President of the New-Hampshire Provincial Congress.

Medford, June 19, 1775.

Sir.—I embrace this opportunity, by Colonel Holland, to give you some particulars of an engagement in battle, which was fought on the 17th inst., between the British troops and the Americans.

On the 16th, at evening, a detachment of the Massachusetts line marched, by the general's order, (General Ward) to make intrenchment upon a hill in Charlestown, called Charlestown hill, near Boston, where they intrenched that night, without interruption, but were attacked, on the morning of the 17th, very warmly by the ships of war in Charlestown river, and the batteries in Boston. Upon this, I was ordered by the general to send a detachment of two hundred men, with proper officers, to their assistance; which order I promptly obeyed, and appointed Lieutenant Colonel Wyman to command the same. At two o'clock P. M. an express arrived with orders for my whole regiment to proceed to Charlestown, to oppose the British who were landing on Charlestown point; accordingly we proceeded, and the battle soon came on, in which a number of officers and men of my regiment were killed and wounded. The officers killed were Major McClury, by a cannon ball; Captain Baldwin and Lieutenant Scott, by small arms.

The whole number, including officers, killed and missing,	15
Wounded,	45
Total, killed, wounded and missing,	60

By Colonel Reed's desire, I transmit the account of those who suffered belonging to that portion of his regiment who were engaged:

Killed, 3; wounded, 29; missing, 1.
Total, in both regiments, 93.

But we remain in good spirits, being well satisfied that where we have lost one, the enemy have lost three. I should consider it a favor if the committee of safety should recommend to the several towns and parishes of New-Hampshire the necessity of detaining and sending back all the soldiers belonging to the New-Hampshire line, stationed at Medford, whom they may find at a distance from the army, without a furlough from the commanding officer.

I am, sir, with great respect,

Yours and the country's,

To serve in the good cause,

JOHN STARK.

NOTES BY EDITOR. Colonel Stephen Holland, of Londonderry, afterward went to New-York and joined the enemy. He received a grant of land in Ireland, as a remuneration for his estate confiscated in America.

General Ward ordered this party to intrench upon Bunker's hill, but by mistake they proceeded a mile farther, to Breed's hill, a lesser eminence, and nearer to Boston. The attempt of the enemy to dislodge them produced the action called the battle of Bunker's hill. This affair gave the enemy direct evidence that the yankees could fight, and the latter confidence in themselves. The enemy intended to possess and fortify Dorchester heights, on the 18th of June, but the operations of the Americans, on the night of the 16th, directed their attention in another direction; very fortunate for the Americans, as they were enabled to fortify the heights themselves, and force the enemy to evacuate Boston.

Marching Orders for Colonel John Stark, commanding the 5th and 25th Regiments of Foot.

You are forthwith to march, with the regiments under your command, to Norwich, in Connecticut, according to the route indicated; and in case of extreme bad weather or other unforeseen accidents you are obliged to halt a day or more, between this and Norwich, you will acquaint Brigadier General Heath, who is appointed to the command of the brigade, now under marching orders, and receive and follow his directions. You will immediately apply to Commissary General Trumbull, and to Quarter Master General, Col. Mifflin, for an order for carriages and provisions for your march to Norwich. Upon your arrival there, Brigadier General Heath has his excellency, the commander-in-chief's directions for the farther disposal of the brigade.

His excellency expects you to preserve good order and exact discipline upon your march, carefully preventing all pillage and marauding, and every kind of ill-usage, or insult to the inhabitants of the country. As the motions of the enemy, and the advanced season of the year make it of the utmost consequence that not a moment should be lost that can possibly be made use of on your march, the general, depending on your zeal, experience and good conduct, is satisfied that, on your part, no vigilance will be wanting.

Given at head quarters, this 16th day of March, 1776.

HORATIO GATES, *Adj't Gen'l.*

Route from Cambridge to

Framingham,	20
Sutton,	18
Dudley,	20
Mort Lake,	19
Norwich,	20
In all,	97

THOMAS MIFFLIN, *Q. M. Gen'l.*

Colonel Stark, and other colonels, presented a remonstrance to General Schuyler against the removal of the army from Crown Point to Ticonderoga.

GENERAL SCHUYLER'S ANSWER.

Ticonderoga, July 9, 1776, 9 *P. M.*

Gentlemen—Your remonstrance, of yesterday's date, was delivered to me at eight o'clock this evening, by General Sullivan. Previous to any observations on it, give me leave to remind you of a mistake you have made in supposing that I informed you "that Congress had directed that the army was to be removed to Ticonderoga." My expression was exactly in these words: "That it be recommended to General Schuyler to form a strong camp in the vicinity of Ticonderoga or Crown Point." I observed that, as I quoted from memory, and had not the resolution with me, I could not repeat the very words of it. I rather wish to impute your mistake to misapprehension than to any intentional false repetition of what I said, which I can not suppose any gentleman can be guilty of.

The reasons which induced the council of general officers unanimously to give their opinion to move the main body of the army from Crown Point, I can not conceive myself at liberty to give without their consent; for myself, I declare with that frankness which I wish always to characterize me, that the measure seemed not only prudent, but, in my opinion, indispensably necessary for a variety of reasons, against which those you have given do not, in my opinion, bear a sufficient weight to alter it; some of which are evidently nugatory, and all of which might be contrasted with more cogent ones in support of the resolution. I assure you, at the same time, that if I were convinced of the impropriety of the measure, I should not be in the least tenacious of supporting my opinion, but immediately give way to conviction, and rescind the resolution so far as depended on me to do it.

I am happy, gentlemen, that you declare your readiness to obey the resolution of the general officers, although it does not meet your approbation—a sentiment that every good officer ought not only to entertain, but to inculcate on others as a principle on which the preservation of every army in a great measure depends. Such a sentiment will always induce me, and I dare say every other general officer, to receive with patience and pleasure the advice of his officers, and act accordingly, where I or they are convinced.

I am, gentlemen, with great respect,

Your most obedient, humble serv't,

PH. SCHUYLER.

Note by Editor. After events proved that the memorialists were correct. The following extract expresses the opinion of the commander-in-chief to Congress.

In consequence of the evacuation of Crown Point, General Schuyler lost for a time the confidence of many of the northern officers, and many of the people of the north.

Extract from a letter of General Washington to Congress, July 19, 1776.

"I confess the determination of the council of general officers, on the 7th, to retreat from Crown Point, surprised me much; and the more I consider it, the more striking does the impropriety appear. The reasons assigned against it by the field officers, in their remonstrance, coincide greatly with my own ideas, and those of the other general officers I have had an opportunity of conversing with, and seem to be of considerable weight, I may add, conclusive. I am not so fully acquainted with the geography of that country, and the situation of the different posts, as to pronounce a peremptory judgment upon the matter; but if my ideas are right, the possession of Crown Point is essential to give us the superiority and mastery of the lake.

That the enemy will possess it, as soon as abandoned by us, there can be no doubt; and if they do, whatever gallies or force we keep upon the lake, will be unquestionably in their rear. How they are to be supported there, or what succor can be drawn from them, is beyond my comprehension. Perhaps it is only meant that they shall be employed on the communication between that and Ticonderoga. If this is the case, I fear the views of Congress will not be answered, nor the salutary effects derived from them that were intended.

I have mentioned my surprise to General Schuyler, and would, by the advice of the general officers, have directed that post should be maintained, had it not been for two causes: an apprehension that the works had been destroyed, and that if the army should be ordered from Ticonderoga, or the post opposite to it (where I presume they are), to repossess it, they would have neither one place or another secure, and in a defensible state; the other, lest it might increase the jealousy and diversity of opinions which seem already too prevalent in the army, and establish a precedent for the inferior officers to set up their judgment whenever they would, in opposition to their superiors—a matter of great delicacy, and that might lead to fatal consequences if countenanced, though in the present instance I could have wished their reasoning had prevailed."

General Gates and Schuyler took fire at the implied censure of the general officers who had given their opinions to General Washington, against the abandonment of Crown Point, and the preference of Ticonderoga. They made common cause, and in spirited terms vindicated their judgment to the commander-in-chief; reprehended in strong language the general officers to whom General Washington alluded, and carried their complaints to Congress. The steady, temperate course, however, of the commander-in-chief, prevented serious consequences.*

*Wilkinson, vol. 1, page 63.

Ira Allen to New-Hampshire Committee of Safety.

Onion River, July 10, 1776.

Gentlemen—I learn you are alarmed at the retreat of our army out of Canada. I can assure you the savages have killed and scalped a number of men by the river La Cole, on the west side of Lake Champlain. When they will visit us or you, is uncertain; I advise you to look sharp, keep scouts out, but not to move, except some families much remote from the main inhabitants. Last Saturday I was at Crown Point with General Sullivan. He assured me he would do all in his power to protect the frontier settlements.

I proposed a line of forts by this river to Cohos. He said he believed that to be the best place, and made no doubt but it would be done. He immediately ordered Colonel Waite and two hundred men to this place, here to remain, and grant all protection in his power to the inhabitants. Before I left there, Generals Schuyler, Gates and Arnold arrived. I conclude there is a determination, before this time, in regard to all the frontiers. I make no doubt but a line of block forts is agreed on by all, from this river to yours, and so round your frontiers. I had intelligence from St. Johns about twelve days ago. Our enemy had but one hundred tents, which at most could not be more than six hundred men. They did not appear to be in much preparation for war. At Chambly there were but few men. It is thought by some that the enemy are busy in sending provisions and clothing to all the garrisons near the head of the river St. Lawrence, and in supplying the Indians with all necessaries. The small-pox has almost gone through our army; they are in much better health than they were. Gondolas are building; the vessels are preparing for war. I hope, in a short time, they will be able to beat all the powers of Britain on this lake. Crown Point is proposed for head quarters.

In haste, IRA ALLEN.*

* Vol. 1, fifth series, American Archives, page 177.

A PROCLAMATION.

By Lieut. General John Burgoyne, commanding an army and fleet against the revolted Provinces of America.

To the inhabitants of Castleton, Hubbardton, Rutland, Tinmouth, Pawlet, Wells and Granville, with the neighboring districts; also the districts bordering on White Creek, Cambden, Cambridge, &c.

You are hereby directed to send, from your several townships, deputies, consisting of ten persons or more, from each township, to meet Colonel Skene, at Castleton, on Monday, July 15, at 10 o'clock in the morning, who will have instructions not only to give farther encouragement to those who complied with my late manifesto, but also to communicate conditions upon which the persons and property of the disobedient may yet be spared. This fail not to obey, under pain of military execution.

Head Quarters, at Skenesborough House, July 10, 1777.

J. BURGOYNE.

By order of His Excellency, the Lieutenant General—

B. KIMPTON, *Secretary.*

A PROCLAMATION.

By Philip Schuyler, Esq., Major General in the Army of the United States of America, and Commander-in-chief of the Northern Department.

To the inhabitants of Castleton, Hubbardton, Rutland, Tinmouth, Paulet, Wells, Granville, with the neighboring districts bordering on White creek, Cambden, Cambridge, &c., &c.

Whereas, Lieutenant General John Burgoygne, commanding an army of the British troops, did, by a written paper, by him subscribed, bearing date at Skenesborough House, on the 10th day of July, instant, require you to send from your several townships, deputations consisting of ten persons or more from each township, to meet Colonel Skene at Castleton, on Wednesday, July 15th, at ten in the morning, for sundry purposes in said paper mentioned; and that you were not to fail in paying obedience thereto, under pain of military execution.

Whatever, my countrymen, may be the ostensible reasons for such meeting, it is evidently intended by the enemy, then to prevail on you, by threats and promises, to forsake the cause of your injured country; to assist them in forcing on the United States of America, and under the specious pretext of affording you protection, to bring on you that misery which their promises of protection drew on such of the deluded inhabitants of New-Jersey who were weak enough to confide in them, but who experienced their fallacy by being treated indiscriminately with those virtuous citizens, who came forth in defence of their country, with the most wanton barbarity, and such as hitherto hath not even disgraced barbarism. They cruelly butchered, without distinction to age or sex; ravished children from ten, to women of eighty years of age; they burnt, pillaged and destroyed whatever came into their power. Nor did those edifices dedicated to the worship of Almighty God escape their sacrilegeous fury. Such were the deeds—such they were incontestibly proved to be which have marked the British arms with the most indelible stains.

But they having, by the blessing of divine providence on our arms, been obliged totally to abandon that State, they left those who were weak or wicked enough to take protection under them, to bemoan their credulity, and to cast themselves on the mercy of their injured countrymen. Such will be your fate, if you lend a willing ear to their promises, which I trust none of you will do. But lest any of you should so far forget the duty you owe to your country as to join with, or in any manner assist or give comfort to, or hold correspondence with, or take protection from the enemy: be it known to each and every one of you, the inhabitants of said townships, or any other, the inhabitants of the united States, that you will be considered and dealt with as traitors to said states; and that the laws thereof will be put in execution against every person, so offending, with the utmost rigor; and do hereby strictly enjoin and command all officers, civil and military, to apprehend or cause to be apprehended, all such offenders. And I do strictly enjoin and command such of the militia of said townships as have not yet marched, to do so without delay, to join the army under my command or some detachment thereof.

Given under my hand and seal, at head quarters.

PHILIP SCHUYLER.

Fort Edward, July 13, 1777.

By the general's command—

HENRY B. LIVINGSTON.

Manchester, 24*th July*, 1777.

Dear Sir—I learn, by express, from the council of safety and assembly of your State, dated the 19th instant, and directed to the council of this State, that it is expected that one fourth part of twelve regiments are to be immediately drafted, formed into three battalions, and put under your immediate command, and sent forthwith into this State, to oppose the ravages and coming forward of the enemy; and also to desire the convention of this State to send some person or persons to wait on you, at No. 4, this day, to advise with you, relative to the route and disposition your troops are to take, as also the present disposition and manœuvres of the enemy.

By Major Tyler and Captain Fitch I send you an extract of a letter from General Schuyler, relative to the situation of the enemy. And from what intelligence I have been able to collect since that date, I judge there is not less in number than 2,000, at different places in Castleton and Rutland, and a large number at Skenesborough; part of which are (by their motion) making preparations for a very speedy movement toward this camp, which is at present so thinly inhabited that I can by no means be able to make a stand without assistance. It is, therefore, of the most pressing importance that your troops be forwarded to this place with as much expedition as possible. Provision will be made here for their subsistence, on their arrival. The council of safety of this State are present, and join me in urging the necessity of your speedy assistance.

I am, sir, your very humble servant,

SETH WARNER.

BRIGADIER GENERAL STARK.

Address of the Council of Safety of Vermont to the Councils of Safety of Massachusetts and New-Hampshire.

IN COUNCIL OF SAFETY. *State of Vermont*,
Manchester, July 15, 1777.

Gentlemen—This State, in particular, seems to be at present the object of destruction. By the surrender of the fortress of Ticonderoga, a communication is opened to the defenceless inhabitants on the frontier, who, having little more in store at present than sufficient for the maintenance of their respective families, and not ability immediately to remove their effects, are therefore induced to accept such protections as are offered them by the enemy.

By this means, those towns who are most contiguous to them are under the necessity of taking such protection, by which the next town or towns become equally a frontier as the former towns before such protection; and unless we can have the assistance of our *friends*, so as to put it immediately in our power to make a sufficient stand against such strength as they may send, it appears that it will soon be out of the power of this State to maintain its territory.

This country, notwithstanding its infancy, seems to be as well supplied with provisions for victualing an army as any on the continent; so that, on that account, we can not see why a stand may not as well be made in this State as in Massachusetts; and more especially, as the inhabitants are heartily disposed to defend their liberties.

You, gentlemen, will be at once sensible that every such town as accepts protection is rendered, at that instant, incapable of affording any farther assistance; and what is infinitely worse, as some disaffected persons eternally lurk in almost every inhabited town, such become doubly fortified to injure their country, our good disposition to defend ourselves and make a frontier for your State, with our own, which can not be carried into execution without your assistance.

Should you send immediate assistance, we can help you; and should you neglect till we are put to the necessity of taking protection, you know it is in a moment out of our power to assist you.

Your laying these circumstances together will, I hope, induce your honors to take the same into consideration, and immediately send us your determination in the premises.

I have the satisfaction to be your honors' most obedient and very humble servant. By order of the council,

IRA ALLEN, *Secretary.*

Letter from Meshech Weare, President of New-Hampshire, to Ira Allen, Secretary of the State of Vermont.

Exeter, July 19, 1777.

Sir—I was favored with yours of the 15th instant yesterday, by express, and laid the same before our general court, who are sitting. We had, previous thereto, determined to send assistance to your State. They have now determined that a quarter part of the militia of twelve regiments shall be immediately drafted, formed into three battalions, under the command of Brigadier General John Stark, and forthwith sent into your State, to oppose the ravages and coming forward of the enemy; and orders are now issuing, and will go out in a few hours, to the several colonels for that purpose.

Dependence is made that they will be supplied with provisions in your State; and I am to desire your convention will send some proper person or persons to Number Four, by Thursday next, to meet General Stark there, and advise with him relative to the route and disposition of our troops; and to give him such information as you may then have relative to the manœuvres of the enemy.

In behalf of the council and assembly, I am, sir, your most obedient humble servant,

MESHECH WEARE, *President*.

STATE OF NEW-HAMPSHIRE.
In Committee of Safety, July 30, 1777.

To Colonel Samuel Folsom—

You are desired to proceed to No. 4, and if General Stark has marched from there before you arrive, to follow him until you overtake him, and endeavor to find out what circumstances his men are in, how they are supplied, and what they are likely to want that can be supplied from hence.

The State of Vermont having assured us that they would supply them with provisions, dependence is made on them therefor.

You are to inform General Stark that it is expected that he, with the advice of his field officers, will appoint such officers as are wanting in his army.

Beside the ammunition lately sent to No. 4, there is now on the way forty-three bushels of salt, a thousand weight of musket-balls, of different sizes, four hundred flints, and a small cask of medicines, of which you will inform General Stark. If it had been possible to procure tin kettles, they would have been sent, but they were not to be had; and we fear the men will be put to great difficulty for want of them. You will endeavor to be informed what magazine of ammunition there is at Bennington, and whether our men can depend on a supply from thence in case of necessity.

You will inquire of Mr. Grant and Col. Hunt what ammunition they have delivered to Gen. Stark's men, and what is now on hand, as well as stores. On the whole, you are to advise with all persons in the service of this State on such things as you think needful to forward the business we are engaged in, and make report, on your return, of what shall appear to you necessary to be farther done for supplying the troops under Gen. Stark.

The £200 (pounds) delivered to your care you are to deliver to Gen. Stark, if he thinks he shall need it, for contingencies, taking his receipt to account therefor.

MESHECH WEARE, *President.*

General Schuyler to General Lincoln.

Albany, August 8, 1777.

Dear General—Your favor of the 6th instant was delivered me last night. I could not wish you to remain too long at Bennington for the Massachusetts militia, as the enemy point their force down Hudson river; and we can not know how soon we may want your assistance. Please to leave orders for them to follow you, and do the same in respect to those from New-Hampshire, who are yet expected.

I inclose you a copy of a letter from General Washington to General Putnam, which was transmitted me by the latter, and came to hand last evening. You will please to promulgate it as extensively as possible.

I am, with great regard and esteem,

Dear General, your mo. obt. hbl. servt.,

PH. SCHUYLER.

Major General Lincoln.

Half Moon, August 14, 1777.

Dear General—Your favor of yesterday's date, per express, I received on the road to this place. As the troops were not on the march, I am glad you detained them in Bennington. Our plan is adopted. I will bring with me camp-kettles, axes, ammunition and flints. I expect from Albany a surgeon, with a case of capital instruments, bandages, dressing, medicines, &c., &c. You will please to meet us, as proposed, on the morning of the 18th. If the enemy shall have possession of that place, and in your opinion it becomes improper for us to rendezvous there, you will be so good as to appoint another, and advise me of the place. You will give me leave to recommend that all the troops march as light as possible, bringing only their blankets, a second shirt, and a pair of stockings, beside what they have on.

I am, sir, your most obed't humble serv't.

B. LINCOLN.

Brigadier General Stark.

To the Council of New-Hampshire.

Bennington, August 18, 1777.

Gentlemen—I congratulate you on the late success of your troops under my command, by express. I propose to give you a brief account of my proceedings since I wrote to you last.

I left Manchester, Vt., on the 8th instant, and arrived here on the 9th. The 13th I was informed that a party of Indians were at Cambridge, which is twelve miles distant from this place, on their march thither. I detached Col. Gregg, with two hundred men under his command, to stop their march.

In the evening I had information, by express, that there was a large body of the enemy on their way, with field pieces, in order to march through the country, commanded by Governor Skene. The 14th I marched with my brigade, and a portion of the State militia, to oppose them, and cover Gregg's retreat, who found himself unable to withstand their superior numbers. About four miles from this town I accordingly met him on his return, and the enemy in close pursuit of him, within a half mile of his rear; but when they discovered me, they presently halted on a very advantageous piece of ground.

I drew up my little army on an eminence in view of their encampment,—but could not bring them to an engagement. I marched back about a mile, and there encamped. I sent a few men to skirmish with them, who killed thirty of them, with two Indian chiefs. The 15th it rained all day; I sent out parties to harrass them.

The 16th I was joined by this State's (Vt.) militia, and those of Berkshire county. I divided my army into three divisions, and sent Lieut. Col. Nichols with two hundred and fifty men on the rear of their left wing, Colonel Herrick on the rear of their right, ordered, when joined, to attack the same. In the meantime I sent three hundred men to oppose the enemy's front, to draw their attention that way. Soon after I detached Colonels Hubbard and Stickney on their right wing, with two hundred men, to attack that part; all which plans had their desired effect. Colonel Nichols sent me word that he stood in need of a reinforcement, which I readily granted, consisting of one hundred men; at which time he commenced the attack precisely at three o'clock in the afternoon, which was followed by all the rest. I pushed forward the remainder with all speed.

Our people behaved with the greatest spirit and bravery imaginable. Had they been Alexanders, or Charleses of Sweden, they could not have behaved better.

The action lasted two hours; at the expiration of which time we forced their breastworks, at the muzzle of their guns; took two pieces of brass cannon, with a number of prisoners; but before I could get them into proper form again, I received intelligence that there was a large reinforcement within two miles of us, on their march, which occasioned us to renew our attack; but, luckily for us,

Colonel Warner's regiment came up, which put a stop to their career. We soon rallied, and in a few minutes the action began very warm and desperate, which lasted until night. We used their cannon against them, which proved of great service to us.

At sunset we obliged them to retreat a second time; we pursued them till dark, when I was obliged to halt for fear of killing our men.

We recovered two pieces more of their cannon, together with all their baggage, a number of horses, carriages, &c.; killed upward of two hundred of the enemy in the field of battle.

The number of wounded is not yet known, as they are scattered about in many places. I have one lieutenant colonel, since dead (Colonel Baum), one major, seven captains, fourteen lieutenants, four ensigns, two cornets, one judge advocate, one baron, two Canadian officers, six sergeants, one aide-de-camp, one Hessian chaplain, three Hessian surgeons, and seven hundred prisoners.

I inclose you a copy of General Burgoyne's instructions to Colonel Baum, who commanded the detachment that engaged us. Our wounded are forty-two—ten privates and four officers, belonging to my brigade; one dead. The dead and wounded in the other corps I do not know, as they have not brought in their returns yet.

I am, Gentlemen, with the greatest regard, your most obedient and humble servant,

JOHN STARK,

Brigadier General Commanding.

P. S. I think in this action we have returned the enemy a proper compliment for their Hubbardston engagement.*

* Historical Collections and Monthly Literary Journal.

Van Schaik's Island, August 18, 1777.

Sir—I have the honor to congratulate Congress on a signal victory obtained by General Stark, an account whereof is contained in the following letter from General Lincoln, which I have this moment had the happiness to receive; together with General Burgoyne's instructions to Lieut. Col. Baum, a copy whereof is inclosed.

I am in hopes Congress will very soon have the satisfaction to hear that Gen. Arnold has raised the siege of Fort Schuyler. If that takes place, I believe it will be possible to engage two or three hundred Indians to join the army, and Congress may rest assured that my best endeavors shall not be wanting to accomplish it.

I am informed that General Gates arrived at Albany yesterday. Major Livingston, one of my aids, will have the honor to deliver this dispatch.

I am, with every sentiment of respect,

Your obedient servant,

PH. SCHUYLER.

Hon. John Hancock, Pres't of Congress.

The following private letter to General Gates, is copied from General Stark's first draft. He would not write to Congress; but wrote to his old friend, General Gates.

Bennington, August 23, 1777.

Dear General—Yours of the 19th was received with pleasure, and I should have answered it sooner, but I have been very unwell since. General Lincoln has written you upon the subject, with whom I most cordially concur in opinion.

I will now give you a short account of the action near this place. On the 13th of August, being informed that a party of Indians were at Cambridge, on their way to this place, I detached Lieutenant Colonel Gregg to stop their march, and, in the night, was informed that a large body of the enemy were advancing in their rear.

I rallied my brigade, sent orders to Colonel Warner, whose regiment lay at Manchester, and also expresses to the militia to come in with all speed to our assistance; which orders were all promptly obeyed. We then marched with our collected force in quest of the enemy, and, after proceeding five miles, we met Colonel Gregg in full retreat, the enemy being within a mile of him.

Our little army was immediately drawn up in order of battle; upon which the enemy halted, and commenced intrenching upon very advantageous ground. A party of skirmishers, sent out upon their front, had a good effect, and killed thirty of them, without loss on our side. The ground where I then was not being fit for a general action, we retired one mile, encamped, and called a council of war, where it was determined to send two detachments to the rear, while the remainder attacked in front. The 15th, proving rainy, afforded the enemy an opportunity to surround his camp with a log breast work, inform General Burgoyne of his situation, and request a reinforcement.

On the morning of the 16th, Colonel Symonds joined us, with a party of Berkshire militia. In pursuance of our plan, I detached Colonel Nichols, with two hundred men, to the left; and Colonel Herrick, with three hundred men, to the right, with orders to turn the enemy's flanks, and attack his rear. Colonels Hubbard and Stickney, with two hundred men, were posted upon his right, and one hundred men stationed in front, to attract their attention in that quarter.

About three o'clock P. M., Colonel Nichols began the attack, which was followed up by the remainder of my little army. I pushed up in front; and, in a few minutes, the action became general. It lasted about two hours, and was the hottest engagement I have ever witnessed, resembling a continual clap of thunder.

The enemy were at last compelled to abandon their field pieces and baggage, and surrender themselves prisoners of war. They were well inclosed by breast works, with artillery; but the superior courage and conduct of our people was too much for them.

In a few moments we were informed that a large reinforcement of the enemy were on their march, and within two miles of us. At this lucky moment, Col. Warner's regiment (one hundred and fifty men) came up fresh, who was directed to advance and commence the attack. I pushed up as many men as could be collected to his support, and the action continued obstinately on both sides until sunset, when the enemy gave way, and was pursued until dark. With one hour more of daylight, we should have captured the whole detachment.

We obtained four pieces of brass cannon, one thousand stand of arms, several Hessian swords, eight brass drums, and seven hundred and fifty prisoners. Two hundred and seven were killed on the spot; wounded unknown. The enemy effected his escape by marching all night, and we returned to camp.

Too much honor can not be awarded to our brave officers and soldiers, for their gallant behavior in advancing through fire and smoke, and mounting breast works supported by cannon. Had every man been an Alexander or Charles XII.,* they could not have behaved more gallantly. I can not particularize any officer, as they all behaved with the greatest spirit. Colonel's Warner and Herrick, by their superior intelligence and experience, were of great service to me; and I desire they may be recommended to Congress.

As I promised, in my orders, that the soldiers should have all the plunder taken in the British camp, I pray you to inform me of the value of the cannon and other artillery stores.

* The general was an enthusiastic aamirer of Charles XII. The memoir of that intrepid warrior was the companion of all his campaigns; and, even to the last of his life, he dwelt with pleasure upon the daring exploits of that Alexander of the north.

I lost my horse in the action, and was glad to come off so well. Our loss is inconsiderable—about thirty killed and forty wounded.

Very respectfully,

Yours, in the common cause,

JOHN STARK.

Hon. Major General Gates.

N. B. In this action, I think we have returned the enemy a proper compliment for their Hubbardston affair.

NOTE BY EDITOR. This letter differs in a few particulars, of no importance, from the dispatch to the New-Hampshire council. Not considering himself as acting under the orders of Congress, he forwarded them no account of the action. General Schuyler, however, dispatched an aid-de-camp to that body, with the intelligence of his success.

Copy of a handbill issued at Boston, August 22, 1777.

Boston, (12 *o'clock*) *Friday*, *August* 22, 1777.

The following letter from Hon. Maj. Gen. Lincoln to the honorable council is just received by express.

Bennington, *August* 18, 1777.

Gentlemen—I most sincerely congratulate you on the late very signal success gained over the enemy, near this place, by a few continental troops, the rangers from the grants, some of the militia from the State of Massachusetts, and those from New-Hampshire and the Grants, under the command of Brigadier General Stark. Officers and men, stimulated by the most laudable motives, behaved with the greatest spirit and bravery; entered the enemy's several intrenchments with fortitude and alacrity, amid the incessant fire from their field-pieces and musketry. Our loss, killed, is supposed to be between twenty and thirty—wounded in common proportion. The enemy were totally defeated. The number of their slain has not yet been ascertained, as they fought on a retreat, several miles, in a wood; but is supposed to be about 200. A large number of the wounded have fallen into our hands.

We have taken one lieutenant colonel, mortally wounded; one major, five captains, twelve lieutenants, four ensigns, two cornets, one judge advocate, one baron, two Canadian officers, and three surgeons. Beside the above officers and wounded, there are in our hands thirty-seven British soldiers, three hundred and ninety-eight Hessians, thirty-eight Canadians, and one hundred and fifty-five Tories; four brass field-pieces, with a considerable quantity of baggage. The number the enemy had in the field can not be ascertained—perhaps one thousand five hundred.

It is very unhappy for the wounded, and painful to us, that such is our situation that we can not afford them all that speedy relief which their distresses demand of us. We were under a necessity to forward the prisoners to the State of Massachusetts. They are now under the care of General Fellows. He will wait the order of the council with respect to them.

I was ordered by General Schuyler, a few days since, from this place, to join the army at Stillwater, and was on my return when the action happened. This is the best account I can obtain of matters at present. It appears, by one of the enemy's journals, that the day before the general action they had thirty killed, and two Indian chiefs, and some wounded.

I am, gentlemen,

With sentiments of esteem and regard,

Your very humble servant,

B. LINCOLN.

Published by order of council—

JOHN AVERY, *Dep. Sec.*

Captain Barnes, who brought the above letter, was in those gallant actions, the following particulars of which were taken from his own mouth: viz., that on Saturday, the 16th instant, about one thousand six hundred militia from New-Hampshire, Massachusetts, and the Grants, under the command of Brigadier General Stark, about five miles west of Bennington, at a place called Loomschork, attacked a body of the enemy, consisting of about one thousand five hundred, in their intrenchments; and, after an obstinate engagement, dislodged them from their strongholds, making prisoners of upward of three hundred men, and taking two field-pieces.

General Stark, having been reinforced with one hundred and fifty continental troops, under Colonel Warner, took advantage of the confusion of the enemy's retreat, and pursued them, with great slaughter, about two miles and a half, where the enemy were reinforced with one thousand men and two field-pieces. A second and very severe engagement ensued, and after continuing about two hours, the enemy beat a retreat. The militia rushed on with a universal shout, which put the enemy into such confusion, that they left their wounded behind, and General Stark complete master of the field.

In the second onset, two more field-pieces, together with three hundred more of the enemy were taken; among whom was a lieutenant colonel, a major, the general's aid-de-camp, and thirty other officers. The prisoners arrived at Lanesborough last Tuesday night. The enemy left nearly two hundred dead on the field. Our loss was twenty-five killed, and a number wounded. Among the prisoners were one hundred and forty-seven tories, belonging to this and other States; that the parties sent out by General Stark, the day after the engagement, brought in about one hundred more prisoners. In the whole, the prisoners amounted to more than seven hundred.

The number of the enemy, in the lines first attacked by the militia only, were, as Capt. Barnes was informed by the aid-de-camp of the general commanding, fifteen hundred;

and that their reinforcement consisted of one thousand. About one thousand stand of arms, and eight loads of baggage was also taken, and twenty horses, supposed to belong to the dragoons.

The lieutenant colonel, who was taken, is since dead of his wounds.

General Stark is the same person who commanded a regiment at the famous battle of Bunker's hill, and behaved there with great intrepidity and courage.

Captain Barnes says that, after the first action, General Stark ordered a hogshead of rum for the refreshment of the militia; but so eager were they to attack the enemy, upon their being reinforced, that they tarried not to taste it, but rushed on the enemy with an ardor perhaps unparalleled.

State of New-Hampshire. In Committee of Safety.

Dear Sir—The committee received yours, of the 18th instant, with the greatest pleasure, and have directed me to present their very sincere thanks to you, the officers and soldiers under your command, for their brave and spirited conduct manifested in the late battle, and for the very essential service done to the country at this critical period. I hope, sir, that this success may be a prelude to greater things of the same kind; and that heaven will yet bestow many blessings upon our country, through your hands.

Fervantly praying that the God of armies may protect you in the day of battle, and be a shield and buckler to our countrymen under your command, and that he may give success and victory to all your undertakings, I do, in behalf of the committee, subscribe myself

Your most obedient

And very humble servant,

M. WEARE, *Chairman.*

Hon. General Stark.

A collection of trophies, similar to those presented to Vermont and Massachusetts, were sent to New-Hampshire. The drum and one or two other articles have, after being missing more than forty years, found their way to the State Capitol at Concord. The cannon might also have been there, had the legislature of New-Hampshire ever considered them worth the trouble of application to Congress. Vermont applied, and obtained two of them in 1848.

To Brigadier General Stark.

Vanshaik, August 19, 1777.

Dear Sir—I do myself the pleasure to congratulate you on the signal victory you have gained. Please accept my best thanks. The consequence of the severe stroke the enemy have received can not fail of producing the most salutary results. I have dispatched one of my aids-de-camp to announce your victory to Congress, and the commander-in-chief.

Governor Clinton is coming up the river with a body of militia; and I trust that, after what the enemy have received from you, their progress will be retarded, and that we shall yet see them driven out of the country.* General Gates is at Albany, and will this day resume the command.

I am, dear general, your most obedient serv't,

PH. SCHUYLER.

*** Better still—they were driven to Boston.—Editor.**

To Brigadier General Stark.

STATE OF VERMONT, *in Council of Safety,*
Bennington, September 6, 1777.

The council's compliments most cordially wait on his honor, Brigadier Gen. Stark, with their sincere thanks for the honor the general has been pleased to do them, by presenting a Hessian broad-sword, taken by a number of troops from the State of New-Hampshire and elsewhere, under his immediate command, in the ever memorable battle fought at Walloomschaik, near this place, on the sixteenth day of August last;' and also for the honor the general has been pleased to do them in applauding their exertions as a council.

In the House of Representatives,
September 18, 1777.

"*Voted*, To choose a committee of three, to join such as the honorable board shall appoint, to take into consideration a letter from Congress respecting General Stark, and to draft an answer thereto, and lay the same before this house; and that Col. Peabody, Capt. Martin and John Dudley, Esq., be the committee of this house for that purpose. Sent up by Col. McClary."

September 23, 1777. "Sent the copy of a letter from Gen. Stark, to Col. Evans, and another copy of the same to Col. Drake, with a letter from this house to each of them."

In Congress, September 18, 1777.

"Vote for a committee to draw an answer to a letter just received from Congress, respecting the conduct of Brig. General Stark, brought up and read, and concurred, and Mr. Bartlett, Mr. King and Mr. Thompson added."

We have not been able to obtain the report of the committee above named upon the subject. But the Bennington success probably superseded all farther action upon the case. And the vote of thanks of Congress, and the promotion of General Stark concluded the matter.

From the President of the Council of Safety of the State of Vermont.

Bennington, Sept. 20th, 1777.

The council beg leave to return their sincere thanks to the Hon. Brig. Gen. John Stark for the infinite service he has been pleased to do them, in defending them and their constituents from the cruelty and bloody rage of our unnatural enemy, who sought our destruction on the 16th of August last.

They also return their grateful acknowledgements for the honor the general has been pleased to do the council, by presenting them with one Hessian gun, with a bayonet; one broad-sword, one brass barreled drum, and a grenadier's cap, taken on the memorable 16th of August, for the use of the State.

The general may rely upon it they will be reserved for the use they were designed.*

I remain, dear general,

With sentiments of esteem,

Your most ob't serv't,

THOMAS CHITTENDEN.

Hon. Brigadier General Stark.

In Congress. The Delegates of the United States of New-Hampshire, Massachusetts Bay, Rhode-Island, Connecticut, New-York, New-Jersey, Pennsylvania, Delaware, Maryland, Virginia, North-Carolina, South-Carolina, and Georgia,

To John Stark, Esquire.

We, reposing especial trust and confidence in your patriotism, valor, conduct, and fidelity, do, by these presents, constitute and appoint you to be brigadier general in the army of the United States, raised for the defence of American liberty, and for repelling every hostile invasion thereof. You are, therefore, carefully and diligently to discharge the duty of brigadier general by doing and per-

* Mr. Butler, in his address, inquires where are they now? Lost, we suppose.

forming all manner of things thereunto belonging; and we do strictly enjoin, charge, and require all officers and soldiers under your command to be obedient to your orders, as brigadier general. And you are to observe and follow such orders and directions, from time to time, as you shall receive from this or a future Congress of the United States, or committee of Congress, for that purpose appointed, or the commander-in-chief, for the time being, of the army of the United States, or any other, your superior officers, according to the rules and discipline of war, in pursuance of the trust reposed in you. This commission to continue in force until revoked by this or a future Congress. Dated October 4, 1777.

By order of the Congress—

JOHN HANCOCK, *President.*

Attest. CHAS. THOMPSON, *Secretary.*

To General Stark, from President Hancock.

Yorktown, Pa., October 5, 1777.

Sir—It is with the greatest pleasure I transmit the inclosed resolve of Congress, expressing the thanks of that body to you, and to the officers and troops under your command, for the signal victory you obtained over the enemy in the late battle of Bennington.

In consideration of your distinguished conduct on that occasion, and the service you rendered the cause of freedom and your country, the Congress have been pleased to appoint you a brigadier in the army of the United States. Be pleased to communicate to the officers and troops, under your command, this mark of the approbation of their country for their exertions in defence of American liberty.

I inclose your commission, and have the honor to be, with the greatest esteem and respect, sir, your most obedient and very humble servant,

JOHN HANCOCK, *President.*

In Congress, October 4, 1777.

Resolved, That the thanks of Congress be presented to General Stark, of the New-Hampshire militia, and the officers and troops under his command, for their brave and successful attack upon, and signal victory over the enemy, in their lines at Bennington; and that Brigadier Stark be appointed a brigadier in the army of the United States.

By order of Congress—

JOHN HANCOCK, *President*.

Camp at Saratoga, October 18, 1777.

Dear Sir—Inclosed, I send you an exact copy of the Convention, signed by Gen. Burgoyne, and ratified by me. I will forward every thing necessary for your assistance. Colonel Warner had my verbal instructions last evening. Let me very frequently hear from you by express, and be sure to keep a sharp look out upon Lake George and South Bay, and between Fort Ann and Fort Edward.

I am, dear general,
Your affectionate
Humble servant,
HORATIO GATES.

The Hon'ble Brig. Gen'l Stark.

Proceedings in the Legislature of Massachusetts in regard to the Bennington trophies.

To General Stark.

Sir—The general assembly of this State take the earliest opportunity to acknowledge the receipt of your acceptable present—the tokens of victory gained at the memorable battle of Bennington. The events of that day strongly mark the bravery of the men who, unskilled in war, forced from their intrenchments a chosen number of veteran troops of boasted Britons, as well as the address and valor of the general who directed their movements, and led them on to conquest. This signal exploit opened the way to a rapid succession of advantages most important to America. These trophies shall be safely deposited in the archives of the State, and there remind posterity of the irresistable power of the God of armies, and the honors due to the memory of the brave. Still attended with like success, may you long enjoy the just reward of your grateful country.

I have the honor to be,

Your obedient servant,

JEREMIAH POWELL,

President of the Council.

In Council. Read and concurred, and ordered that the above letter be taken into a fair draft, and the president of the council be directed to sign the same; and that it be transmitted to the Hon. General Stark.

Consented to by fifteen of the Council.

Thursday, December 4, 1777.

In the House of Representatives.

Resolved, unanimously, That the board of war of this State be, and hereby are directed, in the name of this court, to present to the Hon. Brigadier General Stark, a complete suit of clothes becoming his rank, together with a piece of linen, as a testimony of the high sense this court has of the great and important services rendered by that brave officer, to the United States of America.

In Council. Read and concurred, and consented to by fifteen of the Council.

Friday, December 5, 1777.

NOTE BY EDITOR. The trophies consisted of a musket, sword, brass barreled drum, and a Hessian helmet. They are suspended in the senate chamber of Massachusetts.

War Office, 24th January, 1778.

Dear General—The honorable Congress having thought proper to direct an irruption to be immediately made into Canada, and their design being in part communicated to you by Hon. James Duane, Esq., I am directed by that honorable body to acquaint you that, for wise and prudential reasons, they have appointed Major General the Marquis de Lafayette, first in command, and Major General Conway, second in command, who will act in concert with you in promoting the interest and political views of the United States in Canada.

I am confident, from my knowledge of your attachment to the freedom of America, that you will cordially coöperate with them in every measure and move to the public service. My experience convinces me, and the opinion I entertain of you and your associates, the general officers, upon this important service, induces me to believe that the expectations of Congress will be fully answered by your hearty agreement with, and officer-like assistance to the gentlemen above mentioned. There is not any thing that will more recommend your many and great services to Congress than your implicit compliance with their wishes upon this occasion.

I am, dear general,

Your most obed't humble serv't,

HORATIO GATES, *President.*

Hon. Brigadier General Stark.

Instructions for Captain Patrick, Commanding officer at Schoharie.

Sir—You will keep continual scouting parties in the adjacent country to where you are posted, to discover the motions and movements of our internal enemies. If any of them should be found under arms, aiding, assisting, or holding correspondence with our enemies, you will forthwith detect them (if in your power), and with their crimes send them to me or to the commanding officer at this place. You will do the utmost in your power to find out if any British officers should come into that country, as it is highly probable they will do, because they have there so many friends; and let no pains be spared in detecting and securing them, making report of your proceedings, from time to time, to me or the commanding officer at this place. Putting great trust in your vigilance, valor, and good conduct, I subscribe myself

Your very humble ser't,

JOHN STARK.

Given at Head Quarters, at Albany, this 20th day of April, Anno Domini 1778.

Fishkill, May 18th, 1778.

Dear General—Your letters of the 3d, 7th and 13th of this month are just now put into my hands by General McDougal. Being detained some days at a council of war, held at Valley Forge, I did not arrive here until this morning. I must therefore beg you will, with all convenient expedition, embark Colonel Greaton's and Colonel Allen's regiments, with the artillery under Lieut. Col. Stevens, as directed in my last letter from the war office, of the 17th ult., and command them to proceed immediately to Fishkill. This being executed, you will, as speedily as may be, repair to the army in this department.

Please acquaint Col. Stevens that the military stores and fixed ammunition are to be removed down the river, agreeably to my former orders.

I am, sir, your most obedient

And humble servant,

HORATIO GATES.

The Hon'ble Major General Conway.

To Brigadier General Stark.

Fishkill, May 18, 1778.

Dear Sir—This instant I received your favor of the 19th of April last. I hope that this letter will find you in Albany, from whence I have desired General Conway to remove, the moment he has embarked the troops and stores to be sent down the river. As the committee at Bennington have offered to recruit Colonel Warner's regiment with three hundred men, I desire you will immediately transmit them the inclosed requisition for that number. I will write to Congress for the commission for your son,* and shall, the instant I receive it, transmit it to your hand.

I am, dear sir, your affectionate humble serv't,

HORATIO GATES.

To Brigadier General Stark.

Albany, May 18, 1778.

Sir—We have raised a few rangers to apprehend and secure such persons whose going at large may be dangerous to the liberties of America. We want now to send them out, and would be glad if you would give an order that they may be supplied with ammunition. They are fifteen in number.

We are, with great respect,

Your most obedient serv'ts,

MAT. VESSEKER,
ISAAC D. FONDA,
JOHN M. BEECKMAN,
Commissioners.

* Archibald Stark, then a youth of eighteen.—EDITOR.

Oneida, May 19, 1778.

Sir—Your favors of 12th and 16th inst., together with the inclosed speech, this day, came safe to hand. I believe it most prudent to defer communicating your answer to the Senecas until I have had an opportunity of consulting the Oneida chief upon the subject. The meeting at Onondaga is this day dissolved. Not one of the Quigogas attended; nor any of the Seneca chiefs, but a number of their warriors.

They have not yet taken up the affair of the commissioner's speech at Johnstown. The whole concern of the Senecas has been to fall upon some plan to recover their prisoners out of our hands. Some friends of ours returned from Onondaga this evening, and inform that three considerable parties of Senecas and Quigogas—one consisting of one hundred and twenty-four men—have some time since gone to war upon the frontiers of Virginia, and that another party set out yesterday for Quigoga to ravage the frontiers of Pennsylvania, and that Butler is now at Kanadasega, with a large quantity of arms and ammunition for the Indians, where the remaining part of his friends are to meet him. I shall give you a farther account, as soon as the sachems, who are now on their way, return. I am informed that another council is summoned to meet at Onondaga, when the commissioner's speech at Johnstown is to be taken into consideration. But from present appearances, I think there is little reason to expect such an answer as will, or can be accepted. From the character of my informer, and from several concurring circumstances, I have reason to think the above articles of intelligence are too true, and that we shall soon receive a disagreeable confirmation.

I am, sir, your most obedient

And very humble servant,

JAMES DEANE.

General Schuyler.

To the Hon. General Stark.

Albany, 20th May, 1778.

Sir—The mayor, aldermen and commonality of the city of Albany being convened in common council, in consequence of your honor's letter to General Ten Broeck, of this date, informing him that the troops are ordered to Fishkill, and requesting him to relieve the guards in the city.

The common council beg leave to observe that they consider themselves in duty bound to inform you that, from the weakness of the militia in this city (owing to the number in public service) it will not be safe to leave the stores, provisions, hospital, sloops and vessels, the regular and other prisoners (the latter exceeding one hundred), beside the disaffected in and about the city, to so small a number as one hundred and fifty, being the whole number of the militia that are subject to military duty ; for should any accident happen, by means of the disaffected, either in destroying the stores or in discharging the prisoners (ten whereof are now under sentenee of death), it would distress not only this city, but the service of the continent generally.

The common council farther beg leave to observe that about six weeks ago the troops were also ordered down, but upon the committee's representing to the Hon. Major General Conway the above matters, and the necessity of having a body of troops in this city, to succour the northern and western frontiers in case of an attack, General Conway, then commanding at this post, wrote upon the subject to Major General McDougal, and his excellency, the Governor, who thereupon ordered the troops to remain here. The common council farther beg leave to observe that in case your honor can not detain one of the regiments stationed here, that at least one hundred and fifty men ought to be detained, and they doubt not that your honor will concur with them in sentiment.

The bearers hereof, Mr. Recorder and Aldermen, members of this board, can inform your honor of many other reasons for the detention of part of the troops.

We are your honor's obedient servants,

JOHN BARCLAY, *Mayor*.

By order of Common Council.

To Brigadier General Stark.

Head Quarters, Valley Forge, 20th May, 1778.

Sir—In a letter from Maj. Gen. Sullivan of the 1st instant, he complains of wanting assistance in his command, and begs that you may be desired to take post with him this campaign. You will therefore be pleased to join him as soon as possible.

I am, sir, your most obed't

And very humble serv't,

GEO. WASHINGTON.

To Hon. Major General Gates.

Albany, May 21, 1778.

Dear Sir—In consequence of the remonstrance from the mayor and aldermen of this city, in committee assembled, which I inclose you, I have detained a regiment of troops destined for Fishkill, and think it highly necessary for the security of the citizens and commonality.

Murders and robberies are daily committed in the adjacent counties by our *internal enemies*. The militia, it is possible, could be raised, but you know that there is no dependence to be put in them; and by letting these infamous villains at large, we should greatly endanger our most valuable friends.

I am sensible, after mature consideration, you will approve of my conduct, sir; waiting with impatience for your answer, I subscribe myself

Your affectionate and most humble serv't,

JOHN STARK.

Hon. Major General Gates.

To Colonel Safford.

Albany, May 21, 1778.

Sir—Doctor Smith complains that the troops at Fort Edward are turning out the inhabitants and destroying the buildings at that place. I should be glad that such disorders should be suppressed, and the inhabitants' property secured.

I received a letter from you, directed to General Conway, informing him that you expected that the cannon would be at Fort Ann. I should be glad to know where they are now. You mentioned teams to be sent from this place. Col. Lewis not being here, I can give no information in that matter. I expect him soon, when I can give you an account. Keep a good look out for the enemy, so that they do not come upon you unawares.

Your most ob't humble serv't,

JOHN STARK.

To Major General Schuyler.

Fort Schuyler, May 23, 1778.

Sir—Your favor of the 10th instant came safe to hand, and I have now the happiness to acquaint your honor that things have taken a very different turn from what they promised when I did myself the honor to write you last. I left the Oneidas yesterday. Your agent, Mr. Deane, requested me to inform you that the reason of his not writing now, was the uncertainty which attended the result of the meeting at Onondaga. However, in his opinion, from what he could collect, there remained very little prospect of a reconciliation with the Senecas; that the Oneidas would soon stand in need of your protection; that the German Flats, and Cherry Valley would soon be attacked by the Indians, in scouting parties, some time next month. Mr. Butler is on his way down through the Six Nations. He was left at Kanadasega (the first Seneca village west of Cayuga) six days ago, where, by the way, he was met by his son, ensign Butler, and a number of tories.

Mr. Butler's address to the Indian's, and professed design, will be transmitted to your honor, by your agent, the moment the Oneidas determine what course to take. I left them yesterday, full of resentment against the Cayugas and Senecas. They were then upon the point of giving them up to deserved punishment, and immediately call upon your honor for a sufficient force to crush them. The Oneidas now find they have been very much imposed on by their brothers, the Cayugas, who had the impudence to frame a great part of that speech sent you with four strings of wampum. When the Oneida sachems left Onondaga they could not determine what effect their declarations and advice would have upon the minds of the Seneca warriors there convened; whether they would return from thence to meet Mr. Butler, or proceed with their prisoners down to Albany. Mr. Butler strictly enjoined them to go no farther than Onondaga, or Oneida at farthest, and then, by the hands of the Oneidas, demand of General Schuyler their prisoner, "Atskeara," to be delivered up at one of those places for an exchange; but this the Oneidas peremptorily refused.

This morning two runners came from Oneida, with a letter from Mr. Deane, informing that three Senecas had arrived there, and the others were on their way with their prisoner. This, said Mr. Deane, changed the face of things.

I am fully of your opinion that a conference with the Six Nations, at Fort Schuyler, if attainable, would be attended with good consequences; but at present it appears to me impracticable, unless you had such a force at this garrison as would strike terror through those haughty, insolent Senecas, and a speech sent them of a like import, closing with some words of clemency; and then, it is my opinion, you might effect it. I propose going down, the beginning of next week, by which time I expect Mr. Deane will be able to transmit to you something decisive as to affairs in this quarter. You can hardly conceive what artifices and barefaced lies the enemy make use of to evade the force of argument, and misrepresent every thing you say to the Indians, particularly among the Senecas.

I have the honor to be

Your obedient and humble serv't,

S. KIRKLAND.*

P. S. Mr. Butler has said, as related by the Indians, that Sir John Johnson † is repairing to Oswego, to take post there, and Mr. Butler is collecting the Indians for a conference at that place.

To Honorable President of Congress.

Albany, 24th May, 1778.

Dear Sir—I received your favor of April 18th, for which I am greatly obliged to you and my country, for the honors bestowed upon me. The cause of my country appears the noblest for which man ever contended; and no measures should be neglected, or sacrifices withheld, which will support it to a favorable result. In such a cause we may despise even death itself. You may assure Congress that I am most happy when I can do my country the greatest service.

Some time ago Congress appointed me to raise a force to destroy the British shipping at St. Johns. For this purpose I raised a number of soldiers, but as the expedition was abandoned, they were dismissed.

I hope Congress will allow them some recompense for their zeal in volunteering at so unpleasant a season of the year.

I ask this favor, inasmuch as Congress made no provision for them in case they did not succeed. To grant this favor might prove an encouragement to others to engage in similar cases.

I am, sir, &c., &c.,

JOHN STARK.

* Rev. S. Kirkland was the father of the late Rev. John Thornton Kirkland, President of Harvard College. He was, in 1778, a missionary among the Indians of the western part of New-York.

† Son of Sir William Johnson. He joined the enemy in 1775.—EDITOR.

Albany, 24th May, 1778.

Dear General—I received a letter from Governor Chittenden, of Vermont, of the 21st inst., informing me that you had written to that State for three hundred men to be sent to Albany. I think it will be an injury to have them leave that section, except they can be replaced by the like number from some other quarter. We expect an invasion, for the enemy's vessels are now at Crown Point, cruising along the lake, which lies sixty miles on the frontier of that State. I have ordered Colonel Bedel to keep scouts at Onion river and St. Johns, and make report to me of any movements of the enemy in those parts.

You wrote, some time since, that General Fellows was to command on the Grants. He has not yet arrived. I should like to know if he is to take that command, and likewise how far eastward my command extends, that I may govern myself accordingly. Colonel Safford informs me that he has brought all the cannon as far as Fort Ann.

As I have a great deal of writing, I should be much obliged to your honor to allow me a clerk; or if I employ one, to inform me what I shall promise him.

I am, &c., JOHN STARK.

Hon. General Gates.

To the Hon. Major General Schuyler.

Oneida, May 25, 1778.

Sir—I have deferred writing for several days, after the return of the Indians from Onondaga, in hopes of being able to give you a just account of the situation of affairs among the Six Nations. But the intelligence I receive is so various and contradictory, that it is impossible to determine what are their real intentions.

It is, however, now publicly known that three different parties of Quigogas are already gone to war upon the frontiers of Virginia and Pennsylvania. It is also said that Joseph Brandt is at the head of a fourth, and that he is to collect his friends upon the Susquehanna, and attack Cherry Valley. The party of one hundred and twenty-four Senecas, mentioned in my last, are since returned from war. They have taken thirteen scalps and two prisoners, with the loss of several of their party.

From the best accounts I have been able to collect, it appears that the Onondagas are much divided in sentiment; and that a party of the Senecas have observed a neutrality since the beginning of the war, and still wish to live in friendship with the United States. Upward of twenty, mostly of this party, arrived here yesterday, on their way to Albany, to procure an exchange of prisoners. I expect them to leave here to-morrow. They are determined to proceed to whatever part of the States you shall direct them, to effect their purpose.

They were ordered by their sachems to go no farther than the boundary line, and procure an exchange there; but the Oneidas, presuming upon their influence with the commissioners, encouraged them (at the late council at Onondaga), with assurance of personal safety, to proceed to Albany, or whatever place the prisoners they are in quest of, may be confined.

The other part of the Senecas, which is by far the most considerable, seem resolved to make no terms with us, though I believe there is no danger of their attacking Tryon county, while so large a party of their people are down in our country.

The Onondagas have sent three runners successively to the Quigogas and Senecas, to call them to the intended meeting; but, hitherto, to no purpose. They have therefore declared their final resolution not to address them again upon the subject, but return the commissioner belts, at Albany. All the Quigogas, not gone out to war, are now attending a conference with Mr. Butler, at Kanadasega.

Upon the whole, there appears but very little prospect that any considerable council will be held to deliberate upon the commissioner's speech. Or should such an event finally take place, I do not expect they will make such satisfaction, for their repeated violation of treaties, as can be accepted. Your speech, of the 11th instant, I have communicated to the Oneidas and Tuscaroras, to their great satisfaction, and yesterday repeated the same to the Senecas, now here.

The Oneidas have of late been under great apprehensions of danger. Not long since two of their young men were fired upon by a party of the enemy, not far from this village; but as it was in the dark of the evening, they both fortunately made their escape unhurt.

They are much concerned that there are no troops near their country to march to their assistance, in case of a sudden invasion. I have just received an intimation from the sachems that they determine to address a speech to the commissioners, as soon as they can find leisure and opportunity, from whence you will be able to collect their sentiments upon the present situation of affairs here. I have not been able to procure any more warriors to join General Washington's army. Their apprehensions of danger are such that they think it their duty to stay and protect their women and children.

I am, sir,

Your obedient humble serv't,

JAMES DEANE.

To Governor Chittenden.

Albany, May 25, 1778.

Dear Sir—I have received yours of the 22d inst., and noted the contents. You state that General Gates wrote to you to raise three hundred men to recruit Colonel Warner's regiment, and for their being removed to this place. I have written to the general against it, setting forth the necessity of their remaining on that station; but have received no answer yet. I have likewise written concerning the quarter master's want of money, and of the necessity of his being so paid; also to know how far my command extends to the eastward. When I receive the answers, I will give you farther intelligence. In the meantime, I should be glad if the three hundred men should be made up the general mentioned.

Your most obed't serv't,

JOHN STARK.

Albany, May 25, 1778.

Dear General—This morning a letter came to hand from the governor and council of the State of Vermont, which I inclose to you, and recommend to your consideration.

I am, dear sir,

Your humble serv't,

JOHN STARK.

Hon. Major General Gates.

To General Gates.

Albany, (Sunday) 31*st May*, 1778.

Dear Sir—I this instant received an express from Schoharie (a copy I enclose), informing that a party of the enemy have made a descent at Cobuskill, and destroyed a great part of that place. I have ordered out the militia to put a stop to farther proceedings, which I hope will have the desired effect for the present. But they can not prevent it effectually; for, as soon as they return, the enemy will make farther descents, and get away before the militia are collected. I think it highly necessary that a party should be raised for some certain time, and equipped, to march at the shortest notice to any quarter where the enemy may happen to be in force. Without some such method, I fear they will lay waste a great part of our frontiers. I leave it to your wise consideration.

I remain yours, &c.,

JOHN STARK.

To General Stark.

Headquarters, Robinson's House,
May 30th, 1778.

Sir—I have received your favor of the 21st inst. My reason for demanding three hundred men from the committee at Bennington, was in consequence of their having offered to supply that reinforcement to protect Albany, and the upper part of Hudson river, from the tories and scouting parties of the enemy.

Col. Bedel's regiment was thought sufficient to cover the north-western frontiers of the Grants, and all Gen. Nixon's brigade was to come to Fishkill. In case Col. Warner's regiment can not be supplied with the drafts requested from Bennington, you will apply, in my name, to the generals commanding the militia in Hampshire, and Berkshire, State of Massachusetts, for the purpose above recited.

I must desire you will immediately apply to the deputy quarter master general to provide a sloop to carry the convalescent British prisoners of war, now at Albany, to Fishkill, from whence they are, by his excellency, General Washington's command, to be sent in the same vessel to New-York, where a like number of our soldiers, prisoners with the enemy, are to be returned.

As the artillery stores, hospital and prisoners of war are now removed, or removing from Albany, I think Alden's regiment should be without delay sent from thence, as I can not conceive but the inhabitants of Albany can at least protect the town until the militia from the Grants, or Massachusetts, arrive to defend it, especially as Warner's regiment to the northward, Gansevoort's to the westward, and the militia of the whole country in the immediate space, cover that city.

As to the extent of your command under me, it was intended that it should be confined to the State of New-York, northward and westward of Albany; and as far as the manor of Livingston, inclusively, to the south; and on both sides of Hudson river. The governments of the adjoining States will no doubt provide for their own defence respectively. But this, as circumstances require, will be altered hereafter. If your brigade major can not do all your writing business, you must doubtless employ a clerk. His wages must be what is at present customary for such services.

I am, sir, your affectionate
Humble servant,
HORATIO GATES.

To Major General Gates.

Albany, 31*st of May*, 1778.

Sir—I inclose you copies of two letters received from Schoharie. The tragical scheme has been some days brewing. I shall send them all the relief in my power; but, I assure you, it will be a slender reinforcement. I have applied to Gen. Ten Broeck for his militia, and he has promised to assist me as soon as church is over. He can not do any business before, for fear of frightening the town into fits. I should be glad of some few field pieces for the protection of this quarter, as we are weak in men and weaker in artillery. If you could spare me one regiment more, I think it would be highly necessary for the benefit of the United States.

I am, in a great hurry,
Your aff. humble serv't,
JOHN STARK.

P. S. I wrote you about moving the British hospital to New-England. I must desire you would immediately order it to be removed.

To the Mayor and Common Council of Albany.

Albany, June 1, 1778.

Gentlemen—As I am ordered by the Hon. Major General Gates to send to Fishkill all the continental troops from this place, with the British hospital, I must beg the favor of you to mount the guards for the security of the city and the stores in it. Your compliance will much oblige your friend, and very humble servant,

JOHN STARK.

To General Ten Broeck.

Albany, June 1, 1778.

Dear General—I have this instant received orders from General Gates to call upon you to send, without loss of time, one hundred men from your brigade to garrison this city, and protect the stores in it, as the militia can not be depended upon.

The Indians and tories have made a descent upon a place called Cobuskill, about forty miles from this place, and destroyed some part of it. A party of continentals, posted not far off, attacked them; while a company of these militia poltroons looked on, excepting six, who behaved well. This is all the news. I have written to the brigadier of Hampshire county for the like number.

I am, sir, &c.,

JOHN STARK.

Albany, June 2, 1778.

Dear General—I received yours of May 30th, informing of the British hospital's removal, which gives me pleasure. Your orders for sending down Alden's regiment shall be obeyed as soon as the wind will admit. No news could give the troops here more pleasure than to hear of their being removed, as they have lost all confidence in the militia since the affair at Cobuskill. I wrote you some time since concerning Bedel's regiment being mustered by a continental muster master, but you have given no answer to that part of my letter. I think it highly necessary that they, having been all this time at home doing nothing, should be employed some where; I think on Otter creek or at this place. If on Otter creek, Warner's corps could be moved this way. I have sent orders to the brigadiers of Hampshire and Berkshire counties to send me two hundred men to garrison the city and the places hereabouts. I likewise send you a copy of a journal I received this day, informing of the situation of the enemy's shipping on the lake.

Yours, &c.,

J. STARK.

Hon. Gen. Gates.

Hon. Brigadier General Stark.

Cohnawaga, 3d of June, 1778.

Sir—We were this day at the fort at Johnstown, with a few invalids, and about six o'clock of said evening, one Philip Pellet, an old servant of Major Fonda, who is a worthy man, came and informed us that about half way between Sagondawa and Johnstown he saw about one hundred Indians, painted, in the woods, near his house. He also says he knew some tories who were there, who took George Cook and his son prisoners, together with Charles Maresius and several others; and as we were busy swearing to this purpose, two other expresses arrived at the fort, who said the Indians were busy destroying all before them in that part of the country, and were then near Johnstown; upon which we thought proper to go home and bring our families into Cohnawaga church, having only seven armed men to defend that fort. All our militia have gone to the relief of those at Cobuskill and Cherry Valley, on the German flats. We are only about ten men strong in the church, with about one hundred women and children, and expect to be attacked this night by the best accounts we can get. For God's sake, send reinforcements, or I am afraid we shall fall an easy prey to the enemy; and we are also much afraid that some of our neighbors will act against us.

We are, your most obed't serv'ts,

FREDERICK FISHER,
ZEPHANIEL BACHELDER,
JAMES VEDEN,
THOMAS ROMEA,
C. F. M. ADAMS,
GILES FONDA.

Received at Albany, June 4th, 1778.

Note by Editor. A party was dispatched to their relief by General Stark, and the besiegers were themselves surprised and defeated; and some of them, brought in as prisoners, proved to be tories, and hanged.

General Stark to General Gates.

Albany, June 4, 1778.

Dear General—By the inclosed, you will find how deplorable my condition is; and I do not in the least doubt an immediate assistance will be granted.

Colonel Herrick has been here this day, applying for pay for part of a regiment he raised to go to Canada last winter. Among my inclosures, is a letter from Colonel Bedel, who says his regiment is full, and ready for the field, waiting for nothing but provisions.

I should be glad to have Colonel Ethan Allen command in the Grants, as he is a very suitable man to deal with tories, and such like villains.

Colonel Herrick, whose bravery and good conduct is a sufficient recommendation to him, I look upon, would be a very suitable man to be in this western quarter to scourge these tories and Indians. Your sentiments on the above will add greatly to the former favor conferred on

Your affect. humb. serv't,

J. STARK.

Hon. Major General Gates.

Albany, June 5, 1778.

Honored Sir—I last night received your kind favor, of 20th ult., informing that General Sullivan desires me to join him this campaign. Had it been the pleasure of Congress to have ordered me to that station, I should have thought myself very happy to have served a campaign with that worthy officer; and would still be glad to join him, if it could be for the public good.

I look upon myself in a disagreeable situation here, with nothing to do but guard the frontier; with no troops but militia, who are engaged but for a month at a time. I can not obtain any great advantages to the public, nor honor to myself.

But I shall cheerfully obey any orders that are entrusted to me, and proceed wherever Congress * shall think I may be of most service. I have no will of my own; the good of the common cause is all my ambition.

I remain, dear sir, your

Devoted and very humble servant,

JOHN STARK.

His Excellency, General Washington.

* Congress ordered him to the command of the northern department.

To the Hon. General Stark.

Highlands, 8*th June*, 1778.

Sir—I have received your letters of the 18th and 20th instant, and now inclose two to Colonel Ethan Allen, and one for Colonel Bedel, both of which you will please to forward immediately by express. I have ordered Colonel Bedel to send you one hundred of his regiment, properly officered, without delay, to Albany; which, with the militia from Hampshire and Berkshire counties, will be a good reinforcement. The governor farther assures me you have all the support he can furnish.

Mr. Winship, when he was here, said that there were only twenty men at Fort Edward, and that Warner's regiment was at Saratoga; of course the issuing commissary might from thence have supplied the few men at the upper post. If it is absolutely necessary that an issuing commissary should reside at both places, you will order Mr. Winship to place them accordingly.

You will please to acquaint Colonel Varick with my orders to send one of his deputies immediately to Coös, to muster Colonel Bedel's regiment; and direct the colonel himself to set out directly for Fishkill to muster the eastern reinforcements that are daily expected. As to the employment of Colonel Bedel's regiment, I am satisfied with whatever you may determine; but it may not be amiss to take Colonel Ethan Allen's opinion upon the subject, with whom I wish you to open a correspondence. I I have no doubt but an issuing commissary is employed with Bedel's regiment; if not, one must be appointed. Colonel Bedel has my orders to obey your commands.

I am, sir, your affectionate, humble servant,

HORATIO GATES.

To Colonel Klock.

Albany, June 14, 1778.

Sir—I am desired by his excellency, Governor Clinton, to order you to fill up the two companies of rangers that were proposed to be raised in Tryon county, at the last session of the assembly. He is much surprised that it has been delayed so long, since your all is at stake. Your exertions in this affair will do you honor, and your neglect will be your disgrace and your country's ruin. You can not expect that the people of this State and the neighboring States will leave their farms and families to relieve you, when you will do nothing for yourselves. If you expect relief, you must first exert yourselves; and then, I make no doubt but your neighbors will cheerfully assist you. I give this order first for your own safety, and next for the public good.

Your obed't serv't,

J. STARK.

N. B. By having such a number of alert men (and no others are fit for such a service) on your frontier, you will not only disconcert the plans of the enemy, but oblige them to watch their own frontiers, and leave yours in peace. You complain from that quarter that you can not carry on your business; but if there are a number in the service, there will remain less to be provided for, and the country made safe. Were such men to be found as could go into the enemy's country, and serve them as they have served you, it would put a stop to their progress, and render you entirely secure; and without such measures are taken, you may depend upon it you will be harrassed to the last degree. J. S.

To the Committee of Safety of Tryon County.

June 16th, 1778.

Gentlemen—I received yours, of 14th, wherein you complain that you are in bad circumstances. I am of the same opinion with you; but you may blame yourselves for it in a great measure. The governor ordered the officers in your county to raise two companies of rangers for the defence of your frontiers, and exempted you from making up your proportion of the continental troops. Had that order been complied with, you might have been safe; but it was neglected, and you suffer. The reason for your not having the men proposed for that place, is on that account. They say that they are obliged to raise their proportion for the army, while you were exempted, and now you want them to guard your frontier.

Respectfully,

JOHN STARK.

To Brigadier General Stark.

Peekskill, 17th June, 1778.

Sir—I am favored with the receipt of your letter, of the 13th instant, from Albany. I am much pleased that the counties of Hampshire and Berkshire have so readily complied with my request for the two hundred militia to be sent to Albany. These, with what Colonel Allen will do for you, the reinforcements from Bedel's regiment, will, with the State militia, secure the frontier.

From my conversation with the Senaca chiefs, and the complexion of affairs here, I am inclined to think you will not have many real alarms in your district.

I have for some time been dissatisfied with these matters (as you emphatically call them). Let me know, as soon as possible, the names and officers of those you think necessary to be continued in the service, and I will lay it before Congress; and I wish you to recommend the dismission of the rest; but I desire that the armory may remain as it now stands.

Issuing commissaries are only to be placed at the magazines where you think proper to post troops. Lieut. Col. Safford was yesterday furnished with my orders upon the agents for the clothing, etc., so much wanted for Colonel Warner's regiment, and dispatched immediately therewith to Boston.

Please to acquaint Colonel Wynkoop, that when he has worked up his materials, and finished the ten gun boats he mentions, I would not have him build any more, or collect any more materials. As the boats are finished they should be sent to Fishkill landing, to be rigged and equipped. If Colonel Wynkoop is able, I should be glad if he would come to me, when the boats come down, and bring the abstract of the pay due to Captain Low's company of carpenters, that their demands may be satisfied.

I am, sir,

Your most ob't humble servant,

HORATIO GATES.

Hon. General Stark.

Bennington, June 18th, 1778.

Dear Sir—I have lately received a letter from Gen. Gates, requesting me to furnish you assistance in defending the northern frontier. I shall be happy to render any aid in my power for that service. Your reputation, and the hatred and fear with which you are regarded by the tories, those infernal enemies of American liberty, induce me to propose a visit to your head quarters in Albany, so soon as our affairs are in a little better way. The tories, and the friends of tories, give us some trouble yet. Their management in a great measure keeps alive the anarchy which has heretofore disturbed the peace of Vermont.

I am of opinion that we shall never be at peace while one of the traitors is suffered to remain in the country. I hear you are doing well with some of them.* I hope, in a few days, to pay my respects to a man for whose republican character and important services I have the highest veneration and respect.

I am, sir,

Your most ob't serv't,

ETHAN ALLEN.

To Col. Ethan Allen.

Albany, June 20th, 1778.

Dear Sir—Your favor of the 18th has just come to hand, wherein you promise me a visit. You may be sure that I shall be happy in receiving one from a man whose fame has been so extensive, and whom I never have had the pleasure of seeing. As for the political matters you now have in hand, I cordially agree with you in sentiment. You may rely upon my coöperating with you in purging the land of freedom from such most infamous and diabolical villains.

As for Bedel's regiment, if any iniquity has been practiced upon the public, I hope in a few days to discover it. I shall be obliged to you for using your best endeavors to ascertain their numbers, employments, &c.

Please accept my best wishes for your success and happy settlement of the business now on hand.

I am, sir,

Your obedient serv't,

JOHN STARK.

* Doing well, here, means hanging; several tories this time having been hanged at Albany.—EDITOR.

To Major General Gates.

Albany, June 20th, 1778.

Dear General—I wrote to you some time ago to send me a few small field pieces, with a proper quantity of ammunition for them, but they have not yet arrived. I would be much obliged to you for them. We have here two iron three-pounders, which I intended to send to Cherry Valley, but find there is not one shot for them. And as that is a place very much exposed, I think that they might be of great service, as that post covers all the Mohawk river, and stops all passages from Unadilla to that place. I herewith inclose you a return from the commissary of issues, which surprises me. There you will find seven hundred and fifty rations, delivered out in a day, upon an average, in the month of May, without any to the troops or hospital. What these men are doing I do not know; but if there are as many at every post, according to the number of troops, I think it is no wonder that provisions are scarce and dear. I should be glad to have the matter inquired into, as also the state of Bedel's regiment. It is much doubted whether he has half the number enlisted which he returns. Agreeably to your order, I have sent for one hundred of them to come to this place; but I think it would be best to send for them all, and then we shall find out the iniquity, if any there be. He has drawn for a regiment last winter, to go to St. John's, double pay and rations (and none of them ever left their homes; and whether any of them were enlisted or not is uncertain), to the amount of $1,400; and now he is uneasy because he is not paid for his regiment, of which no man knows where it is. I think it the duty of every lover of his country to endeavor to find out such people, which, without ordering them some where else, is impossible; for he can muster all the inhabitants, and as soon as they are mustered, they go to their own business again, and cheat the continent of their wages and provisions.

I should be glad of your opinion on this subject, and as you order I will do.

A nest of villains are lurking about Unadilla, sixty miles from Cherry Valley, and have given us all this uneasiness. I have thoughts of trying to remove it if practicable. I have sent scouts to ascertain the strength and situation of the country. I should be glad of your opinion on this subject.

Your most ob't serv't,

JOHN STARK.

Albany, 21*st of June*, 1778.

Dear Sir—I received yours of the 11th, as to the expedition to Unadilla. I have ordered scouts to be sent from Cherry Valley to reconnoitre that part of the country, and find out the enemy's strength, and the situation of the country. When they return, I shall be able to give you a more particular account; but, till that time, I must rest content. I expect the scouts back in a week. I should be obliged if you would forward the letter, by express, to Gen. Gates.

I am, your ob't serv't,

JOHN STARK.

To General Fellows.

Albany, 22*d June*, 1778.

Dear General—I received your favors, for which I am obliged. You wrote that you would send one hundred men, to guard the frontiers, which have arrived, and inform me that they are raised for one month. I should be glad to have them replaced by that time, as they will not tarry any longer. Your compliance with this request, will much oblige

Your friend and obedient servant,

JOHN STARK.

To the Brigadier of Hampshire County, Mass.

Albany, June 22d, 1778.

Dear General—I received orders, some time ago from Gen. Gates, to call on the militia of Hampshire and Berkshire, to assist in securing the frontiers against the ravages of the enemy. In pursuance of said orders, I wrote to you and Gen. Fellows for one hundred men each, properly officered, to be stationed on the frontiers, where it was thought necessary. Gen. Fellows sent his proportion. But I have not heard from you since. I wish that you would make up your proportion, and send them as soon as possible. Gen. Fellows proposes to relieve his men every month. If you should be put upon the same footing, it would perhaps be not amiss. You can best judge of that matter. The western frontiers are in great distress, and unless speedily relieved, the settlement must be broken up, which will be a great injury to the United States. As it is the best country for bread in America, which is much wanted for the use of the army, I hope you will succeed in sending the men, so that I shall rest assured of your vigilance and good wishes toward the welfare of your country and the common cause.

Your ob't serv't,

JOHN STARK.

To Captain Ballard.

Albany, 23d of June, 1778.

Sir—You are to proceed with the party, under your command, to Cacknawaga, there, or as near that place as you shall, with the advice of your colonel, and other officers in that quarter, judge most convenient to defend, and stop the progress of Brandt (the Indian commandant). Nevertheless, you are not to begin an engagement, but to suffer the militia from this quarter to make the first attack, and you are to support them as you may think most proper.

If you should find that Brandt has crossed the Mohawk river on his way to Crown Point, you will then return with the detachment. Wishing you a happy and successful voyage,

I am, sir, your obed't serv't,

JOHN STARK.

To Captain William H. Ballard.

If you should stand in need of any horses or carriages, you are to apply to the quarter master; and all officers, both civil and military, are ordered to supply you with any thing you may want.

Given under my hand and seal.

JOHN STARK, *B. G.*

To General Gates.

Albany, June 25, 1778.

Dear General—This morning came to hand a letter, the copy of which I inclose. Since that, another from Schoharie brings much to the same purport. I must beg your immediate answer and instructions. There are here a number of bateau men, and no employment for them. Please instruct me in regard to them. Here are a number of British prisoners. I should advise to send them to some part of New-England, as the scarcity and dearness of provisions here renders them very costly; and, likewise, the number of disaffected make it dangerous. Upon the above matters I should be glad of your immediate advice.

I am, &c.,

JOHN STARK.

To General Stark.

Peekskill, 26th June, 1778.

Sir—Having received no letter from you since that dated the 14th inst., I conclude all is calm and serene in your quarter. Inclosed is a letter for Colonel Bedel, which the bearer is charged to deliver to him at Coös. You will, after perusal, seal and forward it as directed.

I have no account from General Washington later than the 21st instant, when his army was on the east side of the Delaware, at Corgel's ferry, and the head of the enemy's column at Mount Holly, moving slowly through the Jerseys.

As General Washington declares in his letter, Philadelphia was evacuated the 18th inst., at sunrise. Our parties who entered the city that day, took Cunningham, provost marshal, and seven of the enemy's officers, prisoners. I hope soon to give you joy of some capital stroke in our favor.

I am, dear sir, &c.,

HORATIO GATES.

To Major General Gates.

Albany, 26th June, 1778.

Dear General—I received yours of the 17th, and it gives me great pleasure to learn that you agree with me in sentiment in regard to those supernumeraries, or rather cormorants, that "devour the childrens' bread." I inclose you a list, as you desired.

You will find one colonel, one major, twelve captains, four clerks, and fourteen other officers; but they can not be in lower stations than that of captains in the battalions, as I am informed their pay is a great deal more.

I think two assistant quarter masters sufficient to be stationed at Albany for all the business to be done there; one at Schenectady, one at Fort Schuyler; and, as all the timber is obtained at Coeyman's, there is no more to be done there than one barrack master, one forage master, and clerk, and one wagon master can do.

We have not more than five or six wagons in the public works. There are many carpenters at work here, building store-houses, which I think of no service at present; and God forbid they should go on, if there is any business for them elsewhere. If they could not be better employed, I think they had better be discharged, as we have now more store-room than provisions.

As to the names of those to be retained in service, I can not give them, as all are strangers to me. I have been informed by some country people that the scheme which the purchasing commissaries pursue is a great damage to the public. The more they give for any article, the more profit they have; which seems to be the drift of every body here, come of the public what will.

I understand that people have taken men out of the regiments for clerks to them, giving to them sixty dollars per month, which puts them above all officers of the regiments, the colonel excepted; which makes the troops very uneasy. And I think they are not far from right, since the soldier, who is despised, must run all the risks for nothing, while these others are devouring the fat of the land.

I think that these things should be remonstrated against to Congress, as they must be deceived in the manner these people in their pay are spending the public money. I leave them to your farther consideration, and conclude by subscribing myself

Your obedient serv't,

JOHN STARK.

NOTE BY EDITOR. This letter caused much commotion in the *hive*. Those who disliked the prospect of losing profitable sinecure offices, were particularly indignant.

To the President of the New-Hampshire Congress.

Albany, 28th of June, 1778.

Dear Sir—I take this opportunity, by express, to inform you of my situation at this place. I arrived on the 18th of May, and found the greatest irregularity in the army. There were then two regiments here, and both ordered away. I detained one of them for the security of this city, and the stores, as I could place no dependence upon the militia; such a set of poltroons is not to be found on the face of the earth. When their all is at stake, they rather choose to see it destroyed than to hazard any thing in its defence. On the 13th of May, a party of continental troops, who were stationed at a place called Schoharie, about thirty or forty miles from this place, being informed that a party of the enemy were advancing to destroy it, marched out, but could not induce the militia to follow them, except seven or eight; and in a short time were engaged with a party of the enemy, in which action the captain, and the lieutenant, and fifteen men were killed, while the militia coldly looked on, but did not go to their assistance. Such is their conduct; and when I applied to them for a guard for their State prisoners, they told me there were so many tories among them that they could not be depended upon.

The Indians and tories are making depredations daily at the westward. They have burned many houses, and killed and driven away a great number of cattle.

The enemy have been very still at the northward, but I expect they will break out soon, as they visit Crown Point sometimes. If they should appear in that quarter, none can be depended upon for the security of that country but you.

Gen. Bayley informs me that he has sent one Major Wright, of Peters' corps, to Number Four, but could not get the people of that place to take him into custody, which is similar to their conduct last year. I wish their conduct to be inquired into. He was obliged to send him to you. I would take it kind if he were secured, as he is an arrant poltroon.

It is reported here that General Howe has left Philadelphia, and Gen. Washington is on his march for New-York. How that may be, I do not pretend to say; but it is certain they have put their baggage on board some time ago. Gen. Gates is on his march for New-York. They (the people) do very well in the hanging way. They hanged nine on the 16th of May; on the 5th of June, nine; and have one hundred and twenty in jail, of which, I believe, more than one half will go the same way. Murder and robberies are committed every day in this neighborhood. So you may judge of my situation, with the enemy on my front, and the devil in my rear.

I am your obedient humble servant,

JOHN STARK.

To Colonel Hay.

Albany, June 30, 1778.

Dear Sir—I received yours of the 26th inst., and have noted the contents. As for sending Mrs. Chesley and Mrs. Cooper to Canada, I can not see any damage they can do us by their going; and there is one other, ****** and his wife, had best go along with them. If you send your letter, I will lay them under an obligation to convey it safe. You wrote for some large cannon that were brought from Ticonderoga, to put on board the gun-boats. They are not mounted. I have ordered them to be put in order; but I believe they will not do, as they are very long. The two eighteen-pounders are twelve feet, and the twelve-pounders nine feet long; but, if they will answer, I will send them as soon as they can be put in order.

There are a few anchors here; but I can not obtain them any other way than by pressing them, as it grieves the inhabitants to the soul to think that they can not help the enemy. For all the disappointments the enemy have met with, they are still in hopes they may recover, and then it will be out of their power to grant them any relief.

I am, sir, &c., JOHN STARK.

To General Stark.

June 30, 1778.

Sir—I received yours of the 27th instant, and much approve of your plan. I shall do every thing in my power to have it put in execution. The field pieces you mentioned, I will send for, and I think there will be no obstacle in the way, but the want of men, who I hope will be got out. Should it meet with success, it would in all probability put a stop to the ravages of the enemy in your quarter, and chastise the pride and insolence of that abandoned savage crew. And unless such measures are taken, you will be kept in a continual alarm, and your country ravaged.

I am, sir, &c.,

HORATIO GATES.

To the Hon. General Gates.

July 1*st*. 1778.

Dear General—I have some thoughts of sending a party to Unadilla, to try to break up a nest of tories—which nests give us all our trouble in this quarter. To promote my plan, I beg you would be so good as to send me the field pieces I wrote you about some time since. This Unadilla is about sixty miles from Cherry Valley. It is concluded that the expedition can be made in a month. Should the party meet with success, they will secure all our western frontiers, and give such a check to the tories in these parts that they will never dare to lift up their heads again. I have received no answers to my three last letters. We live in a suspense about the transactions of the southern army. I wish to learn the truth.

I am, dear sir,

Your sincere friend,

And humble servant,

JOHN STARK.

[Press Warrant]

Albany, 2*d of July*, 1778.

Sir—The general finds that the inhabitants of this place are so lost to all sense of their duty to the continent, that they will not assist him in any thing they can help, which puts him to the disagreeable necessity to order you to take such a number of bateau men as shall be necessary to assist you in pressing one anchor from Martin G. Van Burgan, one from William Winne, and from one Lucas, into the public service, and one from Dow; the one from Dow, you will pay for. The other three you will give your receipt for, they being all for the service of the continent; and this shall be your sufficient order for so doing.

Given the day and date above mentioned.

JOHN STARK.

[Supposed to Colonel Alden.]

Albany, 4*th of July*, 1778.

Dear Sir—I received yours of the 1st instant; and concerning those disaffected persons, if they will not come within the lines, and swallow the oaths of allegiance with a good stomach, you must take the trouble to bring them in, and use your utmost endeavors (by usage becoming such villains) to make them (after a season) valuable subjects.

I send you three quires of paper by the bearer. The ammunition you write for shall be sent by the first safe opportunity. I shall make inquiry about the salt provisions and rum; if to be spared, they shall be sent to you. The militia from Berkshire county must be sent down; but you are to stay until farther orders.

I am, sir, your obedient serv't,

JOHN STARK.

To Captain William H. Ballard.

Sir—You will proceed immediately with a number of tories (whom you brought to this place prisoners), to Albany. You are to take a guard sufficient for you from the militia. When you arrive at Albany, you will deliver the prisoners unto General Stark. Then you will return and join your regiment.

ICHABOD ALDEN, *Colonel.*

Note by Editor. Colonel Alden commanded the post at Cherry Valley, and was surprised by the Indians under Brandt and Walter Butler, in the autumn of 1778, and slain. The fort was not taken, but the houses of the settlement were mostly burnt, and the inhabitants nearly all massacred. Colonel A., very imprudently, was accustomed to sleep outside of his fort. He was in a house outside on the night of the surprise.

Albany, 9th July, 1778.

Honored Sir—I received a letter from Col. Ganesvoort, informing that he has received intelligence the enemy are making preparations against Fort Schuyler ; on which I ordered Colonel Alden's regiment to reinforce him, which leaves me without any troops but a few militia, and without a field officer. I should be glad of a few continental troops, if not more than one company, as there is not one officer here that can parade a guard. As to the affair of Fort Schuyler, I refer you to Colonel Ganesvoort's letter, of which you have a copy.

Yours, &c., JOHN STARK.

General Gates.

To Colonel Warner.

Albany, July 9, 1778.

Dear Sir—An alarm from Fort Schuyler has put me under the necessity of sending Colonel Alden's regiment to reinforce that post, which has left me without a field officer to command the militia. I should be obliged, if your health will permit you to come and take command of them, and assist me in the farther operations of the campaign. Your compliance with this request will much oblige your friend and

Humble servt.,

JOHN STARK.

To General Gates.

Albany, 15*th July*, 1778.

Dear General—I send you by the bearer, Captain Clark, eight of those people, called tories, who have been found so inimical to their country that the council of our good friends at Bennington have thought proper to send them as a present to their friends, to obey their laws and worship their gods in future. I would to God every State on the continent would follow their example. If this meets your approbation, you will send them to the enemy's lines, where they will be received. The good people of Vermont have suffered too much from them already to permit them any longer to be their neighbors.

I am, &c., JOHN STARK.

To His Excellency, Gov. Chittenden.

Albany, July 5th, 1778.

Sir—I received yours of the 22nd instant, with the prisoners, and have given orders for them to be sent to the enemy's lines; all except one Minors, whom I have examined before the officers who brought him in, and can find no crime against him worthy of banishment. The only crime is that his wife told him "that she saw one Simons, and that he did not tell it again."

I hope your committee do not banish every body on so slight an accusation, for if every one should be banished for such slight crimes, I am afraid that there would be but few left. I shall detain him here until I have your answer on the subject, and beg the proofs may be sent.

I am, sir,

Your most obedient

JOHN STARK.

To Brigadier General Stark.

HEADQUARTERS HAVERSTRAW,
July 18, 1778.

Dear Sir—I this day received your letter of the 14th instant, and am sorry to find you so circumstanced as to render a reinforcement necessary, which I can hardly spare in the present critical and interesting state of things. I have, however, ordered Colonel Butler, with the fourth Pennsylvania regiment, and a part of Morgan's rifle corps, to march to the village Mawarsink, in Ulster county, from whence they may be called either to Albany or farther to to the westward, as the exigencies of affairs will point out. These, with the troops which General Gates informs me are to march to your assistance, will, I expect, prove sufficient to repel any attack which may be made upon you; and I hope, in a little time, to be in a situation that I can give you every necessary support.

I am, dear sir,

Your very humble servant,

GEORGE WASHINGTON.

Albany, 7th July, 1778.

Dear General—I received yours of June 26. The letter to Colonel Bedel I have sent as directed. Colonel Whitlock arrived yesterday, and informs me that about sixty of Colonel Bedel's regiment will be in this day, but it will be difficult to get the remainder. I believe my prediction will turn out true that those men have never been raised for any service but to stay at home. I have sent to Col. Bedel to march the remainder agreeably to your orders, which will discover the truth of that matter. I beg he may have no orders to the contrary, until he arrives. I send you a return of Colonel Alden's regiment for the month of June.

We have need of a paymaster at this place, as a part of Bedel's men are expected in this day, and they want money of course; likewise the militia, whose time is out, complain that it will cost them more to go down to you than their pay will come to. If they can not be paid when their time is out, it will discourage others from coming, which may be a damage to the service. I should be pleased to afford them no opportunity of complaint.

I have met with some difficulty in getting down the gun boats. When I applied to the quarter master for pilots, and inquired if they had not a number of assistants that were pilots, Mr. Van Vonter told me they had, and he would send them. When they heard it, they complained that it was degrading their rank to take charge of these boats, and employed others. Four boats have gone, and the other two are left, I suppose, for the above reason. I sent you a list of these gentlemen's names in a former letter, with their employ. I will not trouble you farther in this matter. Your wisdom is sufficient to settle the case. We have had no alarm lately, though duly threatened.

Your humb. serv't,

J. STARK.

To General Gates.

White Plains, 13*th July*, 1778.

Sir—Yesterday I received your last favor, with the intelligence from Colonel Ganesvoort inclosed. The two pieces of brass artillery, &c., must be at Albany by this time, where Col. Stevens acquaints me you have some good iron guns mounting; so your demands on that head are satisfied. Should the intelligence from Oswagathie continue to obtain credit, and the alarm from that quarter increase, you will immediately apply in my name to Hampshire and Berkshire for more militia, and acquaint Col. Ethan Allen it is my request that he immediately march out all the militia he can, without delay collect, to Albany.

It may not be amiss, at the same time, to intimate to the council at Bennington that I desire their assistance and concurrence in every measure you think indispensably necessary for the public service. Bedel's regiment has my orders to be at Albany the first day of next month, where they are to receive pay and clothing. I will immediately send a deputy paymaster to Albany with fifty thousand dollars for the payment of the troops, continental and militia, but I shall command him not to advance one penny either to the quarter master general or to the commissary of purchases, as Gen. Greene has directions to take care for them. As to the sending you more continental troops, that is not in my power; but Gen. Washington, who is just at hand, has received your last letter with the inclosure, and will himself determine upon that subject.

I am, &c.,

HORATIO GATES.

Hon. Brigadier General Stark.

White Plains, July 14, 1778.

Dear Sir—This instant your favor, dated the 10th, from Albany, is put into my hand by the express. All accounts and reports received from you, General Schuyler, and the Indian commissioners, have been regularly transmitted to Congress, and his excellency, General Washington, and every means in my power constantly supplied for the defence of both the northern and western frontiers, as my letter to you of yesterday's date, by Lieutenant Trowbridge, will evince. The money sets out this morning for Albany.

You need be under no manner of concern of another Canada expedition being heedlessly undertaken. The period is not far distant when that province must join the great confederation, without any force being raised to effect it; or if any, such only as is merely necessary to take possession.

Colonel Alden's behavior is exactly what it was last year. Be assured that he shall be made to answer for his conduct. I have this moment ordered General Nixon to ransack the State stores, and send the shoes and stockings so much wanted by that regiment. The paymaster, who is now here, has received the subsistance due to the corps, to the 1st June; shall have charge of what shoes, &c., can be procured for them.

Colonel Trumbull says Ganesvoort's regiment is paid up to April; Warner's and Whitcomb's rangers, the same. So the continentals with you are full as well paid as any this way.

Inclosed, I send you all the late glorious news. It is so positively asserted, from all quarters, that the French fleet are off New-York, that I have the utmost belief in the news. You may depend upon my sending you all the good news that arrives.

I am, sir, &c., &c.,

HORATIO GATES.

To Hon. Brigadier General Stark.

To General Washington.

Albany, 24th July, 1778.

Dear Sir—The Pennsylvania regiment, and a detachment of the second rifle corps arrived here the 27th inst., but in a very miserable condition for want of clothing. I inclose a return of what is wanted by them at present, without which they will not be fit for scouting, which appears the only business on hand. I shall send them immediately to the frontiers to protect the affrighted inhabitants, whose fears are but too well grounded. I think the western frontiers will never be at peace until we march an army into the Indian country, and drive these nefarious wretches from their habitations, burn their towns, destroy their crops, and make proclamation that if ever they return they shall be served in the same manner.*

I hear of nothing from Fort Schuyler of late, worthy of notice. An officer of Colonel Butler's regiment will wait for the clothing and answer.

With due respect, &c.,

JOHN STARK.

His Excellency, General Washington.

To Governor Chittenden.

Albany, 29th July, 1778.

Dear Sir—I received yours of the 27th, and noted the contents. But finding some difficulty in sending the prisoners to New-York, I would advise that they be sent back to Bennington, and left in the public works, for several reasons.

1st. If they are sent to New-York, they will be the best spies that can be let in to them; and if sent into Canada, can give information of the defenceless state of our frontiers, and send a sufficient force to destroy them this season.

* This plan was carried into effect by General Sullivan in 1779, who defeated the Indians under Brandt, the tory Butlers, and the sons of Sir William Johnson, John and Guy—laying waste all the hostile Indian settlements from the Susquehannah to the Genessee.

2d. If I detain them here, I must put them into the city hall, which, if I do, will bring them under the inspection of the committee of this place, who do not love you so well as to wish you any peace; but, in my opinion, would be glad to have your settlement broken up. Therefore, putting all these reasons together, I think it best to keep them until the end of the campaign, when, if you find you can not trust them any longer, you can send them to Canada, or any other place which you think proper.

I am, sir, &c.,

JOHN STARK.

Hon. Thomas Chittenden.

To General Washington.

Albany, 31*st July*, 1778.

Dear General—I received orders last January to raise a number of volunteers to burn the shipping at St. Johns, a copy of which I inclose. I proceeded to raise a party for that purpose, and had them ready to march, when the expedition was abandoned; which put both me and the officers to considerable expense, and the men I raised are troubling me every day for wages.

I should be glad if your Excellency would be so good as to put me in a way to obtain some remuneration for my extra expenses, and those of the officers and soldiers whom I engaged for that service.

We have a number of State prisoners in this jail, who draw provisions; who I think ought not to draw them from the continent, as they are prisoners belonging to this State. Your orders on this head will much oblige

Your friend and hbl serv't,

JOHN STARK.

N. B. Besides these, a number of soldier's wives in this city are starving, with no person to help them. I have applied to the corporation to take care of them, but was denied any help. Would likewise be much obliged by your order on this head. Nothing new since I wrote.

J. S.

To His Excellency, General Washington.

Albany, August 10, 1778.

Dear General—Your letter of the 5th instant has come to hand by express. I am very happy to hear that the disposition of the troops in this department will so well agree with your sentiments.

The posts of Schoharie and Cherry Valley I look upon as exposed to equal danger. For that reason I have stationed Colonel Butler at one, and Colonel Alden at the other.

By the inclosed letters, you will perceive the progress Colonel Butler has made, since he took the command at Schoharie; and if he should be removed, and form a junction with Colonel Alden's regiment, I shall find some method to remove Colonel Alden, so that Butler may have the command, and Alden be satisfied. Concerning the provisions, that have been issued to the State prisoners, upon inquiry, I find it to be by some general order a year ago; but I shall stop it until farther orders. We are in daily expectation of some important news from you.

I am, sir,

Your humble servant,

JOHN STARK.

To Colonel Alden.

Albany, 15th August, 1778.

Sir—I received yours of the 12th, and am happy to hear of the success of your scout. A few such strokes will teach the enemy to watch their own frontiers, and give us peace on ours. As to the tories you sent, I shall take care that they be properly treated.

As for the plunder Captain Ballard's scouts have taken, you will order it to be divided among the people who took it. If any has fallen into their hands belonging to the honest inhabitants, you will please to deliver it up to the proper owners. Captain Ballard and his party are to choose such person to make division, as they think will do the most justice to the party.

You will order a court of inquiry to examine the matter, and see what part ought to be condemned and what returned to the owners, and make report.

You write that you have been obliged to employ some of the inhabitants to assist in building your fort. The accounts must be sent down, properly attested, and I make no doubt will be allowed; but I can not send you any money before I receive orders for so doing. If your scouts should be fortunate enough to fall in with any more of those painted scoundrels,* I think it not worth while to trouble themselves to send them to me. Your wisdom and your scouts may direct you in that matter.†

I am, sir, &c.,

JOHN STARK.

To Colonel Butler.

Albany, 16*th of August*, 1778.

Dear Sir—I received yours of the 14th instant, and am glad to hear that you have got the enemy and tories in so good a way. I am in hopes, in a few weeks, that they will all be convinced that it is neither through fear nor want of strength that we have spared them so long.

As for the cattle your scouts have brought in, such of them as do actually belong to friends of the country, I would be glad might be given up to the proper owners; the others, which belong to the tories who have taken up arms against us, I think ought to be sold for the use of the party that brought them in. As to that portion of the inhabitants who have been disaffected, but have not taken up arms, I think it would be well to admit them to their oath; but the others keep on suspense at present, informing them that their future behavior must determine their fate, and that the blood they have been instrumental in

* Tories painted like Indians for disguise.

† Meaning, in other words, "knock them on the head."

shedding, calls aloud for vengeance on their guilty heads. As to advancing on the enemy at present, I am of your opinion it would be impolitic, before we first find out their strength and situation. I would be glad that it should be done.

I have sent a small scout from Cherry Valley for that purpose, and if they bring in any intelligence worth communicating, I will send it to you. Lest they fail, I would be glad if you could send a small scout of good woodsmen, with a good pilot, for the same purpose. As for the pack-horses and saddles you mention, I have not had an opportunity to learn what number could be provided; I shall make enquiry, and let you know.

As to the number of continental troops with you and at Cherry Valley, I believe they will amount to the number you mention; but cannot tell you what the militia will amount to at present.

If the enemy should attempt to attack your post, you will find it out, before they can come, long enough to send away the women and children.

Of the shot you mention, I have not one here, or else I would send them to you. I have written to General Washington on the subject, but have received no answer. If he sends them, I will forward them to you. Captain Scoul, whom you recommend to me, answers the desired recommendation. I think him a very intelligent young gentleman, and worthy of acquaintance.

I am, sir,

Your most obedient serv't,

JOHN STARK.

N. B. My best respects to Majors Posey and Church, with all the other brave officers of your corps.

Albany, August 18, 1778.

Dear Sir—An exchange is proposed from Canada of Captain Brunson, of Warner's regiment, now a prisoner there, for one Smith, son of Doctor Smith, a State prisoner in the City Hall.

I can not but consider the exchange a good one. Brunson has given most undeniable proofs of his soldiership and firm attachment to his country's cause.

He has been in service ever since the commencement of the war, and discharged his duty most satisfactorily. Such men are ornaments to their country, and through the exertions of such men may we hope to see the liberties of this country established by an honorable peace. The other proposal for exchange is but a youth, who can not render any essential service to the king; and any injury he may do this nation we may look upon with contempt. If there is nothing in the case of Smith more than I have heard, I have no reason to doubt your excellency's consent to an exchange, every way in our favor.

I have the honor, &c., &c.,

JOHN STARK.

His Excellency, Governor Clinton.

His Excellency, General Washington.

Albany, 19th August, 1778.

Dear Sir—I yesterday wrote you concerning clothing for Major Whitcomb's corps of rangers, and sent a return of the said corps. The bearer hereof waits on you for clothing, and can inform you of the sad condition of the men.

I understand that Colonel Winship, deputy commissary general, has resigned. I know of no person so attentive to his business as Bethuel Washburn, assistant deputy commissary general at this place. I hope he may be appointed, as his fidelity may be relied on.

Inclosed is the report of Lieutenant Colonel Wheelock,* who has been upon a scout to Unadilla, which will inform you of the situation of the enemy. If an expedition should be made to that quarter, a number of pack-saddles will be necessary. Colonel Wheelock's information may be depended on, as he is a gentleman of undoubted character.

I am, sir, your ob't serv't,

JOHN STARK.

To General Washington.

Albany, August 21, 1778.

Dear Sir—I am under the disagreeable necessity of complaining of the quarter master general of this department, although I could wish never to be under such a necessity. Not only myself, but almost every other person who has any business to transact with him, have reason to complain, as he seems very unwilling to oblige any person whatever.

He has no tents, nor can I learn that he has tried to get any; by which neglect, Colonel Alden's regiment is in a suffering condition, with no probability of their wants being supplied.

I have, after several applications for some kind of grain for my horses, been informed that I can have none unless I advance hard money for the same. I think it a very surprising affair if the continental money will not purchase a little grain for some horses; but I am fully of the opinion that such gentlemen, by demanding hard money, have been very influential in reducing the continental money to

* He was afterward president of Dartmouth College. Several years after the war, General Stark, having business to transact in the vicinity of Hanover, called upon President Wheelock, at whose house, on a pressing invitation, he passed the night. In the evening a large party of his fellow-citizens called on the president, to whom he said he was happy to have an opportunity of presenting them to his veteran commander.

An escort of citizens on horse-back attended him a few miles on his return, President Wheelock riding in the escort.—EDITOR.

its present low state. I must beg, if he can not be removed or reformed, that I and some other officers may be recalled.

I am, sir, &c.,

JOHN STARK.

To the Commissioners of Albany.

Albany, August 22, 1778.

Gentlemen—I received yours of yesterday, informing me of your desire to have the tories Captain Ballard brought here the other day.

I assure you I have no intention to keep them. You write for twelve, as being inhabitants of this State, one of whom I look upon as a prisoner of war, and shall detain him as such. The other eleven I have given orders to be delivered up to you.

As to the cattle and sheep brought in by Captain Ballard, I have directed Colonel Alden to have a court of inquiry sit upon them, and make report to me, as I thought the owners had not been concerned in any conspiracy against the United States.

I am, &c.,

JOHN STARK.

Albany, September 15th, 1778.

Dear Sir—I beg to be excused for not writing to you sooner; but, not having any thing worth communicating, I deferred it. The enemy at the northward have given us no trouble as yet. Major Whitcomb is daily watching their motions, and often bringing in their sailors. Four came in the other day, with two deserters, who agree that they have but three or four vessels on the lake.

Three prisoners brought from Unadilla inform that Brandt is mustering his forces in order to pay us a visit. Whether he is in earnest or in jest, is uncertain; but if he should be fool enough to attempt it, I hope to be able to give a good account of him.

Colonel Blair informs me that a small scout of his militia found two brass howitzers in the river by Saratoga, after the army left that place, and turned them into the stores and took a receipt.

I would beg your honor to make them some allowance for the same. He farther informs me that one hundred dollars has been paid for such pieces found before.

The quarter master general is building a large store house at this place, which is putting the continent to an amazing expense, to little or no purpose, as I can not see the most distant prospect of so extravagant a building ever being wanted in this department. I should be much obliged to you to let me know whether it was by your order, or that of any other general officer, or not.

I have the honor, &c.,

JOHN STARK.

His Excellency, General Washington.

To the British Commander at Crown Point.

Albany, 24*th September*, 1778.

Sir—I am not a little surprised to think of the conduct of the master of your vessels on the lake at Crown Point, who says that, by your order, he has detained Captain * * *, whom I sent with a flag of truce, in order to carry over to you a number of people in your interest. If that was not the case, you must be sensible that it is contrary to the law of nations to detain such a flag; but also the laws of humanity forbid it; and as I have a number of prisoners in my custody, it is in my power to make retaliation. You may depend upon it I shall not let that piece of broken faith pass unnoticed.

I am, sir, your most humble servant,

JOHN STARK.

To His Excellency, Governor Chittenden.

Albany, 24th September, 1778.

Sir—I received yours of the 22d instant, informing me that some of the inhabitants are detained on board the enemy's vessels at Crown Point, whom you wish to redeem. I send four French prisoners, who were taken at Ticonderoga last year, for that purpose, whom you will keep until you have a like number in return. I have information that the enemy is forming a design against you this Fall. I should think it advisable for you to send a strong reinforcement to your frontiers; as the time is short, and the season so far advanced, it can not put you to much trouble; otherwise, your frontiers may share the fate of German flats. A few days will decide the matter; and as I have nothing more at heart than your welfare, I give you this advice. I know that you have enemies here, which induces me to give it, as your own exertions must be your salvation.

Your humble serv't,

JOHN STARK.

To Colonel Alden.

Albany, 3d of October, 1778.

Sir—Yours of the 30th of September has come to hand. I highly approve of your proceedings concerning the tory effects. I should advise you to keep the money in your own hands at present.

I shall reserve the prisoners in my hands, for the purpose of exchanging yours with Brandt.

The French king has published a declaration that his army and navy are to seize, take and destroy all the property of the king of Great Britain, wherever they can find it, either by sea or land. This order was sent to Mons le Compte Durbarè, supposed to his prime Minister of State.

I am, your humble serv't,

JOHN STARK.

Brigadier General Stark.

Fishkill, 8th of October, 1778.

Dear Sir—I have been favored with yours of the 31st of August, and 7th, 15th and 28th of September. The subject of Mrs. McNeil's petition comes under the notice of the quarter master general, General Mifflin, who was in that office at the time the grievance complained of was committed. He has lately had one million of dollars put into his hands for the purpose of discharging all demands; and I see that Col. Hughes is appointed to adjust and settle all those in the State of New-York. To him, therefore, Mrs. McNeil must apply.

The proceedings of the court martial, had at Schoharie, never came to hand. The inclosed paper, which appears by the endorsement to have contained the proceedings, was all that you sent.

The quarter master should make a reasonable compensation to those persons who take up shot or any stores from the North river and deliver them to him. I have laid your several complaints against Col. Lewis before the quarter master general. Col. Lewis has sent down a vindication of his conduct, and desires a proper enquiry, which the quarter master general must make.

I would not have you build barracks at Fort Edward. The troops now there may winter at Saratoga, where are good barracks for three hundred men.

If there should be a necessity of keeping a small command at Fort Edward, a hut or two may be easily erected for that purpose.

If Col. Butler undertakes the Unadilla expedition, I hope he may have success. I am glad to hear of the blow struck by the Oneida Indians upon the rear of Brandt's party.

I am, sir,

Your most obedient servant,

GEORGE WASHINGTON.

Albany, 9th October, 1778.

Dear Sir—Being employed the last winter to prepare an expedition to the northward, I enlisted a number of men for that purpose, who are demanding pay, and give for reason that Bedel's regiment received their pay for like service. I should be glad if you would lay the affair before Congress, and see if they will not make some allowance for the extra expenses of the *voyage*.

I likewise understand that a major general, when on a separate command is, by order of Congress, entitled to extra allowance for his support; but can find no resolve where a brigadier is allowed any more than his bare wages, which, at this time, are very inconsiderable for a maintenance, more especially on a separate command; and being willing, for the honor of my country and the noble cause we are engaged in, to live up to my station, I desire you will let me know whether I can not be allowed my table expenses, &c.

I am in hopes, in a few days, to be able to give you a good account of the enemy at the westward. Colonel Butler, with his detachment, has marched to Unadilla. His success will probably finish the campaign in this department. I inclose a return of the garrison of Fort Schuyler.

I am, sir,

With great respect and esteem,

Your most obedient

And very hbl. serv't,

JOHN STARK.

Hon. President of Congress.

In September, 1778, some prisoners brought information that Brandt was mustering a force of tories and Indians at Unadilla, on the Susquehannah, with an intention of laying waste the western frontiers of New-York. Upon this information being received at head quarters, Colonel William Butler,* of the Pennsylvania line, was detached with a force of continentals and militia to divert the threatened danger. Of the success of this expedition, General Stark gives the following account in a letter to General Washington.

Albany, Oct. 23, 1778.

Dear Sir—I have just returned from Schoharie, and find that the enemy have been driven too far from the frontier for me to overtake them this season, as it is so far advanced. Too much honor can not be given to Colonel Butler and his brave officers and soldiers, for their spirited exertions in this expedition against the Indians. They have put it entirely out of the power of the enemy to do our frontier any serious injury for the remainder of the campaign. I beg of your excellency that they may be relieved, as soon as the nature of the service will admit, as both officers and men are much fatigued.

I must beg also that clothing may be sent them, for want of which they are neither fit for duty where they are, nor in a condition to be removed. It grieves me to the soul to see such brave troops in so miserable a condition.

I am, sir, &c.,

JOHN STARK.

His Excellency, General Washington.

* Colonel Butler marched from Schoharie and penetrated into the Indian country in October, with great difficulty crossing high mountains and deep waters, and destroyed the towns of Unadilla and Anaguaga, the latter being the head quarters of Brandt, lying on both sides of the Susquehanah where it is two hundred and fifty yards wide. Many farm houses and about four thousand bushels of grain were destroyed.—ALLEN.

Bennington, 19*th May*, 1779.

Dear General—The men I sent into Canada (by your orders) in the last part of 1777, or beginning of '78, as spies, and who were made prisoners, have all returned safe, and have made repeated applications to me for the reward promised them. I have it not in my power to discharge these demands, as my expense, as well as that of several other officers (by endeavoring to carry your orders into execution), is very considerable to us. I therefore desire your advice in the premises; and beg leave to propose whether it would not be advisable for you to inclose to me a letter to the commanding officer at Albany, purporting the nature of your orders to me, which occasioned the expense, and desire me to wait on him for an adjustment, or to direct to any other measures in the affair that you may judge proper. I could wish you to write me, by the bearer, on this subject (should you see this person), as the men are poor, and are under real necessity for their pay. Your endeavors to serve them will much oblige them, as well as, dear general,

Your most obedient humble servant,

SAMUEL HERRICK.*

Brigadier General Stark, Derryfield, N. H.

Archibald Stark, a young lieutenant of 18, who accompanied Gen. Sullivan against the Six Nations in 1779, wrote the following minutes:

"Dance at head quarters; the Oneida sachem was master of ceremonies."

"September 3d. The army is preparing to march for Wyoming."

"4th. The army marched fifteen miles down the river."

* Colonel Herrick, as also Colonel Seth Warner, were good penmen, as appears by their original letters to General Stark.

"5th. The whole army embarked on board boats, except what were necessary to drive the pack-horses and cattle; and on the 7th arrived at Wyoming, in high spirits. During the whole of this severe campaign, our loss in killed, died of wounds, and sickness, did not exceed sixty men."

"8th. General Sullivan received an express this evening from General Washington, informing him that Count de Estainge is on the coast near New-York, with a French fleet and army; in consequence of which, General Sullivan's army is ordered to march the 10th inst. for head quarters."

"10th. The army march for Easton, and the 15th arrived there. This army has marched from Tioga to Easton (one hundred and fifty miles through a mountainous, rough wilderness) in eight days, with their artillery and baggage. A most extraordinary march indeed."

"16th, 17th, 18th. Remain at Easton. We are informed that Count de Estainge has taken several ships-of-war, with all the transports and troops the enemy had at and near Georgia. He is expected daily at New-York."

"25th. Our army is to march the 27th inst. towards head quarters."

To General Stark.

Bristol, R. I., 25th of October, 1779.

Sir—This morning I received a dispatch from his excellency, Gen. Washington, dated the 2d instant. He informs me that the evening of the preceding day the enemy burnt and destroyed the works at Stoney and Verplanck's Points, and retreated down the North river. His excellency also sent me the copy of the inclosed intelligence from the southward which he says, came from such men and such authority as induces him to believe it substantially true. I give you joy of this extraordinary flow of good news.*

I am, sir, your aff. humb. serv't,

HORATIO GATES.

* The arrival of the French fleet under Count de Estainge.

West Point, December 14, 1779.

Dear Sir—Since the death of the late worthy General Poor, I am led to suppose you have had no regular correspondent from the army. The fluctuating state of our affairs, since that time, has prevented my writing; but now, since all hopes of active operations for this campaign are laid aside, I can write with more propriety than before.

Representations in regard to this important fortress must have been made you before this; but still, it can be no injury farther to show the absolute necessity of its being well supplied the ensuing winter; and still farther, to urge the importance of the place. It is beyond a doubt the keystone of America. The enemy, possessing it, would infallibly cut off all communication between the northern and southern States.

You may be assured that every supply within the power of the army will be attended to with the greatest alacrity; but their endeavors, without your assistance, must be altogether useless. While, on the other hand, their industry, with your care and assistance, will effectually secure the garrison, and place matters upon a proper footing for the opening of another campaign.

To relate the difficulties of last winter at Morristown, with the unequalled sufferings of the troops at that place, would wound the feelings of every one who had the misfortune to hear them. That period having passed (though by no means forgotton), I shall not enlarge upon the circumstances, but leave you to judge what must have been their calamity to be for six or seven days destitute of flour, and with very little meat, and sometimes several days without either.

It was then supposed to be owing to the indigence of the States at large. Upon the present system of supplying the army, it would be an insult to the judgment of any man to suppose they could not be procured, when every one acknowledges that there is more provision by far in the country than when the war was commenced.

Every one knows how liberally a much larger army was supplied at that time. The next thing that occurs to me, is in regard to the next campaign. We ought to exert every nerve to procure soldiers to fill up our battalions, agreeably to the establishment now on foot in Congress, of which you will probably soon receive notice. Although this new arrangement may occasion a diffidence in officers, and a negligence of the service, still, if Congress thinks it just, it is not our business to find fault. I have been told that a number of soldiers and some officers, belonging to the sixteen additional regiments, have made application to their respective States for their depreciation money. I can not see the propriety of its being paid, for they were not considered as belonging to any State in particular, nor were their vacancies filled by any particular State. As for their services, I don't think ten more soldiers enlisted on account of their appointment than would otherwise have done. It was only creating a multiplicity of officers, which the public would now willingly be rid of. However, as that matter more particularly concerns you than me, the farther progress of it rests solely with you.

I am, sir, your obedient humble servant,

JOHN STARK.

To Hon. Meshech Weare.

[Circular.]

HEADQUARTERS. *Morristown,*
January, 6, 1780.

Sir—As it will contribute in some degree to relieve our distress on the subject of provisions, I am to desire that you will discharge all the men in the brigade under your command whose enlistments and terms of service will clearly expire by the last of this month.

In conducting the matter, you will call upon the commanding officers of regiments to prevent the discharge of any not coming within the above description.

I am, sir, your most obedient serv't,

GEO. WASHINGTON.

Brigadier General.

To the Commissioner of Indian Affairs and the Commander-in-Chief.

Albany, June 26, 1778.

Pursuant to orders received from Colonel Bedel, by direction of the commanding officer at Albany, I set off with my party ye 28th of March last, and with a design to visit the Penobscot tribe of Indians.

On our arrival at Penobscot we found they were principally absent, which detained us nearly ten days. On their return, the chiefs being called together, we delivered them the belts and found them very friendly disposed. They appointed three of their chiefs to wait on the commander-in-chief of the northern department, who will inform him of the particular condition, disposition, and intention of the tribe. Before we came away, they had sent off the belts, ordering them to be transmitted to the Indians at Machias, St. Johns, &c. We returned to Colonel Bedel's on the 22d instant.

LOUIS VINCENT, *Interpreter.*

To General Stark.

HEADQUARTERS. *Kamaporuh,*
June 30th, 1780.

Dear Sir—You will be pleased to repair immediately to the State of New-Hampshire, in order to receive and forward to the army the levies required of the State, by the honorable the committee of Congress, for filling their three battalions. I have not heard from the State upon the subject, and therefore can not inform you of the place which may have been appointed for their rendezvous ; but this you will learn, and, if you do not already find the levies assembled at it, you will exert every degree of industry in your power to effect it.

You know how precious moments are to us ; and I am pursuaded your efforts, both to collect and forward the levies, will correspond with the exigency. That the business may be more facilitated, you will take with you four officers from General Poor's brigade, to whom I wrote on the subject, if this number should not be already in the

State, and with whom you will forward the levies, either in a body or in detachments of from one hundred and fifty to two hundred men, as circumstances best suit, with all possible expedition. If there are more officers in the State than this number, you may retain them for this service.

In receiving the men, you will pay particular attention to their being sound and healthy, and in every respect fit for service; and none but such as answer this description must be taken, as they would otherwise prove an incumbrance and a great expense, without being of the least advantage.

Besides the levies for filling the three battalions, it has been deemed essential, to render the success of our operations the more certain, to call upon the State for between nine hundred and a thousand militia to join the army in service for three months from the time of their arriving at Claverack, on the North River—the place assigned for their rendezvous—by the 25th of next month.

It is much my wish that you should have the direction and command of those. You will therefore use your best endeavors to have them assembled, armed and equipped in every respect in the best manner circumstances will admit, for taking the field, and march with them so as to arrive with certainty at Claverack by the time I have mentioned.

I shall only add that I shall be happy to hear from you very frequently on the subject of this important and interesting business, both as it respects the levies for the battalions, and the militia; and, entirely confiding in your greatest address and assiduity in promoting it,

I am, dear sir,

With much regard and esteem,

Your most ob't serv't,

GEO. WASHINGTON.

Brigadier Gen. Stark.

To President Weare.

Ramapough, June 30, 1780.

Sir—I send Brigadier General Stark to your State to collect and forward the drafts for your battalions, and the levies for three months to the appointed place of rendezvous. The zeal which the State of New-Hampshire has always manifested, gives me the fullest confidence that they have complied with the requisitions of the committee of Congress in all their extent, though we have not yet heard from thence what measures have been taken.

This is the time for America, by one great exertion, to put an end to the war; but, for that purpose, the necessary means must be furnished. The basis of every thing else is the completion of the continental battalions to their full establishment. If this is not done, I think it my duty to forewarn every State that nothing decisive can be attempted; and that this campaign, like all the former, must be chiefly defensive. I am sorry to observe that some of the States have taken up the business on a less extensive scale. The consequences have been represented with candor and plainness; and I hope, for the honor and safety of America, the representation may have the weight it deserves. The drafts can not be forwarded with too much expedition; but as to the militia, under present appearances, I think it advisable to suspend the time fixed for their rendezvousing to the 25th of next month, at which period I shall be glad they may be without fail at the place appointed; and it would be my wish that they should come out under the command of General Stark.

I entreat your excellency to employ all your influence to give activity and vigor to the measures of your State. Every thing depends on the proper improvement of the present conjuncture. We have every thing to hope on one side, and every thing to fear on the other.

With perfect respect, I have the honor to be

Your Excellency's most obed't humble serv't,

GEO. WASHINGTON.

P. S. The suspension of the period for the assembling of the militia is founded on the French fleet's not being arrived; if this event shall have taken place before this reaches your excellency, the suspension is not to have effect. The militia can not be too soon at the place of rendezvous after the fleet arrives.

[Opinion sent to a Council of War held near Tappan, New-Jersey, 1780.]

Agreeably to your excellency's request, I send you my opinion of what we ought to do for the safety of the country this fall and winter.

Question 1. To what object our attention ought to be directed this fall and winter?

Answer. To try to reënter as many of the soldiers now in the field as can be engaged, either for the war or for one year from the first of January next, and in case the second division of the French fleet should arrive, to push with all our force against New-York; should that not be the case, to keep as near to the enemy as our circumstances will admit of, so as to prevent their obtaining any supplies from the country.

Question 2. Whether we ought to send any part of the army to the southward?

Answer. As the army at present does not amount to many more than that of the enemy, and is in expectation of the second division of the French fleet, I do not think it advisable to detach any part of it.

JOHN STARK.

[Resolve of the State of New-York.]

In Senate, October 10, 1780.

A message of the honorable, the House of Assembly, was received with the following resolution for concurrence: viz.,

Resolved, unanimously, That the delegates from this State be instructed to declare in Congress, that it is the earnest wish of this State that Congress should, during the war, or until a perpetual confederation should be completed, exercise every power which they may deem necessary for an effectual prosecution of the war; and that, whenever it shall appear to them that any State is deficient in furnishing the quota of men, money, provisions, or other supplies required of each State, that Congress direct the commander-in-chief, without delay, to march the army, or such parts of it as may be requisite, into such State, and by military force compel it to furnish its deficiency.

Resolved, That his excellency, the governor, be requested to transmit a copy of the foregoing resolution to the delegates from this State in Congress.

Resolved, That this Senate do concur with the honorable, the House of Assembly, in this said resolution.

Extract from the minutes.

ROB'T BENSON,

Cl'k of the Senate.

To Major General Heath.

November 23, 1780.

Dear Sir—Yours of this date was received by Major Fisk, but previous to the receipt I had ordered the troops to march; those of the centre column I halted, and gave the necessary directions to the right and left columns.

I hope the forage will turn out according to your wishes, but it does not equal my expectations. The country below White Plains is almost desolate on account of the ravages of both armies. Scarcely a farmer has more than one cow, and many who were once in affluent circumstances are now reduced to indiscriminate poverty.

I sent Col. Sheldon's light dragoons to Fort Clinton yesterday, and moved with the troops within eight miles of King's bridge, to cover them in case of necessity. But the caution, however prudent it may appear, was needless, for the enemy either did not know of our approach, or did not choose to meet us.

Twenty militia light horse, who proceeded in front of the cavalry, took prisoners two of DeLancy's men: one Bumour, cousin of the famous Major Bumour, and one Ferrett, a noted cow-boy, and of course a villain; he has once been condemned to be hanged, but made his escape. I have sent them to you under a guard.

While the cavalry were formed upon a hill in our advance, one of them left the line and proceeded a few rods to the rear to water his horse. Curiosity led him to a house near by, when a cow-boy came up, dismounted him, and rode away his horse in triumph.

If my instructions would have permitted, Morrisania, that noted nest of tories, might have been plundered and burnt, but I think it too late now.

I am, sir,

Your obedient humble servant,

JOHN STARK.

To General Stark.

HEADQUARTERS. *West Point*, November 23, 1780.

Dear Sir—Your favor of yesterday came to hand this morning. I am glad to hear that everything goes on well with you. The weather is disagreeable, but your troops will endure anything. I apprehend that some rum and bread will have reached you before this does.

I am anxious to hear from you to-day, and hope an express is now on the way with an account of something very interesting. Heaven grant that it may be equal to our most sanguine expectations. Please give me notice when you are on your return, and the time you will probably reach this place, that provisions may be in readiness for the troops. I have sent you a few sheets of paper.

I am, with great regard,

Dear sir, your obed't serv't,

W. HEATH.

P. S. Please give the inclosed to Major Cartwright, if he is not gone; if he is, please send it back to me.

W. H.

General Stark.

About eight miles from King's Bridge,
November 23, '80—5 o'clock *P. M*

Dear Sir—Yours of 12 o'clock is received, and I am very happy to hear of your success; and am in hopes mine will be equal. I believe the enemy are surprised to find us so near them. We have taken three prisoners, but can learn nothing of consequence from them; one of them is a cousin of the famous Maj. Bumour. Col. Cilley, with the left, is now, I suppose, at Maroneck; he marched from White Plains at about 1 o'clock. I have not heard from him since.

As to your movement, I approve of the hour of 10 o'clock for the march to commence. You will move very slowly until 1; and then, in case you hear of no alarm, you will, by proper marches, retire. But in case of alarm, you will have recourse to the copy of Gen. Heath's instructions. I beg that the greatest vigilance may be observed in loading and forwarding the teams. I expect you will hear from me before 10 o'clock in the morning; if not, the preceding instructions will be your guide, together with your own prudence.

Wishing you success, I am,

Dear sir, your most obed't serv't,

JOHN STARK.

To Colonel Shrieve.

To His Excellency, General Washington.

Peekskill Hollow, November 30, 1780.

Dear Sir—The impaired state of my health, and the unsettled state of my accounts with the State of New-Hampshire; renders my presence in that State the ensuing winter highly necessary. I have never as yet settled my depreciation, or received any cash from that source. Without an arrangement of these matters, it is impossible for me to subsist in the army.

The many favors I have received from you, and the zeal you have manifested for the interest of the officers under your command, induces me to ask leave of absence until spring.

The brigade I have the honor to command is now under orders to join its several States; therefore it is not probable it will be in my power to render the country any essential service until the next campaign.

I have the honor to be, sir,

Your most obed't serv't,

JOHN STARK.

To the Officer commanding the New-Hampshire Line.

GARRRISON. *West Point*, December 12, 1780.

Dear Sir—I apprehend some of the officers will wish to go on a furlough during the winter. They may be indulged, the following order being strictly observed: Each brigade, which has not a brigadier, is to be commanded by a colonel. Each regiment at all times to have one field officer with it. The colonel commanding a brigade not to be considered as answering for the regiment to which he belongs. Two commissioned officers to be with each company, if convenient; but one is indispensable. The officers will agree who shall go first, and divide the time, so that those who go first may return in season to give a reasonable time to those who remain, if they choose it—

always bearing in mind that all officers are to join their respective corps by the first of April next. The brigadier or officer commanding the brigade will certify which of the field officers are to go first, and that others are satisfied as to the length of the furlough; this, on being shown here, will be approved. The colonel or commanding officer of each regiment will certify the same, respecting the commissioned officers, which is to be shown and approved by the brigadier or officer commanding the brigade.

I am, with great regard, your ob't serv't,

W. HEATH.

GARRISON. *West Point,*
December 19, 1780.

Dear Sir—I have just received a letter of this date from Major Maxwell, at Crom pond, informing me that the enemy are in motion at Morrisania; and it is supposed that Crom pond is their object, and that they will be up this evening or early in the morning. I therefore request you would order about one hundred and fifty or two hundred men from the New-Hampshire line to move down towards Crom pond immediately. Let them take one day's provisions with them. Perhaps Colonel Delancy may be cleverly handled.

I am, with great regard, dear sir,

Your obed't serv't,

W. HEATH.

General Stark.

Peekskill Hollow, Jan. 1, 1781.

Sir—Your letter of the 31st ult. I have been honored with, together with the resolution of Congress. If my health permits, I shall endeavor to pursue my journey by the last of this week. But my finances are exhausted; neither do I know where they can be replenished, unless by application to your excellency. I believe five thousand dollars may answer my purpose. If you can grant me that sum, it will be considered as an infinite obligation. I beg your excellency to consider that I have not drawn a single farthing of cash since the last of December, 1778; and only four thousand dollars, on account, since then. Therefore, as my demands have not been great, and my present necessity is very urgent, I flatter myself your excellency will furnish me with the cash. As to the term of my absence, it is a matter of indifference to me whether your excellency or Congress limit it. But, either way, I shall return as soon as my health will permit.

Wishing your excellency a happy new year, and an agreeable winter,

I have the honor to be

Your most obed't serv't,

JOHN STARK.

His Excellency, Gen. Washington.

GARRISON. *West Point,*
January 1, 1781.

Dear Sir—I am just honored with yours of the last evening; am happy to hear, and much approve of the measures you have taken to support Col. Hull, and hope they will be crowned with deserved success. Wishing that the new year may be productive of honor, peace and happiness to our country, to you and your family,

I am, with great regard, dear sir,

Affectionately yours,

W. HEATH.

General Stark.

P. S. A few boards arrived last evening; three or four of them are at your service, agreeable to your former request.

To Major General Heath.

Peekskill Hollow, Jan. 2, 1781.

Dear Sir—Your favor of the 31st was delivered by express, with the letter from his excellency. You apologize for breaking the seal of the letter superscribed to me, but, convinced that it was a mistake, you are excusable.

Yours of the 1st instant was received, and I am very happy that my conduct has met with your approbation. Major Waite, who was sent with the party, has returned. He went to Pines bridge, found Colonel Hull, and that the enemy had retired. I can not learn that they did any thing of consequence.

I have the honor to be

Your obedient humble servant,

JOHN STARK.

To Colonel Pickering, Quarter Master General.

Peekskill Hollow, 2d January, 1781.

Sir—Having received his excellency's approbation for leave of absence for the recovery of my health, I propose setting out the last of the week; but am absolutely destitute of cash to perform my intended journey, or for the transportation of my baggage. If you can furnish me with a sum sufficient for the purpose, I shall be very glad. I have certificates from the quarter master and forage department for nearly ten thousand dollars, but I suppose you do not take them; therefore, I must solicit to have some cash advanced on account. I wish you to let me know as soon as possible what assistance you can afford me.

I am, sir, your obedient humble serv't,

JOHN STARK.

General Washington to General Stark.

HEADQUARTERS. *New-Windsor*,
Jan. 3, 1781.

Dear Sir—I am favored with yours of the 1st instant, and wish it was in my power to gratify you in your request. But as there is not a single farthing in the military chest, it will be absolutely impossible to furnish any part of the sum solicited.

I am, dear, sir, with very great regard,

Your most obed't hble. servant,

GEO. WASHINGTON.

P. S. I have not been able to obtain any money, for my own expenses or table, for more than three months.

General Stark.

To the Hon. Meshech Weare.

Derryfield, 18*th March*, 1781.

Sir—I have received two letters from Lieutenant Howe. The one informs that he shall be able to muster forty recruits to-morrow, and the other gave intelligence of some persons tracked from Long-Island to Amherst, who were supposed to belong to the Dunbarton tory club. I sent Lieutenant Stark to examine the suspected houses, which, I suppose, was executed this morning at day-break.

The furloughs of the officers are almost expired, and they can not tarry unless business requires it. If you should think proper to have them detained to conduct parties of recruits, the measure could not fail to meet with universal approbation.

I was, day before yesterday, taken suddenly unwell, and am not able to go out yet; but, as soon as I am able, I shall come to Exeter. In the meantime I should be glad of a list of officers in the western district, and the number of troops that Brigadier General Nichols is to muster, that they may be equally divided and officered according to our circumstances.

If you should think proper to place some money in my hands, to give to the officers with their instructions, I should be accountable for it by their receipts, by your letting me know the quantity each is to have. I have written to Lieutenant Colonel Dearborn to receive, and with your approbation to forward, those from Exeter.

Your most obedient servant,

JOHN STARK.

General Washington to General Stark, appointing him Commander of the Northern Department.

HEADQUARTERS. *New-Windsor,*
June 25, 1781.

Dear Sir—Upon finding it necessary, for the operations of the campaign, to recall the continental troops from the north, I have ordered six hundred militia from the counties of Berkshire to that quarter, in addition to the militia and State troops of New-York; and I have now to request that you will assume the general command of all the troops in that department, as soon as conveniently may be. I am induced to appoint you to this command on account of your knowledge and influence among the inhabitants of that country.

You will be pleased, therefore, to repair to Saratoga, and establish your head quarters at that place, retaining with you four hundred of the troops from Massachusetts, and sending the other two hundred to Col. Willet, who will remain in command upon the Mohawk river, as his popularity in that country will enable him to render essential services there.

In case of an incursion from the enemy, you will make such dispositions, as you shall judge most advantageous, for opposing them and protecting the frontier, not withdrawing the troops from the Mohawk river. I rely upon it you will use your utmost exertions to draw forth the force of the country from the Green mountains and all the contiguous territory. And I doubt not your requisitions will be attended with success, as your personal influence must be unlimited among those people, at whose head you have formerly fought and conquered with so much reputation and glory.

I request you will be particular in keeping up proper discipline, and preventing the troops from committing depredations upon the inhabitants.

Be pleased to let me hear from you from time to time, and, believe me, dear sir,

Your most obedient humble servant,

GEO. WASHINGTON.

Note by Editor.—The expedition against Lord Cornwallis, in Virginia, was now in secret contemplation. The movement was only known to Congress, to General Washington, Robert Morris, Count de Rochambeau, the French agent, the Chevalier de La Lucerne, and General Lafayette. Previous reports had been circulated, that, on the arrival of the French army, an attempt would be made upon New-York. The British general in New-York, therefore, when too late to remedy the matter, received with astonishment the information that the American army was in Virginia, and soon afterward, that Lord Cornwallis was shut up at Yorktown by a French fleet on one quarter, and a superior American and French force on the other.

HEADQUARTERS. *Peekskill,*
June 28, 1781.

Sir—On your arrival to take the command of the northern frontier, you will be pleased to advise with General Schuyler with respect to the disposition of the troops destined for the defence of that quarter. As that gentleman's knowledge of every part of that exposed country is very good, his assistance and counsel may be very useful to you. From this motive, I am induced to give you this direction. You will also consult with him with respect to furnishing the means of subsistence to the troops under your command, should you at any time find the public stores to be exhausted.

With much regard,

I am, sir, your most obed't

Humble serv't,

GEO. WASHINGTON.

Brigadier General Stark.

To Governor Clinton.

Albany, 1781.

Dear Sir—An instance, which I think is unusually alarming, has lately transpired in this department, and which I think is a design of no less consequence than the dissolution of the army. The plan seems to be to try the superior force of the civil government over that of the military, in seizing, imprisoning and detaining soldiers from their duty, at a time when the public are under the necessity of giving such enormous prices to induce men to enter the service, and the demand is so pressing. This instance happened in this city on the body of one Hoar, a soldier in the Massachusetts line, but detained here in the useful works of the armory. He was seized on a pretended debt of about six pounds, that it was said he owed a tavern-keeper as a tavern bill. The tavern-keeper took the advice of a young fubble of a lawyer who, ready to undertake anything that would make him popular in knavery, and perhaps possessed of some glimmering hopes of future favors from the tory's sovereign for the bold and daring attempt, readily engaged in the design, and granted a writ, by force of which he now lies in jail.

I need not relate to your excellency the fatal consequences resulting from such a procedure; they are too plain to need a moment's animadversion. However, I am not apprehensive of any imminent danger from the loss of a single soldier, though a very useful man; but the precedent, I must own, alarms me. What shall hinder a body of the enemies to the country (of which, to my sorrow, I must own that I think this city is replete), to either trust, or pretend to trust soldiers, and then commence actions against them? The answer must be, they must be immediately laid in jail, and by the same authority that puts one in can a brigade be put in; and, if a brigade goes, I know nothing to prevent the whole army from sharing the same fate. And farther, sir, I am fully confident that George the III., of Great Britain, has many subjects in this city who would willingly lay down half, nay, even the whole of their estates in this service, and trust in his royal clemency for the repayment of the money so profitably laid out for his great advantage. But it is unnecessary to enlarge upon a subject so explicit, and I shall only beg leave to be considered yours, and my country's sincere friend.

I am, sir, your faithful friend

And obedient servant,

JOHN STARK.

To His Excellency, General Washington.

Albany, 9th of August, 1781.

Dear Sir—In compliance with your orders, I arrived at Bennington on Friday last, and on Saturday made a visit to their governor, who, together with the leading men of the country, have promised me every assistance in their power to repel the common enemy. I have reason to believe, from their conduct, that their promises are not fallacious; for, before I came to Bennington, Major McKinstry, who has command of the troops at Saratoga, sent an express to apprise them of the enemy's advance for his post. The alarm was spread, and in a few hours one hundred and fifty men, on horseback, marched to his assistance. The alarm proved false, and next day they returned, but not till they had visited Saratoga.

On Monday last, at sunrise, a party of eleven was discovered in the south-east part of Bennington, supposed to be a party of tories from Hoosac, passing to Canada. The people were instantly in arms, pursued them until 1 o'clock, when three of the pursuers came up and made them prisoners. They were instantly marched to Bennington. Upon examination, I find them to be a party from Canada, which first consisted of six. They made prisoners of Esquire Bleeker and two servants, when they were joined by other tories, making up the eleven. I inclose you their instructions. For my part, I think they ought to be considered as spies, and beg your excellency's opinion on the subject.

Perhaps you will be surprised when I inform you that the militia from Berkshire and Hampshire counties have not yet arrived at Saratoga. Upon being apprised of it at Bennington, I wrote to Gen. Fellows by express, begging that they might be hastened without loss of time. I likewise wrote Major McKinstry to send me a return of the garrison at Saratoga, and find it to consist of but ninety men, including officers; for which reason, I thought it most prudent for me to return to Albany and wait until a larger number can be collected; but be assured that when a number arrives that will render my presence necessary, I shall lose no time in repairing to my post.

I should be remiss in my duty not to inform your excellency that it was with the greatest difficulty I procured an express to go to Saratoga, for want of something to pay his expenses; and in a department that requires so much intelligence to be communicated, if possible, some provision ought to be made. Knowing that your excellency will do all in your power for the public good, your directions on this, and every other subject, shall be my invariable and certain guide.

Your letter, of the 28th of June, is just placed in my hand. I will show it to General Schuyler, who is polite enough to promise me every assistance in his power, either in advice, or knowledge of the country and property, if required.

I congratulate your excellency on his fortunate escape, the night before last. He writes by this conveyance, otherwise I should give you the particulars.

There is not a drop of public rum in the department. I wish that a quantity may be ordered this way, as large as would amount to our proportion. Your excellency must know that, if I do my duty, I must keep scouts continually in the woods, and men on that service ought to have a little grog in addition to their fresh beef and water.

Every intelligence worthy of your excellency's notice shall be regularly communicated, if in my power.

Wishing your operations against our enemies all the success that the virtue of our cause deserves,

I have the honor to be,

Your excellency's most ob't,

And very humble servant,

JOHN STARK.

To His Excellency, General Washington.

Albany, August 15, 1778.

Dear General—The deputy paymaster of this department informs me that he is recalled, and that your excellency is of opinion that we have no occasion for one. Your excellency must be deceived as to the distances of our detachments from head quarters.

One body is stationed at Otter creek, one hundred and thirty miles north-east of this place; one at Fort Edward, fifty miles; one at Fort Schuyler, one hundred and twenty miles; and Alden's and Butler's regiments are posted on two other stations. Beside these, the militia are employed for short terms, and the wages they earn will not justify the expense of sending to you. Under these circumstances, a deputy paymaster is often of the greatest importance at this place. I leave the matter, however, for your judgment.

As Congress has been pleased to make provision for the battalion officers, but not any as I have heard for the generals or staff, I should be glad of your opinion in what manner I shall make up my accounts, as I am in a separate command, which makes my expenses much greater than if I acted with the army. I wish to be able to live up to my station, which can not be done by the bare allowance of a brigadier, as I am obliged to purchase everything at a high price: for instance, for a gallon of rum, $14; a pound of sugar, $2.50; and every thing in proportion.

Capt. McKean is with me, and informs that he can raise a company of good rangers to scour the woods on the western frontier, if he can have proper encouragement. He served with me in the ranging service during most of the last war.

I have ordered him to raise them, which I hope you will approve, as I think one company of such men can do more than a regiment of militia.

I am, sir, your ob't serv't,

JOHN STARK.

HEADQUARTERS. *Dobbs' Ferry,*
August 16, 1781.

Dear Sir—I have received your favor of the 9th, and am very well pleased with the account you give of the disposition and behavior of the people of Vermont. The party you mention to have been captured by them, I think must be considered as prisoners of war, and ought to be closely confined, to prevent all possibility of escape until they are exchanged.

I hope the militia have arrived before this time, as I have been obliged to order the remainder of the continental troops to join the main army.

I am fully sensible of the embarrassments the several departments labor under for the want of money, especially to pay the expenses of expresses and persons employed to carry intelligence; and after informing the quarter master general of your situation in this respect, shall be very happy if he can devise ways to remedy the evil in future. The commissary will have directions to send a proportion of whatever rum we may receive for the use of your department.

I am, dear sir, with great regard,

Your most obed't serv't,

GEO. WASHINGTON.

Brigadier Gen. Stark.

Instructions to Captain Livingston.

Headquarters, Albany.

By John Stark, Esq., Brigadier General in the Army of the United States, and Commander of the Troops in the Northern Department.

You will proceed, with the party under your command, to Schoharie. On your arrival at that place, you will establish your post on the most convenient and advantageous piece of ground in your power, to act either offensively or defensively, as circumstances may require—immediately detaching and keeping out such scouts as may be necessary to give you intelligence of the advance of an enemy, and save you from a surprise.

In case, on your arrival, the militia of that place should join you, they are to be allowed provisions in the same manner as the other troops under your command.

You will take particular care that no wanton mischief is committed either upon the persons or property of the inhabitants by your soldiers.

The commissary has my orders to send some cattle along with you. Flour, I presume, can be got upon the ground; if it appears otherwise, I shall take care that you shall be equally supplied with the other troops in the department. Should any public teams come to Schoharie during your stay, you will lend them what aid you can with safety, to assist in loading.

Placing full confidence in your address, activity and experience as an officer, I shall omit particulars not essentially interesting, in regard to which your prudence must be your guide—and wish you every success and honor due to military glory.

Done at Albany, this 16th of August, 1781.

JOHN STARK.

Albany, 18*th August*, 1781.

Dear Sir—Application has been made to me by several gentlemen of reputation, for permission to send a flag of truce to Canada for the exchange of persons, inhabitants of this State, who are now there in captivity. If you should think proper to signify your approbation to such exchange, I will furnish them with a flag. The bearer will give you the names of those proposed for the purpose.

As the command of this department may require me upon occasion to impress wagons for the transportation of provisions, &c., I must request your excellency to grant me a warrant for that purpose.

I have the honor to be, &c.,

Your Excellency's most obed't serv't,

JOHN STARK.

His Excellency, Governor Clinton.

HEADQUARTERS. *Albany.*
22d August, 1781.

Dear Sir—I am informed that a large quantity of grain is at Schoharie, and that the inhabitants would willingly part with it upon terms highly beneficial to the United States; and, as so large a granary as that of Schoharie may be a considerable object to induce the enemy to destroy it, I have had it in contemplation to remove it to Schenectady. To do this will be impossible unless a large number of teams can be collected, which I am told can not be done without your warrant to impress them. If you should judge the matter worthy of attention, it will be then necessary to give a press warrant to me, or some person whom you shall think more proper, to execute the business.

I am, sir, &c.,

JOHN STARK.

To His Excellency, Governor Clinton.

Albany, 23d August, 1778.

Dear Sir—I have ventured to detain three armorers in this department until your pleasure shall be known, two of whom I determine to send to the westward under the direction of Col. Willet, and the other is to go to Saratoga with me. Your excellency will be pleased to consider that when a gun is out of repair (though perhaps a trifle would put it in order), a soldier is rendered unfit for duty; and it is very improbable that any man can be found with the militia capable of performing the service. But, nevertheless, if your excellency should disapprove of the measure, and think they can be of more service any where else, I shall send them immediately.

Two hundred of the militia have arrived. I hope the remainder will come in soon. I am just told that seventy will be in to-morrow.

I have likewise detained one, of Col. Vanschaik's regiment, to serve as a pilot on the frontiers. Gen. Schuyler can inform you of the necessity of his tarrying. He is a man that he enlisted on purpose for a guide.

I am, dear sir, &c.,

JOHN STARK.

His Excellency, Gen. Washington.

Brigadier General Stark.

HEADQUARTERS. *Peekskill,* August 24, 1781.

My Dear Sir—His excellency, the commander-in-chief, having crossed the Hudson river, the command of all the troops, posts, etc., in this department, have devolved on me. By his special instructions he has been pleased to enjoin on me attention to the security of the northern and western frontiers of this State. I have, therefore, to request of you stated reports and returns of the state of things, and of the troops in your district, and of all important intelligence or occurrences that may come to your knowledge. Please to endeavor to obtain the earliest and best intelligence of any motions or designs of the enemy, and advise me from time to time how your troops are supplied with provisions, etc., etc. A quantity of rum is on its way from Springfield to Claverack, as the nearest point of embarkation on the Hudson, and designed for the use of the army. About one tenth part of the rum which goes to Claverack is designed for the troops under your command. Please direct Mr. Commissary Gamble not to detain a larger proportion. The remainder must be forwarded to West Point for the use of the garrison and this army. The latter now consists of eighteen regiments of regular troops, without a single drop of rum in the hands of the commissaries. Please let me hear from you as often as opportunity offers.

I am, with great regard, dear sir,

Your most obe't serv't,

W. HEATH,

M. General.

Poughkeepsie, August 25th, 1781.

Dear Sir—I am favored with your letter of the 23d inst. Although I fully agree with you in the importance of removing the grain from Schoharie, as it is yet the property of individuals, I am not authorized to grant warrants of impress for the purpose.

If the commissary general or State agent should purchase the whole or any part of the grain in that quarter, for the use of the army, I shall then be authorized and will cheerfully grant him my warrant for impressing as many teams as may be necessary to remove the quantity they shall certify to be so purchased. Should they decline selling in the first instance, I hope your influence with the inhabitants, and their own safety, will induce them to remove their crops to the interior parts of the State, and not leave it as an incitement to the enemy to repeat their ravages against that place.

I am informed that Captain Dunbar and Lieutenant Grant, of the levies of this State, are apprehended and sent to Albany on a charge of deserting to the enemy. As these troops are subject to the command of the commander-in-chief, and, as a sufficient number of officers to constitute a court for the trial of these officers may not conveniently be convened at Albany, I submit it to you whether it would not be more expedient to order them, with the evidence, to West Point, to be tried there.

With greatest respect, &c.,

GEORGE CLINTON.

Brigadier General Stark.

To General Stark.

Fort Rensselaer, 25th Aug., 1781.

Dear General—Your favor of the 23d instant has come safe to hand. The arrival of only part of the rum is a disappointment; yet, it is a true old saying that "half a loaf is better than no bread." This disappointment, however, for the present does not affect me so much as the backwardness of the troops designed for this quarter. The want of rum is quite a small evil in proportion to what the want of men would be, in case of a visit from the enemy, which we have continual reason to apprehend in these parts; for our situation is vulnerable for a large extent on both sides of the river; and this is the most convenient frontier we have for the enemy to approach, either from Niagara, Buck's island, or Oswegotchie (from all which places we have been visited this campaign); nor would it be a new thing for the enemy to move this way through Lake Champlain.

But the immediate painful part of my business here, is the daily applications that are made to me by numbers of suffering inhabitants (whom I class among the best of whigs, being always ready to turn out in case of alarm), for guards to enable them to save their grain—a considerable quantity of which is still in their fields, in great danger of being spoiled—and it is not in my power to help them. Very considerable quantities of grain may be had in these parts for public use, if we are fortunate enough to have the grain all secured. But, in order to procure grain for the public use, the quarter master should furnish us with bags; indeed, this appears to me to be an object of such importance that it ought to spur the quarter master to make large exertions, in order to procure bags. I should be glad if you would urge him to attend to this business. At present I have a large guard at Turloch, with a number of hands at work endeavoring to secure as much of the harvest of that place as possible. This makes my force, which was otherwise very scant, bare indeed.

The whole force now at this place, including ten who are sick, is fifty one; and most of the posts above and below are entirely destitute. I am not a little desirous of removing a part of the stores from Fort Herkimer, agreeably to an order I received some time ago from his excellency, Gen. Washington, which the want of strength has hitherto prevented. I can not therefore help thinking it strange that one hundred men, beside the two companies stationed at Schoharie, and which is the full proportion for that place, should be sent for and detained there, while this more exposed and extensive country remains so exceedingly bare. Of this I imagined Gov. Clinton was well apprised. By his letter to me of the 13th inst., immediately after the disaster at Haversink, in which, after continuing to guard against a possible appearance of that party of the enemy in this quarter, he lets me know that he had ordered reinforcements for Schoharie from General Ganesvoort's brigade of militia, until the entire departure of the enemy should be ascertained. Yet after this, his reinforcing that place with part of the quota of troops intended for this river, which is more exposed than that place, is what I could not have expected. There is no doubt, however, that if it is with you to have this matter rectified, it will be done without loss of time; but, should it be still necessary to wait for directions from the governor upon this head, I shall be much obliged to you to mention the difficulties I labor under to him, yourself, as well as make me acquainted with it, that I may likewise write upon this business as soon as possible, as much may depend upon it. I am in danger of having a famine of paper. I shall therefore be much obliged to you, sir, to order some this way.

I am, sir,

Your most obed't serv't,

MARINUS WILLET.

P. S. Flour we shall be able to furnish ourselves with if we have no assistance, but beef I must request you to order this way, or we shall soon be meat less.

To Colonel Pickering.

HEADQUARTERS. *Albany,*
August 25th, 1781.

Dear Sir—My situation in this department is the most disagreeable I was ever in. There is no forage for horses; no horses to transport any kind of provisions in this extensive department; there are no camp-kettles for the use of the troops. And unless some of the above mentioned grievances are redressed, and very speedily, I shall expect the troops on the frontiers will disperse and go to their homes.

I can not say it is the fault of the quarter master, for I do not know his authority; but, unless he can or will do something more than he has since I have been here, he is entirely useless here.

I applied to him a fortnight ago for a wagon to transport my baggage to Bennington; I have not got it yet, nor do I see any probability of it.

I must beg an answer from you on the subject; and do let me know what I am to expect from the quarter master's department—whether assistance or not.

I am, sir, your most obedient serv't,

JOHN STARK.

To Colonel Henry Laurens.

Albany, August 27th, 1781.

Dear Sir—By a spy, who has been on board the enemy's ships at Crown Point, we learn that their intention is to make a push upon this place, to alarm the New-Hampshire Grants by way of Castleton, and gather all the tories in this quarter, who are to be met by General Howe's army near this place. Therefore I should advise you to keep your men in readiness.

Your obed't serv't,

JOHN STARK.

To Governor Chittenden.

Albany, 27th August, 1781.

My Dear Sir—I only waited the prudent and happy determination of Congress, to congratulate you upon the interesting and important decision in your favor. Be assured, sir, that no intervening circumstance on the grand political system of America, since the war began, has given me more real pleasure than to hear of your acceptance into the Union*—a measure that I do now, and always did think, was highly compatible with the real interest of the country. It is with difficulty that I can determine in my own mind why it has been postponed to this late hour; but perhaps Congress had motives that we are strangers to. The best and wisest mortals are liable to error.

I am very happy to acquaint you that the people in this city show very much of the highest solicitude upon the matter, fully convinced that to be separate will be more for the interest of both States than to be united. In my opinion, nothing can wound a generous mind more than the mortifying thought of making a large country miserable; and the people of your State, by their utter detestation of the management of New-York, must have been wretched under their government.

To have been connected with New-Hampshire is what many in the State would have been very sorry for, as very inconvenient and expensive for both bodies of people, and no real good resulting from such a connection; therefore I am of the opinion that every man, who consulted the public interest, must be an advocate for a separation. For, had they been connected, there would ever have been a jealousy between the two States, which would have been infallibly dangerous to both; but that jealousy, by the separation, must entirely subside, and New-Hampshire and Vermont live in perfect friendship as sister States.

That Vermont, in its government, may be happy, and a stranger to internal jars, is the ardent wish, my dear sir, of your most obed't serv't,

JOHN STARK.

*This was premature: Congress offered, but Vermont would not accept.

Bennington, 28th August, 1781.

Sir—From the slight acquaintance I have made with you, and your known humanity, I am induced, in behalt of my good friend, Captain Brownson, to ask the favor ot you to use your good influence to procure the release ot Doctor Smith's son, who is confined in Albany gaol; and for whom, by my request, application has been made to you before. Capt. Brownson's exchange can be effected for him, and a servant, McFall, taken at the battle of Bennington; and, as there is no probability of any farther exchange taking place, I must earnestly entreat your kind interposition in this case.

General Safford, who will deliver this, will consult you more fully on the subject, to whom I beg leave to refer you. I have the honor to be, sir,

With respect and esteem,
Your most obed't and most
Humble servant,
JOSEPH FAY.

Hon. General Stark.

Fort Rensselaer, 28th August, 1781.

Dear General—Yours, of the 26th inst., is come to hand. The prospect of a supply of beef relieves me from a considerable deal of anxiety. Yesterday, just at dusk, I was advised of the enemy's having been early the day before at Cobuskill, where it is said they have burned several houses and barns. How it came to pass that I did not receive this account sooner, I am unable to devise, as the distance is little more than twenty miles from this place, and only eight miles from Turloch, where I have a large party at work procuring the grain of that settlement. Had I have known it at the time, I think the chance would have been in my favor of falling in with them before they could have reached the Susquehanna, as I had a party out that night as far as Cherry Valley, in consequence of having discovered ten or twelve Indians at Bowman's creek. I shall endeavor to find out the reason of this delay in sending this account this way.

No people can be more alert and ready to turn out on news of the approach of an enemy than the militia of this quarter; consequently none deserve more attention. We shall, therefore, look to you for our quota of men, and every thing else that may be necessary to make our situation as comfortable and agreeable as possible.

I am, sir, your most obedient humble serv't,

MARINUS WILLET.

Hon. General Stark.

To Brigadier General Stark.

Poughkeepsie, 28th August, 1781.

Dear Sir—Your letter of the 11th instant is this moment received. I can have no objections against your sending a flag to Canada, to negotiate an exchange of the inhabitants who are prisoners with the enemy, as their liberation is an object I have frequently attempted, although in vain, and most ardently wish.

I need not mention to you, sir, the great care that ought to be taken, especially in our present situation, in the appointment of an officer to conduct this business, as your own good sense will dictate that he ought to be a man of address and firmness; and no person should be permitted to accompany him but such as merit the most perfect confidence.

I inclose you a list of the persons transmitted to me by the commissioners of Albany, to be offered in exchange, and against which I have no objection, provided that those that are marked as inhabitants make their application to me, for the purpose, in writing, agreeable to law, to be filed in the Secretary's office of the State.

If the enemy should consent to an exchange, due attention must be paid to give preference to those of our friends who have been longest in captivity, as this is consonant with justice, and the contrary would occasion discontent.

Agreeable to your request, I transmit your inclosed warrant of impress for forty wagons for ten days. You will please to observe that you may, by the letter of the warrant, in the first instance, employ the whole number of wagons for ten days, to transmit provisions or public stores, and the warrant would expire. But I conceive the public service would be advanced by employing a small number of them only at a time; and that in this way they will be sufficient, with what the quarter master may furnish, to transmit provisions for your troops during the season. It is justice to make the disaffected, who in other respects bear least of the common burthen, the objects of the impress, which I am sure will not be disagreeable to you.

I am, with great respect and esteem,

Dear sir, your most obed't serv't,

GEO. CLINTON.

Albany, 29th August, 1781.

My Dear Sir—Your letter of the 24th was delivered me last evening. I am very sorry it will be impossible for me to transmit a regular return of the state of the district, in my present circumstances. Paper, that necessary article for the transaction of business, we are wholly destitute of; and the troops in the department are so scattered that it would be a work of considerable time (under the best circumstances), to collect and digest the state of the department into a single return. Much more must be the difficulties in the present, which are very far from coming within that description. I desired Col. Willet to send me a return twenty days ago, but it has not come yet, nor can I guess when it will. He has nothing to make it on.

I shall regularly communicate every intelligence that comes to my knowledge, worthy of attention; and shall begin with the common, but ever disagreeable news of twelve houses and fourteen barns being burnt, by a party of the enemy, at Cobuskill, and three men and five boys taken prisoners; and a number of cattle and horses driven away. I can not learn who had the command, nor their exact number; but they bent their course towards Cherry Valley, where it is very probable we shall hear of some other instances of their unparalleled clemency.

I shall strictly adhere to your directions with respect to the commissary; and, at the same time, must beg you would attend to the indispensable wants of this department. It is not in my power to send an express forty miles, for want of cash, be the emergency ever so pressing. There is not a camp-kettle for all the militia, and not half enough for the three years' men; and you are too well acquainted with those gentry to think they will rest easy under such circumstances. There is no forage in the department, nor means to provide any.

The commissioners of accounts and the quarter masters draw provisions from the department, which I think directly contrary to a positive resolution of Congress; but I shall suspend directing to the commissary not to deliver it until your pleasure shall be known.

There are a number of prisoners of war and convention in this department: some under bonds for their appearance on certain days; and others at large. I have ventured to give orders for the seizing of all that can be found. A number are already collected, and I expect to get a number more. I could wish that they could be exchanged for some of Alden's or Warner's regiments that were taken in this quarter. But, at all events, they are very improper persons to be at large, especially in this country.

I am, dear sir,

With much respect and esteem,

Your ob't serv't,

JOHN STARK.

Major General Heath.

To his Excellency, Governor Clinton.

Albany, 31*st August*, 1781.

Dear Sir—My embarrassments in this department are almost intolerable. I have not a single grain of forage, nor can I procure any. When I apply to the quarter master, he says, "what can I do?" and this is all I can get from him. It is all that he does, and almost all that he says. You must be sensible that it will be impossible to transact the business without some magazine of forage is laid up, or at least some for immediate consumption.

It is a month since I have been on the ground, and I have received nothing from the quarter master except a little swamp hay, and none of that for these ten days.

I have almost daily calls from the frontier for provisions, but am not able to send them any assistance, as the quarter master has no money to hire teams, and no authority to impress them; and as you promised me every assistance in your power, to facilitate my command and the public business, I must now claim the benefit of your promise, and beg your assistance at this critical period. Major Shurtliff, who will have the honor of delivering this, can enumerate many difficulties I have not mentioned, and which, if mentioned, would stretch this letter beyond its designed length. I shall be very happy to be favored with your advice, and shall apprise you of all intelligence that shall appear to affect the State.

Your most obedient servant,

JOHN STARK.

To the Honorable President of Congress.

Albany, September 1*st*, 1781.

Dear Sir—Perhaps the topic that I take the liberty to address you upon, is so common that it is no longer noticed; if that be the case, my labor is lost. However, the high opinion I have formed of the rectitude, virtue and justice of the august body over whom you preside, leads me to hope that my request, which I think reasonable, may be taken into consideration and granted.

I must inform you that it is going on the third year since I have received any cash from the public as pay, or on account (except two thousand dollars at Providence, R. I., in 1779), which you must know is very incompetent to the expenses of a general officer since that time. However, I have tamely waited the liberality of Congress, without asking what was my due, until my means as well as my credit are entirely exhausted.

Necessity now induces me to ask that from you which I endeavored to keep off as long as possible. I do not indeed recollect ever troubling your excellency with a request of this kind before, nor should I now, were there any other method within the compass of my knowledge.

It may be necessary to inform your excellency that I applied to New-Hampshire last winter for a settlement of accounts. They returned for answer that "Congress had not recommended it to them to take up the matter with respect to the general officers; and without that recommendation, they did not conceive that it was in their power, as Congress might determine to do it themselves, as they had their sole appointment." But they advanced me a little paper money upon my own credit, which I hold myself bound for the payment of; and a little of it still remains in my hands. There it must remain, for I can get nothing for it.

I could, I own, when I procured the paper, have exchanged some of it for hard cash, but the precedent I did then, and still do, despise; and I trust you will not permit me to be a sufferer by that.

I have no doubt but that Congress are too much troubled with requisitions of this kind; but, at the same time, I must, among others, request a little cash—not that I expect or wish all that is my due, but something that shall be equal to what Congress shall think a general officer ought to have, on a separate command.

I have the honor to be

Your most obedient humble servant,

JOHN STARK.

To Brigadier General Stark.

Poughkeepsie, 1*st Sept.*, 1781.

Dear Sir—When in Albany last winter, I addressed a letter to Governor Haldiman, respecting the exchange and liberation of a number of women and children, captured by the enemy on the frontiers of this State, which was to be forwarded by a flag. Brig. Gen. Clinton intended sending to Canada to effect the exchange of Dr. Smith and others, but it seems the situation of our affairs, while he had the command, rendered such communication inexpedient, and he has returned me the letter and papers; but the forwarding of them at this late day might be deemed improper.

I now take the liberty of inclosing them to you, and to request that the letter be forwarded by the first flag.

As the letter is sealed, I inclose you a copy of it, to which, and the other inclosed papers, I beg leave to refer you for information. It is only necessary for me to observe, that I am possessed of the obligation of Mr. Stuart, executed by himself and two freeholders, for complying with the conditions expressed in the papers, signifying my consent to his being exchanged, and for the liberation of an inhabitant of this State, a prisoner with the enemy, for a negro man he is to take with him; and also Dr. Smith's obligation, subscribed by two other persons, for the exchange of Captains Wood and Drake, agreeable to the State commissary's certificate.

You will find, among the papers now transmitted, a petition from Margaret McKenny, supported by one in favor of her request by a number of the most respectable inhabitants of Schenectady.

I should be happy if I were at liberty to grant her the indulgence she asks, as I believe her case (and it is an extremely hard one), is truly represented by the gentlemen of Schenectady, who have interfered in her behalf.

But, however insignificant the character, I do not conceive myself authorized to permit subjects of this State to change their allegiance without their compliance with

16

a law of this State, which empowers me to exchange them on making proper application for the purpose, as mentioned in my certificate at the foot of the petition.

Mr. McFarland's character, as a zealous whig, induced me to consent to his accompanying the flag, and I believe he may be confided in. You will please to return me the papers respecting Mrs. McKenny, when you have perused them. I transmit them to you, under the idea of her applying to you on the subject, and perhaps she may conceive herself able to comply with the law, to facilitate which I will agree to take the most insignificant characters in exchange for her family, on her engagement to return when required, if she can not effect any.

I am, with great respect, dear sir,

Your most obed't serv't,

GEO. CLINTON.

To Brigadier General Stark.

HEADQUARTERS. *Peekskill,*
September 3d, 1781.

Dear Sir—I addressed you a few days since, but, as the conveyance was not direct, am uncertain whether my letter reached you. I wish you to write me very frequently, and give me a particular state of affairs in your district—the number of troops, and where stationed; what works are in the district, in what condition, and how garrisoned; what supplies of ammunition, provisions, &c., you have.

Whenever you can obtain any intelligence of the motives or designs of the enemy, please give me the earliest notice of them. Please, also, to direct the person who is directed to do the duty of deputy adjutant general, to make accurate monthly returns of all the troops in your district, in continental pay, to Lieutenant Colonel Grosvenor, the deputy adjutant general of the department at this place, or wherever this army may be at the time of making such return.

Such return should be made punctually by the first of each month, that the general return may be made to Congress. Please, by the first opportunity, to order a return of your present strength to be sent, that, if there is any deficiency in the militia levies, the States may be called upon to complete them.

A British fleet, of fourteen sail-of-the-line, under the command of Admiral Sir Samuel Hood, arrived at Sandy Hook last Tuesday, from the Wes-Indies: one ship of 90 guns; thirteen, of 74; three, of 44; one sloop and one fire-ship. It is said three old British regiments came in the fleet: viz., 1st battalion of royals, 13th and 69th; but these must have been much reduced by sickness in the West-Indies.

I congratulate you on the safe return of Colonel Laurens from France, and the success of his embassy. A large sum of specie, and a quantity of clothing of all sorts, are safely arrived at Boston.

I am, with great regard,

Dear sir, your most obedient serv't,

W. HEATH, *Major General.*

City Government of Albany to Governor Clinton.

Albany, 4th September, 1781.

Sir—We have received undoubted information that a party of the enemy from Canada intend to burn and destroy this city.

The corporation and field officers of this city have had a meeting on the subject, and conceive it absolutely necessary that some troops be stationed in town to protect the city, and the public buildings, stores and magazines in it.

We conceive the city guards and night watches to be insufficient to ward off the impending danger. An undisciplined militia, whose city duty is frequent, are inadequate to the task. We have requested General Stark to detain in town a sufficient guard or company for the purpose, and to be held in readiness to assist the city guards and patrols; but, though willing, he does not conceive himself authorized to grant this request without orders for the purpose from the commander-in-chief of the department.

We therefore beg your excellency to write to General Heath on the subject, and endeavor to prevail on him to send a company (or two if possible) of troops, of at least sixty men each, or to order General Stark to send a company of the troops now at Saratoga, to be stationed in this city for the above purposes.

We are, &c.

His Excellency, Governor Clinton.

To His Excellency, Frederick Haldiman, Esq., Governor-in-Chief of Canada, and Commander of the Britannic Majesty's forces in the same.

HEADQUARTERS. *Saratoga,* September, 1781.

Sir—The British military prisoners in this department are as anxious to be released from captivity as I suppose are the Americans in your power. Wishing to alleviate, as far as in me lies, the calamities incident on captivity, I have to propose to your excellency the exchange of all prisoners within my power, either agreeably to the mode settled between his excellency, General Washington, and his excellency, General Sir Henry Clinton, or on any other we can agree upon. Should you prefer the former, you will please to advise me thereof as soon as may be; to transmit me a list of the numbers and rank of the prisoners in your power, and to signify at what place you would wish to deliver and receive such as may be exchanged.

Should your excellency deem it more eligible to settle the terms of exchange between us, I conceive it would tend to expedite the business, if commissioners were appointed on both sides, to meet either on this or the other side of lake George, and settle the terms.

Captain —— is the bearer of this, attended by ——, one non-commissioned officer and — privates, and, having orders to return as soon as he has delivered this, as a flag he is entitled to, and will doubtless be treated according to the laws of war. I am, with due respect,

Your Excellency's most obedient servant,

JOHN STARK, *Brigadier General*,

Commanding the Northern Department.

To Captain E. Marshall.

Albany, September 4, 1781.

Dear Sir—Finding it necessary, for the good of the service in expediting public stores to the frontiers, to have an officer in whom I can confide stationed in this city—from your long service in the army, and, consequently, knowledge of your duty—I am induced to appoint you to this command; and, from and after my leaving the city, you are to consider yourself commanding officer on this ground, unless relieved by me, the commanding officer of the northern department, or the commanding officer of the main army, either of whose orders you are to obey.

As I have reason to think there will be several militia men who will arrive after this date, to go either to the westward or northward, those you will victual and send to their regiments, in such a manner as you shall think proper, reserving in the city twenty men, who are to be a constant guard until farther orders.

I must request you to employ some of your leisure moments in inspecting the public works of all kinds, as I have every reason to think that the most flagrant abuses are committed, and the most wanton dissipation of public property too familiar in them. In case you meet with any instances of the kind (which I think that you can hardly fail of), you will take the earliest opportunity of reporting them to me. You will do all in your power to facilitate the public business of all kinds in the department, and strenuously urge on supplies while it is practicable. I shall leave you power to impress teams, but that power is not to be made use of when it can be well avoided, and then is to be to the reputed friends of the country; and the carriages of persons of suspicious character are to be taken.

You will give no orders for provisions except to the quarter master's department, and then agreeably to the return and list he shall make out, in compliance with my orders of the 3d instant: one ration per day to Mrs. Orson, Lieutenant Lee's regular allowance, and to all officers on command (they producing their instructions), and to the Indians of the Oneida tribe, upon the order of John Bleeker, Esq., of this city.

You will see that my orders of the 3d instant are distributed, and when the returns and reports are delivered to you, forward them by the first conveyance to my headquarters.

You will not allow Mr. Commissary to repay any rum which he has borrowed heretofore, unless the supply of that article will justify it.

Should any of the Massachusetts levies come on without arms, you will furnish them, and endeavor to obtain receipts from their officers for the same, making them accountable to the commissary of military stores.

I am, &c., JOHN STARK.

[Copy of an extract from General Washington's Letter to the President of Congress.]

Philadelphia, September 5, 1781.

"With the highest pleasure I do myself the honor to transmit to your excellency a copy of a letter from Gen. Gist, which announces the safe arrival of Admiral De Grasse in the Chesapeake, with twenty-eight ships-of-the-line. On this happy event, I beg your excellency to accept my warmest congratulations."

Baltimore, September 4, 1781.

Sir—I have the pleasure to inform you that the Serpent, (cutter of eighteen guns), Captain Arme de Luane, has this moment arrived here with dispatches to your excellency from Count de Grasse, who arrived in the Chesapeake, with twenty-eight ships-of-the-line, the 26th ult. The next day he landed three thousand troops on the south side of James river, in order to form a junction with the Marquis de la Fayette. The fleet, on their passsage, took a packet from Charleston, with Lord Rawdon on board, bound for Europe.

The grand fleet has taken its station from the middle ground to Cape Henry, from whence have been detached three ships-of-the-line and one frigate to York river, where one twenty-six-gun-ship fell into their hands. Captain De Luane informs me that he left the fleet the day before yesterday, and that he had particular directions from the admiral to forward these dispatches to you by one of his officers; but, as this gentleman can not be in readiness to proceed immediately, I have thought it expedient to forward the intelligence by express, to assist your excellency in the government of such movements as it may be judged necessary to adopt on this occasion.

I do myself the honor to inclose a list of the fleet, delivered to me by the cutter, which will wait here for your orders. I have ordered all the vessels to sail immediately for the troops at the head of the Elk.

I am, &c., M. GIST.

NOTE. The above fleet is exclusive of that under the command of Count Barras. New-York news, which may be depended on, states that two frigates, conveying three transports from that place, having on board three Hessian regiments, were captured; only one frigate returned, which brings the news.

Albany, September 12, 1781.

Dear General—I this moment received a letter from Colonel Willet, dated Fort Plain, 10th inst. The following is an extract:

"I am just returned to this place. The party that Lieutenant Woodworth fell in with, which occasioned the late alarm, was not so strong as was represented to me. They were too far gone before I got to Fort Herkimer.

Poor Woodworth was taken in by their ambuscade, and was unfortunately killed the second fire. It cost us dear; only fifteen men out of thirty-nine, and two officers, have escaped; eleven of our men, including Woodworth, were found dead. The remainder, with Lieutenant Wilson, we have no account of. Wilson, no doubt, did all in his power. The enemy were too heavy for him; and I fear some of his men left him in the lurch. It has been an unfortunate affair. We must hope for better luck hereafter. Please communicate this to the governor and General Stark. Want of paper and time prevented me from doing it myself."

Inclosed you have a copy of a hand-bill from below. I give you my warmest congratulations on the flattering aspect and prospect of our affairs.

I am, &c., dear sir,

Your obed't serv't,

E. MARSHALL.

Hon. General Stark.

[Extract from Rivington's New-York paper, dated September 5, 1781.]

By a letter from the Chesapeake, dated the 31st ult., the French fleet or squadron, consisting of twenty-three sail, including frigates and inferior vessels, were arrived at Lynn Haven bay, in Virginia, from whence a sixty-four and two frigates were detached up York river, and had taken a station off Yorktown. Every preparation was making by our noble general to defend the important posts his lordship there possesses; and, as a very formidable and truly well appointed squadron of the British line, commanded by Admiral Graves, is, through much exertion, supposed to be now in the vicinity of our combined enemies, we may conclude the present to be the most interesting and critical era since the commencement of the American rebellion—for an expected action at sea is likely to become decisive of the inadmissible idol, Independence.*

We have at present the satisfaction to perceive a great part of the French navy in a more peculiar, and, perhaps, a more dangerous position than they were ever yet reduced to. Granting that the French West-India and Rhode Island fleets should have both reached the Chesapeake before Admiral Graves, we trust the following statement, as accurate as we can present it of the British navy when arrived in the bay, may inspire every true Briton with a firm confidence of its fair pretensions to brilliant success.

A list of the British fleet, commanded by Thomas Graves, Esq., rear admiral of the Red: "One of 98 guns, twelve of 74 do., one of 70 do., four of 64 do., two of 50 do., four of 44 do., three of 32 do., five of 28 do., one of 24 do."

* During the month of October, 1781, poor Mr. Rivington had the mortifying opportunity of dressing his paper in mourning for the capitulation of a second British army to the American rebels, which settled the question of the *admissibility* of the "idol, Independence."

[Extract of a Letter from Virginia, dated Yorktown, August 31.]

I now inform you that we are blocked up by a French fleet of twenty-three sail; one of sixty-four, and two frigates lie in sight of us.

Yesterday came up two victuallers, committed to the protection of his majesty's frigate, Pegasus, and dispatched by Rear Admiral, Sir Samuel Hood, to New-York. The Pegasus and her convoy, on their passage, fell in with a French squadron of line-of-battle-ships, supposed to be Mons. Barras. It was apprehended that the whole, consisting of six victuallers, and a vessel with the 40th regiment on board, had fallen into the hands of the enemy, until happily these two effected a safe arrival in our harbor.

HEADQUARTERS. *Peekskill,*
September 7, 1781.

Dear Sir—By a letter from General Ganesvoort, and the mayor of the city of Albany, to his excellency, Governor Clinton, with a copy of which I have been honored, it appears they are apprehensive that a party of the enemy have a design to burn and destroy that city; that they had requested of you a company of the troops under your command for its protection, which you would gladly grant, but was doubtful of doing it without my sanction.

I wish you immediately to afford the protection requested, if the state of the troops under your command, and the safety of the other posts will admit it; or, if not in your power to grant effectual support, you would do it as far as circumstances will allow, and give me notice, if you apprehend it necessary, what farther aid may be requisite.

I am, with great regard,

Dear sir, your most obed't serv't,

W. HEATH, *Major General.*

Brigadier General Stark.

Schenectady, 8th September, 1781.

Dear Sir—As the inclosed is so wet by the rain, I am afraid you will not be able to read the whole. By the letter of Lieutenant Fonda, it appears that Lieutenants Woodworth and Wilson, with a party of forty, including themselves, went from Fort Plain yesterday in the forenoon, and were attacked between the Indian castle and Fall hill; both lieutenants are killed, and tweny-six privates, and four wounded. I can not learn the enemy's strength, nor what number are killed on either side.

Captain V——, and the small party, with some pork, beef, salt, &c., &c., are gone off.

Yours, sincerely, in haste,

H. GLEN.

To Captain E. Marshall.

HEADQUARTERS. *Peekskill*,
September 8, 1781.

Dear Sir—Apprehending that the city of Albany may be in some immediate danger, and that it is not in your power to afford the aid requested, without too much weakening your other posts, I have ordered two companies of Colonel Weisenfel's regiment, under the command of the Major, immediately to Albany. This detachment, while in the northern district, will be subject to your orders; but I wish not to have it removed beyond the city, unless some particular occasion shall require it. In consequence of this measure, you will not call any of your troops from Saratoga to cover Albany.

I am, with great regard, &c.,

W. HEATH, *Major General.*

Brigadier General Stark.

To the Worshipful Abraham Ten Broeck, Mayor of Albany, and Brigadier General Gansevoort.

PLEASANT VALLEY, *Duchess County,*
September 8, 1781.

Gentlemen—I have the honor of inclosing a letter from Major General Heath, commanding the department, to Brigadier General Stark, (which you will please to have delivered), authorizing him to afford the city of Albany the protection you request, and directing him, in case the state of the troops under his command will not admit of effectual support, to give the general notice what farther aid may be requisite. You will readily perceive the propriety, on this occasion, of not only transmitting the substance of any intelligence you may receive of the designs of the enemy, but also of giving the manner of acquiring it, and every circumstance attending it, to enable me to form a proper judgment of the credit it may merit, and back your application with confidence.

I have the pleasure, also, of transmitting the inclosed extracts from Rivington's New-York paper, of the 5th instant, announcing the arrival of twenty-three sail-of-the-line, belonging to our illustrious ally, in Lynn Haven bay (Chesapeake), and that Lord Cornwallis is completely blocked up, &c., &c., which you will please to communicate to your fellow-citizens in such manner as you may deem proper.

On Mons'r Barras' junction, which, from the inclosed account, must long since have taken place, our fleet will consist of thirty-one sail-of-the-line, besides frigates, etc., from which, when compared with the enemy's lists, you will be able to judge of the event of an action.

I am, with great respect, gentlemen,

Your obed't serv't,

GEO. CLINTON.

Albany, September 9th, 1781.

Dear General — The letter, per bearer, came to hand yesterday, about an hour after the express went off for you. In expectation, then and now, of farther intelligence from the westward, I retained, and still do, the only express horse here, or I should have sent them forward immediately. You may depend upon the earliest notice.

The same slothfulness, too prevalent here, has prevented me from sending the rum and other stores this day. They will, at all events, go off to-morrow morning, and will be at Stillwater on Tuesday morning. The commissary here, says wagons generally came from Saratoga to receive them at that post. I believe you may venture to send some men on that day. There came but two hogsheads of rum from Claverack. I have ventured to let the commissary repay Mr. Glen sixty gallons, of whom Mr. Gamble had borrowed one hundred and eighty, two months ago, and entered into a private obligation to repay the same in ten days, or pay for the rum in specie; this both parties mutually did for the benefit of the public. The rum Mr. Glen was selling for a merchant in Boston, whom he expects every moment will call for the money; but he said if I would let him have two barrels he would wait for the other. I hope these considerations will justify proceedings.

I am, sir, &c.,

Your obed't serv't,

E. MARSHALL.

Hon. General Stark.

Saratoga, 9th September, 1781.

Dear Sir—This will be handed you by Captain Brady, who has suffered a long and tedious imprisonment in Canada; but, by good fortune, made his escape from Montreal, on the — of August. He is now nearly two thousand miles from his place of residence, and no friends or money to assist him. The public finances in this department not enabling me to grant him any aid, I have taken the liberty to recommend him to you. He can give you a tolerable account of affairs in Canada.

My letters of yesterday, from Albany and Schenectady, give an account of a body of the enemy being on the Mohawk river; and that they had killed two lieutenants and twenty-five privates, and wounded four more. I can not learn the particulars of this sad disaster, but hope to be able to inform you in my next, together with their capture by the brave and intrepid Colonel Willet, who is collecting in force to oppose them.

I must beg you to send me a supply of ammunition as soon as possible, as the department has not sufficient for a single action; which, by the accounts I can learn from Canada, we may daily expect.

I am, sir, &c., JOHN STARK.

Major General Heath.

Schenectady, September 9, 1781.

Sir—I wrote to his excellency, the Governor, relative to those women whose husbands are with the enemy, and in his answer, which I have just received, he approves of sending them off; but directs that a list of their names should first be sent to him (which I shall do without delay), and then he will signify his approbation to you of sending them off as soon as you think it expedient. As you may not have seen the law relative to this matter, I here inclose you a copy of it.

Mr. Ellis informs me that he is going to wait on you on business relative to Mrs. Constable's going to Canada. I have only to observe that she had the necessary leave when she had obtained yours.

Before your arrival at Albany, to take the command, I applied to Colonel Willet to station twelve or fifteen of his men in this town, to assist us in the commissionary business, in apprehending disaffected persons, and small parties of the enemy, who came in a private manner, in order to enlist soldiers amongst us, and get intelligence. He promised to comply with my request; but, I suppose, from the multiplicity of business, and scarcity of men, he has neglected it. I should be glad if you would order us a few men here for those purposes, for the militia will not answer.

With respect, your most ob't serv't,

HUGH MILLER.

Brigadier General Stark.

Albany, September 10, 1781.

Dear General—Yours of yesterday came to hand last evening. I believe you may dispel your fearful apprehensions of Colonel Willet's suffering for want of cartridges. When I came from that quarter, his men were supplied, and he had nine thousand on hand (and the artillery making more), and a large quantity of loose powder. The whole, fixed and unfixed, amounted, by the artillery officer's calculation, to nearly three tons. I send per bearer the things you demanded of the surgeon of the hospital. Major's Stark's horse is recovering. No news from either quarter.

I am, &c., E. MARSHALL.

To Major General Heath.

Saratoga, 11th September, 1781.

Dear Sir—Yours of the 3d and 7th inst. are now before me; the former was received last night, and the latter this day. By your not acknowledging the receipt of my former letters, I am led to believe you never received them, for certainly they must have reached you long before this. In them you will find the reason of my not sending you a return; and the same difficulty that then existed is not yet removed. Therefore, you must not expect a return until the materials are supplied to make it with. However, I can tell the number in this garrison, which consists of two majors, seven captains, eleven lieutenants, twenty-seven sergeants, and three hundred and sixty rank and file. We have about ten rounds of cartridges per man, and no more ammunition in store. I wrote to General Knox for a supply some time ago, but have neither received the ammunition, nor any answer; but hope for them every hour. I have no deputy adjutant general, nor have I one that I can appoint, capable of the business, who is willing to undertake it. Be assured, sir, whenever you shall think proper to order a supply of paper, and appoint a deputy adjutant general, either from your army, or some one that you know in this district, the business shall then be done with regularity, and, I hope, to your satisfaction; but till then, I can not tell how it will be transacted. You will perceive, by the number of men in this garrison, that it would be very imprudent to detach any of them to Albany; but I expect a few more in every day. Notwithstanding this, I can not think myself justifiable in sparing any men from this, or any of the frontiers, without your positive orders, until we are stronger than we are now.

And, indeed, was I ever so strong, Albany is a very dangerous place to put men into; for, were I to send a company there, I should expect they would have one half of them in jail, and the other half to keep them there, in a month. For I can inform you, sir, that they have had more than one continental soldier in jail, for debts, or pretended debts; now they are calling for more, for perhaps the same purpose. It appears, sir, that some villains have determined to try whether they can detain a soldier in jail for debt or not; and, by the assistance these patriotic gentlemen have had from the magistrates of Albany, they have been enabled to carry their nefarious plans into execution.

Farther, sir, Albany is able to turn out five hundred men for its own defence; and a larger body than fifty can not well come against them ; and, if ten virtuous citizens are not able to defend themselves against the assaults of one sculking rascal of a tory or an Indian, it is very remarkable, as they have got forts and walls to cover them, almost beyond the power of human force to shake. But, my dear sir, if you have men to spare from the army, I expect they will be soon wanted at this place, as I have this day almost certain intelligence of there being a large detachment of the enemy at St. Johns, destined for this quarter. Perhaps they may come before you can possibly send me any assistance ; but I hope not.

I am sorry that, among the rest of my calamities, it is not in my power to send an express forty miles, unless by detaching a soldier on foot, with his provisions on his back ; and, in case the enemy shall approach, I shall be under the necessity of sending expresses to Hampshire and Berkshire counties, to Albany, and to the Grants. This, sir, requires good horses and horsemen. Neither of them are to be had here ; and, were there any horses, there is no money to pay their expenses, nor forage to keep them on ; nor any of either can I get.

I have applied to the governor for forage, but he says that Congress has never required it of the State, and, without that requisition, he can not give a warrant to impress it ; and that he supposes Congress has lodged the money in the hands of the proper officers, to procure it.

I am, sir, your obedient

Humble servant,

JOHN STARK.

To General Stark.

Albany, September 11, 1781.

Dear General—Your favor of this day's date has just now come to hand. You may rely that every intelligence I can procure, from Canada or elsewhere, worthy of your attention, will be immediately communicated. I have now the pleasure to inclose a farther communication of the account I wrote you in my last, with some agreeable additions, to which I add, as may be relied on, that the British fleet, which Rivington, in a paper of the 5th inst., declared was gone in quest of the French fleet, has returned to New-York, where it remains; and will perhaps remain, as it can not face the formidable fleet of our illusritous ally.

Governor Clinton writes that all our prisoners who were at New-York, have been sent out on exchange and parole; and that, from the best, nay, certain accounts, the greatest consternation prevails in that place among the British and their infamous friends. God increase their apprehensions. It was this morning reported that the infamous Arnold had made a descent at New-London, in Connecticut, and burnt that town, * but it has since been contradicted, and will, I hope, prove without foundation.

With my compliments, please advise Major Stark that I feel with pleasure his polite attentions, both as it endears him to me, and that such a line of conduct is ever attended with happy results in a young gentleman. I should have written him, but the express waits.

I am, sir, your most ob't serv't,

PH. SCHUYLER.

* This report proved true. The fort on Groton heights surrendered September 6, 1781, and Colonel Ledyard was slain with his own sword after he had delivered it up as a token of submission. A large portion of New-London was at the same time laid in ashes by the traitor, Arnold.

Saratoga, September 13, 1781.

Dear Sir—I am honored with yours of the 11th instant. The extra flood of good news it contains diffuses a joy through my senses little short of delirium, and makes me almost forget my declining years, and wish for health and vigor, and an opportunity of distinguishing myself in the presence of our illustrious general, in aiding to humble the haughty, arrogant, and ostentatious Earl Cornwallis. I should be very happy to have a share in his defeat and capture—two events which either already have occurred or infallibly must take place in a few days.

Poor Rivington must now be in a wretched dilemma. What excuse can he make? How extricate the British from their present difficulties? If he, or any other power short of omnipotence can, they must be adepts indeed.

I am so pleased with the good news you send me, as almost to forget to thank you for your generous offer of sending me intelligence. Be assured, sir, that I feel exceedingly grateful for this and every other expression of your favor.

I have no doubt of the willingness of that infamous traitor, Arnold, to do his country all possible injury, but hope he has not been able, in the case you mention, to give us fresh evidence of his hateful disposition.

With esteem, sir, your friend,

And most humble servant,

JOHN STARK.

Hon. General Schuyler.

Albany, 15th September, 1781.

Sir—Agreeably to your orders, which I received yesterday, I marched on my men this morning for Saratoga; but the corporation of Albany, conceiving this place to be in danger, sent me a note, the copy of which your honor has inclosed, requesting me to halt till they could write to you upon the subject.

If your honor reconsider my orders from General Heath, you will find that Albany is the post I am at present to command, and to consider myself under your command while here. Notwithstanding, sir, I can assure you there shall be nothing lacking in my power to serve the common cause of America.

I am, with proper respect,

Your most obed't hbl. serv't,

SAM'L LOGAN.

Brigadier General Stark.

Albany, September 15, 1781.

Sir—We are just now informed that you have ordered one company of your detachment to march to Saratoga, in consequence of orders received for that purpose from General Stark. As we conceive, from your orders from General Heath, that you was sent here for the purpose of affording protection to this city, and conceiving that General Stark has not adverted to your orders from General Heath, we wish you to halt the company on the march, and to wait yourself until we receive an answer to the letter directed to General Heath, herewith delivered, which we beg may be forwarded on by express.

We are, sir, your very humble servants,

ABRAH'M TEN BROECK, Mayor.

LEONARD GANESVOORT, Recorder.

To Major Logan.

Albany, September 15, 1781.

Dear Sir—The mayor informed me just now that Major Logan, with the troops under his command, were ordered from hence, and wished me to write you on the subject. As those troops were expressly sent for the protection of the city, the citizens are much alarmed that they should be removed at a time when parties of the enemy are lurking about with the express intent of burning the city.

You doubtless have your reasons for the disposition, but if they are not of a very pressing nature, I would advise you to dispense with their going up, as they can be drawn to your assistance on the shortest notice, should there be occasion, and I may also hasten on the militia, should you find it necessary to call for them.

General Washington embarked at and sailed from the head of Elk, with five thousand and five hundred of his troops, on the 8th instant. The remaining two thousand and five hundred were expected there on that day, and would immediately follow. Both French fleets are now in the Chesapeake.

An account is current in Philadelphia that the French, Dutch, and Spanish fleets had formed a junction, and sailed on an expedition with a large army of land forces, under convoy, their destination not known.

I am, with great respect,

Dear general, your obed't serv't,

PH. SCHUYLER.

Hon. General Stark.

To Major General Schuyler.

Saratoga, 16th September, 1781.

Dear Sir—Yours, of yesterday, was delivered to me last night by express. I only ordered Major Logan, with half of his troops, to this post. The remainder, with the united efforts and spirited exertions of the citizens of Albany, must, in all human probability, be competent to its defence.

You must be sensible, sir, that no party of more than fifty or sixty could get there undiscovered; and even of these, ten parties would be discovered where one would miss. On the other hand, Albany may for a few days turn out one hundred and fifty men for guards, every night. These, sir, with the regular guards of troops which will be left, will be an infallible bar against any descent upon the city.

In case of an attack here (which I am in daily expectation of), I can assure you, sir, that I have no hopes of any assistance from Albany; and, should I receive any, it will exceed my expectations; as the delays that attended their late march to Schoharie, at a time when we had every reason to expect they would be hourly wanted, are still fresh in my memory, and affords convincing proof that it is not their inclination to fight away from their own castle.

I think, by this time, my Lord Cornwallis has his hands full of business, and I fancy, if the truth was known, would rather be arguing the cause of America in the British Commons (however irksome that task might be), than in his present situation. Pray, sir, continue to give me the news, as you are the only gentleman from whom I can expect it authentically. That God may prosper the alliance, and render us a happy peace, is the most ardent wish of,

Dear sir, yours, with respect and esteem,

JOHN STARK.

To Brigadier General Stark.

HEADQUARTERS. *Continental Village,*
September 17, 1781.

Dear Sir—I have received repeated information that the enemy have been building canoes and small bateaux for some time, at St. Johns, and sending hard bread from Montreal to that place; and it is now said that a number of troops have arrived there. Whether their design is to cross the lakes and advance toward you, or toward the towns on the Connecticut river, for which the light craft seem rather calculated, is uncertain.

You will please to keep a sharp look out, and be in readiness to oppose them, should they advance. I have ordered Colonel Weisenfels to move to Albany immediately. The troops he will take with him, with those lately sent under the command of Major Logan, will make about three hundred and fifty men. They are an exceedingly fine corps, and generally officered with old continental officers.

I would have one company left at Albany for the security of the city. The remainder you will dispose of in such manner as you may judge most conducive to the public service and security of the frontiers.

From the high opinion I have of Colonel Willet, and his knowledge of the country, I would have him continued in command in the quarter where he has been. Colonel Weisenfels is a brave and good officer; will answer your expectations whenever employed. Let me hear from you often. I have not yet received a return of the troops in your district, which leaves me in uncertainty whether your force is sufficient, or that reinforcements are necessary.

Some soldiers have deserted from the troops gone to the southward—several Canadians from Colonel Hazen's regiment; probably they will steer for Albany. Please direct your guards to examine such as appear suspicious, and, if any are detected, send them down.

With great regard, etc.,

WM. HEATH, *M. General.*

Albany, September 19*th*, 1781.

Dear General—Some prisoners came to town last evening from Montreal. They had the liberty of that town, and say that, two days before they left that city, a body of two hundred and fifty men crossed for St. Johns; it was said they were to be joined by a body of whites and

Indians at that place, and, in conjunction with a body from Buck's island, were to fall upon and destroy the remainder of the country on the Mohawk river. I have no news from below.

I am, with esteem, sir, yours, &c.,

E. MARSHALL.

Hon. General Stark.

To Major General Heath.

Saratoga, September 20, 1781.

Dear Sir—I am somewhat alarmed that no answers have been received to my several letters addressed to you. I think it improbable that all should have miscarried; and have considered some of them of sufficient consequence as to have required an answer. By them you will ascertain that this department is destitute of ammunition, there not being ten pounds to a man at his post; and none at Albany, subject to my order. There are no horses for expresses, or to convey provisions to the several posts, and if there were, they would starve for want of forage. We have not even paper to transact our business with, nor can we obtain it.

Now, sir, if you will cast up the account, you will find the public much in our debt, and unless these debts are paid, or more regular provision made for supplies, I hardly know what consequences may follow—no good ones can come, unless miracles interpose in our behalf.

Intelligence from Canada, through sound sources, leads us to conclude that an attack is designed, either upon this post or the Mohawk river. From the situation of the country I think the attempt will be made upon this post, as the enemy can come here with twenty-five miles land carriage; while, on the other quarter, the distance is six times that number. However, if ammunition is supplied me, I hope to give any that may come such a reception as will make them glad to return if they have an opportunity.

The people of Albany are greatly alarmed for their city. They require all the troops of this district, or a major part of them, to prevent about fifty tories from burning them, their sloops, wives and houses; for it appears these turbulent sons of rapine have given out most fearful threats against that sacred place. However, sir, unless you order to the contrary, I shall venture, in case I feel confident of the enemy's approach, to order all the troops now at Albany to this post, or to the Mohawk.

The resolutions of Congress, allowed to every general officer, I have not seen for nine months. I wish they may be sent me.

With respect, I am, dear sir,

Your obed't humble serv't,

JOHN STARK.

Dear General—Since my last, nothing extraordinary has turned up in this department, except seven deserters, who shall be sent to you as soon as possible; and a few tories that have been taken on the frontiers. I inclose you a copy of a letter found with one of them, and am in hopes, by this time, that the writer is a prisoner likewise.

I am informed that forty-seven of the enemy's Indians are coming down here to make a treaty with us, while their young men are cutting our throats. I think, until their insolence is chastised in a severe manner, we never can expect peace in this quarter. The bearer of this, Major Guather, has found fifty-five shells, twelve boxes musket balls, one vise, and one pair hand-screws in the river near Saratoga. It is reported that the enemy sunk some cannon in the river. I should think a farther search would be necessary, but, by reason of the scarcity of men, it has been neglected.

I am, sir, &c., &c.,

JOHN STARK.

His Excellency, General Washington.

Saratoga, 24th September, 1781.

Dear Sir—Your letters of 24th August, 3d, 7th, 8th, and 17th of September, came safely to hand; to all of which, except the latter, I have written particular and descriptive answers, and given you an account of the department as near as was in my power; and, by what unfortunate accident they are kept from you, I can not imagine; but perhaps some of them may have reached you before this, and will clear up the mystery; but, lest they should not, it will be necessary to be particular in this.

Your suggestions in your last, with respect to a visit from Canada, I think very probable; for it is no longer a doubt that the enemy have put eighty or a hundred bateaux in repair for some purpose; and, as they are boats well calculated for making a descent upon this post, or some part of this frontier, it is very likely that we are the object of their design; and to my sorrow I must inform you that, should they make an attempt now, we should be able to make but a faint resistance. Ammunition, that life of an army, we are scant of; the troops have not ten rounds per man, and none can I get from Albany; but, lest you should think I have been remiss in not giving you this intelligence earlier, I have written three times to you, and once to General Knox, for a supply; but have received neither answers nor ammunition in return for any of them, for which reasons I must suppose they never came to your hands.

I have written particularly for some horses and forage to be procured for this quarter; for at present I have no other method of keeping up a line of correspondence with the frontiers, but by sending soldiers on foot with their provisions on their backs; and, in case the enemy should come in force, that, sir, would be but a sorry method for the commander of a district to communicate his orders, and call in the country to his assistance.

Thus, sir, you will see the necessity of sending some cash to enable me to send expresses, and some provision for horses for the purpose, and pointing out some method of procuring forage and other necessaries for the use of the district, and which are absolutely necessary to facilitate the public business.

There are in this neighborhood about thirty persons, who lately came from Canada, as I suppose to bring dispatches to Albany, and to find out the situation of the country. I have taken every possible method to trepan them, and hope to succeed; but, at the same time, the slowness of my dispatches gives me some reason to fear that I shall not. One of the parties, employed for the purpose, shot one man through the arm, as he was endeavoring to pass them last evening. He is likely to suffer amputation.

You must not expect any regular returns from this quarter, unless you supply paper; for there is none here to transact any kind of public business. This, sir, has been, and still is, my apology for not sending you a return.

The people of Albany seem in a mighty fright about their devoted city, and would willingly, if they could, call all the troops in the district to its protection, but, for my part, I have not penetration enough to see any impending danger; for they have five hundred citizens able to bear arms, and nothing else to do but to protect themselves, and the most that can ever come against them (unless I am withdrawn from this place, which shall not be if I can help it) can not be more than fifty. Now consider the odds, and you will find it to be infinitely in their favor.

Captain King, of the Massachusetts militia, will have the honor of delivering this. He has offered his service to perform the business, which I was glad to accept, as the only sure method of conveying a letter to you. His conduct in this and every other branch of his duty appears uniformly good, and merits my highest approbation.

September 25th. This moment are brought in five of the party I mentioned, supposed to be in this neighborhood, but they will give no satisfactory account of the remainder of the party. They were taken by Captain Dunham and two more persons this morning. Too much honor or praise can not be bestowed on these three brave militia men, for this special and meritorious conduct.

I am, sir, your obedient, humble servant,

JOHN STARK.

To Major General Heath.

To Brigadier General Stark.

HEADQUARTERS. *Continental Village,*
September 24, 1781.

Dear Sir—Your favors of the 9th and 11th did not come to hand until last evening. I have received but one other letter from you, since my return from the eastward. That letter I inclosed to Congress, with a general representation of the situation of the army, and I believe omitted writing you an answer at that time.

I was surprised, by yours of the 9th, to find your district so short of ammunition, and last night sent an express to Colonel Crane, at West Point, to forward immediately to Albany thirty thousand musket cartridges, four barrels of powder, fifteen hundred flints, some cartridge paper, thread, etc., subject to your orders. I apprehend the ammunition is by this time on the water. Paper was some time since sent to Albany, and must have arrived. I must again request a return of the several corps of troops as soon as possible. I assured Congress, in my last, that yours should be in the next, which must be made the 1st of October.

Weisenfel's regiment will have joined you before this reaches you. I request you to dispose of it in such a manner as to cover the country and promote the public service. A company, or part of a company, I would have stationed at Albany. Ballstown is, I am told, a pass through which the enemy will probably advance; but, as you are on the spot, you are the best judge. Endeavor to have every thing arranged in the best manner for immediate defence. Your brigade major or inspector is, of course, to do the duty of deputy adjutant general. If you have not a brigade major or inspector appointed, it belongs to the eldest majors. If they decline, a capable captain is commonly appointed.

We are equally embarrassed with you in our finances, sending expresses, etc. I have represented your situation, and will do it again.

Every account we receive from below announces that the British have had a very severe drubbing from the French. The last occasion says two British seventy-four gun ships were sunk, three ships driven on shore, four or five taken, five or six missing; the remainder returned to New-York; the admiral's ship so much damaged that he would not return in her; the inhabitants of New-York in the greatest consternation, packing up their effects.

I am, with equal regard,

Dear sir, your obedient servant,

WM. HEATH, *Major General.*

Albany, September 24, 1781—1 o'clock, A. M.

Dear Sir—Your favor of yesterday's date was this moment delivered. This morning I had intelligence of a party's having crossed the Mohawk river, and of their being discovered near Canastighuma; a party is gone out after them. We have not had any farther accounts from the southward than what I have already transmitted. I have letters from Philadelphia, but they contain nothing but very great hopes that Cornwallis will soon be in our power. Indeed, it seems almost impossible for him to escape, as both our naval and land force is so infinitely superior to the British.

General Heath informs me that the enemy are embarking their stores at New-York; what their object may be he cannot learn; but is under no apprehensions for West Point, as his force is equal to that of the enemy at least.

With compliments to the major,

I am, dear sir, very sincerely,

Your obedient servant,

PH. SCHUYLER.

Hon. Brigadier General Stark.

[Instructions for Captain Hickoks, with a Flag of Truce.]

By John Stark, Brigadier General in the army of the United States, and commander of the Northern Department, &c.
Done at head quarters, Saratoga, 26th September, 1781.

Sir—You will proceed with the flag under your direction to the British shipping on Lake Champlain. On your arrival, you will tarry until you find out whether Captain ——— will have it in his power to negotiate his business there; if so, I have no objection to your tarrying a few days, until that can be transacted; but, should he be under the necessity of going to Canada, it is by no means probable that you will be permitted to attend him, for which reason you will return by the route you go, and make report of your proceedings.

It will be necessary for you to keep up your flag ever after you leave Skenesborough, and frequently order your drums to beat a parley, especially should you discover any boat or party. Wishing you a pleasant voyage,

I am, dear sir,

Your most obed't serv't,

JOHN STARK.

To Captain Hickoks.

To Brigadier General Stark.

HEADQUARTERS. *Continental Village,*
October 1st, 1781.

My Dear Sir—Since Captain King came here, Major Villefranche has returned from the Mohawk river, from whom I learn that your district is very far from being short of ammunition. Indeed, I think the quantity is much too large for the places where it is at present deposited. I learn that there is not less than twenty odd casks of powder, each containing two hundred pounds, beside a large quantity of fixed ammunition on the Mohawk river, and that a great part of it is at Fort Herkimer, which is one of the most advanced posts. There are also at the same place a number of spare cannon. The powder ought to be divided to the different posts in such quantities as, from the particular situation and the importance of the posts, may be necessary. After each post is properly supplied, your reserve ought to be at some safe post in the rear, from which each advanced post may draw supplies, when they are wanted. The spare cannon should be deposited in the same manner. I request you to write Col. Willet immediately upon the subject; and have such arrangements made as may appear most eligible, without risking more ammunition than is necessary, at the advanced posts.

I am informed that paper was sent to Albany for the use of your district, as early as the beginning of the last month. As I observed in my other letter, you must call on Mr. Quackenbush, at Albany, for what you want. I must renew my request for a speedy return to be made of the troops, etc., in your district. I hope Col. Weisenfel's regiment will give you a force adequate to any occasion you may have for it.

I am, with great regard, etc.,

WM. HEATH, *M. General.*

To Brigadier General Stark.

Fort Rensselaer, 6*th October*, 1781.

Dear General—The murder of Mr. Werner Taygert, and the captivity of one of his sons, two days ago, at their uninhabited house upon Fall hill, by three or four rascals, nobody knows who, comprehends the substance of our present intelligence in this quarter, and it is disagreeable.

I have, for the present, fixed Major Logan, with his detachment, at Johnstown, and directed him to keep guards at Fort Hunter, and at Veeder's mills, in Caghnawaga. Johnstown is the best place to cover Caghnawaga, and is an additional protection to Stony [not legible]. I have sent Captain Marshall's company from Johnstown to relieve Captain White at Ballstown; and ordered Captain White to this place with his company. I could wish to know from you when you conceive the service of the Massachusetts troops to expire.

This department is badly furnished with surgeons. The surgeon of my regiment is at the German flats, and can not attend any other place. My surgeon's mate is at Saratoga. At this place we have a mate from the general hospital, and this quarter is all that he can attend. Major Logan has requested me to supply him with a doctor at Johnstown. You can easily perceive that this is not in my power. I shall be glad if you can order him one from Saratoga, or any other place you please.

I am, &c., MARINUS WILLET.

Albany, October 7, 1781.

Dear General—When Major Logan took the command at this post with two companies, he told me it was at the particular request of this city, from which, I concluded he might continue some time. I therefore sent the twenty men I had retained by your order, to their several corps, knowing they were much wanted. The remaining part of Shepherd's company consists of about twenty-seven men, from which, I am so often obliged to detach small parties, that I have not relieves for a guard of six men. If you could think it convenient to station a small guard at the Half-Moon, it would ease me much, for, whenever flour goes on for your quarters, I am under the necessity of sending men to press teams to carry it into Stillwater.

Twenty head of cattle, out of forty-eight just arrived, go to Saratoga; part of the remainder I shall send westward. I see but faint hopes of any more rum.

Letters from the south mention only that De Grasse drove the British fleet from the Virginia coast, without capturing any capital ship. Rivington tells us they had two or three sunk after the action. Admiral Digby has arrived at New-York with three ships, only. This is nearly the state of affairs.

I am, with highest respect,

Your obed't serv't,

E. MARSHALL.

Brigadier General Stark.

To Major General Heath.

Saratoga, 8th October, 1781.

Dear Sir—Yours of the 24th and 25th ult., and the 1st inst., are now before me, and the ammunition mentioned has come to hand. What quantity of that article has been received on the Mohawk river, I am ignorant of; but it is certain that Colonel Willet, some time in the beginning of August last, took a quantity from Albany for the use of that quarter, and I have never been able to procure a return of the stores, &c., for want of paper.

You are pleased to observe that paper was sent as early as the beginning of last month. That might be the case, but the portion allotted to this post never arrived until yesterday, and then we got but ten quires, part of which being for the use of the garrison, and a part for my office, which you must be sensible is a very inadequate supply, and can not last but a few days.

By every appearance, it is plain that the enemy in Canada are either meditating an attack on this place, or that they are very anxious for intelligence from the westward. Their small parties are continually among us. Last night I sent a party who took two more of them prisoners, who are now safe in my guard-house. They say that they came over the lake with three more in company, who parted with them about five miles above my garrison; I am in hopes to take them, but can not insure success.

I shall instantly dispatch orders to Colonel Willet to send the spare ammunition now at his post to Schenectady, where I presume it will be secure.

This day Thomas Lovelace, the commander of the party whose instructions I sent you, was hanged, in pursuance of the sentence pronounced against him by a court-martial. The remaining four taken with him are sentenced to imprisonment during the war. They are already sent to Albany, and under close confinement.

You will perceive by the returns that go with this conveyance, our strength, and then, if you think a reinforcement necessary, you can act your opinion. I would only observe, that in case any men are to be sent, no time should be lost, as the season is far advanced, and, should the enemy come, it will be impossible for me to give you notice early enough to reap any advantage from a reinforcement that could come afterward. I have promises, in case of an attack, that the Vermonters shall once more come to my assistance. I am in hopes to give you an account of a small acquisition in the course of a few days. Any thing extra you must not expect, as I am only prepared to act on the defensive.

You can not think how disappointed I was when Capt. King returned, without bringing any official account of the French fleet, or our southern army. I hope, before this comes to your hand, that I shall have a confirmation of the great events that our country seems now to be pregnant with. Pray omit no intelligence, as the least gives great pleasure to me in this obscure and melancholy quarter. I have no accounts from the Mohawk river of a late date. When any thing occurs worthy of notice, you may depend upon the earliest intelligence which my circumstances will permit me to furnish.

I am, sir, with respect and esteem,

Your most obed't serv't,

JOHN STARK.

To Brigadier General Stark.

Poughkeepsie, October 8, 1781.

Sir—By some unaccountable delay, your letter of the 4th ult. (which appeared by a mark on the back to have been in the post-office) did not come to my hand until this evening. I have had frequent representations of the abuse you complain of, in the arresting and confining soldiers for tavern debts, and thereby depriving the public of their services; and I am so fully impressed with its destructive consequences, that it is my intention to apply to the Legislature, who are now convened at this place, to make provision, as far as possible, to prevent such abuses in future.

I am, with the greatest respect,

Your most obedient servant,

GEO. CLINTON.

P. S. I am happy in transmitting you the inclosed account of an action between General Greene and the enemy, and congratulate you on the occasion. I hope to receive a confirmation of it.

To Brigadier General Stark.

HEADQUARTERS. *Continental Village,*
October 10th, 1781.

Dear Sir—Your favor of the 7th and 8th have just come to hand. I have ordered the 2d New-Hampshire regiment immediately to embark and proceed to Albany, with a detachment of artillery, and one field-piece. I have sent the 2d regiment, because it has more field officers than the first, and will admit of some companies of levies being incorporated into it, if necessary; for, of itself, it is but weak in numbers, but excellent troops.

A few days since I directed Colonel Reynolds, who is at Number Four, to detach his major and two hundred men to join you. He will have two hundred left to move to your aid, or to the upper settlements on Connecticut river, should the enemy attempt them. These, I hope, will be a force sufficient to repel any that may come against you. Keep a sharp look out, and endeavor to develope the designs of the enemy, and keep me frequently advised of what passes, if possible.

We have as yet no official accounts of the naval engagement between the two fleets. The British were severely mauled, and have ever since been refitting. It is said they intend again to try their fortune. It will probably be their ruin.

It is said General Greene has had a bloody action with the British in Carolina, and that the advantage was in his favor; many are said to have been killed and wounded on both sides. The particulars are not yet come to hand.

By the last accounts from General Washington, every thing was in a prosperous way, and I hope soon to give you some important news from that quarter.

I am, with much regard,

Dear sir, your obed't serv't,

WM. HEATH, *Major General.*

To General Stark.

Albany, October 11, 1781.

Dear General—My knowledge of the scantiness of your present supplies makes me intensely uneasy. I have met with a number of inhabitants of this town who appear determined to give every aid in their power, but as we can not expect a quantity of flour, equal to what we have undoubted reason to believe you will soon want, I have requested the bearer, Bethuel Washburn, Esq., to assist in procuring whatever supply of flour he possibly can in your neighborhood, and desired him (provided you will ascertain the necessity of and furnish him with men for the purpose), even to use force, especially with those he can find possessed of any considerable quantity, and are disaffected to the general cause in the districts of Saratoga,

Schoharie, or Half Moon—these districts being most contiguous to you.

Be so good as to let me know your real situation, both as to beef and flour, the first convenient opportunity, directed to Major Shurtleff, at this place. General Schuyler has been kind enough to desire I would request you to take whatever beef he has fit for the knife, ordering the issuing commissaries to give receipts for the same, as received from me, mentioning the weight of each; and to have all the wheat he has at that place threshed out and ground immediately, should you find it necessary, the commissary giving receipts for the quantity of flour produced therefrom, in the same manner.

I am, sir, your most ob't serv't,

E. MARSHALL.

From Captain Marshall, commanding at Albany, to Major C. Stark, aid-de-camp to General Stark.

Albany, October 15, 1781.

Dear Sir—A very curious, sublime, and masterly performance. The penman must have been much exercised with indignation, or he never could have written with such force and energy. Then the grammar and consistency outshine all pieces of the kind I ever perused; although there are some few lies in it, yet I don't mind trifles. I never denied him subsistence. Am I obliged to become an historiologist?

The Seven Wise Masters, the Arabian Nights entertainments, Tom Thumb, &c., were always beyond my capacity. Your Bohemian kings may be hippo-centaurs for aught I know. This I know, I will never divulge the secret. He might have eat the tavern keeper's family, horses, barns, wood-piles, and all the mynheers in the city—he never asked me for an ox or barrel of flour.

I suppose you are under no great apprehensions while the Albanians and the contiguous militia are at your backs. Their patriotic spirit never shone more brilliantly than at this juncture. And then, their resolution and firmness, I am sure you cannot doubt; for larger numbers of them have been severely handled heretofore by the Governor (Clinton), for their —— in —— activity on similar occasions, notwithstanding they now, like a firm couraged horse, will stand the second spur, and even wait a third before they will kick. * * * * * * if he had asked me, had it been for no more than a day's allowance, humanity would have urged me to have given it to him.

Great spirit and determination is evinced by their officers—swearing death and vengeance against the delinquents. Of some companies two, and of some three have already marched. I heard a certain general swear, "God d—m him, if he did not make them smart."

So the next account, after the alarm subsides, will be bloodshed and slaughter among our friends in this quarter; shrieks, cries, and deadly agonizing groans already vibrate on the drums of my ears.

But you have not told me how the general treated the sensibly feeling injured men on the presentation of their learned remonstrance. Where, or how is Ford? Have you given any charge against him? If not, and you think the following one will answer, exhibit it:

"Sir, you are confined for unofficer-like behavior in combining with, and aiding and assisting Captain Dunham in making his escape, when he was under sentence of a court-martial for treasonable practices, in holding correspondence with the enemy when he was under your charge."

Do as you think best on the occasion; this, or something similar, I wish might be presented against him. Why don't you tell me what you are about? The 2d New-Hampshire regiment and a six-pounder, with a detachment of artillery, arrived this morning. They will go on as soon as we can procure wagons. Your intelligence will oblige me.

Yours, &c.,

E. MARSHALL.

Major C. Stark.

To Brigadier General Stark.

Albany, October 12, 1781—1 o'clock, P. M.

Dear Sir—At 6 o'clock this morning I was favored with yours, announcing the arrival of the enemy on the south end of Lake George. I immediately called on General Ganesvoort, and have already sent two expresses to every quarter of the country, to hasten on the militia. Some will move from hence to-day. I have also wrote two letters to Generals Rositer and Fellows; and, as the officer whom you had sent there, requested me to call on General Rositer to march, if I thought it necessary, I have ventured to request him in your name to proceed.

The night before last I intercepted a letter going to the enemy. It acknowledges the receipt of dispatches from Canada, and clearly points that this place is their object, the disaffected districts of N—— Helleburgh, and others in the vicinity. The writer says we are ready to execute the business as soon as the party that is to conduct it arrives. This business a former intercepted letter affords me the means of knowing: and it is to burn the city. I have ordered a scout of Indians to join the militia, and try to discover the party before it arrives. The remainder of the Indians are ordered to join you. If I was to leave this before the militia arrive, I fear the consequences would be disagreeable. I shall tarry at least a day longer to put matters in a good train.

I am, &c., Dear General, your ob't serv't,

PH. SCHUYLER.

Brigadier General Stark.

HEADQUARTERS. *Continental Village,* October 12, 1781.

Dear Sir—I wrote you the 10th, which I hope you have received before this time; and that the second New-Hampshire regiment will join you, before this reaches you, as they embarked and sailed the night before last. I have ordered a chain of expresses to be immediately established between this place and your army, for the immediate conveyance of intelligence. Please to improve them, and give the earliest intimations of whatever occurs.

Please carefully to watch the motions and advances of the enemy, and endeavor to ascertain their force, and who commands. A gentleman, not long since from Canada, gave it as his opinion that, from the size of the batteaux, he apprehended they had a design to pass by the rivers toward the head of Connecticut river. While they remain at Point Ofer it remains uncertain which way they will proceed, and they will probably display much deception. I early gave notice to the State of New-Hampshire, and north-western parts of Massachusetts, to keep a look out in that quarter. Please advise me of every movement the enemy make; it will reach me in about thirty hours.

I am, with great regard, &c.,

W. HEATH, *M. Gen'l.*

Brigadier General Stark.

Albany, October 13*th*, 1781.

Dear Sir—Too much indisposed from yesterday's fatigue, I have not been in town to-day, but believe a considerable body of militia has marched, as I have seen many come across the ferry.

By letters from Virginia of the 29th ult., I learn that our army have begun their approaches, and that they hoped in a little while to send us accounts that he* is captured. General Greene, it is said, has defeated a very considerable body of the enemy at Monks corner. I expect letters by this day's post, and if any thing interesting occurs, shall send an express. With best wishes to the major, I am, Dear General, with

Great regard, your most obed't serv't,

PH. SCHUYLER.

Hon. General Stark.

* Lord Cornwallis.

Fort Rensselaer, 11*th October,* 1781.

Dear General—By the best advices from Montreal, it appears that eight hundred men went up the St. Lawrence early in September. The report was, that they were intended to relieve their western garrisons; but it is by no means improbable, even if they were intended as a relief, that, while they have such an augmentation of their force to the westward, they will make an incursion into this quarter.

I beg leave to submit whether it is eligible to draw any of the troops from this quarter, as our situation is so advanced from the thickly inhabited parts of the country, as will not admit of our receiving speedy succors from any other place. I can only promise, if they come, that everything in my power shall be done to cause them to regret their enterprise.

I am, sir, your very humble serv't,

MARINUS WILLET.

General Stark.

HEADQUARTERS. *Continental Village,*
October 14th, 1781.

Dear Sir—A copy of yours of the 4th, to General Ganesvoort, announcing the advance of the enemy to this side of Lake George, was handed me last evening. The first New-Hampshire and tenth Massachusetts regiments, with a detachment of artillery, are ordered to march to your support immediately. I hope they will arrive, to enable you to defeat the enemy, if you are not fortunate enough to do it before. The moment these regiments are no longer necessary in your quarter, order them to return.

I am, with great regard, &c.,

W. HEATH, *M. Gen'l.*

Brigadier General Stark.

To Colonel Tupper.

HEADQUARTERS. *Continental Village,* October 14, 1781.

Sir—You will immediately select the best clothed men of the brigade under your command, with them a detachment of artillery, and one field-piece from the company under Captain Vose, and march for Albany. If the wind should be favorable when you get to Fishkill, you may embark on board vessels for your greater dispatch ; but if the wind should continue to blow down the river, proceed with all possible dispatch by land. On your arrival at Albany, send off an express to General Stark, informing him of your arrival, and then continue your march to Saratoga, or wherever General Stark may be, or you receive his orders to march. If the enemy should have gone back before you reach General Stark, on certain accounts of it, halt your troops; and, upon your receiving notice from General Stark that your aid is not necessary, return to this place with the troops that march with you, except such as belong to the 2d New-Hampshire regiment, who are to join their regiment. Take three days' provisions with you, and draw what may be necessary at Fishkill to support you to Albany.

Beside the ammunition in the men's boxes, take about fifteen thousand spare musket cartridges with you. Advise me frequently of your situation, and all occurrences of consequence.

I am, sir, with great regard,

Your ob't serv't,

W. HEATH, *M. General.*

Albany, October 15, 1781.

Dear Sir—Your favor of yesterday's date was delivered me in the course of the night. I am much obliged, and pleased by your attention to the ladies.

Yesterday morning I was advised that you had written to General Ganesvoort for some of the militia, and also to the Massachusetts. I went to the general and urged him to be pointed in his orders, and to point the necessity there was for General Rensselaer to march up his brigade. He had wrote, but not so fully as I wished. I therefore addressed myself to General Rensselaer, and doubt not but we shall have a respectable body to oppose the enemy, should they venture down. I have ordered the Indians to hold themselves in readiness, and some to scout between Schoharie and Batts' hill. I think it will be right in you to renew your request to Ganesvoort, and to press him to hasten up the militia. In no season of the year can they leave home with so little inconvenience, especially as this will be the last occasion during the campaign.

My disorder has taken a favorable turn, and I hope in a few days to join you, and shall take the advantage of an escort from the militia. I forgot to mention, in mine of the 4th inst., that I had advised Colonel Willet of the intelligence contained therein. With best wishes for your health and happiness,

I am, Dear General,

Your obed't serv't,

PH. SCHUYLER.

Hon. General Stark.

Bennington, October 16th, 1781.

Dear General—I am surprised to learn that the militia of Albany county have no other business upon their hands, at this time of general alarm and danger, than to distress the inhabitants of Vermont, as if they considered the British from Canada not sufficient for our destruction, at a time when all our militia are under marching orders, and most of them have already marched. This they think a proper time to manifest their spite and malice.

Part of my regiment has marched to Castleton. I shall this morning follow with the remainder. If your honor can not find the militia of Albany some other employment, I shall march my regiment to that quarter, and try powder and ball with them, which I have as well as they. I pray your honor to check them if possible.

I am, Dear General, your very humble servant,

SAM'L ROBINSON.

Hon. General Stark, Saratoga.

Honorable General Stark.

Albany, October 16, 1781.

My Dear Sir—The inclosed was delivered to me and opened before I discovered that it was directed to you.

General Heath advises me that the second New-Hampshire regiment, and some artillery, are on the way up; I will press the quarter master to expedite them to you. General Heath also informs me that General Greene has defeated the enemy in Carolina, and obtained a complete victory, though dearly bought, as it has cost us many valuable officers and three hundred men. The enemy's loss trebles ours.

Mrs. Schuyler arrived last evening, and has detailed the various attentions you and your worthy son have paid to herself and her daughters.*

I feel it with pleasure and with gratitude, and hope to return you personal thanks as soon as the severe fit of the gravel, which now confines me, will permit.

I am, dear sir,

Your most obedient humble serv't,

PH. SCHUYLER.

* In 1781 the headquarters of the northern department was established at Saratoga, on or near one of the estates of General Schuyler, whose lady and daughters came to the farm in the autumn to prepare their winter stores. At this time General Stark, with his son, Major Caleb Stark, frequently called upon them, and detached a sergeant, with a party of soldiers, for their protection, and to assist their servants in securing the winter supplies. The foregoing letter refers to these attentions.

To Brigadier General Stark.

Bennington, October 17, 1781.

Sir—In consequence of your request to me of the 11th, I sent orders to the militia, now considered in this State, in the neighborhood of the New City. Lieutenant Colonel Fairbanks is present with me, and informs that, in obedience to my orders, he had mustered a number of men to march to your assistance on Sunday morning. Saturday evening, Colonel Van Rensselaer came with a party of men from Albany, and its vicinity, and took them prisoners, broke open their houses, and much distressed their families.

Such conduct appears very extraordinary at this time, when every man ought to be rather employed in the defence of his country, than in destroying his neighbors' property. What Colonel Van Rensselaer designs, is best known to himself; but it has the appearance of preventing men going to defend the frontier at this critical moment. I have ordered one half of our militia to the north, and the remainder I expect must shortly follow. The inhabitants of this western territory are willing to do their duty under Vermont, but are prevented by York. And now, sir, if you judge it lies within your province to quiet those disorders, I must entreat you to do it. That we may be united, is my sincere desire. The dispute of jurisdiction must be settled between the States; but if such conduct is persisted in before, I must repel force by force, and the hardship fend off.

I am, with sentiments of esteem,

Your obed't serv't,

SAM. SAFFORD.

Brigadier General Stark.

HEADQUARTERS. *Continental Village,*
October 20th, 1781.

Dear Sir—Your favor of the 15th came to hand the last night, by which I learn that the report of the advance of the enemy to the south end of Lake George was premature. If there is a doubt whether the enemy will advance, I advise you not to detain the militia. They are wanted at home to gather their harvest, and the state of our provisions will not allow us to feed them, unless absolutely wanted. The New-Hampshire brigade, Col. Willet's regiment, Weisenfel's, McKinstry's, Sear's, and that part of Reynolds' ordered from Number. Four is a very respectable force; and, with such part of the militia as are at hand, and can be collected on the shortest notice, superior to any force that will come out against you. If you, on such intelligence as you can depend upon, are of the same opinion, I advise that the militia be permitted to return home immediately. I have requested Lord Stirling to go as far as Albany, to advise on the present occasion. We are at present exceedingly short of flour, and have not the best prospect of a supply speedily. Please let me hear from you frequently.

I am, your obedient humble serv't,

W. HEATH, *M. General.*

P. S. October 21. Upon farther consideration on the state of our provisions, and some other circumstances, I am fully of opinion that unless something has turned up since you wrote to convince you that a contrary measure is expedient, that, on receipt of this, it will be for the good of the service to dismiss all the militia called out on the late alarm; and that the New-Hampshire brigade remain with you for the present, with such levies and militia as were with you before. Please present my thanks to the militia, for the spirit with which they have turned out on this occasion, and my assurance of their doing it again, should it be necessary.

I am, as before, WM. HEATH.

To Governor Clinton.

HEADQUARTERS. *Saratoga*,
26th of October, 1781.

Dear Sir—For the protection of the northern frontier, it becomes absolutely necessary (in my opinion) that a post be established at or near this place. Barracks are already built here, and other advantageous circumstances point out this as the most proper place; and I have it now in contemplation to establish a garrison for the winter. But, unless my design is seconded by some authority, who have it in their power either to procure supplies, or advance money for those necessaries—that the troops can not exist without—among which, I may name wood and forage, I can not succeed. The former, the troops can not live without; and the latter is absolutely necessary to keep up a communication with the country, and remove and transport supplies for the use of the garrison. My patience is already exhausted in making fruitless applications to the officers, acting by the authority of Congress, to procure supplies. They either will not, or can not, grant them. I have now no other recourse than to make application to you, who seem to be more interested in the protection of this frontier than any other man—being the father and guardian of the people. Now, sir, I have told you my wants, and it remains next to inform you of the consequences, if they are not supplied: viz., that the northern and western frontiers must be evacuated as far as Albany; and, indeed, Albany itself, unless some speedy measures are fallen upon to lay in magazines for the consumption of a garrison. The season is now so far advanced that measures must be taken speedily, or they will prove ineffectual. However, I am convinced that the State will see the absolute necessity of interfering, and will do all in their power, which I hope will be sufficient, to save this unhappy frontier from impending ruin, which will probably be its fate, unless these garrisons are continued for its protection.

I have the honor to be your obed't serv't,

JOHN STARK.

To Brigadier General Stark.

HEADQUARTERS. *Continental Village,*
October 25, 1781.

Dear Sir—Your favor of the 18th, with its inclosures, come to hand this evening. I think it yet rather doubtful whether the enemy will advance—they possible may; but I would not call out many militia until it is pretty certain. Our scantiness of provisions will not admit of it, unless indispensably necessary; and your regular troops and levies, and the three months' militia, are a very respectable force. The conduct of the Berkshire militia does them much honor.

When matters looked very threatening, and the troops to the northward were greatly increasing, I desired Major General Lord Stirling to repair toward Albany, and even to take the command during the emergency, should it be necessary. You will find great relief and support from his lordship, should the enemy advance in force. If they should not come in force, he will not interrupt you in your command.

I would have the tenth Massachusetts regiment, and the detachment of artillery, with the six-pounders which went with the New-Hampshire brigade, return as soon as they can be safely spared; that is, after you are pretty certain the enemy are not in considerable force, or are turned back, or do not advance. Some troops will be necessary in your district during the winter. Colonel Weisenfel's regiment, I believe, is engaged only to the beginning of December; Colonel Willet's to the first of January. I have, therefore, determined that the two New-Hampshire regiments shall be assigned to you. The detachments absent from them shall be ordered up, when the army moves to winter quarters, to join their corps. I would have you consult with Lord Stirling, and also take the advice of General Schuyler, where it may be best to station the troops, and in what numbers, during the winter. You must take into view the Mohawk river, as well as the other parts of the frontiers; and the best preparations in your power should be seasonably made of provisions, fuel and forage, as well as covering for the troops. If any of the posts are difficult of access, when the cold season sets in, provisions, etc., sufficient for the subsistence of the troops designed for such posts, should be previously deposited. These several matters will claim your immediate attention.

Assure those regiments who are to remain with you, that they may depend on equal justice being done them in the distribution of clothing, or any public stores.

Advise me often of your situation, and all remarkable occurrences, that I may advise or direct as may be necessary.

I am, with great regard,

Your obedient serv't,

W. HEATH, *Major General.*

P. S. We have a report that Lord Cornwallis, with his army, surrendered on the 17th instant. We impatiently wait a confirmation.

Albany, Octboer 22, 1781.

Dear Sir—Your favor of yesterday's date, covering letters for General Heath and Lord Stirling, I received about 7 o'clock last evening: the former I shall forward, and the latter detain, as Colonel Tupper informs me his lordship is on the way to this place. But I believe your conclusion is not very just, that you will be relieved from the fatigue and trouble you undergo, as I believe his lordship will return from hence.

The conduct of the Berkshire militia is one of those events which place human nature in an amiable and dignified light. How ridiculous is the idea of conquering a country whose inhabitants, with so much alacrity, abandon the sweets of domestic ease and private concerns, when put in competition with their country. This is the true spirit of patriotism, which I earnestly hope will pervade every quarter of the United States. My thanks are small matters, but as they are gratefully bestowed, they acquire some value on that account. I have endured the most severe torment for forty-eight hours past, from a fit of the gravel; about two hours ago voided a considerable quantity, and am now much relieved. The moment I am able, will do myself the pleasure of a visit. Nothing new now.

I am, Dear General, with great respect, esteem, and every friendly wish, your obed't servant,

PH. SCHUYLER.

Hon. General Stark.

General Enos to General Stark.

HEADQUARTERS. *Castleton,*
October 26, 1781.

Dear Sir—Captain Salisbury this instant returned as a scout from the Mount, which he left last evening. He lay in sight of the enemy's works the chief part of the day. They are repairing the fortification at (Ticonderoga), and have covered the long barracks. Nearly two hundred cattle were employed in drawing cannon, &c., from their boats.

Behind the old French lines appeared a large number of smokes, where it is supposed the chief part of their army is quartered. Colonel Walbridge informs me, by express, that he has not as yet made any discovery from Lake George and that quarter. He has my directions, in case of any important discoveries, to make immediate returns to you.

I am, sir, your most obed't hh'bl serv't,

ROGER ENOS.

Hon. Brigadier General Stark.

Albany, October 15, 1781.

Dear Sir—General Rositer, with a few of his brigade, arrived yesterday afternoon; the remainder, to the amount of eight or nine hundred, will be in this evening. As Colonel Reid, with the second battalion of New-Hampshire continental troops, has arrived here, subject to your command, I advised General Rositer to tarry here, until we received farther advices from you, as perhaps you might think it unnecessary for him to proceed. You will be so good as to dispatch your orders to the general, with as much speed as circumstances will permit. Should he not be wanted, it will save provision to the public to permit him to return the soonest possible. Governor Clinton has ordered up all the militia from below, and the whole, we understand, are on the move. Colonel Willet, in a letter of 13th, advises that all is well in the west quarter, &c.

I am, Dear General, with sentiments of great esteem, your obedient servant,

PH. SCHUYLER.

Hon. General Stark.

Albany, 29th October, 1781.

Dear Sir—Your favor of yesterday's date, covering a copy of a letter from General Enos, was delivered me last evening. As it seems impossible that the reconnoitering officer can be mistaken, I conclude the enemy intend a permanent post at Ticonderoga. Perhaps it may prove a cage in which we shall secure them.

To-morrow, if the weather be good, I shall set out on a visit to you. We have as yet no official account of the surrender of Lord Cornwallis; but the intelligence we have bears such strong marks of veracity, that I have not a doubt but we shall receive authentic advices in a day or two. Please to make my sincere and best wishes to the major, and to thank him.

I am, Dear General, with great esteem and regard, your most obedient servant,

PH. SCHUYLER.

Hon. General Stark.

HEADQUARTERS. *Continental Village,* October 30, 1781.

Dear Sir—Please to forward the inclosed to Colonel Willet. It contains the appointment of Major Hitchcock to muster and inspect his regiment, as the dispersed situation of it will prevent an inspector attending that duty. I trust you will direct Captain Robinson, inspector of the New-Hampshire brigade, to muster and inspect Colonel Weisenfel's regiment, and other regiments of levies, if any are with you, except Colonel Willet's.

I am impatiently waiting to hear some thing very interesting from your quarter.

I am, with great regard, dear sir,

Your obedient servant,

W. HEATH, *M. General.*

Brigadier General Stark.

Fort Ann, November 2, 1781.

Dear Sir—I arrived at this place last evening with the number of men as mentioned in my last, with five days' provisions of beef, and one of bread; was disappointed in every way of procuring the latter article, of which I am now destitute.

I am extremely sorry and much disappointed that you did not furnish me with the number of cartridges required. As the Hampshire forces are destitute of ammunition, I judge it improper to proceed to Fort Edward, unless there shall be absolute occasion. I have this instant heard a firing of cannon and small arms at Fort Edward, and shall immediately send a scout to that place, for intelligence. If no discovery of the enemy be made, I shall be under the necessity of returning to Castleton.

I am, dear sir, your obedient servant,

ROGER ENOS.

Hon. Brigadier General Stark.

To Governor Chittenden.

Saratoga, November 5th, 1781.

Sir—Ordered by his excellency, the commander-in-chief, to assume the command of the northern department, and to call if necessary upon the militia of this State and those of Vermont, for protecting the frontiers of both States, I have observed, with great satisfaction, the alacrity with which both have taken the field on every requisition; but, accountable as I am to superiors, and inexcusable as I should be if I neglected to advise them of any circumstances which carry the aspect of iniquity, I wish to receive the most authentic information respecting the sergeant of the Vermont militia who was slain, and his party captured by the enemy.

I expect your excellency will enable me to furnish a minute detail of it to Congress, by affording me a perusal of the original letter, which the British commanding officer is said to have written to you upon the occasion. This will be returned you by a safe hand, and a copy transmitted to Congress.

The report, as brought to me, is that, upon the party's arrival at Ticonderoga, the British officer expressed great displeasure that the citizens of Vermont had been disturbed; that he sent for the corpse of the deceased sergeant, caused it to be interred with military honors, and then dismissed the captured party with what liquor and provisions they chose to carry away, and delivered them a letter of apology to your excellency. If this be true, it indicates a deep stroke of policy on the part of the enemy, to raise a suspicion in the minds of all Americans that the Vermonters are friendly to them or that they have really some encouragement from some people in Vermont.

That the principal portion of the people of Vermont are zealously attached to the American cause, no honest man can doubt; but, that like every other State, it contains its proportion of lurking traitors, is a reasonable supposition; and if these, by their machinations, have brought upon the people injurious suspicions, there is no doubt but the latter will severely punish the miscreants as soon as their misdeeds are fully developed.

No exertion on my part shall be wanted to eradicate every suspicion injurious to the people of Vermont. Your compliance with my request will probably afford me one of the means; and I pray most earnestly your acquiescence, that I may detail the whole business in its true light.

I congratulate you, with the most heartfelt satisfaction, on the glorious event which has placed another British army in our power, which was announced on the third instant by a discharge of fourteen cannon,* and yesterday by that of a like number of platoons, in honor of the United States of America.

I am, sir, respectfully,

Your humble servant,

JOHN STARK.

Governor Chittenden to General Stark.

Arlington, November 14th, 1781.

Dear General—Your kind favor of the 5th inst. was received on the 10th, but through the extreme hurry of business, and for a want of a proper conveyance, I have neglected the answer till now.

The particular account you have requested me to send you in regard to the slain sergeant of the Vermont militia, and the return of the party with him, who were discharged by the British officer commanding, I have thought it my duty to transmit to his excellency, General Washington, together with every other public movement in this vicinity, that in any manner relates to the welfare of the inde-

*Vermont was not at this time a State. The fourteenth cannon was however fired, as a compliment to her good services in the war, and a hope that she might soon become a state of the Union.—*Editor*.

pendent States of America. This I doubt not will be satisfactory.*

I take this opportunity to return my thanks for the honor done this State, by your directing the discharge of the fourteenth cannon, on your late public day of rejoicing, occasioned by the capture of Lord Cornwallis and his army. A like day will probably be observed in this State on the same occasion.

I am, Dear General,

Your most obedient, humble servant,

THOS. CHITTENDEN.

Brigadier General Stark.

* In a communication to General Washington this matter was explained. Vermont not having been acknowledged by Congress as a State, her people contended for independence, and were threatened by the enemy in Canada. Some little management was necessary.

A correspondence was opened with the enemy, who were flattered for two or three years with the expectation that the people of Vermont were about to become subjects of the king. Thus a meditated invasion was averted, and the Vermont prisoners returned. At the same time, the possibility that Vermont would desert the American cause, was held up to Congress; and, in consequence, the settlers were not compelled to submit to the claims of New-York. Such was the political course Governor Chittenden thought necessary to pursue.—*Allen Biog. Dict.*

We quote the following from Butler's Address:

"Our truce with Canada was rather a help than a hindrance to the last great struggle of the war—the operations against Cornwallis. It was either unknown to Washington, or understood by him to be a political manœuvre. In the midst of the armistice, he wrote to Stark, commander of the northern department: 'I doubt not that your requisitions to call forth the force of the Green Mountains will be attended with success.' Requisitions remember—to defend New-York, their bitterest foe. Stark's reply was that his requisitions were attended with success; that upon a sudden alarm, five hundred and fifty mounted men from Vermont joined his troops in a few hours. Near the beginning of the armistice, Schuyler had written to Washington: 'It is believed that large offers have been made the Hampshire Grants, but that nothing will induce the bulk of them to desert the common cause.'

"Washington was privy to the secret policy of Vermont for some time—probably a month before the surrender of Cornwallis. This fact, stated by one of our historians, seems to have been discredited by all the rest. It is established by a letter long given up for lost (but recently discovered), and so alluded to by our historians as to excite suspicions that they had never seen it. Washington does not appear to have been perplexed by a British officer's apology for killing a Vermonter in a skirmish—an apology which enraged General Stark, and filled Vermont from side to side with indignation."

By this policy of Governor Chittenden, an army, equal in force to that of Burgoyne, was kept inactive in Canada—amused by the *finesse* of the governor, and his able coadjutors, till the war was virtually ended by the surrender at Yorktown.

To General Stark.

HEADQUARTERS. *Albany,*
November 6, 1781.

Dear Sir—Since my leaving Saratoga I have received a letter from Colonel Willet, giving a particular account of the action near Johnstown, and his pursuit afterward. The enemy were very precipitate in their retreat, leaving behind their packs, blankets, &c., which were found strewed through the woods. He pursued them eight miles beyond Canada creek. Before his arrival at that place, he fell in with about forty who were left in the rear to procure provisions. He instantly dispersed them.

At the creek he came up with their rear, when an action commenced, in which Major Walter Butler fell with a number of others. Finding his own provisions were very short, and the probability of coming up with their main force not very great, he wisely gave over the pursuit, leaving them in a situation promising little less than certain death. Cold, and the excruciating pains of hunger, will, in my opinion, produce a death more becoming such a plundering pack of murderers, than the bayonet or ball; and as they must have been, at his quitting them, at least eight days' march from any place where they could procure provisions, the purpose of an entire defeat must be very well answered. Inclosed is an order which I have received from General Heath. The returns I wish may be forwarded as soon as possible.

I am, sir, &c.,

STIRLING, *Maj. General.*

Brigadier General Stark.

To Major General Heath.

Saratoga, November 6th, 1781.

Dear Sir—I am honored with your letter of the 30th ult., and have directed Captain Robinson to inspect the troops you mentioned; but it will be very difficult to perform the business without paper, and I do not think there is at present enough in the garrison to make the rolls proper for inspection.

I have ordered all the teams I can possibly collect, to draw timber for two block-houses that Lord Stirling has directed to be built on this ground. I hope to get them finished in the course of a fortnight.

I have engaged with Colonel Sears that, in case his regiment will cut and collect the timber for one of them, they shall receive a discharge. I think this a very good bargain, and they have fallen to work with unremitted vigor. But, sir, remember the poor continental soldiers. They are now half naked and many of them unfit for duty, merely for want of clothing. If any can be sent to them, I beg no time may be lost, as the doctor tells me that inflammatory disorders are very epidemical in camp, and farther says the want of comfortable clothing is the occasion.

In case the regiments now here are destined to tarry the winter, I beg you to order the detachments to join them, as you must be sensible how inconvenient it is to have regiments mutilated as these are.

I beg, sir, you will accept my warmest congratulations on the late important event, that has crowned our wishes with another British general and his army. This event, I hope, will convince that infatuated nation how chimerical is the attempt of subjecting these States to her lawless will; and open their eyes to their true interest, which is Peace to themselves, and Freedom to America—the latter of which they cannot hope to enjoy.

I beg leave to suggest whether it would not be for the interest of the public to discharge Col. Reynolds' regiment immediately, as this frontier can be in no danger of an invasion between now and the 20th of January; and they are in reality using public provisions, and doing no service to the States, especially if continued on this frontier. If your opinion should coincide with mine, I beg you would let me know it as soon as possible.

I am, sir, your obed't serv't,

JOHN STARK.

[General Orders.]

HEADQUARTERS. *Continental Village,*
November 9, 1781.

The general has the pleasure of acquainting the army that the enemy have been completely disappointed in their designs on the northern frontiers of this State, in consequence of the measures adopted to receive them in the vicinity of the lakes, in which the general is much indebted to Major General Lord Stirling, Brigadier General Stark, and the officers and soldiers both of the regular troops and militia, who, with great zeal and alertness, pressed forward to meet the enemy.

That part of their force which was coming by way of the lakes not having dared to land on this side of them, Major Ross, who had advanced from the westward as far as Johnstown, with a body of six or seven hundred troops, regulars, Yaugers, and Indians, was met by Col. Willet, defeated and pursued into the wilderness, where many of them probably must perish. The number of the enemy killed is not known.

Major Butler, who has so frequently distressed the frontiers, is among the slain. A number of prisoners, chiefly British, have been taken and sent in.

The general presents his thanks to Colonel Willet, whose address, gallantry, and persevering activity on this occasion, do him the highest honor; and while the conduct of the officers and soldiers in general who were with Colonel Willet, deserves high commendation, the general expresses particular approbation of the behavior of Major Rowley, and the brave levies and militia under his immediate command, who, at a critical moment, not only did themselves honor, but rendered essential service to their country.

W. HEATH, *Maj. General.*

Extract from general orders.

THOMAS T. JACKSON, *Aid-de-Camp.*

HEADQUARTERS. *Albany,*
November 10, 1781.

Dear Sir—Your letter of the 7th came to hand yesterday evening. I think, by the accounts of Captains Emerson and Senter, it is reduced to a certainty that the enemy to the northward are returned to Canada, yet I could wish to hear from Captain Carr soon ; as, if the enemy do not accept of my proposals, I would send the prisoners of war now here down the river before the winter sets in, and let them take New-York in their way to Canada. Their number is increased to fifty odd. I have ordered some very good German steel to be sent you ; paper and wafers shall follow as soon as they can be procured. I will inquire into the state of the iron cannon, and send you two of the best of them. What you propose in regard to Colonel Reynolds' men, I will communicate to General Heath, and you shall have his answer in a very few days. I shall request him to send up the carpenters belonging to your brigade, who are now with the quarter master general's department. I send you inclosed a copy of Colonel Willet's loss in his late encounter with the enemy. I do not doubt but this will be the destruction of their whole party.

I am, sir, your most obedient, humble servant,

STIRLING, *Major General.*

General Stark.

To Brigadier General Stark.

HEADQUARTERS. *Continental Village,*
November 14, 1781.

Dear Sir—Your favor of the 6th instant came to hand last evening. I am sorry to hear you continue so short of paper. We suffer here equally with you; however, if possible, let the monthly returns be sent down in season.

I would have Colonel Reynolds' regiment discharged immediately, and the Massachusetts militia as soon as you can spare them. All camp utensils, ammunition, etc., drawn from the public, must be returned previous to their discharge.

I am happy in the prospect of the army's receiving a competent supply of clothing this year. A part of it is now in the store made up, and a large quantity of materials are near at hand. These must be made up by the regimental tailors. Every regiment, whether present or not, will have strict justice done it. I think the paymasters of the two New-Hampshire regiments had best come down immediately with their returns, made out and signed, conformable to the ordinance of clothing and late order, that they may be present at the distribution. I trust the tenth Massachusetts regiment and detachment of artillery are now on their way to this army.

It was my intention that the two New-Hampshire regiments should winter in the northern district. It is now rather uncertain, but the circumstances whether they will or will not are so nicely divided, that I can not now determine which will take place. They must, therefore, make every preparation as if to stay. I shall reserve their last year's huts for them, until the matter is determined. The artificers of the two regiments are ordered to join them. The detachments will do it also, as soon as it is known where the regiments take winter quarters, and they obtain some clothing. At present they are nearly naked. Please to forward the inclosed as speedily as possible to Colonel Reynolds.

With much regard, I am your obedient servant,

W. HEATH, *M. General.*

To Major General Heath.

Saratoga, 29th November, 1781.

My Dear Sir—Your two letters of the 14th and 21st inst. came safe to hand. I have discharged Col. Reynolds' regiment. The militia and levies at this post were dismissed previous to the arrival of your letters. The two block-houses mentioned in my last are nearly completed. The barracks are repairing by the soldiers, as well as they can be done without materials, but I can not hope that the soldiers can be rendered very comfortable without considerable alterations in clothing, fuel, &c. With respect to the latter, you observe that I have it "at command." In that suggestion you are certainly mistaken, for it can not be got without going a mile and a half for it. In your observations on the clothing, you mention that the materials are to be sent, and the clothes to be made by the regimental tailors. I must observe that there is but one tailor in the New-Hampshire line, and he a drunken rascal, that could be hardly compelled to make three coats in a winter.

You observe that few horses should be kept with the troops, and that the remainder should be sent to places where forage can be obtained. This argument I think very reasonable; but I can not find a man in this district who knows where that place is. But I suppose it is romantic to issue any more complaints, when experience has taught me that they are of so little value.

I can not sufficiently admire the magnanimous conduct of our soldiers. They certainly put knight errantry out of countenance; and all those whimsical tales which are generally supposed to have existed no where but in the brains of chimerical authors, seem realized in them.

But I fear that this virtue will not last forever; and, indeed, it is my opinion that nothing but their too wretched situation prevents an insurrection. However, I have not heard a syllable of the kind yet, and shall take every imaginable precaution to hinder it; and I hope that their firmness and my endeavors will prove efficacious.

Colonel Willet writes me that he has between eighty and one hundred men in his regiment, engaged for three years, and he is of opinion that two hundred men ought to be kept on the Mohawk river for its protection. This number, I believe, would be sufficient; a less number, I think, would be dangerous. But until the men are clothed, they can not be sent. Indeed they can hardly leave their barracks; and their distress is so great that it is difficult to keep the necessary guards.

When I have finished the block-houses, and got the barracks repaired, as well as our circumstances will admit, I shall retire to Albany, after which, as there can be little business for a general officer in this district, and the number of men will be so greatly diminished, and those scattered on the frontiers, I must beg leave to make a visit to New-Hampshire. I hope this request will meet your approbation, and that you will be pleased to signify it as soon as convenient.

I shall be ready to take the field whenever my services are required, but at present my domestic affairs strongly press my attendance. I have the honor to be, with the greatest respect and esteem,

Your most obed't serv't,

JOHN STARK.

To Brigadier General Stark.

HEADQUARTERS. *Highlands*, December 5, 1781.

Dear Sir—Your favor of the 22d ult., came to hand yesterday by Captain Carr. Upon having recourse to my files, I find my letters to you are two to one received from you; so that either you do not give me credit for all, or else part of yours to me, and mine to you, miscarry.

I most sincerely condole with you under our wants and embarrassments, for we experience every one of them equally with you, and some which you do not. In October the troops were ten days without bread—the last month more. We are equally naked and destitute of pay.

Materials are collecting for clothing—the whole army and every man will be clothed; but it will be late before it can be effected. It is said Mr. Morris is in hopes of making the army three months pay, at least in the course of this winter. You may assure the regiments with you that they shall have equal justice done them. My heart bleeds for their distresses, but the means of relief are not in my power.

The pay-masters of the 1st and 2d regiments will wait and receive the clothing for the regiment. The Honorable Mr. Morris, our financier, I hope will be able to put matters in a good way, but he must have time.

The time for which Colonel Willet's regiment is engaged expires the last of this month. If you have not already made a distribution of the regular troops to all the posts and places necessary, I would recommend to you to do it immediately. Please send Colonel Reid's regiment toward the Mohawk river, and let them seasonably relieve Colonel Willet's. Probably you may think it best to station a part of the regiment at Schenectady, and send detachments to the principal posts above, some of which are important. Fort Herkimer, in particular, has a considerable quantity of ordnance and military stores, which must be preserved, and the country protected as much as possible.

Please, therefore, to have such disposition made as will best effect the preservation of the public property, curb the enemy, and afford protection to the country. As soon as these arrangements are made, which should not be delayed a moment, please take effectual measures to have a supply of provisions sent up at the best season, sufficient to subsist the troops until the season arrives when they may obtain supplies again.

I have been informed that, in the late alarm, a number of public arms were delivered the militia, which have not been returned. I request you to inquire of Mr. Rensselaer, and find to what regiments they were issued, and let measures be taken to call them all in immediately. Colonel Dearborn, D. Q. M., has just arrived from the southward; he informs me he shall be able soon to send you some paper, etc. I am sorry to hear of your indisposition. I hope that you will soon recover your health.

I have the honor to be

Your obedient humble serv't,

W. HEATH, *Maj. General.*

To Major General Heath.

Saratoga, 12*th December,* 1781.

Dear Sir—I am honored by your favor of the 5th inst. I should have written an answer before, but I have sent to Bennington to gain the particulars of a riot raised some time ago, and which still continues at St. Coicks. The particulars are as follows: Men, under the direction of a Captain Abbot, assaulted a public house at Hoosac; seized upon Colonel Rensselaer and some others, who considered themselves under the government of New-York, and abused them in a most outrageous manner. After which they carried them to Bennington, and called upon the magistrates acting under the authority of Vermont for warrants to arrest them in (as they term it) a legal manner; but, upon the magistrates refusing to interfere in the matter, they were dismissed. Rensselaer, upon his liberation, represented the matter to General Ganesvoort, and invited his neighbors to join him and protect him from a second abuse, with which he was severely threatened. Ganesvoort approved his conduct, and ordered the militia on both sides of the North river above Albany to join them. Those persons called Vermonters discovered the motions of the Yorkers, and immediately collected their force within half a mile of the quarters of the Yorkers; and in this position the two detachments have continued nearly a week.

Yesterday, about twelve o'clock, the Yorkers were about two hundred strong, and the Vermonters about two hundred do. What I mean by Vermonters is those acting under Vermont within the twenty-mile line; for I can not learn that any have joined them belonging to old Vermont.

What the result of these two armies will be, I can not say, but hope they will compromise the matter without bloodshed. I think Congress would do well to interfere in the matter, pass some severe and decisive edicts, and see that they are put in execution before spring; otherwise, the consequences may be exceedingly serious, and perhaps dangerous.

I am sorry to hear that any troops suffer more than those in this quarter, (our enemy excepted); but, since some are more wretched, we must submit to our fate like good soldiers. I am sure it is not practicable for the troops that are here to go to the Mohawk river until they are clothed. Indeed, I am obliged to detain the six months' men to do the necessary camp duty, on account of the nakedness of the continental troops. In the last duty report, only thirty-six "three years" and "during the war" men, including sergeants, were fit for duty in the two regiments. The remainder are so naked that they can not procure fuel for their own use.

If there is any possibility of sending some blankets, shirts, overalls, stockings, and shoes, they might afford a temporary relief, and I dare say would prove satisfactory.

My predictions in my last were realized on the evening of the 10th instant. The troops mutinied; but, by the seasonable interposition of the officers, it was quelled very easily. But, sir, this may be but a prelude to an insurrection of a more serious nature.

Some of the most forward of the mutineers are in custody, and are to be tried by a court-martial. Mutiny is certainly a crime that deserves the severest punishment, but to punish one soldier for it, is unjust and cruel to the last degree. Whenever it is possible, I shall send the second regiment to the posts on the Mohawk river; but you must not expect impossibilities. However, Colonel Willet has between eighty and one hundred men engaged for three years. Those can garrison the posts until the continental troops are clothed.

I shall make inquiry of Mr. Rensselaer what arms were delivered out to the militia, and shall endeavor to have them returned. I never knew of any being delivered until your letter informed me.

You complain that my letters to you are not so frequent as yours to me. I have not received a single letter from you that I have not acknowledged; but I have been apprehensive that some of mine to you have miscarried, and am convinced that some of yours to me have never come to hand, but I am not able to determine the reasons for their miscarriage.

I am, dear sir, with regard and esteem,

Your obed't serv't,

JOHN STARK.

P. S. I never saw a thanksgiving before that was so melancholy. I may, I believe with safety, affirm that there will not be a thankful heart in this garrison, nor one that has cause to be satisfied with his circumstances. It may be argued that it is a blessing to have trials; but life without enjoyment, and replete with misery, is rather (in my opinion) a curse than a blessing.

To Brigadier General Stark.

HEADQUARTERS. *Highlands,*
December 12th, 1781.

Dear Sir—Your favor of 29th ult. came to hand last week. The soldiers will receive ample supplies of clothing, but it will be late before it is all ready. The paymasters of the New-Hampshire regiments have drawn shoes, hose, some overalls, shirts, &c., for the most necessitous men. These will be conveyed to Albany in a few days, when all the detachments will join their corps. The paymasters of the regiments think that the clothing can soon be made up for the men of your line.

Mr. Morris, the financier, wrote me yesterday that he had settled the arrangements of the forage with the quarter master general; so that, as soon as matters can operate, we shall have a supply. Colonel Pickering was expected at New-Windsor night before last. A quantity of paper, etc., is on the road from Philadelphia, and Colonel Dearborn, the deputy quarter master, assures me a supply shall be sent you. The good temper and patience of the troops, exhibited on all occasions, does them honor. I am happy in having the evidence of a prospect of their being well fed and well clothed; and I hope they will receive some pay.

I have not yet fully ascertained whether Colonel Willet's men, engaged for three years, will remain where they are this winter, or not. I have written Governor Clinton respecting them, but have not received his answer; I expect it hourly. I believe the posts usually occupied in the winter, and probably the best calculated to cover the country, are Saratoga, to the northward (from whence detachments can be made to Ballstown aud White creek); and Fort Herkimer, Fort Rensselaer, and Johnstown, on the Mohawk river, from which detachments can also be occasionally made to other small posts, in their respective vicinities, and Schoharie, about thirty miles west of Albany.

I am not so intimately acquainted with the importance of these different places, relatively considered, as to be able to determine what proportion of the troops each ought to have; but I think Colonel Reid's regiment ought to be destined to the western posts above mentioned, and not to be diminished by any detachments which may be necessary to leave at Albany or Schenectady for the security of the public stores. The northern frontier is not so extensive as the western, and can be easier supported by the militia. Let each post be properly and seasonably supplied with provisions. I wish to gratify your inclination in visiting your family, but wish you to remain a few days, as I hourly expect General Hazen in this quarter. As it may be equally agreeable to him to spend the winter at Albany, and as I should prefer having a general officer in the northern district, I will request him to repair there; if he declines it, Colonel Reid must exercise the command.

The light infantry have returned from the southward. No news in this quarter.

I have the honor to be, with great regard,

Dear sir, your obedient serv't,

W. HEATH, *M. General.*

To Colonel Yates.

HEADQUARTERS. *Saratoga,* 14th December, 1781.

Sir—Upon anxiously examining the nature of the disputes between New-York and Vermont, I am of opinion that violent measures at present would be attended with very evil consequences. If, therefore, Col. Rensselaer can be assured of protection of his person and property, together with positive assurances that his adherents shall remain in peaceable and quiet possession of their estates, and that their persons shall be preserved from indignities or insults until Congress shall determine the jurisdictional boundaries—till then, I say, I should think hostilities very dangerous.

Now, sir, considering the inconveniences of keeping men in the field at this season of the year, I imagine, if the above mentioned preliminaries are agreed to and ratified by responsible men on the part of Vermont, it would be prudent for you to withdraw your men; but, if your orders are to continue in your present station, you must obey. In that case, it would be advisable to apply to General Ganesvoort, or the officer who gave the orders, that they might be remanded.

I am, sir, your most obedient servant,

JOHN STARK.

Hon. Meshech Weare.

Saratoga, 14th December, 1781.

Dear Sir—Notwithstanding my letters to you seem to be treated with silent contempt, yet, when any thing intervenes where I think my country or the State of New-Hampshire in a particular manner deeply interested, I conceive it my duty, apart from common politeness, to inform you of it. Such I deem the late riotous conduct of the State of Vermont, in extending their pretended claim to the westward, and threatening to support it by a military force; and, indeed, those within the twenty-mile line are actually in arms, in open defiance and violation of the rules of Congress; and are actually opposing themselves to the troops raised by the State of New-York to put their constitution and laws into execution. Two detachments, one acting under the authority of Vermont, and the other under officers owing allegiance to the State of New-York, are assembled now at St. Coick, in opposition. For farther particulars I refer you to Captain Fogg, who will have the honor of delivering this.

I have been favored with a perusal of the proceedings of the legislature of Vermont State, on the subject of their being received into the Union of the United States, and find that they have not only rejected the resolutions of Congress, but in reality have disavowed their authority;

and I farther perceive that, in their great wisdom, they have thought proper to appoint a committee to determine whether New-Hampshire shall exercise jurisdiction .to Connecticut river or not. This proceeding appears too weak and frivolous. For men of sense to suppose that New-Hampshire would ever consent to an indignity so flagrant, and an abuse so pointed as this seems to be, is what I own surprises me. However, I hope, and indeed have no doubt, that New-Hampshire will be more politic than to take notice of this daring insolence. What I mean by notice, is to think of treating with them upon this or any other subject until Congress shall come to a final determination with respect to these people.

I am, sir, with high respect,

Your most obedient serv't,

JOHN STARK.

Arlington, December 15, 1781.

Dear Sir—I have consulted my council on the perplexed situation of this State, and have resolved to call the Legislature thereof to meet at Bennington, as soon as may be; at which time they will doubtless consult such measures as may tend to the peace and tranquility of this State and the United States.

In the meantime I earnestly request that you write to the officers of New-York, that are daily making depredations to the west, to suspend any farther operations of that kind until the assembly meet; and that, if they do not comply, you will not interfere with your troops. And I do assure you that if they comply with said request, and liberate the prisoners they have taken, I will suspend the exercise of jurisdiction or law over any person or persons who profess themselves subjects of New-York, during that time.

I am, sir, with sentiments of esteem,

Your most obed't and most hbl. serv't,

THOMAS CHITTENDEN.

To General Washington.

Albany, 21st December, 1781.

My Dear Sir—Although I am not the first that has addressed a congratulatory letter to you on account of your late glorious and unequalled success in Virginia, yet be assured that I am not behind the others in respect, or in the high opinion I entertain of the important and very essential service rendered my country by your capital acquisition. British standards will no more be the dread of neighboring nations, nor will her armies in future be deemed invincible. You have taught them the road to submission, and have manifested to the world that they are vulnerable; and no doubt the warlike nations with whom they are at variance, stimulated by your noble example, will give them farther proofs of their inability to trample on the laws of equity, justice and liberty with impunity. I hope that this may be the case, and that they may shortly be brought to a sense of their duty, and relinquish to us the invaluable blessings that the power of Omnipotence has placed in our view, and leave our country once more to taste the sweets of tranquil peace.

My exile has not been attended with any very interesting events. The enemy, to be sure, came as far as Ticonderoga; but when they learned the alacrity with which the militia turned out to defend their country, they returned, with shame and disgrace, without striking a blow at the northern frontiers. But the Mohawk river felt some of the effects of their inveterate malice. However, by the timely interposition of Colonel Willet, they were driven from that country with indignity. As the particulars must have come to your knowledge before now, I will not give you the trouble of reading them here.

During the time the enemy were hovering about Ticonderoga, a sergeant and a scout of the Vermont militia were attacked by a scout of the enemy. They killed the sergeant and took his party prisoners. When the party was brought to Ticonderoga, the commanding officer showed great dissatisfaction at the accident, treated the men with all imaginable tenderness, sent for the sergeant, and had him buried with the honors of war; after which he released the prisoners, with what provisions they chose to take, and they returned home with a letter from Lt. Col. St. Leger to Gov. Chittenden (as it was said), apologizing for the accident. Upon this coming to my knowledge, I addressed a letter to the governor, of which I inclose a copy, as likewise a copy of his answer. You will perceive, by his letter, he gives his reason for not sending to me, by affirming that he has sent the account of it to you. If so, I should be much obliged for a copy of the letter. I shall be farther obliged if you let me know whether he sent you the original or a copy. If he sent you the original, it must be satisfactory; otherwise, the case will still be doubtful in my opinion. I shall think that they dare not produce the original.

The proceedings of the Vermonters have been very mysterious, until about ten days ago, when they in a manner threw off the mask, and publicly avowed their determination to continue their claim of jurisdiction to the North river on the part of New-York, and to Mason's patent on the part of New-Hampshire, and did actually send an armed force, with a piece of artillery, to protect and defend their adherents on the west side of the twenty-mile line; and indeed have done little less than to wage war with the United States, who, I conceive, are bound, by every tie of justice and policy, to defend all its members from the insults of any enemy, internal or external.

I believe, sir, that I may venture to predict that unless something decisive is done in the course of this winter, with respect to these people, we may have every thing to fear from them that they are capable of, in case we are under the disagreeable necessity of making another campaign.

This may be considered as strange language from me, who have ever been considered as a friend to Vermont; and, indeed, I ever was their friend, until their conduct convinced me that they were not friendly to the United

States. Were I to judge by their professions, they are more mine and the State's friend now than ever; but their actions and their words appear to carry a very different meaning. During my command, I have been promised everything from their government and their leading men that I could wish for; but they have taken particular care to perform nothing, while, on the other hand, the militia of New-York, and those of Berkshire, attended to my requisitions with alacrity and uncommon spirit; and I believe the northern and western frontiers are in a great measure indebted to them for the protection of their houses, etc. I most sincerely wish that matters may turn out better than I expect, and am, with my best wishes for your health and happiness,

Your most obedient humble servant,

JOHN STARK.

Albany, *22d December*, 1781.

Dear Sir—I have received your favor of the 12th inst., and am under infinite obligations for the indulgence you are pleased to grant me. However, I shall not hasten from the district until matters are duly arranged, and I hope not till General Hazen arrives to take the command. If he is not already on the road, I should take it as a singular favor if he might be directed to proceed as soon as possible.

Colonel Reid addresses a letter by this conveyance. His domestic affairs are in a very fluctuating state, and render his presence very essential to his interest. It must be unnecessary to mention the difficulties officers and soldiers labor under for want of proper supplies, wages, &c. When all these difficulties are enumerated, you will easily perceive that the indulgences become almost necessity; and, without them, no officer, with a large family and in common circumstances, can continue in service. If, therefore, it is compatible with the public interest, it would certainly be a great favor if he could be permitted to visit his family in the course of the winter.

Your letter of the 17th has just come to my hand. I shall order the return you require to be made, and hope to be able to transmit it in a few days.

I am, dear sir, your obed't serv't,

JOHN STARK.

Major General Heath.

To General Stark.

Saratoga, 22d December, 1781.

Dear General—Here I am, alone, not a soul to speak a word to me but bruin and Mony. A dismal gloom overspreads this quarter at present. However, two d—m'd Indians favored me with their company this afternoon, and gave me a piece of venison, on which I intend to dine to-morrow. No —— but what the cursed Irishman asks too dear for. I am invited to keep Christmas with Mr. Ensign. I think that man must be a christian.

How did you get down to Albany? I hope you have good quarters. Pray let me hear from you every opportunity; in particular, I wish to have your directions with respect to the leather at Dickerson's. If you have not already wrote to General Heath, I pray you to write as soon as possible, representing my situation, and the pressing necessity of my being at home, and also please to forward any letters.

My kind compliments to Major Caleb. I wish to hear how my book comes on. No more writing—this is the last inch of paper I have.

Your prediction was right. I am informed, by a man from Peterborough, that your cousin Nathan and my cousin Abraham are really in the horse-stealing way.

I am, with esteem,

Your most obed't humble serv't,

GEO. REID.*

General Stark.

* Afterwards general of State militia, and father-in-law of late Governor Samuel Dinsmoor, Senior.

To General Stark.

HEADQUARTERS. *Highlands*,
December 25, 1781.

Dear Sir—Your favors of the 2d and 12th instants have come to hand; that of the 2d, by Major Villefranche, not until yesterday. The attention and abilities of that officer deserve commendation in every quarter where his services have been experienced.

I am very sorry to hear of the conduct of the Vermonters and Yorkers with you. I fear that there will, sooner or later, be serious consequences produced by their disputes. I transmitted your intelligence to Congress, and I request you will be pleased from time to time to communicate to me such other circumstances as may come to your knowledge.

The paymasters of the New-Hampshire regiments have drawn clothing of every kind, and will convey it up as soon as possible. The naked condition of those regiments led me to direct that they should be first served.

I hope that the time will soon arrive when the army will be relieved from many if not all of those distressing wants which they have long experienced. I trust the quarter master has relieved your wants of forage and paper. Please direct the returns to be made with as much punctuality as possible.

Congress has called upon the States to complete their respective quotas of troops by the first of March, determined to improve the late successes, and with the blessing of heaven bring the war to a speedy and honorable conclusion.

I have the honor to be,

With great regard, your obed't serv't,

WM. HEATH, *M. General.*

To Honorable General Stark.

Bennington, 12*th September*, 1786.

Dear Sir—This opportunity of presenting gratitude demands a few lines from me. I have had health in general since we saw each other, but have understood your health was much impaired before you left the camp; and since have learned it is much recovered, and wish you that blessing for a long time to come.

It is doubtless yet in your mind what I have mentioned concerning a right of land granted you in this State, for which I paid the fees. If you choose to hold the land, it is agreeable to me; but, when you wrote me last, you proposed quitting your right to me, and that without any pay. I send you a deed; if it is your choice to execute it, then I am secured for the money I have paid; and if you will take the ten dollars which I heretofore proposed, on your letting me know by a line, it shall be conveyed to you by the first safe opportunity; or if Mr. McGinnis satisfies you there, I will repay him here.

I am, sir, with respect,

Your obedient servant,

SAM'L SAFFORD.

N. B. Mine and Mrs. Safford's best compliments to the General, Mrs. Stark, and the Major.

To General Stark.

Monticello, August 19*th*, 1805.

Respected General—I have lately learned, through the channel of the newspapers, with pleasure, that you are still in life, and enjoy health and spirits. The victories of Bennington—the first link in the chain of successes which issued in the surrender at Saratoga—are still fresh in the memory of every American, and the name of him who achieved them dear to his heart.

Permit me, therefore, as a stranger who knows you only by the services you have rendered, to express to you the sincere emotions of pleasure and attachment which he felt on learning that your days had been prolonged—his fervent prayer that they still may be continued in comfort, and the conviction that whenever they end, your memory will be cherished by those who come after you, as one who has not lived in vain for his country.

I salute you, venerable patriot and general,

With affection and reverence,

THOMAS JEFFERSON.

[Answer.]

Derryfield, October, 1805.

Respected Sir—Your friendly letter of August 19th came to hand a few days since; but, owing to the imbecility inseparably connected with the wane of life, I have not been able to acknowledge it until now.

I have been in my 77th year since the 28th of August last; and, since the close of the revolutionary war, have devoted my time entirely to domestic employments, and in the vale of obscurity and retirement, have tasted that tranquility which the hurry and bustle of a busy world can seldom afford. I thank you for the compliment you are pleased to make me, nor will I conceal the satisfaction I feel in receiving it from a man who possesses so large a share of my confidence.

I will confess to you, sir, that I once began to think that the labors of the revolution were in vain, and that I should live to see the system restored which I had assisted in destroying.

But my fears are at an end; and I am now calmly preparing to meet the unerring fate of men, with, however, the satisfactory reflection that I leave a numerous progeny, in a country highly favored by nature, and under a government whose principles and views I believe to be correct and just.

With the highest considerations of respect and esteem, I have the honor to be, sir, your most obed't serv't,

JOHN STARK.

To the Hon. Maj. Gen'l John Stark.

Bennington, 16th August, 1806.

Respected Sir—By direction of a numerous and respectable body of Republican citizens of this and the adjoining towns, convened for the purpose of commemorating the glorious battle fought on the 16th of August, 1777, commonly called the Bennington action, the undersigned, in their behalf, are instructed to inform you of the grateful feelings they entertain for your person; that they duly appreciate the important and eminent services you rendered your country, and more especially the people of this vicinity, on this auspicious day.

They ever have and still consider your fortunate success on that day, achieved by the wisdom of your plans and the promptness of their execution, to have been a fatal check to the success of General Burgoyne, and which shortly after produced the surrender of his whole army to the American troops.

The few officers and soldiers yet living, who were immediately under your command, still hail you as their fortunate and brave general; while those who were their children or unborn, hail you as the patriot of your country, and acknowledge the blessings they enjoy from the prosperity of your arms.

The citizens, composing this meeting, are highly gratified when they learn, through the channel of the newspapers, that you still retain your affection and first love for your country, while many of your compatriots, in their opinion, have apostatized, and forgotten the important object of the American Revolution.

You have their fervant prayers that your days may be prolonged; not doubting (when they shall end) that posterity will hold you in honorable remembrance for the noble deeds you have done.

We tender you, venerable General,

Our warmest affection and esteem,

JOSIAH WRIGHT,
DAVID FAY,
JONAS GALUSHA,
JONATHAN ROBINSON,
WILLIAM TOWNER, } *Committee.*

To General Stark.

Bennington, July 22, 1809.

Honored and Respected Sir—You can never forget that, on the memorable 16th of August, 1777, you commanded the American troops in the action called Bennington battle, and that, under divine providence, astonishing success attended our arms. Our enemy was defeated and captured, and this town and its vicinity saved from impending ruin. It has been usual to hold the day in grateful remembrance, by a public celebration.

On Thursday last, a large and respectable number of leading characters in this and the neighboring towns, met to choose a committee of arrangements for a celebration on the 16th of August next. More than sixty of those who met were with you in the action. They recollect you, sir, with peculiar pleasure, and have directed us to write and request you, if your health and age will permit, to honor them with your presence on that day. All your expenses shall be remunerated.

No event could so animate the brave "sons of liberty," as to see their venerable leader and preserver once more in Bennington; that their young men may once have the pleasure of seeing the man who so gallantly fought to defend their sacred rights, their fathers and mothers, and protected them while lisping in infancy.

Should this request be inconsistent with your health, we should be happy in receiving a letter from you, on that subject, that we may read it to them on that day. Sentiments from the aged, and from those who have hazarded their lives to rescue us from the shackles of tyranny, will be read by them with peculiar pleasure, and remembered long after their fathers have retired to the silent tomb.

Accept, sir, our warmest wishes for your health and happiness, and permit us, dear general, to assure you that we are, with great esteem,

Your cordial and affectionate friends,

GIDEON OLIN,
JONATHAN ROBINSON, } *Committee.*
DAVID FAY,

[Answer.]

AT MY QUARTERS. *Derryfield,*
31st of July, 1809.

My Friends and Fellow Soldiers—I received yours, of the 22d instant, containing your fervent expressions of friendship, and your very polite invitation to meet with you to celebrate the 16th of August in Bennington.

As you say, I can never forget that I commanded American troops on that day at Bennington. They were men who had not learned the art of submission, nor had they been trained to the arts of war; but our "astonishing success" taught the enemies of liberty that undisciplined freemen are superior to veteran slaves.

Nothing could afford me greater pleasure than to meet your brave "sons of liberty" on the fortunate spot; but, as you justly anticipate, the infirmities of old age will not permit it, for I am now more than fourscore and one years old, and the lamp of life is almost spent. I have of late had many such invitations, but was not ready, for there was not oil in the lamp.

You say you wish your young men to see me; but you who have seen me can tell them I never was worth much for a show, and certainly can not be worth their seeing now.

In case of my not being able to attend, you wish my sentiments. These you shall have, as free as the air we breathe. As I was then, I am now, the friend of the equal rights of men, of representative democracy, of republicanism, and the declaration of independence—the great charter of our national rights—and of course a friend to the indissoluble union of these States. I am the enemy of all foreign influence, for all foreign influence is the influence of tyranny. This is the only chosen spot of liberty—this the only republic on earth.

You well know, gentlemen, that at the time of the event you celebrate, there was a powerful British faction in the country (called tories), a material part of the force we contended with. This faction was rankling in our councils, until it had laid a foundation for the subversion of our liberties; but, by having good sentinels at our outposts, we were apprised of the danger. The sons of freedom beat the alarm, and, as at Bennington, they came, they saw, they conquered.

These are my orders now, and will be my last orders to all my volunteers, to look to their sentries; for there is a dangerous British party in the country, lurking in their hiding places, more dangerous than all our foreign enemies; and whenever they shall appear, let them render the same account of them as was given at Bennington, let them assume what name they will.

I shall remember, gentlemen, the respect you and the inhabitants of Bennington and its neighborhood have shown me, until I go to the "country from whence no traveller returns." I must soon receive marching orders.

JOHN STARK.

Hon. Gideon Olin,
Jonathan Robinson, Esq., } *Committee.*
David Fay, Esq.,

Note. The general forwarded in this letter, as his volunteer sentiment: "*Live free, or die*—Death is not the worst of evils."

To the Hon. General John Stark.

Bennington, July 25th, 1810.

Once more the season has arrived for the celebration of that auspicious day, when you sir, at the head of our brave yeomanry, under the benevolent hand of a superintending providence, led our troops to victory on the memorable hill of Walloomsack. The people of the adjacent counties have resolved to celebrate the day on the consecrated ground. For this purpose they have chosen a large and respectable committee from the surrounding towns. The governors of the States of New-York and Vermont will be invited, and probably attend; hundreds of your fellow-citizens, who fought by your side, and thousands of other republicans, will be present on the pleasing occasion. Nothing can be wanting, to make our joys complete, but the presence of our venerable friend and commander, whom, with American pride, we style "the hero of Bennington."

In your patriotic address to us last year, we regret that you tell us that the oil is almost extinguished in the lamp, and that age has rendered it impossible for you to attend, although we are again pressed by our fellow-citizens to give you an invitation to come and join in the festivities of the day. The toast, sir, which you sent us in 1809, will continue to vibrate with unceasing pleasure in our ears: "*Live free, or die*—Death is not the worst of evils."

Never, never, sir, shall we cease to recollect, with the most ardent affection, the man who made the arrangement, and who, at the hazard of his life, executed the plan with such decision and success. And while your sword was waving on the high places of the field, the cries of thousands of our oppressed fellow citizens, like a cloud, rolled before the Eternal. Heaven heard, and led you and your brave fellow-citizens to glory and victory.

Accept, Dear General, the expression of our warmest gratitude, and of our highest esteem, and believe us to be

Your cordial friends,

JONATHAN ROBINSON,
ELEAZER HAWKS,
DAVID FAY, } *Committee.*

[Answer.]

Derryfield, 20th September, 1810.

My Friends—Yours, of the 25th of July, is but just received, inviting me to partake of your festival. Had not your letter been stopped in its passage to me, its contents could have made no difference, for it is now eighty two years since I have been in wear, and I am worn beyond all hope of repairs. The disease and pain, attending the last stage of life, render many of the surrounding objects that I once delighted in indifferent to me. But if any thing could have given me pleasure, it would to have been with you on the 16th of August.

A scene like that must have brought to my recollection the principal events of my life. I could remember how British tyranny arose, and how it yielded to the untutored bravery of democracy, and particularly, as being on that fortunate spot, with so many of the brave men who taught the tyrant's tools the hard lesson.

In your letter, you praise me extremely for being the fortunate commander of valiant men. To merit the praise of my country, has been a leading motive of my life. Unmerited praise is satire; therefore we should be careful not to bestow too much praise, unless we mean to satirize. You mention being pleased with the toast I gave you last year. I have the best evidence that the people of your rugged country do sincerely accord with such sentiments, for in '77 you displayed evidence by practice. And I have no doubt if we had a Congress now, who had the resolution to express the will of the nation, you would be found as ready as you were then.

Be assured of my friendship for yourselves and the other inhabitants of the Green mountains, and accept my thanks for their respect.

JOHN STARK.

Hon. Jonathan Robinson,
Eleazer Hawks,
David Fay.

President Madison to General Stark.

Washington, December 26, 1809.

Sir—A very particular friend of yours, who has been much recommended to my esteem, has lately mentioned you to me in a manner of which I avail myself to offer this expression of the sense I have always entertained of your character, and of the part you bore as a hero and a patriot in establishing the independence of our country.

I can not better render this tribute, than by congratulating you on the happiness you can not fail to derive from the motives which made you a champion in so glorious a cause; from the gratitude shown by your fellow-citizens for your distinguished services, and especially from the opportunity which a protracted life has given you of witnessing the triumphs of republican institutions, so dear to you, in the unrivalled prosperity flowing from them, during a trial of more than a fourth of a century.

May your life be continued as long as it can be a blessing, and may the example it will bequeath never be lost upon those who live after you.

JAMES MADISON.

Gen. John Stark.

To James Madison, Esqr., President of the United States.

Derryfield, January 21, 1810.

Sir—I had yesterday the pleasure of receiving an address from the first magistrate of the only republic on earth. The letter compliments me highly upon my services as a soldier, and praises my patriotism. It is true, I love the country of my birth, for it is not only the land which I would choose before all others, but it is the only spot where I could wear out the remnant of my days with any satisfaction.

Twice has my country been invaded by foreign enemies, and twice I went out with her citizens to obtain a peace.

When tha objectt was attained, I returned to my farm and my original occupation. I have ever valued peace so highly that I would not sacrifice it for any thing but freedom; yet submission to insult I never thought the way to obtain or support either.

I was pleased with your dismissal of the man* sent by England to insult us: because she will ascertain by the experiment, that we are the same nation we were in '76, grown stronger by age, and having gained wisdom by experience.

If the enmity of the British is to be feared, their alliance is still more dangerous. I have fought by their side, as well as against them, and have found them to be treacherous and ungenerous as friends, and dishonorable as enemies. I have also tried the French: first as enemies, and since as friends; and, although all the strong prejudices of my youth were against them, still I have formed a more favorable opinion of them than of the English. Let us watch even them.

But of all the dangers from which I apprehend the most serious evil to my country, and our republican institutions, none requires a more watchful eye than our internal British faction.

If the communication of the result of my experience can be of any service in the approaching storm, or if any benefit can arise from any example of mine, my strongest wish will be gratified.

The few days or weeks of the remainder of my life will be in friendship with James Madison.

JOHN STARK.

*The British envoy.

CHARLESTON, *South Carolina,*
August 29th, 1811.

Sir—In conformity to a resolution of the "Seventy Six Association" of this State, we, their standing committee, hereby transmit for your perusal a copy of an oration, delivered on the Fourth of July, by Benjamin A. Markley, Esq., a member of that institution.

We remain, sir, with great respect and esteem, your obedient humble servants,

JOS. JOHNSON,
J. B. WHITE,
WILLIAM LAUCE,
JOSEPH KIRKLAND,
MYER MOSES.

To General Stark.

[From the Farmer's Monthly Visitor.]

We received the following letter from that indefatigable antiquarian, Henry Stevens, Esq., of Barnet, Vt. We most cheerfully comply with his request, and give it a place in our columns. We presume the cannon, spoken of by Judge Witherell, is one of the two afterward surrendered by General Hull, which were subsequently recovered by our army at Fort George, and is probably one of the two now at Montpelier, as trophies, having been by act of Congress presented to Vermont. We hope the remaining two cannon, of the four taken at Bennington, which the venerable Stark was wont to call "my guns," may be recovered, and placed by permission of Congress in the State House at Concord, as trophies won by her worthy sons.

Detroit, 26th May, 1811.

Venerable General—On examining the fort of this place, a few days past, I perceived in one of the embrasures a handsome brass cannon, with this inscription on it: "John Stark. Taken at Bennington, the 16th of August, 1777." This, together with the situation in which I found it, forcibly drew my mind not only to a retrospect of the revolutionary war, but still farther back, to the records of transactions too remote for my observation; and I could not but view the fortuitous circumstance of its being placed on these walls, as a sort of pledge for the future safety of this place, as well against those from whose martial hands we wrested it, on the embattled plains of Walloomsack, as the descendants of those savages who felt the chastisement of your arms, near this fort, in the memorable ambuscade of the 31st of July, 1763. I have often contemplated the spot with horror, where fell by your side the brave Captains Dalyell and Campbell; where the bridge, from the blood of two hundred and thirty out of three hundred British troops, and that of one hundred out of two hundred provincials, is to this day emphatically called "Bloody bridge."

I was much gratified with the feeling narration of this transaction, by a man of the name of Maxwell, who served under you in that campaign, who, while he related the events, frequently attempted to wipe away the encrusted tear from his furrowed cheeks, often exclaiming: "Ah, is my old Captain Stark still living?"

But, though death is a severe muster master, you have parried his stroke until he has arrived at the very Zed of the revolutionary alphabet, by which you have been enabled to view and contemplate vast portions of your native country freed from the savage knife, and from civil tyranny; in effecting which, to have borne so conspicuous a part, must remain a fruitful source of consolation, even to the very last fragment of your furlough; at the end of which, when summoned to head quarters, to join the main body of patriots and heroes who have long since marched for that station, that you may pass a good muster, and finally receive a pension which will support you through the war of elements, is the sincere wish of

Dear General, your most obed't serv't,

J. WITHERELL.

The Venerable John Stark, Esq.

Dr. Bentley was born at Boston in 1758; graduated at Harvard College in 1777; and was (September 24, 1783) ordained as pastor of the second church at Boston. He afterward removed to Salem, where he resided until his death, which occurred suddenly December 29, 1819, at the age of 61 years.

For nearly twenty years he edited the Essex Register, a paper which supported the political principles of the democratic republican party.

He collected, in the course of his life, a large library of rare and valuable books, as also a cabinet of curiosities and minerals. He was well versed in ancient literature.

His benevolence was well known, and experienced by all whose necessities demanded his assistance.

Masters of vessels, and even seamen, in requital of his kind actions and friendship, when visiting foreign countries remembered him, by bringing home some rare or curious article to add to his collection.

We have been informed of one instance where a party of American seamen, from Salem, who were in Italy during the victorious career of General Bonaparte, observing the French soldiers taking from churches and palaces the valuable paintings of ancient masters, to be forwarded to Paris to grace the triumph of the conqueror of Italy, during the confusion, secured one of them, which was in due time presented to Dr. Bentley.

His valuable library and cabinet were bequeathed principally to Meadville College, in Pennsylvania, and the American Antiquarian Society, of Worcester.

Harvard College probably expected the donation, having conferred upon him the degree of D. D. some short time before his death; but the honor was perhaps too long withheld.

His library was more needed, and may probably be more useful at Meadville. His eulogy was pronounced by Hon. Edward Everett.

He published a sermon on Matthew 7 : 21, in 1790 ; on the death of J. Gardner, 1791 ; of General Fiske, 1797 ; of B. Hodges, 1804 ; a collection of psalms and hymns, 1795 ; three masonic addresses ; and a masonic charge, 1797–99 ; at the artillery election in 1796 ; on the death of J. Richardson, 1806 ; before the female charitable society, at the election of 1807 ; a history of Salem, contained in vol. 6 Mass. Hist. Collections.

Dr. Bentley was a warm friend and admirer of General Stark, whom he several times visited at his residence on the banks of the Merrimack, and with him kept up a friendly intercourse until his own decease.

On one occasion he informed the general that he intended to deliver his eulogy on the occasion of his demise, and had prepared his notes. "Suppose, my chaplain,"* replied the veteran, "your call should come first ?" The general survived his friend nearly three years, and all the American generals of the Revolution, thus making good the saying formerly applied to him, "First in the field, and last out of it."

Major General John Stark.

Salem, Mass., August 30, 1805.

My Dear General—I have just received, with the greatest pleasure, a letter from the President of the United States, inclosed to me but directed to you. In his letter to me the President writes : "Forward the expressions of my respect and esteem for the venerable General Stark, whose name, lately mentioned in the newspapers, excited in me at the same time the sensations which the recollections of his services were calculated to inspire. Disinterested esteem and approbation can not be unacceptable to any one. I therefore solicit your delivery of the inclosed letter to him, &c."

* The general frequently addressed Dr. B. as "my chaplain."

I doubt not this best attention from the man most deserving of the highest honors of his country, so freely expressed, will be welcome to the hero who gave the first serious check to the military power of Britain, when employed against his country.

I am preparing to obey all your commands. Be pleased to assure the major* and his family of my affection, and ask him to inform me of the receipt of this letter; and believe me, with the greatest veneration, and with the highest sense of your personal merit and public services,

Your devoted servant,

WILLIAM BENTLEY.

Salem, Mass., June 18, 1810.

My Dear General—The likeness my young pupil, Miss Hannah Crowninshield, took, proved to be a good one.† All your friends knew it instantly. The inclosed is a copy. The original is as large as life. She is taking a copy for President Madison; and then I intend to get it engraved, and painted in oil colors. Any corrections will be accepted, as she had only one sitting.

With veneration and respect,

Your sincere friend,

WILLIAM BENTLEY.

General John Stark, Derryfield.

* Major Caleb Stark.

† The likeness taken by Miss Crowninshield was the one from which, with alterations, was engraved the portrait at the head of this volume. We have been informed that the above named lady married Captain Armstrong, of the United States Navy. In the portrait, the artist who prepared Miss Crowninshield's painting for the lithographer, gave too much length to the neck and face. The forehead is also too narrow. He was about five feet nine inches in height. The portrait of Major Stark by S. F. B. Morse resembles the general more than that at the head of this volume. A person came to obtain a likeness of General Stark immediately after his decease. Major S. was there; and the artist, in completing his work, frequently looked from the face of the dead to the living resemblance there present.

Salem, December 1, 1810.

My Good General—My packets of papers will prove that I have not forgotten you. One friend after another has promised to convey them to you from Salem, without going the circuitous route, by your worthy son at Boston; but after repeated disappointments, I return to my old route.

Your southern friends all inquire after, and delight to honor you.

Believe me, that I never am more happy than in every expression of my veneration of General Stark, and every opportunity of evincing my readiness to serve him.

With the highest respect,

Your devoted servant,

WILLIAM BENTLEY.

General John Stark.

Salem, May 31, 1811.

My Father—I long to pay another visit to Manchester. All your friends inquire for you. An officer told me lately, that, on a public occasion, he drank as a toast: "General Stark," and a British officer present remarked, "that is the hero who took me." We have a deep interest in your welfare. If any thing in my power can give you pleasure, command.

With duty and affection,

WILLIAM BENTLEY.

To General John Stark, Manchester, N. H.

P. S. I send you papers by every opportunity; I would send them daily if I could. Please ask your son, when he sees my friend Stickney, to beg of him a few specimens of such fossils, stones, minerals, earths, &c., as are within his reach, and much oblige one who will reward him to his full satisfaction.

W. B.

Salem, August 13, 1811.

My Worthy General—I have inclosed you eight packets of newspapers, &c., which I had no opportunity of forwarding, and now send by your son at Boston.

I am obliged to inform you that your old friend, Captain Addison Richardson, left us last Wednesday, as firm as at the first. The great and the good inquire after, and remember you.

With all my heart, and the highest respect,

Your obedient friend,

WILLIAM BENTLEY.

Hon. General Stark.

Salem, December 2, 1811.

My Good General—The communication between Salem and Manchester is so indirect that I have few opportunities of sending to you, save by the circuitous route of Boston. If you will charge your neighbors, who visit Salem, to call on me, I should have the pleasure oftener of discovering that I remember you. I sent five packets by your son, who lately honored me with a visit.

With the papers, I send you a book which has in it this value: it treats of our Indian affairs, which threaten serious trouble.

Believe me most rich, when I imagine I can afford a momentary pleasure to the man to whom my country owes its salvation.

In all duty,

WILLIAM BENTLEY.

Gen. John Stark.

Copy of a letter from David Pierce, Esq., of Gloucester, Mass., to Rev. William Bentley, of Salem, dated 19th February, 1814, on the subject of the "General Stark" armed ship, in 1780, which captured three large ships from London for Quebec, valued, with their cargoes, at $400,000.

Sir—The "General Stark" was built under my direction. In one cruise, in three weeks, she sent me $300,000, I having sold some part of her.

She was a ship of 350 tons; twenty guns on her lower deck, eight guns on her half deck, and two on her forecastle—a very fast sailer and very stiff. I named her in honor of General Stark.

This copy was sent to the general by Dr. Bentley, accompanied by a drawing of the ship by Miss Crowninshield.

GENERAL JACOB BAYLEY.

THE grand-father of General Bayley, of "French war" and revolutionary notoriety, was the son of Joshua, who was the son of John Bayley, who emigrated from Chippingham (England) in 1635, and settled in Newburyport, Massachusetts. The general was born at Hampstead, N. H., in 1728.

He was well known on both sides of the Connecticut river, from 1759 until his death in February, 1815, and rendered valuable services in the "seven years' war." He afterward served with ability and reputation during the revolution.

In 1755–6 he held the rank of colonel, and in August, 1757, was at Fort William Henry, which, after a siege of nine days, capitulated to the Marquis de Montcalm. On this occasion he is said to have escaped the ensuing massacre, by running bare-footed seven miles, to Halfway brook, outstripping a party of Indian runners, and reached Fort Edward in safety.

He was present in Montreal, at the capitulation of Canada, September 8, 1760; after which, having obtained leave of absence on furlough, he visited his home. Being of an adventurous spirit, rather than pass down the Bennington road, he took a point of compass intending to strike the head waters of the Merrimack, but happening to arrive at the Connecticut, in the northern part of Newbury, (now so called, and named by him) he discovered that most beautiful of all the valleys of New-England, comprising the Great Ox Bow and other intervals.

He selected this interesting location for his future residence, and, after the close of the war, emigrated thither through a wilderness, from the residence of Colonel Webster, in Plymouth—his being the last dwelling-house on the route from the English settlements to Canada.

At the commencement of the revolution he joined the noble spirits of the time—was appointed commissary general of the northern division, and served throughout the war.

His fireside narratives, in after life, were full of interest. "Many thrilling incidents and hair breadth escapes," says his grand-son, "I have heard from his lips, which have now escaped my memory. He once run the gantlet, after capitulation (probably at Fort William Henry). He was once taken by two Indians from his home, to be conveyed to Canada, where a reward had been offered for his capture. He managed to escape by extending his feet, tripping up both of them, and running for his life."

"Many incidents of his history have escaped my recollection. One of much consequence at the time, and of important interest to himself and his posterity, I will state. He furnished and became responsible for supplies, of which the army was in the utmost need. He consequently became involved, mortgaged his property, and finally disposed of it all to discharge his obligations in an honorable manner. I well recollect seeing him writing petitions to Congress for relief; but he never obtained any, nor have his heirs, although the claims were ascertained after his decease to have amounted to about sixty thousand dollars. Republican gratitude—or rather American ingratitude, was in this, as in thousands of other cases, strongly exemplified."

The following anecdote we heard from a revolutionary veteran many years ago:

In the year 1784, an elderly gentleman, in a plain dress, travelling on horse back, stopped for the night at a tavern, near King's bridge, about fifteen miles from New-York city, as it then was. He was conducted to the only spare room in the house, in which he had hardly been comfortably established, when a party of young "roaring blades," the sons of wealthy citizens, arrived at the tavern, "to make a night of it." They called for a private room, but were informed by the landlord that his last spare chamber had just been taken possession of by a respectable appearing elderly gentleman, apparently from the country.

"Try the old fellow," said one of them, "perhaps you can coax him to let us into his room for our spree, and we'll soon smoke him out."

The host applied to his guest, who readily assented. He observed, "he was alone, and would be happy to meet a pleasant company of young gentlemen to help him spend the evening." The party soon assembled; liquors were produced, and an excellent supper brought forward, at which the good natured old gentleman played his part as well as the best of them.

After this, one of the youngsters proposed an agreement that who ever of the company should refuse to perform or submit to any proposal made by either of the others, the recusant or recusants should forfeit the whole bill, and the damages of all the others. To the astonishment of the young gentlemen, the stranger agreed to the terms.

The first proposed to burn their hats, and each threw his hat into the fire; coats, vests, and watches followed, the old gentleman throwing into the fire his old fashioned silver turnip, as a companion to the gold watches of the young rowdies.

When his turn came, he called the landlord and requested him to send for a doctor, and his tooth instruments. The doctor soon appeared. The old gentleman then seated himself in a chair, and said: "I propose that the doctor shall draw out every tooth in the heads of this company. Doctor begin with me." The latter found but one, which he extracted. "Now, gentlemen," said the veteran, "submit to my proposal, and ascertain whether you have turned the flanks of an old soldier."

The young men perceived that they were out-generaled; and learned that General Bayley was the person with whom they had attempted to trifle, and to their cost. They apologized—paid liberally his bill and damages, having learned a valuable lesson for their future government. The general, newly equipped with a better outfit than when he left home, proceeded on the next day to New-York, to settle his army accounts.

Extract from a letter written by General Bayley, at Newbury, many years after the close of the war:

"I could not with safety leave the frontier, where I was settled, and join the army. I thought I could be of more service to our cause by securing an extensive frontier from the depredations of the Indians, which, by making friendship with them, I effected for at least two hundred miles. My exertions were such that I was watched and waylaid night* and day, by the enemy from Canada —my house rifled, papers destroyed, son carried captive, and maltreated only because he was my son, and would not discover to them how his father obtained intelligence of their movements. To the close of the war I was employed by Washington to keep friendship with the Indians, and gain intelligence of the enemy in Canada."

It has lately transpired that President Wheelock interceded with his former pupil, Brandt, the Indian chief, and not without success. Moreover, proof is not wanting that the British colonel, Johnson, was taken prisoner by John Warner, but released on condition of the Indians being restrained from Vermont. But our frontier settlements, however safe, were by no means secure—rather out of danger, than free from apprehensions. One of our his-

*Gen. Bayley was so closely watched by the tories in his vicinity, employed by the authorities of Canada, whose scouts often attempted his capture, that his friends dared only to warn him secretly of the approach of the enemy. To have given him notice openly, would have ensured their own captivity, and the destruction of their dwellings. When a friend desired to put him on his guard against tory liers-in-wait, he dropped in his path a paper on which were written these words: "The Philistines be upon thee, Sampson."

torians narrates a panic in Windham county—he might have spoken of another in Windsor county—when the inhabitants along the White river fled, many of them by night, lighted by brands of fire, down the river to Lebanon, "when," says an eye witness, "families are this moment rushing into Newbury; and for sixty miles they are upon a doubt whether to remove or not.

Women yet live who can testify of such days; when they lived in fear of the fate of Miss McRea, the bride of Fort Edward—that Gertrude of Wyoming in real life; when every rustle of a shaken leaf seemed an Indian tread, every tree an Indian covert, every window a mark for his rifle, and every hamlet fully assured that it was singled out, above all others, as the victim of the savage." *

Extract from Powers' History of Coös.

"I have already stated how desirable an object it was with the British to get possession of Gen. Jacob Bayley. A bold and determined effort to effect this was made on the 17th of June, 1782, while Col. Johnson was at home on *parole.* (He was a prisoner of war).

"Gen. Bayley lived at the Johnson village, in a house where now stands the brick house of Josiah Little. Capt. Prichard (British) and his scout, to the number of eighteen men, lay upon the heights west of the Ox-Bow, and made a signal for Johnson to visit them.† Johnson went, as he was bound to do by the terms of his parole, and learned that they had come to capture Gen. Bayley that evening. Johnson was now in a great strait. Bayley was his neighbor, and a host against the enemy, and Johnson could not have him go into captivity; and yet, he must seem to con-

* Butler.

† Johnson was bound by the terms of his parole, to present himself at all times before the enemy's scouts, upon *certain* signals being made from their places of concealment, and to convey no information of their presence to his friends.

form to the wishes of Prichard, or he would be recalled to Canada himself, and in all probability have his buildings laid in ashes.

"Johnson returned to his house, and resolved to inform Bayley of his danger, at the hazard of every thing to himself. But how was this to be done? Bayley, with two of his sons, was plowing on the Ox-Bow. Prichard's elevated situation on the hill enabled him to look down upon the Ox-Bow, as on a map. The secret was entrusted to Dudley Carleton, Esq., the brother of Col. Johnson's wife. Johnson wrote on a slip of paper this laconic sentence: 'The Philistines be upon thee, Sampson!' He gave it to Carleton, and instructed him to go on to the meadow, pass directly by Bayley, without stopping or speaking, but drop the paper in his view, and return home by a circuitous route. Carleton performed the duty assigned him well. Gen. Bayley, when he came to the paper, carelessly took it up and read it; and as soon as he could, without exciting suspicion in the minds of lookers-on, proposed to turn out the team, and said to his sons: 'Boys, take care of yourselves!' and went himself to the bank of the river. The sons went up to the house to carry the tidings to the guard who were stationed there. The guard consisted of Captain Frye Bayley, commandant; Ezra Gates, Jacob Bayley, Jun., Joshua Bayley; Sergeant Samuel Torrey, a hired man of Gen. Bayley; three boys, John Bayley, Isaac Bayley, Thomas Metcalf; and a hired maid, Sarah Fowler.

"Although the guard was apprised of the general's apprehensions, yet, it would seem, they thought his fears were groundless, for they were taken by surprise at early twilight, while they were taking their evening grog; or, we might more significantly say, perhaps they were taking in a freight of prowess, to be tested at a later hour of the night. The enemy were not discovered until they were within a few rods of the front-door. Sergeant Torrey met them at the door, and presented his piece at them; but Prichard knocked aside the gun, made Torrey prisoner, and the enemy rushed in. The guard dispersed in all directions; Ezra Gates was wounded in the arm by a ball, as he ran from the south front-door, and a gun was discharged at John Bayley, as he was jumping the fence to run for the Ox-Bow, and two balls lodged in the fence close to him. Thomas Metcalf reached the meadow, where he tarried all night. Gates was brought in and laid on the bed, where he lay bleeding and groaning, while the enemy were searching the house for prisoners and papers. 'But there was one belonging to the house who displayed great presence of mind and intrepidity. It was a woman!—woman, who in ten thousand instances has risen superior to danger, and performed astonishing deeds of heroism, when man, her lord by constitution, has forfeited his claim to superiority, by timidity and flight.'

"Sarah Fowler, the servant-maid spoken of, remained upon the ground, with a babe of Mrs. Bayley in her arms, undismayed at the sight of loaded muskets and bristling bayonets, and repeatedly extinguished a candle which had been lighted for the purpose of searching the house. Not succeeding with a candle, one of the parties took a fire brand and attempted to renew the search; the dauntless maid struck it from his hand, and strewed the coals around the room. This was too much for British blood, and one of the soldiers swore, by a tremendous oath, that if she annoyed them any more he would blow out her brains, showing at the same time how he would do it. She then desisted, as she had good reason to believe he would execute his threat.

"Mrs. Bayley had, at the outset, escaped through an eastern window, and lay concealed in current-bushes in the garden. The enemy having destroyed one gun, and taken what papers they could find, commenced their retreat, greatly disappointed in respect to the main object of their pursuit, for the general was resting securely on Haverhill side. They took with them prisoners Gates and Pike, the hired man of General Bayley, and proceeded south. An alarm was given, but not in time to arrest the enemy. About half a mile south, they met James Bayley, son of General Bayley, whom they took prisoner, and kept until the close of the war. * * * * * * * .*

"This failure of the British, in the main object of their expedition, brought fresh trouble upon Colonel Thomas Johnson. The tories in the vicinity, who had laid the plan for taking General Bayley, learning that he was not at home that night, and knowing that he was not in the habit of being absent from his family over night, unless on business out of town, said at once, Johnson was a traitor to their cause, for he must have given Bayley information of his danger. * * * * * * * The disposition to peace in the mother country, and the actual treaty before the year came about, saved Johnson from the calamities threatened.

GENERAL JOSEPH CILLEY.

JOSEPH CILLEY was born at Nottingham, in New-Hampshire, in 1735, of which town his father, Captain Joseph Cilley, was one of the earliest and principal settlers. With few advantages of education, he became a self-taught lawyer in consequence of his residence in the midst of a law-seeking community. Before the revolutionary war commenced, he was one of those ardent patriots who seized and brought away the cannon and military stores from the fort at Portsmouth.

Immediately after the commencement of actual hostility, on the plains of Lexington and Concord, he marched, at the head of one hundred volunteers, to the theatre of action.

He was by Congress appointed a major, and in July, 1777, was colonel of a regiment in the army then occupying Ticonderoga. With his gallant regiment he performed a chivalrous part in the actions with General Burgoyne's invading army, near Behmus' heights, at Saratoga.

On the 19th of September his regiment first encountered the enemy, and suffered a more severe loss than any other regiment engaged.

He heard the British colonel give the order to fix bayonets, and charge those d—d rebels; and retorted, loudly enough for the enemy to hear his words: "that is a game two can play at. Charge, and we will try it."

His regiment advanced, delivered their fire, and, under cover of the smoke, closed with the bayonet. The enemy gave way, leaving on the field sixty killed and wounded. On the 7th of October his regiment captured a portion of the enemy's field artillery; and with the eleventh regiment of the Massachusetts line, forced their way with the bayonet into the British camp. In this encounter, Colonel Breyman, of the German grenadiers, was killed; and the British troops separated from their German allies.

At Monmouth, when General Lee ordered a retreat of his division, Colonel Cilley ordered his regiment to advance. They boldly attacked the advanced guard of the enemy and drove them back. By this timely check, the fortune of the day was retrieved. Washington arrived with the remainder of the army, and the action recommenced. Pleased with the gallant stand made by Cilley, the general inquired, "What troops are these?" "True blooded Yankees, sir," was the colonel's emphatic reply. "I see," said General Washington—"they are my brave New-Hampshire boys."

When the army retreated from Ticonderoga, in 1776, a son of Colonel Cilley (Jonathan) was left behind. He was but a boy, and his captors, learning who he was, brought him to General Burgoyne. The latter treated him kindly, and set him at liberty, with permission to select any article he pleased from the captured* baggage of the Americans. He selected the best regimental coat he could find, which proved that of Major Hull (afterwards General Hull). He was also furnished with an old horse, and a pair of saddle-bags, filled with Burgoyne's proclamations, to convey to his father. He found him in front of his regiment on parade. The colonel seized one of the hand-bills, which,

* After the evacuation of Ticonderoga, many reams of continental paper fell into the hands of the enemy. It was divided in due proportions among the British officers. The younger ones, in derision of the yankee money, used it for lighting their pipes, while the veterans stowed it away among their effects.

After the surrender of Burgoyne's army, this paper was discovered to be of value, and would purchase for the holders as many necessaries as would British gold.

Jonathan Cilley might, under the privilege granted by Burgoyne, have demanded a few quires of these paper apologies for money, and perhaps they would have been given him.

after reading, he tore into pieces, and scattered them to the winds, saying, "thus shall his army be scattered."

He served throughout the war with reputation. On the 22d of June, 1786, he was appointed first major general of the New-Hampshire militia, and served the State in various civil capacities. From this time, he advised the people to compromise their lawsuits. He died in August, 1799, aged 64 years. He was a man of temperance, economy, great industry, decision of character and sound judgment. His passions were strong and impetuous; his determinations prompt, and his disposition frank and humane. He was a decided republican in politics.

Portions of this notice have been gathered from Allen's Biographical Dictionary, and the remainder from the conversations of the late Major Caleb Stark, who, in 1776 and 1777, was adjutant of the first New-Hampshire regiment, commanded by Col. Cilley.

During the confused night retreat from Ticonderoga, General Kosciusko, not finding his own, took the first saddled horse that came in his way. It belonged to the adjutant of Colonel Cilley's regiment, who, not finding his horse where he left it, proceeded on foot until daylight, when he discovered the Polish general mounted upon his horse, and demanded his property, which the other refused to give up. High words ensued, and the adjutant demanded satisfaction. The general replied that "a subaltern is not of sufficient rank to meet a brigadier general." "If he is not," said a third person, coming up on foot, "I am. This officer, general, is my adjutant; the horse is his property, and his demand is a proper one."

"Ah, Colonel Cilley," replied the general, "if that is the case, I will give up the horse." The adjutant recovered his horse, but, in half an hour afterward, Colonel Cilley, who had also lost his horse, said: "Stark, I am tired; you must lend me your horse"—which request was of course complied with.

During the armistice, prior to the peace of 1783, several American officers visited New-York. Rivington, the king's printer, kept a book-store, which was a lounging place for British officers. At this time an American officer entered the store, purchased several books, which he directed to be sent to his lodgings; and, calling for a pen, wrote his name and address. "What," said a British colonel, half reclining on a sofa, "an American officer write his name!" "If I can not," was the prompt answer of Colonel Cilley, "I can make my mark;" and suiting the action to the word, drew his sword, and applied the flat of it to the British officer's face. The latter departed, saying that he "would hear from him." The intrepid colonel, however, heard no more of him.

COLONEL MARINUS WILLET.

Colonel Willet was one of the bravest, most vigilant, and enterprising officers of the New-York line. He was at Fort Stanwix when that post was invested by Colonel St. Leger, with a force of more than 2,500 regulars, tories, and Indians, on the 3d of August, 1777. On the 6th, he sallied out with a party from the fort, and bravely attacked the enemy, to favor the approach of General Herkimer with aid to the garrison. The latter was unfortunately defeated and slain.

In a few days, Colonel Willet and another officer effected a march through the wilderness, to the German flats, to raise a force to succor the besieged fort, which, however, under the command of Colonel Peter Ganesvoort, held out against St. Leger, until a rapid march of General Arnold, with a strong force, and the consequent desertion of his Indians (who learned the fact of the approach of Arnold, when he was thirty miles distant), compelled him to raise the seige and retreat to Canada, thus depriving Burgoyne of the support of 1,500 good troops.

In the years 1780–81, Colonel Willet commanded Fort Rensselaer, on the western frontier. He was charged with the defence of the Mohawk river, and the western settlements, where his prudence, foresight, and decision of character rendered important services. On the 25th of October, 1781, he defeated the enemy at the battle of Johnstown. He died at New-York, honored and respected, in August, 1830, aged ninety years.

In several letters of Generals Washington, Heath, Stark and others, contained in this volume, his services are highly complimented. The latter general, who in 1781 commanded the northern department, often in after years spoke with approbation of the efficient support he received during his command from the gallant Colonel Willet.

[Account of the Battle of Johnstown.]

To Major Rowley.

FORT RENSSELAER, *24th October*, 1781,
9 o'clock, P. M.

Dear Sir—I am this moment informed by Mr. Lewis, of Correytown, that the enemy in considerable force passed through the lower part of that town about sunset, making toward the river. I am collecting all the forces in this quarter, and shall advance toward them as quickly as possible. As they are in your quarter, I have no doubt of your exertions in collecting as many of the men of your regiment as possible. I wish you to have them all collected in a body, without any loss of time. And as it is likely you may be somewhat acquainted with the particular route of the enemy, sooner than I shall, I wish you to take such a position as you may think best, and make me acquainted with it, together with the whole of your situation, and every information you can procure, as fast as possible.

I am, sir, your obed't serv't,

M. WILLET.

P. S. I think it will be best for you to forward this letter to Schenectady as soon as possible, that the people below may be acquainted with this intelligence, that such measures may be taken as the officer there commanding shall see fit.

M. W.

To Lord Stirling.

SCHENECTADY, 26*th October*, 1781,
6 o'clock, P. M.

My Lord—Last night, about 10 o'clock, I sent Mr. Van Ingen, a young gentleman who is my clerk, to Colonel Willet, in order to bring the particulars, who this moment returned. The colonel had no time to write. He has made a statement of what has happened, as near as he can recollect (he has been on the spot where the action was), which I herewith inclose.

Colonel Wimp, with the greatest part of his regiment, and the Albany militia, with about thirty Indian warriors of the Oneidas, left this place in the morning for Colonel Willet. Colonel Schuyler's regiment went on this afternoon. I look out for the ammunition, which will be forwarded the moment it arrives. Please excuse my bad writing. I am in a great hurry.

I am your Lordship's most obed't serv't,

H. GLEN.

Major Ross, commanding officer at Buck's island, with about 550 men, left that place in bateaux, and proceeded to Oneida lake, where they left their boats, some provisions, and about twenty lame men to take care of them. They proceeded from thence by way of Cherry valley, to the Mohawk river, and made their first appearance at a place opposite Anthony's nose. They then proceeded to Warren bush, and in its vicinity destroyed upward of twenty farm houses, with out-houses containing large quantities of grain, and killed two persons.

After this they crossed the Mohawk river at a ford about twenty miles above this place, and proceeded in order to Sir William's hall, where they arrived about a quarter of an hour before Colonel Willet and his detachment, who had crossed the river six miles higher, and marched, also, for the same place.

Colonel Willet commenced an action with the British, which was much in his favor, when part of his troops, who covered a field piece, gave way, which occasioned the loss of the piece and ammunition cart,* but which, a short time after, he bravely recovered. The enemy, however, had stripped the cart of all the ammunition. The evening coming on put an end to the action.

Part of Colonel Willet's men, however, possessed the hall all night. The enemy retreated about six miles into the woods, where the last accounts, just now come in, leave them. About thirty British have been taken during the action and the morning before.

The action commenced yesterday in the afternoon, and Colonel Willet went in pursuit this morning, with a force about equal to the enemy's. An account has also come to hand (although not official), that a party sent from Fort Herkimer took their boats and provisions. Seven of the enemy's dead and three of ours were found on the field of action this morning. Between thirty and forty were killed and wounded on both sides.

6 o'clock, P. M. For Major General Lord Stirling.

This party of five hundred and fifty were so roughly handled by the intrepid Colonel Willet, that they returned to Canada with but two hundred men. Many perished in the wilderness of hunger, their boats and provisions having been cut off, and their retreat greatly harrassed. Colonel Walter Butler, notorious for his cruelties at Wyoming and Cherry valley, was slain.

Colonel Willet had with him a party of Oneida Indians, who, he said, furnished the best cavalry for wood service. The enemy made a precipitate retreat, leaving behind their packs, blankets, &c., which were found strewn through the woods. Colonel Willet pursued them eight miles beyond Canada creek. Before his arrival there, he fell in with a party of forty, who had been left in the rear to procure provisions, whom he instantly dispersed. At the creek he came up with their rear, when an action com-

*At this juncture Major Rowley, of Massachusetts, arrived with a party of Colonel Willet's men, and attacked the enemy with great bravery.

menced, in which Walter Butler and a number of others fell. Butler attempted to escape by swimming the creek, but was fired at and wounded by an Oneida. He turned and called for quarter, but the Indian, throwing down his gun and blanket, dashed into the stream and soon came up with Butler, still earnestly begging for quarter. The Oneida answered, "Cherry valley," buried a tomahawk in his brain, took his scalp, and rejoined his party.

In passing through the region of western New-York at this period, it was easy to ascertain, at a glance, who were whigs and who were disaffected (tories in all else but taking up arms), the houses and estates of the latter being respected by the marauders from Canada, while those of the former were plundered or destroyed.

MAJOR CALEB STARK.

On the 20th of August, 1758, Captain John Stark, of his Britannic majesty's corps of American rangers, while on a furlough from the army, was married to Elizabeth, daughter of Caleb Page, Esquire, who also held his majesty's commission as captain of provincial militia, and was one of the original grantees of "Starkstown," now known as Dunbarton, New-Hampshire.

In the spring of 1759, his furlough having expired, and a new company having been enlisted, the hardy soldier returned to his post at Fort Edward, prepared to perform his part in the next campaign, which, under the vigorous direction of the Earl of Chatham, was destined to reduce Louisburg and Quebec, and open the way to the entire conquest of Canada.

His wife was left at home, with her father, one of the most prominent and wealthy pioneers of the settlement, under whose hospitable roof the subject of this notice was born, December 3, 1759, during the absence of his father. The capitulation of Canada, in 1760, terminated the war in the north, and the provincial troops returned to their homes.

Soon after these events, there being no immediate prospect of active service, Captain Stark resigned his commission in the army, and withdrew, with his wife, to his paternal acres, at Derryfield, now Manchester, New-Hampshire.

The good Captain Page, entertaining a strong affection for the child who had been born under his roof, and had received his christian name, was desirous of retaining and adopting him. To this proposition his father made no objection, and he remained under the indulgent care of his maternal grand-father until the 16th of June, 1775.*

The best works of the time were procured for his improvement, and he obtained a good education for that period. The two principal books were Fenning's Dictionary and Salmon's Historical Grammar, which are still preserved in the family.

The tragedy enacted at Lexington, on the nineteenth of April, 1775, having aroused the martial spirit of New-England, Captain Stark abandoned his domestic occupations, and hastened to the theatre of action, in the vicinity of Boston, followed by most of the old corps of "rangers" who had served under his orders during the previous war, and others from the province, who were eager to prove their devotion to the cause of liberty.

The daring acts of valor, which had so frequently distinguished the career of the veteran Stark, combined with his military experience and success, left him no competitor in the minds of his countrymen in arms, by whom he was unanimously elected colonel, and in a few hours a regiment of nearly nine hundred men was enlisted for one year.

These proceedings were soon known in the northern settlements, and his son, then under sixteen years of age, whose memoir we are writing, made an earnest application to his grand-parent for permission to repair to the camp at Medford. The latter remonstrated with him, on account of his extreme youth, saying that although his father was familiar with scenes of strife and carnage, the camp was not a fit place for one of his years; and there the matter for a short time rested.

* This interest in the child of his adoption continued unabated until the close of his life; and in the division of his large estate, his favorite grandson was assigned an equal portion with his own children.

Not, however, dissuaded by these representations, the young man resolved to go at all events; and having secretly collected his clothing in a valise, without the knowledge of the family, and before day-light on the morning of June 16, 1775, he mounted a horse which had been given him by his grand-father, and with a musket on his shoulder, started for the American camp.

After travelling a few miles he was joined by another horseman. The stranger was a tall, well-formed, fine looking person, wearing the undress uniform of a British officer. He inquired politely of our young adventurer who he was, and where he was going; and upon being informed that he was proceeding to the camp at Medford, to join his father, Colonel Stark, the stranger said: "You are, then, the son of my old comrade. Your father and I were fellow-soldiers for more than five years. I am travelling in the same direction, and we will keep company."

The stranger was the celebrated Major Robert Rogers, of "French war" notoriety. As they journeyed on, the major insisted on defraying all the road expenses, and toward evening took his leave, transmitting to his old associate in arms, Colonel Stark, a message, soliciting an interview at a tavern in Medford.* Upon the arrival of our youthful patriot at the regimental head quarters, his father's first greeting was: "Well, son, what are you here for? You should have remained at home." The answer was: "I can handle a musket, and have come to try my fortune as a volunteer!" "Very well," said the colonel; and addressing Captain George Reid, he continued: "Take him to your quarters; to-morrow may be a busy day. After that we will see what can be done with him."

*We have reason to suppose that the object of Major Rogers' visit to America, in 1775, was to sound public opinion and ascertain the relative strength of the opposing parties, to enable him, in the choice of service, to make the best personal arrangement which circumstances would permit. At this interview, as we have been informed, Colonel Stark assured him that no proffers of rank or wealth could induce him to abandon the cause of his oppressed country. "I have," he said, "taken up arms in her defence, and, God willing, I will never lay them down until she has become a free and independent nation." The veteran lived nearly forty years after this object of his most fervent wishes and laborious toils in the field of honor had been accomplished.

The morrow, in truth, was a "busy day." A force, composed of detachments from the Massachusetts and Connecticut lines, under the command of Colonel William Prescott, moved, on the evening of the 16th of June, with instructions to fortify "Bunker's hill," but misapprehending their orders, proceeded about one mile farther, and commenced an intrenchment on "Breed's hill," a lesser eminence, which was commanded by the guns of the opposite battery on Copp's hill, in Boston, as well as exposed to the fire of the ships of war at anchor in the harbor.

At daylight, on the 17th, a furious cannonade opened upon the half-finished "redoubt," and soon after, in compliance with an order from General Ward, two hundred men were detached by Colonel Stark to support the parties employed on that rude field-work. Later in the day (about 2 P. M.), another order was received, directing him to march with his whole regiment, to oppose the enemy who were landing in great force at "Morton's point."

As previously stated in the preceding pages, the New-Hampshire line, under Colonel Stark, formed the left wing of the American force on this ever memorable occasion, and gallantly repelled the reiterated attacks of some of the choicest battalions of the British light infantry.

Our young "volunteer" proceeded, with the company under Captain George Reid (to whose care he had been so summarily assigned by his father the previous evening), to the position occupied by the regiment at the rail-fence, extending from the redoubt to the beach of Mystic river, where an opportunity was soon afforded for testing the skill and facility with which he could "handle a musket" in his country's cause. Side by side with some of the veteran rangers of the "old French war," he stood at his post on that eventful afternoon; and when their ammunition was nearly expended, and the occupation of the redoubt by the British marines and grenadiers had decided the fate of the day, he returned unharmed* to Winter hill, where the regiment was subsequently intrenched.

* During the action a man was killed at his side, and it was reported to his father that he had fallen.

On this pleasant eminence, a few miles from the city, were located the handsome residences of several wealthy loyalists, whose opinions having rendered them obnoxious to the American party, on the commencement of hostilities, had abandoned their dwellings, and taken refuge in Boston. Among them was a gentleman named "Royal," who, on retiring to the city, had left his lady, with a family of beautiful and accomplished daughters, in possession of his abode. The mansion being conveniently situated for his "head quarters," Colonel Stark called upon the family, and proposed, if agreeable to them, his occupancy of a few rooms for that purpose; to which Madame Royal most cheerfully assented, being well aware that the presence of an officer of his rank would afford her family and premises the best protection against any possible insult or encroachment, not only from those under his immediate command, but also from other detachments of the patriot forces.

His proposal was made, not with the tone of authority, but rather as the request of a private individual; and it is almost unnecessary to add, that during the intercourse which ensued, the family were always treated by Colonel Stark and his officers with the utmost consideration and respect.

During the remainder of this campaign our young soldier was acquiring, as a cadet in Captain Reid's company, the principles and practice of the military discipline of the day; and, when not actually engaged with his new duties, many of his leisure hours were naturally passed at the "head quarters" of his father, where his association with the refined and well educated ladies of the house could not but exert, at his age, the most favorable influence over the formation of his habits and manners. And when referring, in after years, to this period of his life, the subject of this memoir has frequently acknowledged the advantages derived from the intercourse it was then his privilege to hold with this amiable and interesting family.

On the re-organization of the army, early in the succeeding year (1776), young Stark received his first commission as "ensign" in Captain George Reid's company, and proceeded with the regiment, which constituted a portion of Sullivan's brigade, to New-York, and thence, in May, to Canada, where our New-Hampshire troops, under that able and resolute general, rendered important service in checking the advance of Sir Guy Carleton, and covering the retreat of the forces which had invaded that province the preceding season under Montgomery and Arnold.

The retrogade movement of the army, always discouraging to the young soldier, was rendered more so on this occasion by the accompaniment of a dangerous and loathsome malady, the small-pox, which, as innoculation was not in general use in those days, rapidly spread among the officers and men, converting the camp into a vast hospital. Among the victims of this contagious disease was the adjutant of the first New-Hampshire regiment, who died at Chimney point, in July. And Ensign Stark, who had been previously performing, during a portion of the campaign, the duties of quarter master, although then under seventeen years of age, was deemed qualified to succeed to the vacancy, being already distinguished for his energy of character and promptness of action, as well as for the proficiency attained in all the details of military discipline and duty. Promotion to the grade of lieutenant accompanied this appointment.

After the retirement of Sir Guy Carleton to winter quarters in Canada, the regiment, with others from the northern department, marched to reinforce the dispirited remnant of the main army, under General Washington, in Pennsylvania. Cheerfully sharing all the hardships and privations which were endured by the army, at this gloomiest period of our revolutionary struggle, Adjutant Stark was also an active participator in the brilliant operations at Trenton and Princeton, with which the campaign was so successfully closed in New-Jersey.

In January, 1777, the army being cantoned on the high lands about Morristown, the first New-Hampshire regiment was dismissed, the term of enlistment of the men having expired. In company with his father, young Stark was now enabled to revisit his native State, where the next few months were employed coöperating with the other officers of the regiment in raising recruits for the ensuing campaign.

Several junior officers having been promoted to the rank of "brigadier," over the heads of some of the veteran colonels of the army, Colonel Stark could not, consistently with a decent self-respect, continue to retain a commission which compelled him to serve under officers of less experience than his own. On his resignation, the command of the regiment was assigned to Colonel Joseph Cilley, an officer of undoubted courage and firmness, in every respect qualified to succeed him; and Lieutenant Stark, having been re-appointed adjutant, repaired with the troops to Ticonderoga, in the spring of 1777.

Those who are conversant with military affairs will readily appreciate the important bearing of the adjutant's duties on the discipline and efficiency of the regiment. It is no disparagement to the individual courage and conduct of the officers and men composing the same, to remark that the steadiness and precision with which all the evolutions of this regiment were performed, when in the presence of the enemy on various occasions during this campaign, afforded satisfactory evidence of the faithfulness with which the duties of his office were discharged by the subject of this memoir.

After the evacuation of Ticonderoga, and the retreat of the American army to the North river, General Schuyler was superseded in the command of the northern department by General Gates. Young Stark happened to be present on duty at the head quarters of that general,*

* While General Gates was rejoicing at the reception of tidings announcing the first success in the north, an aid-de-camp mentioned to him that a son of General Stark was awaiting an interview, with a message from Colonel Cilley. "Is he?" said Gates; "call him in." When he appeared, the general said: "I am glad to see you, my boy. Your father has opened the way for us nobly. In less than two months we shall capture Burgoyne's army. Don't you wish to see your father?" The adjutant replied, that "if his regimental duties would permit, he should

when the intelligence of the Bennington success was received by express, and being permitted to accompany a small party sent to open a communication with General Stark, he was soon enabled to congratulate his father personally on that brilliant achievement; and, after a few days' absence, rejoined his regiment, which was the first to come into action on the 19th of September.

In the action of October 7, 1777, he was wounded in the left arm. Soon after the capitulation of Saratoga, General Stark, having received from Congress the commission of brigadier general, which had been justly due to him the year previous, selected his son for his aid-de-camp. During the years 1778 and 1781 he discharged the duties of aid-de-camp, brigade major, and adjutant general of the northern department, then commanded by General Stark. He was a good writer for one of his years, and from the period of his appointment as aid-de-camp, wrote the letters of the general's official correspondence. In the campaign in Rhode-Island, in 1779, he acted as aid-de-camp to his father, in which capacity he was present at the battle of Springfield, in 1780.

After the close of the revolutionary war, his attention was directed to mercantile pursuits: first at Haverhill, Mass., and afterward at Dunbarton, N. H. He was for a time concerned in navigation, and owned several vessels.

be glad to visit him." "I will find an officer," said Gates, "to perform your duties, and you may go with the party I shall dispatch to Bennington, and convey a message from me to your father. I want the artillery he has taken for the brush I soon expect to have with Burgoyne." He proceeded with the party. The houses along their route were deserted by their owners, but abounded in materials for good cheer. From the residences of fugitive tories they obtained ample supplies for themselves and horses during their march.

After the surrender, he accompanied General Stark on a visit to General Gates, and at his head quarters was introduced to all the British officers of rank who were there assembled as the guests of the American general-in-chief of the northern army.

He said that Major Ackland and General Burgoyne were, in personal appearance, two of the best proportioned and handsomest men, of their age, he had ever seen.

General Burgoyne held a long conversation with General Stark, apart from the other company, on the subject of the French war, of which the former then stated that he intended to write a history.

In 1805–6, he became an importing merchant at Boston, in the English and East-India trade. In the course of his commercial transactions he visited the West-Indies in 1798, and Great Britain in 1810, where he spent a year making purchases for himself and other merchants of Boston. While in England he travelled through a large portion of the kingdom, and his observations furnished an interesting journal. He also kept a journal during his residence in the West-Indies.

After the declaration of war, in 1812, he closed his mercantile affairs at Boston, and purchased an establishment which a company had commenced at Pembroke, N. H., which he furnished with machinery for manufacturing cotton. To this he devoted his attention until 1830, when, having disposed of his interest in the concern, he proceeded to Ohio to prosecute his family's claims to lands granted for military services, which, in 1837, after a vexatious course of law-suits, were recovered. He died upon his estate in Oxford township, Tuscarawas county, Ohio, August 26, 1838, aged 78 years, 8 months and 23 days.

In 1787 he married Sarah, daughter of Dr. William McKinstry, formerly of Taunton, Mass., (who was, in 1776, appointed surgeon general of the British hospitals at Boston). She died September 11, 1839, aged 72. Of their eleven children (five sons and six daughters), five are now living. Major Stark's remains lie in his family cemetery at Dunbarton. His monument bears the following inscription:

IN MEMORY OF

MAJOR CALEB STARK,

ELDEST SON OF

MAJOR GENERAL JOHN STARK,

Under whose command he served his country in the war of American Independence. He entered the army at the age of 16, as quarter master of 1st N. H. Regiment; was afterward adjutant of the same, and subsequently brigade major and aid-de-camp to General Stark. He was present at the battle of Bunker's hill, in 1775; at Trenton, in 1776; at Princeton, and in the actions of September 19th, and October 7th, 1777, which immediately preceded the surrender of Burgoyne.

BORN DECEMBER 3, 1759: DIED AUGUST 26, 1838.

In person, Major Stark was rather above the middle height, of a slight, but muscular frame, with strong features, deep-set, keen, blue eyes, and a prominent forehead.

He much resembled his father in personal appearance. His characteristics were indomitable courage and perseverance, united with coolness and self-possession, which never deserted him on any emergency.*

He was the youngest survivor of the action who appeared to witness the ceremony of laying the corner stone of the Bunker hill monument, by the Marquis la Fayette, by whom he was recognized at once as a fellow-soldier. During his tour to New-Hampshire, the illustrious guest of the nation and his suite were entertained at his mansion in Pembroke.

Major Stark was one of the twelve revolutionary veterans who stood by General Jackson, at the ceremony of his first inauguration as President of the United States, and was personally acquainted with all the presidents, from General Washington to General Harrison, inclusive.

[Copied from an Ohio paper of August 31, 1838.]

"PATRIOT DEPARTED. Died, on Sunday evening last, at his residence near New-Comerstown, in this county, Major Caleb Stark, of New-Hampshire. Though confident that on this occasion ample justice can not be done to the memory of Major Stark, yet entire silence on the subject would not be tolerated by that portion of the community who know his public services, and his worth.

* When the pension act of 1820–21 was passed, Major Stark (as former brigade major) being personally known to all the officers and most of the soldiers of the New-Hampshire line, his testimony secured pensions to all whose cases he represented at the war department.

Most of the veteran applicants who sought his assistance had some reminiscence of their military days to relate. One of them, Captain Daniel Moore, spoke of the sinking of a flat-boat in the middle of the North river, in which himself, Major S., their horses, and the oarsman were the only passengers. "While I was considering," said the captain, "what excuse I should make to the general for losing his boy, the boy's presence of mind and activity effected arrangements which enabled us all, with the horses, to reach the shore in safety, although in a well-soaked condition."

"He was the son of General Stark, of New-Hampshire, the hero of Bennington. At the age of fifteen he entered the army of the revolution, and commenced his career at the battle of Bunker's hill, as a volunteer in his father's regiment. He remained in service until the close of the war, which found him a brigade major. In the engagements which resulted in the surrender of General Burgoyne, he was adjutant of the regiment commanded by the brave Colonel Cilley, grand-father of him who fell in the duel last winter at Washington.

"At the close of the war he retired to private life. He afterward was extensively engaged as an importing merchant at Boston, and subsequently as a manufacturer of cottons at Pembroke, N. H. He owned and cultivated a large farm, and contributed the results of many agricultural experiments to the public journals.

"He possessed a highly cultivated and active mind, for the improvement of which he suffered no opportunity to pass neglected.

"His memory was strong, and his stores of information, derived from travel or extensive reading, were ever at command. He had the reputation of being one of the best military critics of the nation; and was often consulted, especially during the war of 1812, when our army had but few experienced officers.

"He came to Ohio to prosecute the claims of his family to lands granted to General Stark for military services, in which, after a tedious litigation, he was successful. It was his intention, after he had succeeded in recovering this valuable estate, to have returned to his family in New-Hampshire, but sudden indisposition and death prevented its being carried out.

"Major Stark, in all his acts and movements, exhibited the prompt decision and energy of the soldier. Indeed, his whole course appeared to be influenced by the habits acquired while fighting the battles of freedom in the war of the revolution. At the season of life when habits are generally formed, his education was acquired in the tented field, in the laborious marches, counter-marches and privations of that fearful struggle, devoting his moments of leisure to useful study; and, in his duties abroad, pressing forward with indomitable resolution and confidence in himself.

"From the effects of this habitual perseverance resulted, as is supposed, the immediate cause of his death. He had attended court at New-Philadelphia on the 16th of August; and on the 17th, which was a very warm day, rode a hard travelling horse from Dover to his residence, twenty-three miles, in three hours! On the following week he was attacked with a disease in the head, and suspension of his faculties, which, with some intermissions, continued until his death, on Sunday evening last, at the age of 78 years, 8 months and 23 days."

The subject of the following article, from the pen of Major Stark, has long since been dismissed from public attention, by the adjustment of American claims against France. As it contains the sentiments of an old soldier, of strong mind, as well as an attentive observer of all public events from the commencement of the revolution until his decease, in 1838, it may perhaps be interesting to many yet living, who remember the veteran writer.

[Copied from the Tuscarawas (Ohio) Advocate, of March 31, 1835.]

"*Mr. Douglass.* If you think the following desultory remarks will be either instructive or amusing to the public, you may publish them, unless they are in the way of more interesting matter.

A considerable portion of the historical facts are from memory, many of which I have never seen published; but I can say as Virgil makes Æneas say: "Many of them I saw, and part of them I was."

FRENCH SPOLIATIONS.

This knotty question has called forth the maledictions of the president against the French nation.

The matter has now reached a crisis at which every real American should pause and consider. Let them take a retrospective view of our own history, and see how far we have observed good faith, national honor, and integrity, as well with our own citizens, as with other nations and individuals, who patronized us in the heart-rending struggles which were endured when this country was conquered from Great Britain.

To illustrate these intricate subjects, it is necessary to treat of them under separate heads. I will commence with the French relations.

Early in the revolution, it was considered an object of the first importance to engage, if possible, the French in our cause.

Mr. Silas Deane, and other agents, were sent to France to feel the pulse of the king and nation upon the subject. The French court, smarting under their losses and mortifications incurred in the "seven years war," observed a cautious indifference. They neither acknowledged the agents nor directed them to leave the kingdom.

It was not so with individuals, among whom was M. Beaumarchais, who, on his own account and credit, furnished the United States with twenty thousand stand of arms, and one thousand barrels of powder, of one hundred pounds weight each. These were immediately hurried off to America. Ten thousand of the muskets were landed at Portsmouth, (N. H.), and the remainder in some southern State.

With those landed at Portsmouth, the army stationed at Ticonderoga, for the defence of the northern frontier, was immediately equipped, and great exertions made by the officers to instruct the soldiers in their use.

We will pass over the disastrous retreat from Ticonderoga, during which, although the American army lost their cannon, and most of their baggage, they preserved these precious arms, and reached North river with inconsiderable loss. There the same indefatigable exertions were continued in disciplining the troops for ulterior action.

The first opportunity of testing the qualities of the new French muskets occurred September 19, 1777, when the Americans left their lines and advanced, without trepidation, to meet the veterans of Britain in the open field. The result of that day belongs to history. The two armies, after this action, lay in their intrenched camps (reserved rights) until the 7th of October, when both armies simultaneously quitted their camps and met in deadly contact on the vacant ground between their lines.

On that all important day the Beaumarchais arms, followed by their yankee comrades, after forcing the enemy from the field with great slaughter, leaped boldly into his camp, drove his forces from part of it, capturing a portion of his artillery, and discomfiting his whole army. Ten days afterward that army were prisoners of war, and the corner stone of independence so firmly placed that it could not be shaken or removed. The treaty of 1783 confirmed its foundation.

I firmly believe that unless these arms had been thus timely furnished to the Americans, Burgoyne would have made an easy march to Albany. These same arms, under the direction of the brave and impetuous Colonel Cilley, arrested the British advance at Monmouth, and performed many other notable feats in the course of the war. What then? My pen almost refuses to record the fact that these arms have never been paid for to this day!

When the war was ended, application was made to Congress for payment, which was refused on the frivolous pretext that they were a "present from the French king." Judge Marshall was employed to press the payment, but his efforts were unsuccessful. The claim was referred to the United States attorney general, who reported in substance that he could find no evidence of their ever having been paid for, or that they were presented as a "gift" by the court of France.

Congress, skulking behind their sovereignty, still refused payment. Fifty-eight years have rolled away since the arms were delivered, and forty-eight since the constitution was formed; and, during the latter period, our eyes and ears have been charmed by our presidents and governors, by incessant reiterations, in their annual messages and speeches, of the national health, wealth and unparalleled prosperity. Yet, the cries of Beaumarchais' heirs (by the French revolution reduced to poverty) have not been heeded!

Supposing the most favorable plea of Congress to be true, that there was an underhanded connivance by France to furnish the arms, inasmuch as the king had thought proper to deny it, is it just or magnanimous for the United States to refuse payment? Suppose the arms were clearly "a gift," bestowed on us in our poverty, ought not a high-minded people to restore the value of that "gift," with ten fold interest, when their benevolent friend has become poor, and they have waxed wealthy and strong?

To enumerate the aid we received from France during the revolution, her various gifts, loans, troops furnished, battles fought and severe losses incurred in our behalf, is the work of history; but an honorable remuneration from our government, and a grateful remembrance from every true American, are due to the French nation.

Who has forgotten that by the treaty of 1788 we guaranteed the French West-India possessions? Who has forgotten the proclamation of neutrality crowded upon General Washington by the British faction about him, when the "practice" of neutrality might have answered equally as well, without proclaiming to the world that we had so shortly forgotten our obligations, and were willing to let them know that we hold treaties in contempt, when transient circumstances caused them to operate against our temporary interests?

By the treaty of 1783 it was mutually stipulated that no laws should be enacted to interrupt the collection of debts due to the citizens of either of the contracting parties. Great Britain complied, on her part, with the treaty, while in some of the States stop-laws were passed, and the doors of justice closed against British claimants. The English, in consequence, refused to deliver up the frontier posts they held within the United States, which measure cost us two or three Indian wars, and the posts were still retained.

It was not until after the treaty of Pilnitz, formed by Great Britain and her allies to put down the revolutionary rebels of France, and the consequent invasion of their territory by a Prussian army, that France was supposed to be irretrievably ruined, and the epoch arrived to sweep republicanism from the earth, that the November order was issued by the British cabinet as a step preparatory for that important event, and Mr. Jay was dispatched to England to form a treaty.

In the interim, France had aroused from her slumbers. Her gigantic energies had driven the invaders with ruin and disgrace from her soil, and followed them to their lair. Her masses had become the invaders in their turn!

This unexpected turn of affairs rendered the British government more pliable. They graciously gave us a treaty, by which we might navigate the West-India seas with vessels of seventy tons burthen, and pay the debts of those States who had violated the treaty of 1783 by their stop-laws. These terms being agreed upon, the parties opened an account current. The British surrendered the posts, and agreed to pay for all illegal captures; which terms, at maturity, were complied with by both parties.

Even in this matter we were the aggressors, and suffered severely for violating the treaty. The United States were compelled to pay the damages for the refractory portion of the States who had arrested the course of justice by refusing to pay their debts according to treaty and moral obligation.

How far the license trade was countenanced, it is now difficult to determine; but during the wise experiments of the "embargo" and "non-intercourse," to starve Great Britain into compliance by withholding tobacco from her voracious appetite, licences were very common, very easily procured, and probably the cause of many seizures.

We will now try the honor and good faith of the United States on another tack. How have they fulfilled their contract with the soldiers of the revolution? When it was necessary to continue the army in 1776, Congress, by a resolve of September 16, promised the soldier, in addition to his pay, one hundred acres of land in case they would join the officers and conquer the country. They closed with these terms, and by unparalleled sufferings, exertions, and consummate bravery, in eight years cleared the country of its enemies, leaving the United States government in quiet possession of our immense public domain. Two years after the peace, May 20, 1785, resolves were passed for furnishing the soldiers the promised lands; but especial care was taken to saddle the law with a supplement, requiring the lands to be located in plats of six miles square, so that if two hundred and thirty soldiers could not be collected, and induced to combine in the location, they could not obtain their land.

But Congress, farther to exhibit their love of justice and honor, enacted a law that the soldier might assign his right to the honorable fraternity of speculators, many of whom were members of the honorable Congress.

After the first harvest had been gathered, a considerable number of lots still remained; and it became necessary to enact the law of 1796, reducing locations to five miles square, and permitting lands to be located in quarter townships, so that forty soldiers, uniting, might locate. At the same time, in order to hurry the business, a statute of limitation was added, fixing upon the first day of January, 1800, for the outlawry of the claims. This most "just and salutary" enactment brought many of the claims to the speculators' shops.

The first and second lot of dealers became pretty well gorged, when Congress passed the act of March 1, 1800, confining locations to the original owners, to be transferred according to the laws for the conveyance of real estate. These matters clearly exhibit the spirit of justice and national equity in those early days of liberty and equality.

It may be remembered that although the soldier was promised pay at the rate of $6.66⅔ per month, even of that sum but a small portion was ever paid.

When the war was over, a certificate was handed to the soldier, showing the amount due to him as arrears for past services, with a furlough, and the magnanimous present of his gun and bayonet. With these resources he was turned adrift to wend his way home, distant perhaps from fifty to seven hundred miles; and this was his treatment, after conquering for his country millions of acres, secured to that country by his privations, faithfulness, courage and wounds in the public service.

These papers, in process of time, were embraced in the funding system, but not until the largest portion of them had been swallowed by hawkers and speculators in and out of Congress, at the rate of 80 and 90 per cent. discount.

Those owners who had not parted with their certificates, fondly expected that their principal and interest would be funded at par value. But no! A magnanimous Congress placed the speculator, who had purchased the papers at two shillings and sixpence on the pound, on a par with the soldier who, for a nominal value of six dollars, sixty-six cents and two-thirds of a cent per month, actually received but eighty-three cents per month for his privations, wounds and hardships actually endured in the public service.

When those flimsy papers, called "Pierce's notes," were generally disposed of, a new dish had to be prepared to glut the hungry maw of the buzzards. The soldier's land was the next bill of fare, and this new field of operation was eagerly entered. Several members of Congress, with the aid of smaller outside fry, were engaged to obtain *ex post facto* laws to carry on the operations. The acts of 1785 and 1796 effectually answered the purpose of reducing the soldier's claim from the government price—say from two dollars to twenty and ten cents per acre—and opened such a field for forgery, fraud and chicanery, that many of the soldiers lost the whole. Indeed, if this honorable tribe found the land, they experienced very little trouble in making out the title; and, if made out of whole cloth, not one soldier in a thousand could find out the fraud, and not one in ten thousand carry a suit to the expensive tribunals of the United States, if it was discovered.*

We will now look back to the year 1779. Every American should be familiar with the account of the destruction of that beautiful settlement on the Susquehannah, called Wyoming, and the horrible massacre which ensued. Congress resolved to send an expedition against the Six Nations, to revenge the inhuman murders and savage devastations committed during their expedition to Wyoming.

General Sullivan was appointed to the command. Provisions and military stores were also forwarded to sustain the army. As the march was through an unexplored wilderness, unforeseen obstructions and impediments were found in their way; and before the troops could reach the enemy, their provisions were so far exhausted as to require a speedy return, or a reduction of rations to half allowance. An order of General Sullivan made the proposition in regard to half allowance, forcibly exhorting the army to accept, with a condition that Congress should pay for the deficiency.

The army accepted the terms—pressed on, found, and totally defeated the enemy; pursued him to his den, ravaged his corn fields, destroyed his villages, and returned completely victorious. So effectually was the chastisement

* Having been engaged in prosecuting the claims of his family to military lands, from the year 1826 until their recovery in 1837, the writer had an opportunity of examining all the proceedings of Congress, and of speculators in regard to soldiers' lands.

inflicted, that the States suffered no more from the marauding expeditions of these tribes during the war.

For this signal service, I anticipate the reader's expectations—votes of thanks, medals, swords, &c., and a liberal payment of the detained allowance. I wish I could stop here; but justice forbids the concealment of the true but shameful fact, that Congress even refused to pay for the "half rations." General Sullivan considered his honor insulted by the refusal, and resigned his commission. Thus, by a flagrant act of injustice, the nation was deprived of the skill, bravery and intelligence of one of the most accomplished officers of the army.

* * * * * * *

The above episode affords one specimen of the manner in which the United States Government has treated her military servants.

But to return to our obligations to France. No sooner had that nation recognized our independence, on the 6th of February, 1778, than instant preparations were made to render absolute assistance. Early in the summer, Count de Estainge arrived on our coast with twelve line-of-battle-ships, six frigates, and four thousand troops to aid our cause.

In the attempt on Newport one ship of the line was lost, and the fleet very much shattered by the August storm. Not discouraged in well doing, more French troops arrived, and powerful fleets constantly hovered upon our coast, ready to render assistance (ever attended with great danger, loss and expense), until, to cap the climax, the French fleet and army united with our own force, reduced Cornwallis, and ended the active war upon the continent.

As peace had not yet been agreed upon, to divert the British forces from New-York, Count de Grasse, with the flower of the French fleet, and a suitable land force, sailed for Jamaica, expecting to be joined by the Havana fleet. While pursuing his course, he was interrupted off the island of Dominica by Admiral Rodney, and his fleet nearly annihilated. So decisive was this naval engagement, that France was unable to appear upon the ocean again in any force during the war; indeed, Lord Howe's victory of August, 1794, may fairly be ascribed to the result of that battle, fought at our desire, and to secure our independence.

The expense of that war was as much, if not more, to France than to the United States; and if the latter had only paid the purchasers of soldiers' tickets, "*quantum meruit,*" it would probably have been five times as much as it cost the United States.

It is a matter of historical truth that the expenses incurred in this war by France, bankrupted the nation, and hurried on the terrible events which convulsed the world from the commencement of the French Revolution until the battle of Waterloo.

During all this period of distress and disaster, the Americans were chuckling in their sleeves, and wafting the treasures of the old world to embellish the half-fledged cities of the new world.

Gratitude is a virtue often spoken of with apparent sincerity, but not so frequently exhibited in practice.

It is a notorious fact that the people of the United States were jointly and severally rebels, from the 19th of April, 1775, until the national recognition in 1783. Of course they were guilty of treason, and liable to forfeiture of life and estate, according to the well known law of nations. Now, then, who protected them from the rigor of that law? Is it presumption to say, in answer—their soldiers? How often was it said in conversation, in those days of trial, "if we can only get our liberties secured, we will willingly give all our personal property and half of our farms."

This was the language when the soldier was in the field. The king of England had pronounced them rebels. The soldiers declared them to be freemen. They wiped away the stigma of rebellion and nullified the treason.

"Treason never prospers—what is the reason? When it does, none dare call it treason."

The soldiers redeemed the farms, received very little personal property, generously allowed the owners to retain their lands, and added uncounted millions to the national domain, to which no individual had any pretence of title or claim until gained by the soldiers, by right of conquest, from a declared enemy. While the whole was in jeopardy, the people generously promised them one hundred acres each (it being understood that they must conquer it). Conquer it they did—what then? Why, they quietly laid down their arms, trusting to the magnanimity and justice of their country for that petty pittance of one hundred acres to each soldier. And how was that paid? Answer—Congress, two or three years after the peace, overflowing with gratitude, liberality and justice, passed a law to locate their lands in six-mile square townships, and soon afterward in five-mile square townships, as before mentioned.

If the people should ever look back upon those laws, they would doubtless agree that they ought to be headed acts of abomination, to defraud the soldiers of the revolution of their promised lands, for conquering the boundless regions which compose the geographical chart of the United States.

This was the manner in which Congress paid their soldiers. Their fame, their bravery, their privations and patriotism have been proclaimed to the world in both hemispheres; and this is their reward from an high minded and honorable republic. The same republic is now about to buckle on her armor, and engage in a war with her old patron for a paltry debt of five millions.

In looking over the report of the Senate, we see a temperate, long-winded address, a la mode le Senate; while the more chivalrous spirits of the House, as their "*ultima ratio*," say that the United States will sustain at all hazards the faithful performance of the stipulations of the treaty with France; that is, as much as to say, "pay us, or abide the consequences."

If this laconic paragraph does not give France a fit of the ague, that nation must possess strong nerves and robust bodies.

These historical facts ought to be kept in view, in order to direct our moral obligations and duties; and we ought occasionally to look over a worm eaten authority, seldom used by statesmen excepting upon the eve of elections, which, as nearly as I remember, is, "cast the beam out of thine own eye, and thou wilt see more clearly to pluck the mote out of thy neighbor's eye."

AMERICUS VESPUCIUS.

To the Hon. Senate and House of Representatives of the United States, in Congress assembled:

Respectfully petitions Caleb Stark, and gives your honors to understand that he served in the army of the revolution during the whole of that glorious war: viz., in 1775, as a cadet to learn the active principles of the then military discipline and evolutions, and was present at the ever memorable battle of Bunker's hill.

On the new organization of the army, in 1776, he received the appointment of ensign in Captain George Reid's company in Col. John Stark's regiment, and advanced into Canada, when Gen. Sullivan was ordered to sustain the retreating army from before Quebec. In July, the adjutant died of small-pox at Chimney Point, and he succeeded to the offices of lieutenant and adjutant of the regiment, and proceeded to Mount Independence, where the campaign was closed in that department. On the retreat of the British army [to winter quarters], the regiment was ordered to join General Washington in Pennsylvania. Soon after their arrival, they were ordered to enter New-Jersey, and on the morning following witnessed the capture of the Hessians at Trenton. The regiment was dismissed in January, 1777, their term of enlistment having expired, and the officers returned to prepare new recruits for the next campaign. In the new organization, your petitioner was continued in the same rank, and on the opening of spring repaired to the rendezvous at Ticonderoga, in the regiment of Col. Joseph Cilley, where he continued until the retreat of the army in July, and proceeded with the regiment to the sprouts of the Mohawk, where they joined Gen. Gates, the new commander, and soon afterward took up the line of march to meet the enemy. He was found at Behmus' heights and Stillwater; and your petitioner performed the duties of adjutant in the action of September 19th, and that of October 7th. In the last action he was so severely wounded as to be disqualified to perform the difficult duties of his office.

Colonel Stark having been appointed a general officer, requested your petitioner to accept the office of brigade major to his brigade. Peculiar circumstances, not necessary to be explained, induced him to accept the appointment, and he repaired to New-Hampshire to prepare for the next campaign.

In the early part of 1778 General Stark was ordered to take command of the northern department, and fix his head quarters at Albany. It devolved on your petitioner to perform not only the duties of brigade major but those of adjutant general to that extensive command. At the close of the campaign, orders were received to join General Gates at Providence [R. I.], who charged General Stark with the command from East-Greenwich to Tower Hill.

The same duties devolved upon your petitioner as at Albany. About mid-winter General Gates, by command of General Washington, ordered General Stark to repair to Massachusetts and New-Hampshire to forward the recruiting service, in which your petitioner performed the practical duties.

He repaired early in the spring [1779] to Providence, with General Stark, and was commanded to join General Cornell, to examine and make remarks on all the points liable to attack from Point Judith to Tiverton. About the time this new duty was in progress, by a new regulation of Congress, the duty of brigade major was ordered to be performed by a major of the line, and my office devolved upon Major Bradford, of the Rhode-Island troops.

It was my intention to have retired; but, by the desire of General Stark, backed by General Gates, I consented to the appointment of aid-de-camp to General Stark, and in that capacity passed the campaign. In the same capacity I joined General Washington at Morristown, in 1780, and was present at the battle of Springfield, and also engaged in the great foraging party from West-Point in October following, to mask General Washington's plan of surprising Staten Island.

In 1781, General Stark being again ordered to assume the command of the northern department, your petitioner was called on to perform the same duties which he had discharged at Albany in 1778, and passed the campaign at Saratoga, where he continued until after the reduction of Lord Cornwallis, when General Stark was ordered to leave a small garrison at Saratoga, and prepare for the campaign of 1782.* That year passing without any active service, I pass without further notice; but by command of General Washington I joined the army at Newburg, April 10th, 1783.

The preliminaries of peace suspending military operations, I returned home on the separation of the army.

During all this period, from the close of 1775, I received pay rations and forage as an ensign and lieutenant; from July, 1776, as an adjutant; and from October, 1777, nominally as a major; but was occasionally obliged to draw considerable sums from my patrimonial property to supply my extra expenses, in consequence of the depreciation of paper money, and have received neither half pay, commutation, nor land.

It may appear remarkable that I have not called before. The fact is, I never saw the several laws that gave me a claim until the present season, nor ever heard of them till 1824. I supposed I was precluded by leaving the line. I now perceive a vast train of special acts in favor of the army from September 16th, 1776, to the concluding compliment made to the illustrious la Fayette in 1825.

In corroboration of the above facts, you have the depositions and certificates numbered 1, 2 and 3.

It will now rest with Congress to determine whether I shall perhaps be the only officer in the State not allowed to profit by the public arrangements for the labors of eight dangerous and difficult campaigns.

CALEB STARK.

DEPOSITION.—No. 1.

I, Caleb Stark, brigade major, and aid-de-camp to the late Gen. John Stark in the revolutionary war, do testify and declare that I never received any allowance, as half-pay, or commutation, or land, for my revolutionary services, other than is described in the petition accompanying this affidavit, nor ever applied for the same. I farther declare that I never heard of the several resolutions of Congress in favor of officers of my standing until 1824, and never saw them until the present season.

CALEB STARK.

DEPOSITION.—No. 2.

To whom it may concern. I certify that I have been acquainted with Major Caleb Stark ever since the year 1775; and know that he served in the New-Hampshire line, as adjutant to Col. Cilley's regiment, in the years 1776 and 1777; and that he was wounded in the battle of October 7th, at Stillwater, in 1777; and that he served as brigade major and aid-de-camp to the late Gen. John Stark during the remainder of the revolutionary war.

HENRY DEARBORN,

Maj. Gen. U. S. Army.

DEPOSITION.—No. 3.

I, Robert B. Wilkins, lieutenant in the New-Hampshire line, in the revolutionary army, do testify and declare that I knew Major Caleb Stark as early as 1775, when he served on Winter hill, and afterward as lieutenant and adjutant to the close of the northern campaign, and reduction of Burgoyne; that he was wounded at the battle of the 7th of October, at Behmus' heights; and that he afterward served as brigade major and aid-de-camp to Gen. Stark to the end of the war.

ROBERT B. WILKINS.

In 1828 the petitioner obtained, by a special act of Congress, his land and commutation (or five years' full pay), but without interest; and by the pension act of 1828, full pay for life.

To Hon. Samuel Bell, United States Senate.

Pembroke, 29th November, 1825.

My Dear Sir—Inclosed you have my petition to Congress, with such evidence as I suppose will prove sufficient to establish my claim. Should farther testimony be deemed necessary, I can produe most of the New-England officers now living, as well as all the surviving officers of the State of New-York, of which, I presume, there will be no necessity.

I spoke to your colleague, Hon. Mr. Woodbury, who promised me his influence. I must request you also to make my case known to the several gentlemen of our delegation, that they may be enabled to render you assistance in case it should meet with opposition.

You will find in the inclosed paper a great variety of cases similar to mine, that have been provided for.

I have perused the laws cursorily through four volumes of the digest, but could not find a regular file in the State library subsequent to that publication. I intended to have seen you before your departure, but was detained at Boston longer than I expected.

If, after examining the papers, any deficiency appears, have the goodness to let me know.

I have the honor to be,

Your friend and humble servant,

CALEB STARK.

Hon. Samuel Bell.

Dear Sir—Since writing the above (petition), a circumstance has occurred to me which has hitherto escaped my recollection. It is a fact that the same regiment that first arrested the advance of Burgoyne, on the 19th of September, 1777, and on the 7th of October, in the same year, carried victory into his camp, was the same that retrieved the battle of Monmouth, when our army was retreating under the command of General Lee, and produced the well known anecdote, that after the British were checked and forced to run on their part, our illustrious Washington rode up and inquired of Colonel Cilley: "What troops are these?"

The Colonel, with his usual promptitude and impetuosity, answered: "True blooded Yankees, sir, by G—d."*

In this regiment I served in 1775–6–7, devoting all my abilities to form them for action. Any person in the least acquainted with military affairs, knows the very important duties of an adjutant on such occasions; and their victorious career through the whole of the war, is the best commentary on the faithfulness with which the duty was performed.

I send you these texts to be used for arguments, should you think them worth relating.

I am, sir, &c.,

CALEB STARK.

* "I see," said General Washington—"my brave New-Hampshire boys."

PHINEHAS STEVENS.

To most of the pioneers who sought an abode in the wilds of America, the same circumstances will apply. Prior to the year 1760, the frontier settlers were at all times exposed to the incursions of hostile savages, who were continually on the watch for opportunities of laying waste their homesteads, and to slay or carry away as captives the inhabitants. Necessity, therefore, compelled them to become familiar with danger, and acquire a hardihood of character unknown to their posterity. Whether they attended public worship, or cultivated their lands, they departed from their fortified garrisons with arms in their hands, prepared for instant action, and worshipped or labored with sentinels on the alert.

In their warfare, the Indians preferred prisoners and plunder to scalps. Hence, few persons were slain by them, excepting those unable to travel, those who attempted to escape, and such as appeared too formidable for them to encounter with a hope of success.

Of the latter class was Captain Stevens. He was athletic, hardy and resolute; ever ready to cultivate his acres, or arm in their defence, as well as for the protection of his countrymen. He was truly a martial husbandman—

> "Who, in the reaper's merry row
> Or warrior rank could stand."

A man of self-acquired education, possessing deep penetration and intelligence, he was admirably fitted for the important public services, in the performance of which he was intrusted by the government.

He was the father and defender of the early settlements on the north-eastern frontiers of New-England, where he, like

> "The pastoral hero, assembled his band,
> To lead them to war at his monarch's command."

He was the son of Joseph and Prudence Stevens, and born on the 20th of February, 1706, at Sudbury, Massachusetts, from whence he removed with his father to Rutland, in the same State.

At the age of sixteen, accompanied by his three younger brothers, he was proceeding to a meadow where his father was engaged in making hay, when he fell into an Indian ambuscade. The enemy made him prisoner, slew two of his brothers, and were about to slay the youngest, then but four years of age. He succeeded, however, in making the savages understand, by signs, that if they would spare the life of his little brother, he would carry him on his back. He conveyed him in that manner to Canada. Such tragic events were not uncommon at that period. The captives were soon afterward redeemed.

He received several commissions from Governor Wentworth, of New-Hampshire, and Governor Shirley, of Massachusetts, and rendered important service in defending the frontiers.

In 1747, when Number Four was abandoned by its inhabitants, he was ordered to occupy the fort with thirty men. On the 4th of April, of that year, the garrison was attacked by more than four hundred French and Indians, commanded by Monsieur Debeline. The siege continued three days. Indian stratagem, French skill, and fire, applied to every combustible matter in the vicinity of the fort, produced not the desired effect. Its heroic defenders were not appalled, and would not capitulate. At length the enemy demanded a parley, and the commanders met outside of the fort. The Frenchman declared that he had seven hundred men, and depicted the horrid massacre which must ensue unless the post was surrendered.

"My men are not afraid to die," was Captain Stevens' noble answer. The attack was renewed, and continued with increased fury until the third day, when the enemy again called for a cessation of arms. They then proposed to depart if the garrison would sell them provisions sufficient to support them on their way back to Canada. Captain Stevens replied that he could not sell the supplies of the fort for money, but would give them five bushels of corn for every prisoner they would deliver up to him. Upon receiving this answer the enemy discharged four or five guns at the fort, and departed.

This noble defence of a timber fort, by thirty-one persons, against a force of more than fourteen times their number, confirmed the high opinion already entertained both by the government and his fellow-citizens of the capacity and dauntless valor of our frontier hero. For his distinguished gallantry upon this occasion, Commodore Sir Charles Knowles presented him an elegant sword. From this circumstance the township, when its charter was granted by Governor Wentworth to Joseph Wells, Phinehas Stevens, and others, in 1752, obtained the name of Charlestown.

On two occasions (in 1749 and 1752), if not more, the Governor of Massachusetts employed Captain Stevens to proceed with flags of truce to Canada to negotiate the redemption of captives from the Indians. Of these expeditions he kept diaries, as we have reason to suppose he did of most of his transactions, as well in regard to the affairs of his farm, as of his proceedings in the public service. We have seen his journal of 1749, published in the New-Hampshire Historical Collections, and also his original journal of 1752, which was several years ago found at the bottom of an old churn in a garret in Charlestown. It was afterward lost at the burning of the Vermont State Capitol. The manuscript was written in a plain, legible hand. The language was concise and appropriate. His education, however obtained, must therefore have been superior to that of most of his New-England cotemporaries.

The journal of 1752 contained observations relative to his crops; mentioned the date when the first barrel of rum was brought to number four; detailed a journey to Portsmouth, and another with a flag of truce to Canada. It also contained a description of Montreal. Mr. Wheelwright, of Boston, was his colleague in this mission to Canada.

Captain Stevens died at Chenucoto, in Nova Scotia, April 6, 1756, while engaged in public service, in the fifty-first year of his age. He is the ancestor of many persons of high respectability in New-Hampshire and Vermont. His son, Colonel Samuel Stevens, was the first representative of Charlestown to the General Court. He was a councillor six years, and afterward register of probate until his death, November 17, 1823, at the age of 85 years.

One daughter of Captain Stevens was born in the fort at Number Four, and married to Hon. John Hubbard, father of the late Hon. Henry Hubbard.

The president of the Vermont Historical and Antiquarian Societies, Colonel Henry Stevens, is the grandson of the hero of Number Four. Those societies are indebted to his laborious researches for a large portion of the valuable ancient documents and curiosities in their possession. The State of Vermont should also justly appreciate his exertions in procuring from Congress two of the most important trophies of a victory gained by the valor of the White and Green mountain boys, to adorn her capitol—the Bennington cannon.

He formerly resided at Barnet, Vt., but in 1858 removed to Burlington. As an industrious and scientific farmer, his experiments, his writings and addresses before the State and County agricultural societies, have obtained for him an extensive reputation.

His son, Henry Stevens, junior, was an assistant of Mr. Sparks while preparing those voluminous historical works which, while they reflect the highest honor upon that distinguished gentleman, also cast a brilliant light upon the achievements of the American revolution.

Since the foregoing was written, a communication has been received from Colonel H. Stevens, which we insert in his own words.

I find among my grand-father's old papers the following commissions:

"To Phinehas Stevens, of No. Four so called, on ye East of Connecticut river. You, the said Phinehas Stevens to be Lieut. of the foot company of Militia, in the regiment whereof Josiah Willard, Esq., is Colonel.

B. WENTWORTH.

Dec. 13, A. D. 1743."

"He was commissioned by Gov. W. Shirley, as Lieut. in a company of volunteers, raised for the defence of the western frontiers, on the 26th day of October, A. D. 1744."

"He was appointed captain of a company of volunteers, to be raised for his majesty's service against the French and Indians, January 9, 1745, by W. Shirley."

"He was commissioned first Lieut. of a company of soldiers raised for ye defence of ye western frontiers, for the protection of the inhabitants, whereof Josiah Willard, Jun'r, is Captain, 29th July, A. D. 1745," by W. Shirley.

The following commission I copy from the original, which is all written:

BY HIS EXCELLENCY, THE GOVERNOR.

Province of Massachusetts Bay.

These are to direct you forthwith to enlist sixty able bodied, effective volunteers to make up a marching company on the western frontiers. Twenty-five of which sixty men you may so enlist out of the standing companies in those parts; taking effectual care, that, that enlistment be made with as much equality as may be, so as not much to weaken any particular party of those soldiers, and with the said company to scout during the summer season in such places where the Indian enemies hunt or dwell, keeping one half of your company at the garrison called Number Four, to guard and defend the inhabitants there, and to repel and destroy the enemy that may assault them; and upon return of the half that go out upon the march, the half just mentioned forthwith to march out and scout in the manner above said; and so interchangeably—one part to continue to do their duty at Number Four, and the other to be upon the march above said.

And you, the officer that shall command the said marching party, must keep exact journals of your marches, noting down all circumstances, and making such observations as may be useful hereafter. You must take care to keep an exact discipline among your men, punishing all immorality and profaneness, and suppressing all such disorders in your marches and encampments as may tend to disorder and expose you to the enemy.

Given under my hand, at Boston, the twenty-sixth day of April, 1746, in the nineteenth year of his majesty's reign.

WM. SHIRLEY.

To Captain Phinehas Stevens.

I find also one other commission, bearing date at Boston, 16th June, A. D. 1746.

Also, one other commission to Phinehas Stevens, "to be commander of the fort called Number Four, and the garrison there posted, or to be posted there, and to consist of the first company of soldiers in the said garrison." Dated the 25th of February, A. D. 1747. Wm. Shirley.

Also, one other commission: "You, the said Phinehas Stevens, to be captain of the garrison at the fort called Number Four." Dated at Boston, November 10, A. D. 1747. Wm. Shirley.

Also, a commission of captain of a company at Charlestown. Dated 26th April, 1754. B. Wentworth.

There were other commissions before and after the above, which I have not been able to recover.

I have a commission of Simon Stevens, as a lieutenant in John Stark's company, dated the 14th of January, 1758, signed "Loudoun."

Again, I have Simon Stevens' commission, as captain of a company of rangers, bearing date at Three Rivers, July 9, 1760. Signed, Jeff. Amherst.

Samuel Stevens was commissioned as a lieutenant by Jeffery Amherst, and had command of a party that went from Charlestown up Connecticut river to meet Robert Rogers with provisions, at the time he went to St. Francis, A. D. 1759.

Again, Enos Stevens (my father), was a lieutenant, A. D. 1756. I had his journal of an expedition up West river, and so on to Fort Massachusetts. His diary was burnt in the Vermont State House.

CHILDREN OF CAPTAIN PHINEHAS STEVENS.

Simon and Willard (twins), born February 4, 1735. (Simon died.)

Simon, 2d, September 3, 1737; Enos, October 2, 1739; Mary, March 28, 1742; Phinehas, July 31, 1744; Catharine, November 20, 1747. (The above named were born at Rutland, Massachusetts.)

Prudence, November — 1750, Solomon, September 9, 1753—were born at Charlestown, N. H.

Dorothy, born October 31, 1755, at Deerfield, Mass. Died at Charlestown, September 10, 1758.

Enos Stevens, my father, married Sophia Grout, March 4, 1791. Of their ten children, only three are now living: viz., Henry Stevens, Willard Stevens, of Barnet, Vt., and Sophia, wife of Jonathan Fitch Skinner, of Barton, Vermont.

Our friend, Colonel Henry Stevens, married Candace Salter, March 16, 1815. Of their eleven children, four sons and one daughter are now living.

Enos, the eldest, resides at Boston, Mass. Henry is now in London, agent for the trustees of the British museum, literary agent for the Smithsonian Institute and several other American libraries; also for several private American gentlemen.

Sophia Candace married her second husband, William Page, an artist, celebrated as the greatest colorist since the days of Titian, of whom, in that branch of the art, he has been a distinguished and successful imitator. He resides at Rome, in Italy.

Simon is a distinguished attorney and counsellor at law, in Lancaster, Pennsylvania.

Benjamin Franklin is now engaged at New-York, assisting his brother Henry in purchasing and exchanging books for the British museum and other libraries.

Lieutenant George Stevens graduated at West-Point, in 1843, and was ordered to Fort Jessup. From thence he proceeded, with the army of occupation, to Corpus Christi, and was there attached to May's corps of dragoons. May, with his cavalry, cut their way through the Mexican field batteries, but on returning with five of his company, he found one battery still in operation. He rode up and demanded its surrender, with which demand General la Vega complied. Captain May placed him in charge of Lieutenant Stevens, who, with a sergeant, conveyed the Mexican general of artillery to the rear, and delivered him to General Taylor. After General la Vega recovered his baggage, he presented Lieutenant Stevens with several curiosities, bullets, cigars, &c., which his father now has in possession.

Lieutenant Stevens was drowned in passing the Rio Grande from Fort Brown to Metamoras. The cavalry were dismounted, and he proposed to take the lead on horseback, although advised by General Twiggs not to venture. However, he went on ahead. In passing the river the horses could ford part of the way, and three of the mounted dragoons followed to direct the foremost. When within sixty yards of the Mexican shore, the horses came into a whirlpool. About sixty of them were carried round and round, and Lieutenant Stevens became unhorsed. He kept above water for about sixty rods. Boats were put off from the shore, but could not reach him on account of the roughness of the water. He was recovered on the third day after, and buried on one side of the flag-staff of the fort, Major Brown lying upon its other side.

"How sleep the brave who sink to rest,
By all their country's wishes blest!"

Both for their country, and in danger's face,
Won chaplets which time's hand shall not erase;
Left her foes' cause, for memory stern and just,
To live, though valor's urn has claimed their dust.

Copy of a letter to Governor William Shirley, from Captain Phinehas Stevens, Commander of the Fort at Number Four, forty miles above Northfield, dated April 7, 1747:

"Our dogs being very much disturbed, which gave us reason to think the enemy were about, occasioned us not to open the gate at the usual time; but one of our men, being desirous to know the certainty, ventured out privately, to set on the dogs, about nine o'clock in the morning, and went about twenty rods from the fort, firing off his gun, and saying choboy to the dogs. Whereupon the enemy, being within a few rods, immediately rose from behind a log and fired; but, through the goodness of God, the man got into the fort with only a slight wound. The enemy being then discovered, immediately arose from all their ambushments and attacked us on all sides. The wind being high, and every thing exceedingly dry, they set fire to all the old fences, and also to a log house, about forty rods distant from the fort, to the windward; so that, within a few minutes, we were entirely surrounded with fire—all which was performed with the most hideous shouting and firing from all quarters, which they continued in a very terrible manner until the next day at ten o'clock at night, without intermission, during which time we had no opportunity either to eat or sleep. But, notwithstanding all their shoutings and threatenings, our men seemed not to be in the least daunted, but fought with great resolution, which doubtless gave the enemy reason to think we had determined to stand it out to the last degree. The enemy had provided themselves with a sort of fortification, which they had determined to push before them, and bring fuel to the side of the fort in order to burn it down; but, instead of performing what they threatened, and seemed to be immediately going to undertake, they called to us and desired a cessation of arms until sunrise the next morning, which was granted; at which time they would come to a parley. Accordingly, the French general, Debeline, came with about sixty of his men, with a flag of truce, and stuck it down within about twenty rods of the fort, in plain sight of the same, and said if we would send three men to him, he would send as many to us, to which we complied. The general sent in a French lieutenant, with a French soldier and an Indian.

"Upon our men going to the monsieur, he made the following proposals: viz., that, in case we would immediately resign up the fort, we should all have our lives, and liberty to put on all the clothes we had, and also to take a sufficient quantity of provisions to carry us to Montreal, and bind up our provisions and blankets, lay down our arms, and march out of the fort. Upon our men returning, he desired that the captain of the fort would meet him half way, and give an answer to the above proposal, which I did; and upon meeting the monsieur, he did not wait for me to give an answer, but went on in the following manner: viz., that, what had been promised he was ready to perform; but, upon refusal, he would immediately set the fort on fire, and run over the top, for he had seven hundred men with him; and if we made any farther resistance, or should happen to kill one Indian, we might expect all to be put to the sword. 'The fort,' said he, 'I am resolved to have, or die. Now, do what you please; for I am as easy to have you fight, as give it up.' I told the general that, in case of extremity, his proposal would do; but inasmuch as I was sent here by my master, the captain general, to defend this fort, it would not be consistent with my orders to give it up, unless I was better satisfied that he was able to perform what he had threatened; and, farthermore, I told him that it was poor encouragement to resign into the hands of an enemy, that, upon one of their number being killed, they would put all to the sword, when it was probable we had killed some of them already. 'Well,' said he, 'go into the fort and see whether your men dare fight any more or not, and give me an answer quick, for my men want to be fighting.'

"Whereupon I came into the fort and called all the men together, and informed them what the French general said, and then put it to vote, which they chose, either to fight on or resign; and they voted to a man, to stand it out as long as they had life. Upon this, I returned the answer that we were determined to fight it out. Upon which they gave a shout, and then fired, and so continued firing and shouting until daylight next morning.

"About noon they called to us and said, good morning; and desired a cessation of arms for two hours, that they might come to a parley, which was granted. The general did not come himself, but sent two Indians, who came within about two rods of the fort and stuck down their flag, and desired that I would send out two men to them, which I did; and the Indians made the following proposal: viz., that, in case we would sell them provisions, they would leave, and not fight any more; and desired my answer, which was, that selling them provisions for money was contrary to the law of nations; but if they would send in a captive for every five bushels of corn, I would supply them. Upon the Indians returning the general this answer, four or five guns were fired against the fort, and they withdrew, as we supposed, for we heard no more of them.

"In all this time we had scarce opportunity to eat or sleep. The cessation of arms gave us no great matter of rest, for we suspected they did it to obtain an advantage against us. I believe men never were known to hold out with better resolution, for they did not seem to sit or lay still one moment. There were but thirty men in the fort, and although we had some thousands of guns fired at us, there were but two men slightly wounded: viz., John Brown and Joseph Earl.

"By the above account, you may form some idea of the distressed circumstances we were under, to have such an army of starved creatures around us, whose necessity obliged them to be the more earnest. They seemed every minute as if they were going to swallow us up, using all the threatening language they could invent, with shouting and firing, as if the heavens and earth were coming together.

"But, notwithstanding all this, our courage held out to the last. We were informed by the French that came into the fort, that our captives were removed from Quebec to Montreal, which they say are three hundred in number, by reason of sickness that is at Quebec, and that they were well and in good health, except three who were left sick, and that about three captives had died which were said to be Duchmen. They also informed us that John Norton had liberty to preach to the captives, and that they have some thousands of French and Indians out and coming against our frontier.

"A very beautiful silver-hilted sword has been purchased by order and at the expense of the honorable Commodore Sir Charles Knowles, to be presented to Captain Stevens for his bravery in defence of the fort above mentioned."

The foregoing I copied from a Boston newspaper, with the note at the bottom in relation to the sword. This letter was addressed to His Excellency, Governor Shirley. I have to say that Captain Stevens received the sword, and it was kept, after grand-father's decease, by Colonel Samuel Stevens, of Charlestown. I have been told that Uncle Samuel took said sword to Northampton, to a goldsmith, to have it cleansed. The goldsmith left Northampton, and the sword was not returned.

Your friend,

HENRY STEVENS.

To Caleb Stark, Esq.

Addressed to Honorable Spencer Phipps, Lieutenant Governor of this Province (Massachusetts), and the Council, June 12, 1750.

The memorial of Phinehas Stevens, of Number Four, humbly sheweth:

That, upon his enlisting himself a volunteer in his majesty's service for the then intended expedition against Canada, he removed his family, viz.: his wife and six children, to Rutland, from Number Four, expecting himself soon to set out for Canada, on said expedition; and that, upon the delay of that expedition, he was, by direction from his excellency, the captain general, ordered to the frontiers of the province, and was constantly employed on the frontiers either in guarding stores to Fort Massachusetts or Number Four, or in keeping the fort at Number Four, till the said expedition was laid aside, and the Canada forces dismissed, in which time he defended the said fort, Number Four, from a vigorous attack of the enemy; and his other services, in that term, he humbly hopes were acceptable to the province, where he was at very great expense in supporting his family at a distance from his station; and as his expenses, so he humbly conceives, his constant labors and services for the province in that term, distinguish his case from that of most if not any of the officers who enlisted themselves for the Canada service. He therefore prays your honorable consideration of the premises, and that your honors would grant that he may be allowed the common allowance for a soldier, for subsistence during the said term; and your memorialist, as in duty bound, will ever pray.

PHINEHAS STEVENS.

In the House of Representatives,
June 13th, 1750.

Read, and ordered that the memorialist be allowed out of the public treasury the sum of ten pounds and eight shillings, in full consideration of the above named.

Sent up for concurrence,

D. HUBBARD, Speaker.

In Council, June 13, 1750.

Read and concurred,

SAM'L HOLBROOK, Dep'ty Sec'y.

Consented to,

S. PHIPPS.

COLONEL ROBERT ROGERS.

James Rogers was one of the early settlers of Londonderry, N. H. He afterward removed to the wilderness of the township now known as Dunbarton, where he was killed by mistake by a hunter, who was his intimate friend. The latter, in the dusk of the evening, perceiving a dark object at a distance, supposed it to be a bear, and fired through a thicket with fatal effect. The fur cap and dark clothing of Mr. Rogers occasioned the sad disaster. Mr. Hadley, in his notice of Dunbarton, gives the following account of this catastrophe:

"Mr. Ebenezer Ayer, of Haverhill, Mass., a celebrated hunter of those times, came into these parts to pursue his usual avocation in quest of bears, deer, and other game. He had made a rude camp on Walnut hill, in Bow, near to Dunbarton line. He had been hunting all day, and came to his camp at evening, and it not being late, was still looking out for the approach of a bear.

"Mr. Rogers was an intimate friend of Ayer, and was coming to pay him a visit. He drew near to his camp; he was dressed entirely in black; and the dusk of the evening deceived the eye of the eager hunter. He took the fatal aim, and shot the man! He soon discovered his mistake, and with sorrowing heart stood over the bleeding form of his friend. Rogers did not long survive. He died before he reached his home. Ayer could never after relate the story of the sad event without shedding tears."

Robert Rogers, son of the above, was born at Londonderry, N. H. (or Methuen, Mass.), in 1727. He was from his youth inured to the hardships of frontier life, from which circumstance he acquired a decision and boldness of character which served him in after years.

He was six feet in stature, well proportioned, and one of the most athletic men of his time—well known in all the trials of strength or activity among the young men of his vicinity, and for several miles around. He was endued with great presence of mind, intrepidity, perseverance, and possessed a plausible address.

In 1755 he was appointed by Governor Wentworth captain of a company of rangers. He afterward commanded that celebrated corps, with the rank of major, in the line of the army. With this corps—of which the most hardy and resolute young men New-Hampshire and other provinces could produce, constituted the principal portion—he rendered important services on the northern frontiers, and in the Canadas, until the surrender of those provinces, in 1760, to the crown of Great Britain.

The enemy dreaded him and his daring followers with good reason. The rangers under his command were in their expeditions limited to no season. Summer or winter caused no difference or delay in their arduous duties. They made long and fatiguing marches in winter, upon snow-shoes, often encamping in the forest, without fire, to avoid discovery by the enemy, and with no other food than the game they had killed during their march.

They penetrated into the enemy's country, and destroyed French settlements and Indian villages, sometimes at four hundred miles' distance. They were in truth the most formidable body of men ever employed in the early wars of America, and in every regular engagement proved themselves not inferior to British troops. To their savage and French foes they were invincible.

After the year 1760, he served against the Cherokees in the south, under the orders of General Grant.

In 1765 he proceeded to England to prosecute his claims for services and money advanced during the northern campaigns of the "seven years war."

In 1766 he was appointed governor of Michilimackinac, where, sometime afterward, he was arrested and conveyed in irons to Quebec, charged with an intention to plunder the fort he commanded, and desert to the French.

He managed to be acquitted of this charge and proceeded, in 1769, a second time to England, where he was presented to the king.

While in England at this time, the following characteristic anecdote is related of him.

A mail-coach, in which he was a passenger, was stopped by a highwayman on Hounslow Heath. The robber, thrusting a pistol through the coach window, demanded the purses and watches of the occupants. While others were taking out their valuables, the bold American ranger suddenly seized the man by the collar, by main strength drew him through the coach window, and ordered the coachman to drive on. The captive was an old offender, for whose apprehension a reward of fifty pounds sterling had been offered by the government.

While at a social party of British officers in England, of similar spirits, it was agreed by the company that who ever of them should relate the greatest falsehood, or the most improbable story, should have his bill paid by the others.

When his turn came, Rogers stated that "his father was shot in the woods of America by a hunter, who mistook him for a bear; that his mother was followed by a hunter, who mistook her tracks in the snow, on a stormy day, for those of a wolf; and that he, when a boy, had carried on his back birch brooms for sale to Rumford, ten miles distant from his father's house, following a path through the woods only marked by spotted trees." The company admitted that Rogers had related the greatest falsehood, and the most improbable story, when he had narrated nothing but the truth.

Rogers returned to America in 1775, where, had he not been suspected of being hostile to the revolutionary movement, he might perhaps have obtained an important command, and rendered signal services. He had seen more arduous and difficult service than most of the continental officers.

He visited New-Hampshire, came to Cambridge and Medford, then occupied by continental troops. At the latter place he had an interview with Colonel Stark, who had been his second in command in the ranger service.

Washington suspected him to be a British spy, and prohibited his entering the American camp. He also visited Congress, but his fidelity being considered doubtful, received no appointment.

He obtained, in 1776, the rank of colonel from the Brittsh general at New-York, and raised a corps known as the "Queen's rangers," with which, for a time, he was a scourge to the people in the vicinity of Long-Island Sound.

In October, 1776, he made an attack upon an American outpost near Maroneck, of which a Hartford, (Conn.) paper states the following particulars:

"On Monday last (October 21st) a party of tories (100), some of whom came from Long-Island, under the command of the infamous Major Rogers, made an attack upon an advanced party of our men, when a smart engagement ensued, in which the enemy were totally routed. About twenty were killed on the spot, and thirty-six taken prisoners, who were safely lodged in the goal at White Plains. Their gallant commander, with his usual bravery, left his men in time of action, and made his escape."

He came very near being made prisoner. Soon after this affair, he went to England, and the command of the "Queen's rangers" devolved upon the noted Colonel Simcoe. In 1778 he was proscribed by the legislature of New-Hampshire, who also granted his wife (a Miss Brown, of Portsmouth) a divorce. She afterward married Captain John Roach.

His son, Arthur, resided with his mother, and at her decease inherited the property at Concord. He died at Portsmouth, in August, 1841, leaving two sons and one daughter, then occupying respectable positions in the West-Indies. His eldest son, Robert, now a respectable farmer in Derry, is the only survivor of a family of eight children. For other particulars respecting Colonel Rogers, see the history of Manchester (pages 488–492), from which several of the foregoing statements were obtained.

The following account of his services during the "seven years war" in North America, contains the substance of his journal, published in London in 1765, with information in regard to the same subject obtained from other sources.

ACCOUNT OF THE SERVICES OF COLONEL ROBERT ROGERS.

In 1755 an expedition was organized for the purpose of reducing Crown Point, a post from which had for several years been fitted out most of the Indian scouts which had harrassed the English frontier settlements. Troops were accordingly raised in New England, New-York, and New-Jersey. Albany was designated as the place of rendezvous, and Major General Johnson appointed commander.

Captain Robert Rogers, with a commission from Governor Wentworth, raised a company of rangers in New-Hampshire on account of that province, and made several excursions to the north-western frontiers to prevent inroads from the enemy. On the 26th of August, 1755, he was employed in escorting provision wagons from Albany to the carrying place, since called Fort Edward. At this time, he waited upon General Johnson, to whom he had been recommended as a person well acquainted with the haunts and passes of the enemy, and the Indian methods of fighting. He was by him dispatched on several scouts to the French posts. He was on one of these up the Hudson, on the 8th of September, when General Dieskan was taken prisoner, and his army routed at the south end of Lake George. Johnson's army was composed principally of the troops raised by the above named province for the Crown Point expedition. With the exception of those who were with Rogers on his scout, the remainder of the rangers were engaged in this action.

September 24, 1755. General Johnson ordered Rogers to reconnoitre Crown Point, and, if practicable, to secure a prisoner. He embarked, with four men, and proceeding down lake George twenty-five miles, landed on the west shore. There leaving his boat in charge of two men, he proceeded with the other two, and on the 29th obtained a view of Crown Point. A large body of Indians were observed about the fort, who, from their irregular firing, were supposed to be shooting at marks—a diversion of which Indians are very fond. At night the party crept through the French guards into a small village, south of the fort, and passed through it to an eminence at the south-west, where it was ascertained that the enemy were erecting a battery, having already thrown up an intrenchment on that side of the fort. The next day, having gained an eminence a short distance from the former, an encampment was discovered, extending from the fort south-east to a wind-mill, at thirty yards distance, containing about five hundred men. Finding no opportunity to obtain a captive, and that they had been observed, the scout retreated on the first of October.

On the route homeward they passed within two miles of Ticonderoga, from which a large smoke was noticed, and the discharge of a number of small arms heard; but, as their provisions were expended, they could not remain to ascertain the enemy's force. On the second they reached the place where their boat had been left in charge of two men, who, to their surprise, had departed, leaving no provisions behind. This hastened their return to camp, where they arrived on the fourth, not a little fatigued and distressed with hunger and cold.

October 7th. General Johnson ordered Rogers to embark with five men to reconnoitre Ticonderoga. He proceeded at night to a point of land on the west shore of the lake, where he landed, concealed his canoe, and leaving two men in charge of it, arrived at Ticonderoga point at noon. Here were about two thousand men, who had thrown up an intrenchment, and prepared a large quantity of hewn timber in the adjacent woods. He tarried there a second night, and in the morning saw the enemy lay the foundation of a fort, on the point which commands the pass from Lake George to Lake Champlain, and the entrance to South bay or Wood creek. Having made what discoveries he could, on his return he found a large advanced guard of the enemy posted at the north end of Lake George, near the outlet to Lake Champlain. While viewing these troops, a bark canoe, containing nine Indians and a Frenchman, was observed passing up the lake. He kept in sight of them until they passed the point where his boat and men had been left. They informed him that the party had landed on an island, six miles south of them, near the middle of the lake. In a short time they put off from the island, and steered directly toward their place of concealment. At the distance of one hundred yards, the party gave them a salute, which reduced their number to four.* The party then took boat and pursued them down the lake until they were relieved by two other canoes, upon which the rangers retreated toward the camp at Lake George, where they arrived on the 10th of October.

October 15. Rogers embarked with forty men, in five boats, with orders to ascertain the force of the enemy's advanced guard, and if possible to decoy the whole or part of them into an ambush. The exertions of the party were indefatigable for several days, but to no purpose, and on the 19th they returned to camp.

October 21. Rogers embarked for Crown Point, with four men, in quest of a prisoner; at night they landed on

* Each marksman hit his man.

the west shore, twenty-five miles from the English camp, and marching the remainder of the way, on the 26th came in sight of the fort. In the evening they approached nearer, and next morning were within three hundred yards of it. The men lay concealed in a thicket of willows, while Rogers crept nearer, and concealed himself behind a large pine log by holding bushes in his hand. Soon afterward the soldiers came out in such numbers that the party could not unite without discovery. About 10 o'clock a man came out alone, and advanced toward the ambush. Rogers sprang over the log and offered him quarter, which he refused, making a pass at him with his dirk. This he avoided, and presented his fusee to his breast; but he pressed forward with resolution, which compelled Rogers to shoot him. This alarmed the enemy, and the party retreated to the mountain. They returned, October 30th, in safety to camp.

November 4. Rogers embarked for the enemy's advanced guard, with thirty men in four batteaux, each mounting two wall-pieces, and next morning arrived within half a mile of their position, where the party landed, and concealed their boats. Four spies were sent out, who returned next evening, reporting that the enemy had no works around them, but lay entirely open to assault. Notice was immediately sent to the general, requesting a sufficient force to attack them; but, notwithstanding his earnestness and activity, the force did not arrive until the party were compelled to retreat. On their retreat they met the reinforcement, and turned again toward the French. Two men, sent out next evening to see if their sentinels were on the alert, were fired upon, and so hotly pursued that the whole party was discovered. They obtained the first notice of this from two large canoes, containing thirty men, which were supposed to have come out at the same time with another party by land, to place the English between two fires. To prevent this Rogers embarked with Lieutenant McCurdy and fourteen men, in two boats, leaving the remainder of the party on shore, under the

26

command of Captain Putnam.* To decoy the French within reach of the wall-pieces, they steered as if intending to pass them, which answered the purpose meditated. The enemy boldly headed them, and when within one hundred yards the guns were discharged, which killed several men, and put the boats to flight. They were pursued, and driven so near to the land party that they were again galled by the wall-pieces. Several of the enemy were thrown overboard, and their canoes rendered very leaky. At this time Rogers discovered their land party, and notified his men on shore, who immediately embarked without receiving much injury from the sharp fire which the French for some time kept up in their rear. The enemy were pursued upon the water with diligence, and the wall-pieces again discharged. They were followed to their landing, where they were received, and covered by two hundred men, whom a discharge from the wall-pieces compelled to retire. They were greatly superior in numbers, and it was deemed most prudent to return to camp, which was reached on the 8th of November.

November 12. Rogers proceeded, with twelve men, to ascertain the enemy's strength and condition at Ticonderoga, and on the 14th came in sight of that fort. The enemy had erected three new barracks, and four storehouses in the fort, between which and the water, they had eighty batteaux hauled up on the beach. They had fifty tents near the fort, and appeared busily employed in strengthening their works. Their object being attained, the party returned to camp on the 19th of November.

December 19. After a month's repose, Rogers embarked, with two men, once more to reconnoitre the French at Ticonderoga. On the way a fire was observed on an island near the fort, which was supposed to have been kindled by the enemy. This obliged the party to lay by and act like fishermen, to deceive the enemy, until night came on, when they gained the west shore, fifteen miles north of the English camp. Concealing the boat, the

* Afterward General Putnam.

march was pursued by land on the 20th, and at noon on the 21st the party reached the fort. The enemy were still engaged in their works, and had mounted four pieces of cannon on the south-east bastion; two on the north-west, toward the woods; and two on the south bastion. They mustered about five hundred men. Several attempts were made to take a prisoner by waylaying their paths, but they passed along in too large parties. At night the scout approached near the fort, but were driven, by the severity of the cold, to seek shelter in one of the enemy's evacuated huts. Before day-break, a light snow fell, which obliged the rangers to hasten homeward with all speed, lest the enemy, discovering their tracks, should pursue. They reached their canoe in safety, although almost overcome with cold, hunger and fatigue. They had the good fortune to kill a deer, with which being refreshed, on the 24th they returned to Fort William Henry, which during the year had been erected at the south end of Lake George.

About this time General Sir William Johnson proceeded to Albany to meet the commissioners from the several governments whose troops he had commanded, (New-Hampshire excepted.) These persons were empowered, with the consent of a council of war, to garrison Forts William Henry and Edward, for the winter, with the troops then in service. A regiment was therefore organized, to which Massachusetts furnished a colonel, Connecticut a lieutenant colonel, and New-York a major. The general and the commissioners judged it most prudent to leave one company of rangers under the command of Captain Rogers, to make excursions to the enemy's forts during the winter.

January 14, 1756. Rogers marched, with sixteen men, toward the French forts. They proceeded down the lake on skates until they halted, for refreshments, near the falls between Lakes George and Champlain. At night the march was renewed, and at day-break on the 16th an ambush was formed on the east shore of Lake Champlain, within gunshot of the path by which the enemy passed from one fort to the other. At sunrise two sledges, laden with fresh beef, were intercepted, with their drivers. Their loading was destroyed; and on the 17th, with their prisoners, the party returned to Fort William Henry.

January 26. Colonel Glasier ordered Rogers, with a party of fifty men, to discover the strength of the enemy at Crown Point. On the 2d of February they arrived within a mile of the fortress, and ascended a steep mountain, the summit of which afforded a full prospect, and an opportunity for taking a plan of the works. In the evening they retired to a small village, half a mile south of the fort, and formed an ambush on each side of the road from that to the village. Next morning a Frenchman fell into their hands, and soon after two more men appeared, but took alarm before they could be seized, and fled to the fort. Finding themselves discovered by this accident, they set fire to the houses and barns of the village, containing large quantities of grain, and killed fifty head of cattle. They then retired, leaving the whole village in flames, and with their prisoner reached head quarters on the 6th of February.

February 29. By order of Colonel Glasier, Rogers marched, with fifty-six men, down the west side of Lake George, proceeding northward until the 5th of March, when he steered east to Lake Champlain, about six miles north of Crown Point, where, from intelligence received from the Indians, he expected to find inhabited villages. There he attempted to cross the lake, but the ice was too weak. On the 7th he returned, and passing round the bay west of Crown Point, at night entered the cleared land, among the houses and barns of the French. Here the party lay in ambush, expecting laborers to attend the cattle, and clean the grain with which the barns were filled. They remained there all night, and the next day until dark, when they set fire to the village and retired. Returning, they reconnoitred Ticonderoga, and the advanced guard on Lake George, approaching so near to the fort as to see the sentinels on the ramparts; and, after obtaining all the information desired of their works, strength and situation, on the 14th of March they returned to camp.

The next day Captain Rogers received a letter from Mr. William Alexander,* secretary of Governor Shirley, who last year commanded at Oswego, and who, upon the decease of General Braddock, had succeeded to the chief command of his majesty's forces in North America, stating that, upon General Johnson's recommendation, he was invited to wait upon the governor at Boston, where he was preparing for the next campaign. Thither he repaired, leaving his company in command of Ensign Noah Johnson.

On the 23d the general gave Captain Rogers a friendly reception, and a commission to recruit an independent corps of rangers. It was ordered that it should consist of sixty privates, at 3*s.* (York currency) per day; an ensign, at 5*s.*; a lieutenant, at 7*s.*; and a captain, at 10*s.* Each man was to be allowed ten Spanish dollars toward providing clothing, arms and blankets. The company was to be raised immediately. None were to be enlisted but such men as were accustomed to travelling and hunting, and in whose courage and fidelity the most implicit confidence could be placed. They were moreover to be subject to military discipline and the articles of war. The rendezvous was appointed at Albany, whence to proceed to Lake George, and "from time to time to use their best endeavors to distress the French and their allies by sacking, burning and destroying their houses, barns, barracks, canoes, batteaux, &c., and by killing their cattle of every kind; and at all times to endeavor to waylay, attack and destroy their convoys of provisions by land and water, in any part of the country where they could be found." With these instructions, he received letters to the commanding officers of Forts William Henry and Edward, directing them to forward the service with which he was charged.

* William Alexander was afterward known as Lord Stirling, and a major general in the United States revolutionary army.

When the company was completed, a part of it marched, under the orders of Lieutenant Richard Rogers, to Albany. With the remainder Captain Rogers passed through the woods to Number Four, a frontier town greatly exposed. There he received orders to proceed to Crown Point, for which, on the 28th of April, his course was directed, through vast forests and over lofty mountains. On the second day of the march Mr. John Stark, his second lieutenant, became ill, and was obliged to return with a guard of six men.

May 5. Captain Rogers reached Lake Champlain, four miles from Crown Point, with nine men. They concealed their packs, and entered a village on the east side, two miles from the fort, but found no inhabitants. They waited the whole day following, opposite the Point, for some party to cross the lake. Nothing however appeared, excepting five hunded men, in batteaux, coming up the lake from St. Johns. They kept their stations until ten o'clock next day; but finding no opportunity to trepan the enemy, they killed twenty-three head of cattle, whose tongues were of great service on the march. They now discovered eleven canoes, manned by French and Indians, crossing the lake directly toward them. It was then judged most prudent to disperse, each man taking a different route, and looking out for himself. This course put their pursuers at fault; and the party, assembling at the place where their packs had been left, made a raft, and crossed to the western shore. They obtained a view of the old Indian carrying-place, near Ticonderoga, and reached Fort William Henry on the 14th of May. Mr. Stark and his party reached Fort Edward three days before, having, on their way, discovered and eluded a scout of four hundred Indians. Lieutenant Rogers had arrived some days before, and was then on a scout.

May 20. Rogers was ordered, with eleven men, to reconnoitre the French advanced guard. When viewed next day from the summit of a mountain, their numbers appeared about three hundred, who were busy in fortifying their position with palisades. From the other side of the mountain the party obtained a fine prospect of Ticonderoga and the French camp, which, from the ground occupied, was judged to contain one thousand men. This night was passed upon the mountain, and early next morning the party proceeded to the Indian carrying-path, where an ambuscade was formed between the advanced guard and the fort. About 6 o'clock one hundred and eighteen Frenchmen passed along the path without observing them; in a few minutes twenty-two others came along the same way. Upon this party they fired, killed six, and took one prisoner. The first party returning at the report of the guns, obliged them to retire in great haste.

On the twenty-third they reached Fort William Henry in safety with the prisoner, who reported that two hundred and twenty French and Indians were preparing to surprise the out parties at Fort Edward. This information occasioned Rogers a march, with seventy-eight men, to join a detachment of Colonel Bayley's regiment, and scour the woods as far as South bay, to intercept the enemy; but they could not be found.

June 12. According to orders, in the evening Rogers embarked, with twenty-six men, to visit the French advanced guard. A severe thunder storm compelled the party to land ten miles from their own fort, and spend the night. At sunrise they heard the discharge of about twenty small arms, on the opposite shore, which was supposed to proceed from the enemy cleaning their guns after the rain. The party embarked in the evening, and early on the morning of the 16th drew up their batteaux four miles from the advanced guard, and lay in ambush, by a path leading to the mountain, to surprise the enemy who went there daily in parties to view the lake. They soon afterward discovered that the advanced parties had evacuated their position, and demolished their works. They then approached very near Ticonderoga, and viewed their works from an eminence, judging the garrison to consist of three thousand men. The party returned to their fort on the 18th, excepting one man who strayed away and did not return until the 23d, then almost famished for want of food. About this time the general increased the force of the ranger company to seventy men, and sent them six whale-boats from Albany, with orders to proceed to Lake Champlain, to cut off the supplies and flying parties of the enemy.

June 28. Rogers, with fifty men, embarked in five whale-boats, and proceeded to an island in Lake George. The next day they passed over to the main land, and carried their boats six miles over a mountain to South bay, where they arrived on the 3d of July. The evening following they embarked, and proceeded down the bay till they came within six miles of the French fort. There the boats were concealed. The next evening they embarked again, and passed the fort undiscovered, although so near as to hear the sentinel's watchword. They judged, from the number of fires, that the enemy had two thousand men in his camp. Five miles farther down they lay by all day, concealing their boats. Here several batteaux were seen passing by up and down the lake. At night they put off with the design of passing Crown Point, but afterward, considering it imprudent, on account of the clearness of the night, they lay concealed through the next day, during which a hundred boats passed by them. Seven boats came near their place of concealment, and would have landed there, but the officer insisted, in their hearing, that he would go a hundred and fifty yards farther, where they landed, and dined in the rangers' sight, without discovering them. At nine o'clock at night the latter reëmbarked, passed the fort, and concealed their boats ten miles north of it.

July 7. Thirty boats and a schooner of forty tons burthen passed by toward Canada. In the evening they proceeded fifteen miles farther down, and dispatched a scout, who soon brought intelligence that a schooner lay at anchor one mile distant. The rangers lightened their packs, and prepared to board her; but were prevented by two lighters coming up the lake, whose crews intended to land where they were posted. These were fired upon, hailed, and offered quarter, if they would come on shore; but they pushed for the other side, whither they were pursued and intercepted. Their crews consisted of twelve men, three of whom were killed by the fire, and two wounded; one in such a manner that he soon died. Both vessels were sunk, and the cargoes, consisting of wheat and flour, wine and brandy, were destroyed, except a few casks of the latter, which were carefully concealed.* The prisoners stated that they were a portion of five hundred men, the remainder of whom were not far behind on their passage. This report hastened the return of the scout; which, on the 16th of July, returned to the garrison with their prisoners. The latter reported "that a large force of regulars and militia were assembling at Chamblée, destined for Carillon,† and that large quantities of provisions were on the way; that a new general, with two veteran regiments, had arrived from France; that there was no design against the English forts on this side, but that a party of three hundred French and twenty Indians had already set out, to intercept the provision convoys between Albany and Lake George; that sixty livres was the reward for an English scalp, and prisoners were sold in Canada at fifty crowns each; that the prospect of a harvest was very encouraging, but that the small-pox had made dreadful havoc among the inhabitants."

Upon his return from this expedition, Captain Rogers learned that General Shirley had been superseded in command by Major General Abercrombie, who arrived at Albany, June 25th, with two regiments of regular troops from England. He forwarded to him the report of the last scout, and recommended the augmentation of the corps of rangers. Soon afterward he waited upon him

* A good thought for a soldier.

† Of this fortress, Ticonderoga was the Indian name, and Carillon the French name; each signifying "the meeting of waters."

at head quarters, and received orders to raise a new company, the command of which was given to his brother, Richard Rogers. Of this company Noah Johnson was appointed first lieutenant, Nathaniel Abbot second, and Caleb Page ensign. Of his own company John Stark was appointed first lieutenant, John McCurdy second, and Jonathan Burbank ensign.

August 2. Captain Robert Rogers, by order of General Abercrombie, embarked, with twenty-five men in a lighter, from Fort William Henry, to reconnoitre Ticonderoga and Crown Point. Captain Learned, with sixty provincials, was ordered by General Winslow to proceed as far as the French advanced guard, but not being acquainted with the country, he placed himself under Rogers' command. The latter landed about fifteen miles down Lake George, and on the 4th encamped one mile from the advanced guard. On the morning of the 5th the whole party mustered, and gained the summit of a hill west of the enemy, from which they discovered two advanced posts; one on the west side, half a mile south of Lake Champlain; and the other on the east side, opposite the former, at the old Indian carrying-place. They supposed four hundred men were on the east, and two hundred on the west side.

After deliberating upon the situation of the enemy, it was deemed imprudent to remain there any longer. Captain Learned returned to camp, while the rangers went down toward Ticonderoga. They passed that post, and proceeded toward Crown Point, on the west side of the lake, where they discovered several batteaux, with troops bound for Carillon. They then proceeded to the place where they had burned the village, as before stated, where they observed a party of the enemy sally out, driving horses and cattle to feed.

August 7. They ambushed the road to intercept those who should come to drive in the cattle; but no one appearing, they approached within half a mile of the fort, and were discovered by two Frenchmen before they were in their power. This caused a retreat, during which they killed forty head of cattle. August 10th they reached head quarters.

A company of Stockbridge Indians was this year employed in his majesty's service, officered by Indians commissioned by General Shirley. General Abercrombie was at a loss how to dispose of them; but Sir William Johnson advised him to employ thirty privates* and a lieutenant as scouts, to scour the woods, under the direction of ranger officers. This party Lieutenant Stark had strengthened with some of his own men, and sent on a scout, with particular directions,† the day before the party above named returned.

About this time the Earl of Loudoun had arrived at Albany, and assumed the command in chief. Rogers sent him an account of the Indian scout before mentioned, requesting permission to penetrate into Canada with these Indians, and distress the inhabitants, by burning their harvest (now nearly ripe), and destroying their cattle.

Accordingly, August 16, a party embarked, in whale-boats, in two detachments—one commanded by Lieutenant Stark, and the other by Captain Robert Rogers. The next morning the detachments fell in with eight Mohawks, who had left Fort William Henry the day previous. The whole party then proceeded to the place where the boats had been left, July 7, twenty miles north of Crown Point, on the west shore of the lake, arriving there on the 24th. Embarking again at night, they steered down the lake toward St. John's, and the next day proceeded twenty miles. At midnight a schooner was seen standing up the lake, with a fair wind, toward Crown Point. She passed so swiftly that they could not board her, as was intended. On the 26th they landed, and the Mohawks departed to

* The remainder of the Stockbridge Indians were sent to Saratoga, to serve under Colonel Burton.

† Captain Jacobs, with his Indians, returned a few days after, with four French scalps, taken on the east shore of the lake, nearly opposite Ticonderoga.

join a party of their brethren, then on a scout. On the 27th the rangers ambushed a point of land to intercept the enemy's batteaux, which might pass up and down; but not finding any, they returned up the lake, and landed on the east shore, eight miles north of Crown Point. On the morning of the 29th they entered a French village, east of the fort, and made prisoners of a man, his wife, and daughter, a girl of fourteen, and returned to the garrison September 22.

The Frenchman stated that he was a native of Vaisac, in the province of Guienne, France. He had been in Canada fifteen years; in the colony's service six years; and two years at Crown Point; which fort was garrisoned by only three hundred men, and those mostly inhabitants of the adjacent villages; that four thousand men occupied Ticonderoga, fifteen hundred of them being regular troops, who had plenty of stores and provisions; that he was never at Carillon or the advanced guard, but had heard there were only fifteen men at the latter place; that six hundred Indians were at Carillon, and six hundred more expected; that twelve hundred men had reached Quebec, on their way to Carillon; that the last eighteen hundred were commanded by Monsieur Scipio de la Masure; that Ticonderoga was well supplied with cannon, mortars, shells, shot, &c.; that the garrison expected a reinforcement in two or three days, having sent boats to Montreal to bring the troops; that he had heard, by letter, that Oswego had fallen into the hands of the French, but it was not yet confirmed; that it was understood the English intended to invest Carillon, but did not know what course the French intended to take, should they neglect that step; that they kept a hundred and fifty batteaux on the lake, thirty-five of which plied between Montreal and Carillon; that Monsieur Montcalm commanded at Frontenac, with five thousand men, but he did not know whether they were regulars or militia; that a great many vessels had arrived at Quebec, with provisions and military stores; that he had heard the English had several ships in the St. Lawrence; that Monsieur le Compte Levi commanded Carillon, and came last year from France; that, since the capture of the two last lighters (before mentioned), the number of men on board the large schooner had been increased from twelve to thirty men.

On his return Rogers was ordered by Lord Loudoun to wait upon Colonel Burton, at Saratoga, by whose direction he marched, with his company, from Fort William Henry to South bay; thence east to Wood creek, crossing the creek southerly, opposite Saratoga, and made report to Colonel Burton. During this tour he apprehended four deserters from Otway's regiment, going over to the enemy, who were sent back to Fort Edward in charge of Lieutenant Stark.

At Saratoga the party met Captain Richard Rogers from the Mohawk, with the Stockbridge Indians in company, and all returned to Fort Edward, where an encampment was formed. Part of the Indians were sent out on the east side of Lake Champlain, to alarm the enemy at Ticonderoga; while Captain Robert Rogers, with a detachment of his own company, and that of Richard Rogers, proceeded down Lake George in whale-boats, leaving the remainder of the corps to serve as flankers to the parties conveying provisions to Fort William Henry.

September 7. Captain Robert Rogers embarked on Lake George, with fourteen men, in a whale-boat, which they concealed the evening following on the east side, four miles south of the French advanced guard. There he left seven men in charge of Mr. Chalmer, a volunteer (sent by Sir John St. Clair), with directions, upon discovering the enemy's boats proceeding up the lake, to convey the news, with all possible speed, to Fort William Henry. With the other seven, he arrived, on the 9th, within half a mile of Ticonderoga. The enemy were engaged in raising the walls of the fort, and had erected a large block-house near the south-east corner of the fortress, with ports for cannon. East of the fort was a battery commanding the lake. Five houses were discovered close to the water side, south of the works, one hundred and sixty tents on the south-west side, and twenty-seven batteaux hauled up on the beach. Next morning, with one private, he took a view of the falls between the two lakes, where several discharges of muskets had been heard the evening before. Mr. Henry had been sent to learn the cause, and soon joined Rogers, reporting that the French were building a small fort at the head of the falls, on the east shore; also, that he had discovered their advanced guard on the west side; and estimated both parties at five hundred men. The French were also found engaged in building a saw-mill, at the lower part of the falls. The party returned to their boats and provisions, which Mr. Chalmers had left. He, having executed his orders, had returned to camp, whither the party followed his track, and arrived on the 11th instant.

September 24. General Abercrombie ordered three commissioned officers of the rangers, with twenty privates each, to reconnoitre Wood creek, South bay, and Ticonderoga, who alternately kept up a continual scout for some time.

October 22. The greater portion of the army now lay at Fort Edward, under General Abercrombie; and Lord Loudoun arriving at this time, it was supposed that, notwithstanding the season was so far advanced, an attempt would be made upon the French forts. But his lordship, supposing the lakes would freeze, as they generally do in December, and that no communication could be kept up with Fort William Henry, contented himself with keeping the field until Monsieur Montcalm retired to winter quarters.

October 22. Rogers embarked, with twenty men, being ordered to bring a prisoner from Ticonderoga. He had passed the narrows, twenty miles from the place of embarkation, when his boat was hailed by Captain Shephard, who had been taken prisoner in August last. He knew his voice, and took him on board, with three men, one of whom was taken with him. He left Canada fifteen days before. Continuing his course, Rogers landed, on the night of the 17th, on the west shore, concealed his boats, and travelled by land until within a mile of the fort. The next day two videttes of the French picket guard were discovered, one of whom was posted on the road leading to the woods. Rogers, with five men, marched directly down the road in the middle of the day, until challenged by the sentry. He answered in French, "Friends." The sentinel was thereby deceived, until the party came close to him, when, perceiving his mistake, in great surprise he cried out, "Qui êtes-vous?" The captain answered, "Rogers," led him from his post in great haste, and, with his party, reached Fort William Henry on the 31st of October. The prisoner reported that he belonged to the regiment of Languedoc, and left Brest last April, twelve month; had since served at Lake Champlain, Crown Point, and Carillon; was with General Dieskau last year at Lake George; that the French lost in that engagement a great number of troops; that Ticonderoga at this time mounted thirty-six pieces of cannon, namely, twelve eighteens, fifteen twelves, and nine eight-pounders; that Crown Point was defended by eighteen pieces of cannon, the largest of which were eighteens; that Monsieur Montcalm's forces this year at Carillon were three thousand regulars, and two thousand Canadians and Indians; that General Montcalm was away with one battalion; that the force at Carillon consisted of five battalions and eight hundred Canadians; that the Indians had all gone home, but two hundred of them talked of returning to spend the winter at Carillon; that the advanced guard on the west side, above the falls, were all drawn in, and that on the east consisted of six hundred men, who were to decamp on the 1st of November; that five battalions of infantry of the line and sixty Canadian militia lay encamped half a league from Carillon; that the remainder of the army were in the fort; that the barracks were sufficient for five hundred men, whom he understood were to quarter there; that the French had one schooner and two hundred batteaux on Lake Champlain, and but five or six on Lake George; that the Chevalier Levi commanded in General Montcalm's absence, and that the Canadians were under the orders of Messieurs Corné and Columbié; that, when the general went away, he said "he had done enough this year, and would take Fort William Henry in the spring;" that the French had taken four of Rogers' whale-boats on Lake Champlain; that, when taken, he was within a gunshot and a half of the fort; and that their camp was healthy. From this time the rangers were constantly employed in patrolling the woods about Fort Edward, until November 19, 1756, when they made an excursion down the lake. Captain Abercrombie, nephew of the general, had the curiosity to accompany the expedition; and, although nothing was effected, save obtaining a view of the French garrison, he was delighted with the novelties of a scout, and the noble scenery through which he was conducted. The party returned, on the 25th, at evening. About this time his lordship drew off the main body of his troops, to be quartered at Albany and New-York. Both armies now retired to winter quarters. The rangers were stationed at Forts William Henry and Edward, and were augmented by two new companies from Halifax (N. S.), under Captains Hobbs and Spikeman. These two companies were posted at Fort William Henry, and the other two at Fort Edward. Captain Richard Rogers was sent to New-England for recruits. He waited upon the Boston government to obtain pay for the rangers' services in the winter of 1755; but could obtain none, although Lord Loudoun generously supported the claim.

January 15, 1757. Capt. Robert Rogers marched with Lieutenant Stark, Ensign Page, of Richard Rogers' company, and fifty privates, to Fort William Henry, where they were employed in providing provisions, snow-shoes, &c., until the 17th, when being joined by Captain Spikeman, with Lieutenant Kennedy, Ensign Brewer, and fourteen men of his corps, together with Ensign James Rogers, with twenty men of Hobb's company, and Mr. Baker, a volunteer of the 44th regiment of the line, the whole party proceeded down Lake George on the ice, and at night encamped on the east side of the first narrows. Next morning a portion of the party, who had become lame in consequence of yesterday's exertions, were sent back, which reduced the force remaining to seventy-four, officers included. On the 18th they encamped twelve miles down the lake, on the west side. On the 19th they marched three miles down the lake, and then took to the land with their snow-shoes; and having travelled eight miles north-west, encamped three miles from the lake. On the 20th they marched east all day, and encamped on the west side, three miles from Lake Champlain.

January 21. The party marched eastward until they came to the lake half way between Crown Point and Ticonderoga, where they discovered a sled passing from the latter to the former. Lieutenant Stark, with twenty men, was directed to head the sled, while Rogers, with five of the party, cut off its retreat, leaving Captain Spikeman with the centre. Ten other sleds were discovered following down the lake. Rogers endeavored to give Mr. Stark notice before he shew himself on the lake, but could not. He sallied out, and they hastily turned back toward Ticonderoga. The rangers pursued and captured seven prisoners, three sleds and six horses; the remainder escaped. The captives were separately examined, and reported that two hundred Canadians and forty-five Indians had just arrived at Ticonderoga, and were to be reinforced that evening by fifty Indians from Crown Point; that six hundred regular troops were in that fortress, and three hundred and fifty at Ticonderoga, where they expected a large army which, in the spring, was to besiege the English forts; that they had large magazines of provisions; that the troops were well equipped, and in condition to march at a moment's warning, and intended to waylay and distress the convoys between the English forts. In consequence of this information, and knowing that those who escaped would give immediate notice of the party, orders were given them to march with all expedition to the fires which had been kindled the night before, and prepare for battle, if offered, by drying their guns, as the day was rainy. This was effected, and the party marched in single file—Captain Rogers and Lieutenant Kennedy in front, Lieutenant Stark in the rear, and Captain Spikeman in the centre; Ensign Page and Rogers between the front and centre, and Mr. Brewer between the centre and rear—Sergeant Walker having command of a rear guard.

In this manner the party advanced half a mile over broken ground, and passed a valley fifteen rods in breadth, when the front, having gained the summit of the opposite hill, on the west side, fell in with the enemy drawn up in the form of a crescent to surround the party, and were immediately saluted with a volley of two hundred shot, at a distance of five yards from the nearest, and thirty from the rear of the party. This fire took place about 2 o'clock P. M., and proved fatal to Lieutenant Kennedy and Mr. Gardner, a volunteer, beside wounding several, and Captain Rogers in the head. Rogers ordered his men to retire to the opposite hill, where Lieutenant Stark and Mr. Brewer had made a stand, with forty men, to cover the retreat. They were closely pursued, Captain Spikeman and others killed, and several made prisoners. Lieutenant Stark repulsed them by a brisk fire from the hill, killing a number, and affording those retreating an opportunity to post themselves to advantage. Mr. Stark then took a position in the centre, with Ensign Rogers, Sergeants Walker and Phillips acting as reserves to protect the flanks and watch the enemy's motions. Soon after the party had thus formed for battle, the enemy attempted to outflank them, but were bravely attacked by the reserve, who gave the first fire, which stopped several from returning to the main body. The rangers were then pushed closely in front, but having the advantage of the ground, and being sheltered by large trees, they maintained a constant fire, which killed a number, and compelled the others to retire upon their main force. The enemy attempted to outflank them once more, but were again gallantly repulsed by the reserve. In this affair, Mr. Baker was killed.

A constant fire was kept up till sunset, when a shot through his wrist disabled Captain Rogers from loading his gun. The action continued until darkness prevented the parties from seeing each other. The rangers gallantly maintained their position till the fire of the enemy ceased, and he retired.

During this action, the Indians practiced several stratagems to induce the rangers to submit: sometimes assuring them that reinforcements were at hand, who would cut them to pieces without mercy; that it was a pity so many brave men should be lost; that, in case of surrender, they should be treated with compassion. Calling Rogers by name, they assured him of their friendship and esteem; but he, and the brave men who fought by his side, were neither to be dismayed by their threats, nor flattered by their professions. They were resolved to conquer, or die with arms in their hands.

After the action, a considerable number were so severely wounded that they could not travel without assistance; but as the French garrison was so near, it was thought best to take advantage of the night and retreat. The spirits of the wounded were kept up as well as possible, and the party reached Lake George, six miles south of the French advanced guard, next morning. The wounded men were now exhausted, and could march no farther. Lieutenant Stark volunteered, with Thomas Burnside and another, to proceed to Fort William Henry and procure sleighs for the wounded. They reached the fort at 8 o'clock that night, and next morning sleighs arrived, though the distance was forty miles. Lieutenant Bulkley, of Hobbs' company, came out with fifteen men as far as the first narrows of Lake George; and the survivors of the expedition, consisting of forty-eight effective and six wounded men, arrived with their prisoners on the same evening (Jan. 23, 1757), at Fort William Henry.

Before the sleighs came to their relief, the men, looking back upon the lake, observed a dark object following at a distance on the ice. Supposing it might be one of their wounded stragglers, a sleigh was sent back for him. He proved to be Joshua Martin. His hip had been shattered by a ball which passed through his body, and he had been left for dead on the field of battle; but recovering himself, had followed his comrades' tracks to the lake, and there came in sight of them. He was so exhausted that he sank down the moment the sleigh reached him. He recovered of his wound, became a lieutenant, served through the war, and died at Goffstown at an advanced age.

The number of the enemy in this action was two hundred and fifty French and Indians. Accounts received afterward reported their loss on the spot, and those who died of their wounds, to be one hundred and sixteen—the whole force of the rangers being but seventy-four, officers included. The officers and men who survived the first onset, behaved with the most undaunted bravery, and vied with each other in their respective stations.*

* In regard to this fight, the late Mr. John Shute observed that Rogers did not on this occasion obey his own rules, written out for the guidance of the corps. After taking the sleds, a council of war advised to return by another route than that by which they came, which was their usual practice, and would have saved them the loss incurred by this conflict. The first notice the party had of the enemy was the noise made in cocking their guns, which Shute supposed was occasioned by some rangers preparing to fire at game. He was struck senseless by a ball which ploughed the top of his head. On coming to himself, he observed a man cutting off the ribbon of Rogers' queue, to bind up his wrist, through which a ball had passed. On the night retreat the rangers made a circuit to avoid a large fire in the woods, supposing the enemy were there. This caused them to lose time, so that Joshua Martin, who had kindled the fire by a large dry pine tree to warm himself, was enabled to follow and come in sight of them on the lake; otherwise he must have perished. Stilson Eastman, and the late Colonel Webster, of Plymouth, corroborated the statement of Mr. Shute that the conduct and courage of John Stark saved the party, and that to his activity, enterprise, and example, the corps of rangers were indebted for much of their celebrity during the "seven years war."

RETURN OF KILLED, WOUNDED AND MISSING, IN THE ACTION OF JANUARY 21, NEAR TICONDEROGA.

CAPTAIN ROBERT ROGERS' COMPANY.

KILLED.	WOUNDED.	MISSING.
Mr. Gardner, volunteer,	Captain Rogers,	William Morris,
Mr. Baker, volunteer,	Joshua Martin,	Sergeant Henry,
Thomas Henson.	Thomas Burnside.	John Morrison.

Total—3 killed, 3 wounded, 3 missing.

CAPTAIN RICHARD ROGERS' COMPANY.

KILLED.	WOUNDED.	MISSING.
John Stevens,	David Page.	Benjamin Goodall,
Ensign Caleb Page.		David Kimball.

Total—Killed 2, wounded 1, missing 2.

CAPTAIN HOBBS' COMPANY.

KILLED.

Sergeant Jonathan Howard,
Phinehas Kemp,
John Edmunds,
Thomas Farmer,
Edmund Lapartaquer.

Total—Killed 5.

CAPTAIN SPIKEMAN'S COMPANY.

KILLED.	WOUNDED.	MISSING.
Captain Spikeman,	Sergeant Moore,	Thomas Brown.
Lieutenant Kennedy,	John Kahall.	
Robert Avery,		
Samuel Fisk.		

Total—Killed 4, wounded 2, missing 1.

Total of the four companies—Killed 14, wounded 6, missing 6.*

Captain Rogers forwarded this report to Major Sparks, at Fort Edward, and wrote to Capt. Abercrombie, recommending such officers as were deserving to fill the vacancies occasioned by the late action, as follows:

* The missing men were prisoners.

Lieutenant Stark to be captain of Spikeman's corps, Sergeant Joshua Martin to be ensign of Richard Rogers' company, to which he received the following answer:

Albany, February 6, 1757.

Dear Sir—The general received your report by Major Sparks. He returns you and your men thanks for your good behaviour, and has recommended to my Lord Loudoun that they have pay for their prisoners.

On receiving an account of your skirmish, we sent an express to Boston recommending your brother James for lieutenant of Spikeman's company.

Please send the names of the officers you recommend for your own company, and your recommendation shall be duly regarded.

You can not imagine how all ranks of people are pleased with your men's behaviour. I was so pleased with their appearance when I was out with them, that I took it for granted they would behave well whenever they met the enemy. I am happy to learn that my expectations are answered. I am sorry for Spikeman and Kennedy, as well as for the men you have lost, but it is impossible to play at bowls without meeting rubs. We must try to revenge them. Few persons will believe it, but upon honor I should have been glad to have been with you, that I might have learned the manner of fighting in this country. The chance of being shot is all stuff, and King William's principle is the best for the soldier, "that every bullet has its billet," and that it is allotted how every man shall die; so that I am certain every one will agree that it is better to die with the reputation of a brave man, fighting for his country in a good cause, than by shamefully running away to preserve one's life, or by lingering out an old age to die in one's bed without having done his country or king any service.

The histories of this country, particularly, are full of the unheard of cruelties committed by the French, and the Indians, at their instigation; wherefore I think every brave man ought to do his utmost to humble that haughty nation, and reduce her bounds of conquest in this country to narrower limits.

When General Abercrombie receives his lordship's instructions respecting the rangers, I shall send you notice of it. In the mean time, I hope you'll get the better of your wound. As long as you and your men continue to behave so well, you may command

Your most humble servant,

JAMES ABERCROMBIE, *Aid-de-Camp.*

To Captain Robert Rogers.

The wound of Captain Rogers becoming worse, he repaired to Albany for medical aid, and there received from General Abercrombie the following instructions:

INSTRUCTIONS FOR CAPTAIN ROBERT ROGERS.

His Excellency, the Earl of Loudoun, having given authority to me to augment the companies of rangers under your command to one hundred men each: viz., one captain, two lieutenants, one ensign, upon English pay; four sergeants at 4*s.* each, New-York currency; and one hundred privates at 2*s.*, 6*d.* each, do. per day.

And whereas, certain privates are serving at present in your companies on higher pay than the above, you are at liberty to discharge them, in case they refuse to serve under the new establishment, as soon as you have men to replace them. If they remain and serve, you may assure them that they will be noticed, and be the first provided for. Each man is to be allowed ten dollars bounty money, to find his own clothing, arms, and blankets, and sign a paper subjecting himself to the articles of war, and to serve during the war. You are to enlist no vagrants, but such men as you and your officers are acquainted with, and who are every way qualified for the duty of rangers. Complete the companies as soon as possible, and proceed to Fort Edward.

JAMES ABERCROMBIE, *Major General.*

At this time Rogers wrote to Lord Loudoun, asking his aid in obtaining the amount due to himself and men for services in the winter of 1755. He replied that, as these services were antecedent to his command, it was not in his power to reward them. General Amherst afterward gave a similar answer. His men afterward sued and recovered judgments against him for £828, 3*s.*, 3*d.*, beside costs. For this, and for his own services during that severe season, he never received any consideration.

Captain Hobbs dying about this time, Lieutenant Bulkley succeeded him as captain. From March 5th to April 15th Rogers was confined with the small-pox at Fort Edward, during which time his officers were employed in recruiting, according to the foregoing instructions. Soon after his recovery, he received the following letter:

New-York, April 23, 1757.

Sir—As another company of rangers has been sent to Albany, with orders to proceed to our forts, you will inform Colonel Gage that it is Lord Loudoun's order that the two companies at Fort William Henry, and your own at Fort Edward, proceed immediately to Albany, and embark for this place. Show this letter to Colonel Gage, that he may inform Colonel Munro of his lordship's orders, and that quarters may be provided for your companies at Albany. See that your companies are well equipped, and are good men; if they are found insufficient, the blame will rest on you. If the officers of the new company are ignorant of the woods about Fort William Henry, your brother must send some officers and men to inform them of the different scouting grounds.

I am, sir, your humble servant,

JAMES ABERCROMBIE,

Aid-de-Camp.

To Captain Robert Rogers, Albany.

Richard Rogers, with his own and Bergen's new company of rangers from New-Jersey, being left at Fort William Henry, Stark's* and Bulkley's from the same fort, and Robert Rogers' company from Fort Edward, proceeded to Albany, and thence to New-York, where Shephard's new company, from New-Hampshire, joined them. There they embarked on board a transport, and left Sandy Hook June 10th, with a fleet of one hundred sail, for Halifax; where they soon arrived, and encamped on the Dartmouth side of the harbor, while the main army lay on the Halifax side.

July 3. Rogers went to Lawrencetown, where a portion of his men were employed in making hay for the horses to be employed on the Louisburg expedition. Part of them covered the hay-makers, while others went on scouts, one of which brought in two deserters from the 45th regiment. Toward the end of July, forty rangers were sent across the isthmus of Nova Scotia to the settlements on the Bay of Fundy, and a party down the north-west arm, to scour the woods for deserters, who brought in several, both of the army and navy. At this time Admiral Holbourn arrived with a fleet from England, having on board several regiments of troops, which were landed and encamped at Halifax. All the scouts were now called in, but certain intelligence having been received that a French fleet of superior force had arrived at Louisburg, the intended expedition was abandoned, and the rangers remanded to the western frontiers. During the summer numbers of the rangers were carried off by the small-pox, and several officers were sent on the recruiting service.

The rangers embarked for New-York, and proceeded in small vessels up the Hudson to Albany, where the recruits soon after arrived. They then proceeded to Fort Edward, which was now the only cover to the northern frontiers of New-York, and the more eastern provinces, Fort

*At New-York Captain Stark was taken with the small-pox, and did not accompany the expedition.

William Henry * having been taken in August previous by the French.

General Webb, now commanding Fort Edward, kept the rangers constantly employed patroling the woods between that post and Ticonderoga. Lord Howe accompanied one of these scouts, being desirous of learning their method of marching, ambushing, and retreating; and, on their return, expressed his good opinion of them very generously.

Lord Loudoun now added to the corps a number of volunteers from the regulars, to be trained to wood service under Captain Rogers' inspection, to be hereafter employed as light infantry. Several of them belonged to the 42d regiment of highlanders.†

* Captain Richard Rogers died of small-pox a few days before the siege of this fort; but the enemy, after its surrender, dug him up and scalped him. In consequence of the articles of capitulation, the two companies of rangers were disbanded and dismissed. After the surrender, Samuel Blodget, the ranger sutler, was found concealed under a batteau. He was allowed to go free, after being plundered of every thing but his scalp. He was afterward a sutler in the revolutionary army; became a considerable merchant, a judge, and was the projector of the first canal at Amoskeag falls, on Merrimack river. He lived to a great age, and died at Manchester, respected as an enterprising and public individual.

During Lord Loudoun's absence at Halifax, Fort William Henry was taken, after a siege of nine days, by the Marquis de Montcalm, while General Webb lay at Fort Edward, fifteen miles distant, with more than four thousand regular troops, and made no effort for its relief. The garrison capitulated on condition of quarter, which was shamefully broken by the enemy, and many of the prisoners massacred or carried away captive by the savages. Previous to the expedition against this fortress, ten sachems were sent by the French general as messengers to the northwestern tribes, to invite them to become the allies of France. In consequence of this summons, among others, a party of a tribe called "Cold Country Indians," appeared at the siege. They were cannibals, and many prisoners were by them roasted and eaten. The journal of a French officer, who was in Montcalm's army, and afterward taken in the West-Indies, states "that the Indians roasted several of their English captives, and compelled the survivors to partake of the horrid banquet."—*Hutch. Hist.*

Two savages seized a lad named Copp, and were leading him away by his shirt sleeves, when a ranger, named Benjamin Richards, a bold, athletic man, hearing his cries, broke from the ranks and rushed after them. He snatched away the boy, leaving the shirt sleeves in their hands, and regained his place in the ranks.

† This celebrated regiment in after times repulsed the French on the shores of Aboukir, and covered the landing of Sir Ralph Abercrombie's army in Egypt.

These volunteers formed a separate company under Rogers' immediate orders. For their instruction, he reduced to writing several rules, and a course of discipline, of which experience had taught him the necessity.

December 1, 1757. Lord Loudoun visited Fort Edward, and after giving directions for quartering the army, and leaving a strong garrison under the command of Colonel Haviland, he returned to Albany. The rangers and their volunteers were quartered in huts on an island in the Hudson, near Fort Edward, and were employed in various scouts, which the health of Rogers did not permit him to accompany, until December 17th; when, by order of Colonel Haviland, he marched with one hundred and fifty men to reconnoitre Ticonderoga, and if possible take a prisoner. He advanced six miles in a snow storm, and encamped, the snow being then three inches deep, and before morning it fell to the depth of fifteen. He however pursued his route.

December 18. Eight of the party being fatigued and unwell, returned to camp. The remainder proceeded nine miles to the east side of Lake George, near the place where Mons. Montcalm landed his troops when he besieged Fort William Henry. There they discovered a large quantity of cannon balls and shells, which had on that occasion been concealed by the French, and made such marks at the place, as would enable them to find the articles again. This was their first visit to the ruins since their return from Halifax.

December 19. The march continued on the north-west side of the lake, nine miles, to the head of North-west bay.

December 21. So many of the men became tired, and returned, as to reduce the force to one hundred and twenty three, officers included, who marched ten miles farther, and encamped for the night. Here each man was ordered to leave one day's provisions.

December 22. They marched ten miles, and encamped near the great brook running into Lake George, eight miles from the French advanced guard.

December 23. They proceeded eight miles—the next day six more, and halted six hundred yards from Ticonderoga. Near the mills five Indians' tracks were discovered, supposed to have been made the day before by a hunting party. On the march this day, between the advanced guard and the fort, three places of rendezvous were appointed in case they should be broken in action. Rogers informed the officers and men that he should rally the party at the post nearest the fort; and if broken there, retreat to the second; and at the third make a stand, until night should afford an opportunity of retiring in safety. The road from the fort to the woods was then ambushed by an advanced guard of twenty men, and a rear guard of fifteen. At 11 o'clock a sergeant of marines came from the fort up the road toward the advanced party, who suffered him to pass to the main body, which secured him. He reported the garrison at three hundred and fifty regulars, fifty artificers, and five Indians; that they had plenty of provisions, and that twelve masons were employed blowing rocks in the intrenchment, assisted by a number of soldiers; that Crown Point was garrisoned by one hundred and fifty regulars and fourteen Indians; that the Marquis de Montcalm was at Montreal; that five hundred Attawawa Indians wintered in Canada; that five hundred rangers had been raised in Canada, and were commanded by an experienced officer, well acquainted with the country; he did not know that the French intended an attack on the English fort this winter, but expected a large force of Indians, as soon as the ice would bear, to go down to that post; and all the bakers in Carillon were employed in making biscuit for these scouts.

About noon a Frenchman came near the rangers on his return from hunting. A party was ordered to pursue to the edge of the clearing, take him prisoner, fire a gun or two, and retreat to the main body, and thus by stratagem entice the enemy from their fort. The orders were promptly obeyed, but no one ventured out. The last prisoner gave the same information as the first, and also, that he had heard the English intended to attack Ticonderoga as soon as the lake was frozen hard enough to bear them. Finding that the enemy would not come out, the party killed seventeen head of cattle, and set fire to the wood collected for the garrison. Five large piles were consumed. The French discharged cannon at those who kindled the fires, but did them no injury. At 8 o'clock in the evening the party commenced their march, and on the 27th, with their prisoners, reached Fort Edward. On their return, they found at the north end of lake George the boats the French had taken at Fort William Henry, and a great number of cannon balls concealed. As the boats were under water, they could not destroy them.

On his return from this scout, Captain Rogers was ordered to New-York to confer with Lord Loudoun in respect to the augmentation of the corps of rangers. His lordship gave him a friendly reception, and the following instructions:

By His Excellency, John, Earl of Loudoun, Lord Mackline, and Taireensen, &c., &c.; one of the sixteen Peers of Scotland, Captain General of Virginia, and Vice Admiral of the same; Colonel of the 13th regiment of foot, Colonel-in-chief of the Royal American regiment, Major General and Commander-in-chief of all His Majesty's forces raised or to be raised in North America.*

Whereas, I have thought proper to augment the rangers with five additional companies: viz., four from New-England, and one Indian company, to be forthwith raised and employed in his majesty's service; and having entire confidence in your knowledge of the men fit for that service, I therefore, by these presents, empower you to raise such a number of non-commissioned officers and privates as will complete the companies upon the following establishment: viz., each company to consist of one captain, two lieutenants, one ensign, four sergeants and one hundred privates.

The officers are to receive British pay, that is, the same as officers of the same rank in the line; the sergeants 4*s*.,

*His lordship's list of titles remind one of the Spanish traveller, for whose catalogue of names the landlord could not find room in his house.

New-York currency, and the privates 2*s.*, 6*d.* per day. One month's pay for each of said companies shall be advanced, on condition that it is to be deducted from the first warrants which shall be issued hereafter for the subsistence of said companies. The men are to provide themselves with good blankets and warm clothing; the same to be uniform in each company. They will supply their own arms, which must bear inspection.

The Indians are to be dressed in their own costume, and all are to be subject to the articles of war.

You will dispatch the officers, appointed to these companies, immediately upon the recruiting service, with directions to enlist none for a less term than one year, nor any other than able bodied men, accustomed to the woods, good hunters, and every way qualified for rangers. They are all required to be at Fort Edward on or before the 15th of March next, and are to be mustered by the officer commanding that garrison.

Given under my hand, at New-York, the 11th day of January, 1758.

LOUDOUN.

By His Excellency's command—

J. APPY, Sec'y.

To Captain Robert Rogers.

In pursuance of these instructions, officers were dispatched to the New-England colonies, and the levies were completed on the 4th of March. Four of them were sent to join General Amherst, at Louisburg, and the others remained under the order of Captain Rogers. He was at the whole expense of raising these companies, for which he received no allowance; and by the death of one captain, to whom he had delivered one thousand dollars as advanced pay, as by his instructions he had a right to do, he was obliged to account to government for the same, for which he never received a farthing.

February 28. Colonel Haviland ordered a scout from Fort Edward, under Captain Putnam, who commanded a company of Connecticut provincials, together with a party of the rangers, giving out publicly that upon Putnam's return Rogers would be sent to the French forts with four hundred rangers. This was known to officers and soldiers at the time of Putnam's departure. While this party was out, a servant of Mr. Best, the sutler, was taken by a flying party from Ticonderoga, and one of Putnam's men deserted to the enemy. Captain Putnam returned, reporting that six hundred Indians lay not far from the enemy's quarters.

March 10. Colonel Haviland ordered Rogers to the vicinity of Ticonderoga, not with four hundred men as had been given out, but with one hundred and eighty, officers included. He had with him one captain, one lieutenant, and one ensign of the line, as volunteers: viz., Messrs. Creed, Kent and Wrightson; also, one sergeant and a private, all of the 27th regiment; a detachment from the four companies of rangers, quartered on the island near Fort Edward: viz., Captain Bulkley, Lieutenants Phillips, Moore, Campbell, Crafton and Pottinger; Ensigns Ross, Waite, McDonald and White, with one hundred and sixty-two privates.

Captain Rogers engaged in this enterprise, with so small a detachment of brave men, with much uneasiness. He had every reason to believe that the prisoner and deserter had informed the enemy of the movement intended, and the force to be employed. Yet Colonel Haviland, knowing all this, sent him out with *but* one hundred and eighty men. He probably had his reasons, and could perhaps justify his conduct; but that affords no consolation to the friends of the brave men who were thus rashly thrown in the way of an enemy of three times their force, and of whom one hundred and eight never returned.

The detachment first marched to Half-way brook, in the road leading to Lake George, and there encamped for the night. On the 11th they proceeded as far as the first narrows on Lake George, and encamped that evening on the east shore. After dark a scout was sent three miles down, to ascertain if the enemy were coming toward our fort, who returned without discovering them. The troops were, however, on their guard, and parties were kept out walking upon the lake all night, while sentries were posted at all necessary places on shore.

March 12. The rangers left their camp at sunrise, and, having advanced about three miles, perceived a dog running across the lake. A party was therefore sent to reconnoitre an island where it was supposed the Indians were in ambush ; but, as none were found there, it was thought expedient to take to the shore, and thus prevent being discovered from the surrounding hills. They halted at a place called Sabbath-day Point, on the west shore, and sent out scouts to look down the lake with perspective glasses. At dark the party proceeded down the lake. Lieutenant Phillips, with fifteen men, several of whom preceded him on skates, acted as an advanced guard, while Ensign Ross flanked them on the left under the west shore, near which the main body was kept marching as closely as possible to prevent separation, the night being extremely dark. In this manner they came within eight miles of the French advanced guard, when Mr. Phillips sent back a man on skates to desire the detachment to halt. Upon this the men were ordered to sit down upon the ice. Mr. Phillips soon after appeared, reporting that he had discovered what he supposed to be a fire* on the east shore, but was uncertain. He and Mr. White were sent to ascertain the fact. They returned in an hour, fully persuaded that a party of the enemy were encamped at the place. The advanced guard was called in, and the whole force marched to the west shore, where in a thicket they concealed their sleighs† and packs.

* It was afterward learned that a scout of French had a fire there at the time, but, on discovering the advanced party, put it out, and carried the news to the fort.

† These Indian sleighs were pieces of split wood shaved thin, about sixteen inches wide and six feet long, turned up in front, so as to slide easily over the snow, with two arms and a cross-piece, by which they were drawn. Thus an old ranger described them.

Leaving a small guard with the baggage, the party marched to attack the enemy's encampment, if it could be found. On reaching the place where the supposed fire had been seen, and finding no enemy, they concluded Mr. Phillips had mistaken patches of snow or rotten wood for fire, (which in the night and at a distance resemble it.) They then returned to their packs, and passed the night without fire. On the morning of the 13th a council of officers determined that the best course was to proceed by land upon snow-shoes, lest the enemy should discover the party on the lake. Accordingly the march was continued on the west shore, along the back of the mountains, which overlooked the French advanced guard, and the party halted two miles west of them, where they refreshed themselves until three o'clock. This halt and rest was to afford the day scout from the fort time to return home, before they advanced to ambush some of the roads leading to the fortress that night, in order to trepan the enemy in the morning.

The detachment now advanced in two divisions, one headed by Captain Bulkley, and the other by Captain Rogers. Ensigns White and Waite led the rear guard, while the other officers were properly posted with their respective divisions. On their left they were flanked by a rivulet, and by a steep mountain on their right. The main body kept close under the mountain, that the advanced guard might better observe the brook, on the ice of which they might travel, as the snow was now four feet deep, which made travelling difficult even with snow-shoes. In this manner they proceeded a mile and a half, when the advance reported the enemy in sight, and soon afterward, that his force was about ninety-six, chiefly Indians. The party immediately threw down their knapsacks, and prepared for action, supposing the enemy's whole force were approaching our left upon the ice of the rivulet. Ensign McDonald was ordered to take command of the advanced guard, which, as the rangers faced to the left, became a flanking party to their right. They marched within a few yards of the bank, which was higher than the ground they occupied, and, as the ground gradually descended from the rivulet to the foot of the mountain, the line was extended along the bank so far as to cover the enemy's whole front at once. When their front was nearly opposite his left wing, Captain Rogers fired his gun as the signal for a general discharge. The first fire was given by the rangers, which killed more than forty, and put the remainder to flight, in which one-half of the rangers pursued and cut down several more with their hatchets.

Imagining the enemy totally defeated, Ensign McDonald was ordered to head their flying remains, so that none should escape. He soon ascertained that the party already routed was only the advanced guard of six hundred Canadians and Indians, who were now coming up to attack the rangers. The latter now retreated to their own ground, which was gained at the expense of fifty men killed. There they were drawn up in good order, and fought with such intrepidity, keeping up such a constant and well-directed fire, as caused the enemy, though seven to one in number, to retreat a second time. The rangers being in no condition to pursue, the enemy rallied, and made a desperate attack upon their front and wings. They were so warmly received that their flanking parties soon retreated to their main body with great loss. This threw the whole into confusion, and caused a third retreat. The rangers' numbers were now too far reduced to take advantage of their disorder, and, having rallied, the enemy attacked them a fourth time.

Two hundred Indians were now discovered ascending the mountain on the right, in order to fall upon our rear. Captain Rogers ordered Lieutenant Phillips, with eighteen men, to gain the heights before them, and drive the Indians back. He succeeded in gaining the summit, and repulsed them by a well-directed fire. Captain Rogers now became alarmed lest the enemy should go round on the left, and take post on the other part of the hill, and directed Lieutenant Crafton, with fifteen men, to anticipate them. Soon afterward he sent two gentlemen, who were volunteers, with a few men to support him, which they did with great bravery.*

The enemy now pressed so closely upon the English front, that the parties were often intermixed, and in general not more than twenty yards asunder. A constant fire continued from the commencement of the attack, one hour and a half, during which time the rangers lost eight officers and one hundred privates killed on the spot. After doing all that brave men could do, they were compelled to break, and each man to look out for himself. Rogers ran up the hill, followed by twenty men, toward Phillips and Crafton, where they stopped, and gave the Indians who were pursuing in great numbers another fire, which killed several and wounded others. Lieutenant Phillips was at this time about capitulating for himself and party, being surrounded by three hundred Indians. Rogers came so near that Phillips spoke to him, and said if the enemy would give good quarter, he thought it best to surrender; otherwise, he would fight while a man was left to fire a gun.

Captain Rogers now retreated, with the remainder of his party, in the best manner possible. Several men, who were wounded and fatigued, were taken by the savages who pursued his retreat. He reached Lake George in the evening, where he was joined by several wounded men, who were assisted to the place where the sleighs had been left. From this place an express was dispatched to Colonel Haviland, for assistance to bring in the wounded. The party passed the night without fire or blankets, which

* These gentlemen were both officers of the line, and went out as volunteers, desirous of witnessing the novelty of an Indian fight. Rogers previously requested them to retire, and offered a sergeant to conduct them. They at first accepted the offer; but, being unused to snow-shoes, unacquainted with the woods, and seeing the rangers hardly pressed by the Indians, painted most hideously, and causing the mountains to echo with their horrid yells, like gallant men, came back to their aid. After the fight they escaped, and wandered in the forest and mountains for seven days, enduring great hardships, until the morning of the 20th, when they reached Ticonderoga, and surrendered to a party of French officers, who, observing them, ran out and prevented their capture by a party of Indians. The French treated them in a kind and hospitable manner, and in due time they were exchanged.

were lost with their knapsacks. The night was extremely cold, and the wounded suffered much pain, but behaved in a manner consistent with their conduct in the action.

In the morning the party proceeded up the lake, and at Hoop island met Captain John Stark bringing to their relief provisions, blankets and sleighs. They encamped on the island, and passed the night with good fires. On the evening of March 15, they arrived at Fort Edward.

Regarding this unfortunate enterprise, Rogers says: "The number of the enemy who attacked us was seven hundred, of which six hundred were Indians. From the best accounts, we afterward learned that we killed one hundred and fifty of them, and wounded as many more, most of whom died. I will not pretend to say what would have been the result of this unfortunate expedition, had our number been four hundred strong, as was contemplated; but it is due to those brave officers who accompanied me, most of whom are now no more, to declare that every man in his respective station behaved with uncommon resolution and coolness. Nor do I recollect an instance, during the action, in which the prudence or good conduct of one of them could be questioned."

The only person whose conduct appears censurable was Colonel Haviland, for sending out so small a force, when he had every reason to believe that the enemy was apprised of his intentions, and would without doubt have a superior force in readiness, to compel the rangers to an engagement under every disadvantage.

RETURN OF KILLED AND WOUNDED,

IN THE ACTION OF MARCH 13, 1758.

The captain and lieutenant of the regular troops, acting as volunteers, were made prisoners. The ensign, a sergeant and one private, all volunteers from the same regiment, were killed.

CAPTAIN ROBERT ROGERS' COMPANY—

Lieutenant Moore, Sergeant Parnell, and thirty-six privates, killed.

CAPTAIN SHEPHARD'S COMPANY—

Two sergeants and sixteen privates killed.

Captain James Rogers' Company—
Ensign McDonald killed.

Captain John Stark's Company—
Two sergeants and fourteen privates killed.

Captain Bulkley's Company—
Captain Bulkley, Lieutenant Pottenger, and Ensign Waite killed: 17 privates killed and missing.

Captain William Stark's Company—
Ensign Ross killed.

Captain Brewer's Company—
Lieutenant Campbell killed.

After the return of Captain Rogers from this scout, he was ordered to Albany to recruit his company, where he met with a friendly reception from Lord Howe, who advanced money to recruit men, and gave him leave to wait upon General Abercrombie, at New-York. That general had now succeeded to the command-in-chief, in place of Lord Loudoun, who was about to embark for England. At this time, he received the following commission:

By His Excellency, James Abercrombie, Esquire, Colonel of His Majesty's 44th regiment of foot, Colonel-in-chief of the 60th royal Americans, Major General and Commander-in-chief of all His Majesty's forces raised or to be raised in North America.

Whereas, it may be of great use to his majesty's service in America to have a number of men employed in obtaining intelligence of the strength, situation and motions of the enemy, and other services, for which rangers are qualified: Having, therefore, the greatest confidence in your loyalty, courage and skill, I do hereby constitute you major of the rangers in his majesty's service, and captain of a company of the same. You are therefore to take the said rangers as major, and the said company as captain, into your care, and duly exercise and instruct as well the officers as the soldiers; who are hereby commanded to obey you as their major and captain, respectively. And you are to observe such orders as from time to time you shall receive from his majesty, myself, or any other superior officer, according to the rules and discipline of war.

Given at New-York, this 6th day of April, 1758, in the 31st year of our sovereign lord, the king of Great Britain, France and Ireland, defender of the faith, &c.

JAMES ABERCROMBIE.

By His Excellency's command—

J. APPY, Sec'y.

To Major Robert Rogers.

On the 12th of April Major Rogers reported himself to Lord Howe, at Albany, with whom he conversed respecting the different modes of distressing the enemy, and prosecuting the war with vigor the ensuing campaign. He then proceeded to Fort Edward to take orders from Colonel Grant, then commanding that post. Captain Stark was dispatched to Ticonderoga, on the west side of Lake George; Captain Jacobs (Indian), on the east side; Captain Shephard between the lakes, with orders to take prisoners from Ticonderoga. At the same time, Major Rogers marched, with eighteen men, to Crown Point. Captain Burbank was also detached in quest of prisoners. These scouts were kept constantly out to reconnoitre the enemy from time to time.

April 29. Major Rogers marched, with eighteen men, towards Fort William Henry, four miles, and encamped at Schoon creek, the weather being rainy.

April 30. He proceeded north-east, and encamped by South bay.

May 1. He encamped near the narrows north of South bay.

May 2. He made a raft, crossed the lake, and encamped four miles from it, on the east side.

May 3. He steered north, and encamped three miles from Ticonderoga.

May 4. He marched north-east all day, and encamped three miles from Crown Point.

May 5. He killed a Frenchman, and took three prisoners. With them he reached camp on the 9th instant.

One of the prisoners reported that "he was a native of Lorraine; that he had been eight years in Canada—of which time he had passed two years at Quebec, one at Montreal, and five at Crown Point; that at the latter place were two hundred soldiers, under Mons. Jonang; that Ticonderoga contained four hundred of the queen's regiment, one hundred and fifty marines, two hundred Canadians and seven hundred Indians, three hundred more being expected; that the French did not intend to attack the English fort, but were preparing to receive them at Ticonderoga; they had heard that Rogers was killed in the conflict of last March, but from prisoners taken by the Indians, at Dutch Hoosac, they learned that he was alive, and had sworn to revenge the barbarities with which his men had been treated, particularly Lieutenant Phillips* and his party, who had been butchered in cold blood, after they had been promised quarter. This was talked of among the Indians, who blamed the French for encouraging them to do so."

*A note in the History of Manchester, page 321, refers to this circumstance as follows:

"It is stated in a note, in Rogers' journal, that Lieut. Phillips was killed in this battle; he and his party being tied to trees, and hewn to pieces in the most barbarous manner. This is a mistake. Lieut. Phillips escaped, lived to a good old age, and died in Northfield, N. H., somewhere about the year 1819. The writer of this has often heard Lieut. Phillips relate this and other of his escapes in the 'seven years war.'"

In regard to Phillips, Judge Potter states that "his christian name was William. He was known as 'Bill Phillips.' He was a noted hunter, and lived in the vicinity of Concord, supporting himself principally by hunting. His father was a Frenchman, and his mother an Indian. He partly learned the trade of a blacksmith, but preferred to swing a hatchet or knife to making either; and had rather by far *steal* a hatchet, axe, or knife, than labor in their manufacture, or to purchase them, provided he had money. In a word, he was an excellent hunter and warrior; but, with these characteristics, he had some of the bad habits of both the French and the Indian. He was appointed a lieutenant by Lord Loudoun. He was not killed, as reported by Rogers, in the action of March 13th, 1758, but lived in the Merrimack valley until his death, in 1819. He married Eleanor Eastman, of Rumford (now Concord), daughter of Ebenezer Eastman. He supported himself by hunting and occasional blacksmith work. He became a drunkard, neglected his business, and *would steal*. His wife, in consequence, left him, and joined the Shakers at Canterbury. He lived to a great age, and was supported for a time by the town of Concord. At length, he joined the settlement at Northfield. That town supported him till his death."

Captains Stark and Jacobs returned on the 8th instant. The former brought in six prisoners, four of whom he recaptured near Ticonderoga; they, having escaped from New-York and Albany, were on their flight to the French forts. The latter, who had with him but one white man and eighteen Indians, took ten prisoners and seven scalps from a party of French. About the middle of May a flag of truce was sent to Ticonderoga on Colonel Schuyler's account, which put a stop to all offensive scouts till its return.

May 28. Orders were issued by Rogers to all officers and men of the rangers, and the two Indian companies on furlough, to join their respective corps before the 10th of June. These orders were obeyed, and parties kept on scouts until June 8th, when Lord Howe arrived at Fort Edward with one half of the army.

His lordship ordered Rogers, with fifty men, and his whale-boats, which were conveyed in wagons to Lake George, to proceed to Ticonderoga, to obtain at all events an accurate plan of the north end; also, of the ground from the landing-place to the fort; also, of Lake Champlain for three miles beyond it, and discover the enemy's force in that quarter.

With these orders, he marched on the morning of the 12th, and at night encamped on the site of Fort William Henry.

June 30. He proceeded down the lake in five whale-boats to the first narrows, and to the west end of the lake, where he took the plans required. Part of his men proceeding to reconnoitre the fort, discovered an extensive Indian encampment and a large number of Indians. While Rogers was at a distance from his men, engaged with two or three others taking plans of the fort and camp, the rangers were attacked by a superior number of the enemy who had come between them. Captain Jacobs, with his Mohegans, ran off at the first onset, calling to the rangers to do the same; but they stood their ground, discharged their pieces several times, and at last broke through the enemy, who surrounded them on all sides except their rear, which was covered by a river. They killed three of the enemy, but lost eight rangers in the skirmish. The party rallied at the boats, where Rogers joined them, and, having collected all but the slain, returned homeward.

On the 20th, at Half-way brook, they met Lord Howe with three thousand men, to whom Rogers gave an account of his scout, and the plans he had requested. From him he obtained leave to wait upon General Abercrombie at Fort Edward. He ordered him to join Lord Howe next day with all the rangers, amounting to six hundred, and proceed with him to the lake.

On the 22d his lordship encamped near the site of Fort William Henry. The rangers advanced four hundred yards farther, and encamped on the west side. From this position three small parties were detached, one to the narrows of South bay, one along the west shore of Lake George, and a third to Ticonderoga, all proceeding by land. Another party of two lieutenants and seventeen men were sent down the lake in five whale-boats, on the look out, and were all taken prisoners by two hundred French and Indians.

On the 28th of June General Abercrombie arrived at the lake with the remainder of his troops; and on the morning of July 5th the whole army, of nearly sixteen thousand men, embarked in batteaux for Ticonderoga.

The order of march afforded a brilliant spectacle. The regular troops occupied the centre, and the provincials formed the wings. For the advanced guard, the light infantry flanked the right, and the rangers the left of Colonel Bradstreet's batteau men.

In this order the army advanced, until dark, down the lake to Sabbath-day Point, when it halted to refresh. At ten o'clock at night the force moved onward, Lord Howe proceeding in front with his whale-boat, attended by Colonel Bradstreet, Major Rogers, and Lieutenant Holmes in other boats. Holmes was detached in advance to view the landing-place, and ascertain if the enemy were posted there. He returned at daybreak, and met the army four miles from the landing-place, near the Blue mountains. He reported that he had discovered, by their fires, that a party of the enemy were posted at the landing-place. At daylight his lordship, Colonel Bradstreet, and Major Rogers proceeded within a quarter of a mile of the landing-place, and perceived a small party in possession of it. His lordship thereupon returned to assist in landing the army, intending to march by land to Ticonderoga. At twelve o'clock the landing was effected, and the rangers posted on the left wing. Major Rogers was ordered to gain the summit of a mountain, which bore north one mile from the landing-place; thence to proceed to the river which enters the falls between the landing-place and the saw-mills, and take possession of a rising ground on the side of the enemy; there to await farther orders. After a toilsome march of one hour, he gained the position, and posted his men, to the best advantage, within a quarter of a mile of the post occupied by the Marquis de Montcalm, with fifteen hundred men, as the scouts ascertained. At twelve o'clock Colonels Lyman and Fitch, of the provincials, took post in their rear. While Rogers was informing them of the enemy's position, a sharp fire commenced in the rear of Lyman's regiment, who immediately formed his front, and desired Rogers to fall upon the left flank, which he did. Rogers ordered Captain Burbank, with one hundred and fifty men, to retain their present position, and watch the motions of the French at the saw-mills. With his remaining force he fell upon the enemy's left, the river covering their right, and killed many of them. By this time Lord Howe, with a detachment from his front, had broken the enemy, and hemmed them in on each side; but, while advancing himself with too great intrepidity and zeal, he was unfortunately struck by a shot, and died instantly.*

* This intrepid and accomplished nobleman was beloved by both officers and soldiers, and his fall produced a general consternation.

At six o'clock, July 7th, Rogers was ordered to the river, where he had been stationed the day before, there to halt on the west side, with four hundred and fifty men, while Captain Stark, with the remainder of the rangers, advanced with Captain Abercrombie, and Mr. Clerk, the engineer, to reconnoitre the place. They returned the same evening, and the whole army passed the night under arms. At sunrise, July 8th, Sir William Johnson arrived with four hundred and forty Indians. At seven o'clock the rangers were ordered to march. A lieutenant of Captain Stark led the advanced guard, which, when within three hundred yards of the intrenchments, was ambushed and fired upon by two hundred French. Rogers formed a front to support them, and they maintained their ground until the enemy retreated. Soon after this the batteau men formed on Rogers' left, and the light infantry on his right. The enemy's fire did not kill a man of the rangers. Two provincial regiments now formed in Rogers' rear, at two hundred yards' distance. While the army was thus forming, a scattering fire was kept up between the English flying parties and those of the enemy, without the breastwork. At half past ten, the army being drawn up, a sharp fire commenced on the left wing, where Colonel De Lancy's New York men and the batteau men were posted. Upon this Rogers, with the rangers, was ordered to drive the enemy within their works, and then to fall down, that the pickets and grenadiers might march through. The enemy soon retired within their works, and Major Proby, with his pickets, marched within a few yards of the works, where he unfortunately fell. The enemy keeping up a steady fire, the soldiers were drawing back, when Colonel Haldiman came up with the grenadiers to support them, followed by the battalions of the line. The colonel advanced very near the breastwork, which was eight feet high. Some provincials and Mohawks also came up. The troops toiled, with repeated attacks, for four hours, being much embarrassed by trees felled by the enemy without their breastwork, when the general ordered a retreat, directing the rangers to bring up the rear, which they did in the dusk of the evening. On the 9th, at dark, the army reached the south end of Lake George, where the general bestowed upon them his thanks for their good behavior, and ordered them to intrench. The wounded were sent to Fort Edward and Albany. The loss of the English was sixteen hundred and eight regulars, and three hundred and thirty-four provincials killed and wounded, while that of the French was five hundred killed and wounded, and many prisoners.

Soon after this Rogers went on a scout to South bay, and returned July 16th, having discovered one thousand of the enemy on the east side. This party fell upon Colonel Nichols' regiment, at Half-way brook,* and killed three captains and twenty men.

July 27. Another party of the enemy attacked a convoy of wagons between Fort Edward and Half-way brook, and killed one hundred and sixteen men, sixteen of whom were rangers. Major Rogers attempted to intercept this party with seven hundred men, but they escaped. On his return an express met him with orders to march to South and East bays, and return. On this march nothing material occurred until August 8th. Early in the morning the march commenced from the site of Fort Ann; Major Putnam, with a party of provincials, marching in front, the rangers in the rear, and Captain Dalyell, with the regulars in the centre, the whole force amounting to five hundred and thirty, exclusive of officers. After marching one-third of a mile, five hundred of the enemy attacked the front. The men were immediately brought into line, Captain Dalyell† commanding the centre, with the rangers

* From these and other slaughters this brook is sometimes called "Bloody brook."

† Captain James Dalyell was appointed a lieutenant in the 60th, or Royal Americans, January 15, 1756, and obtained a company in the 2d battalion of Royals, or 1st regiment of foot, on the 13th of September, 1760. On the 31st of July, 1763, he led a detachment against Pontiac, then encamped beyond the bridge on the creek called "Bloody run," near Detroit. The British party was obliged to retreat; but Dalyell, seeing a wounded sergeant of the 55th lying on the ground, gazing in despair after his retiring comrades, ran back to rescue the wounded man, when he was struck by a shot, and fell dead.

and light infantry on the right, and Captain Giddings, with his Boston troops, on the left. Major Putnam being in front of his men when the fire began, the enemy rushed in and took him, one lieutenant, and two privates prisoners, and threw his whole party into confusion. They afterward rallied, and performed good service, particularly Lieutenant Durkee,* who, notwithstanding a wound in the thigh and one in his wrist, bravely maintained his ground, and encouraged his men throughout the action.

Captain Dalyell, with Gage's light infantry, and Lieutenant Eyers of the 44th regiment, behaved with great gallantry. They occupied the centre, where at first the fire was most severe. It afterward fell upon the right, where the enemy made four different attacks upon the rangers. The officers and men behaved with so much courage, that in an hour the enemy broke and retreated; but with so much caution, and in such small squads, as to afford no opportunities to harrass them by pursuit. The English kept the field, and buried the dead. They missed fifty-four men, twenty-one of whom came in afterward, they having been separated from the rangers during the action. The enemy lost one hundred and ninety-nine killed, several of whom were Indians. The party was met, at some distance from Fort Edward, by three hundred men with refreshments, sent by Colonel Provost, and with them they arrived, on the 9th of August, at Fort Edward.

July 11. Colonel Provost, who now ranked as brigadier, ordered Rogers to pursue the track of a large body of Indians, which he heard had passed down the Hudson. The report proving groundless, he returned on the 14th, and proceeded to the camp at Lake George. August 29th, he reconnoitred Ticonderoga, and from that time until the army retired to winter quarters, was employed in various excursions to the French forts, and in pursuit of their flying parties.

* LIEUTENANT ROBERT DURKEE. This brave and skillful partisan served with distinction in the French war, and afterward removed to the settlement in the valley of Wyoming, Penn., and rendered valuable services in the revolutionary contest. He was slain at the battle of Wyoming, July 3, 1778.—*Wilson's Orderly Book.*

Although little was effected by the expedition to Ticonderoga, the British arms were not every where unsuccessful. Colonel Bradstreet, with two thousand men, reduced Fort Frontenac* at Cataraqua; and General Amherst, who had captured Louisburg, now assumed the chief command of his majesty's forces, and established his head quarters at New-York.

Major Rogers proceeded to Albany to settle his accounts with the paymaster, and while there addressed the following letter to Colonel Townshend, deputy adjutant general to his excellency, General Amherst:

Albany, January 28, 1759.

Sir—I herewith send you a return of the present condition of his majesty's rangers at Fort Edward, with a list of officers now recruiting in different parts of New-England, who report nearly four hundred men enlisted, who are now wanted to protect our convoys between Albany and Fort Edward.

In order to urge the recruiting service, I would propose a visit to New-England, and wait upon the general at New-York on my way, to represent the necessity of augmenting the rangers, and the desire of the Stockbridge Indians to reënter the service. The rangers' arms are in the hands of Mr. Cunningham at New-York, and are very much needed at Fort Edward. Will you be good enough to have them forwarded?

Respectfully, your obedient servant,

R. ROGERS.

To Colonel Townshend.

P. S. General Stanwix informs me that a subaltern and twenty rangers are to be stationed at Number Four. I would recommend Lieutenant Stevens, who is well acquainted with the country in that quarter.

* This fort was square-faced, with four stone bastions, and nearly three quarters of a mile in circumference. Its situation was pleasant, the banks of the river presenting an agreeable landscape, with a fair view of Lake Ontario, distant one league, interspersed with many beautiful woody islands. It was erected to prevent the Indians from trading with the English, and became a place of great trade.

[Answer.]

February 5, 1759.

Sir—I received your letter with the inclosed return. The general commands me to inform you that he can by no means approve of your leaving Fort Edward. Your recruiting officers are ordered to send their recruits to Fort Edward, by an advertisement in the newspapers containing the general's orders, as you did not furnish their names and places of duty. The proposals for the Indians must be sent immediately to the general. The arms shall be sent forthwith. Lieutenant Stevens has been notified of the general's intention of leaving him at Number Four. It is a season of the year when you may expect the enemy's scouting parties, and you must see the necessity of remaining at Fort Edward. Your officers will join you as soon as possible. At another time the general would grant your request.

Your humble servant,

R. TOWNSHEND, *D. A. G.*

To Major Rogers.

Rogers proposed to the colonel an addition of two new corps of rangers, on the same footing as those already in service, and that three Indian companies should be raised for the next campaign. To secure them before they went out on hunting parties, he wrote to three of their chiefs: one, to King Uncas of the Mohegans, was as follows:

Brother Uncas—As it is for the advantage of King George to have a large body of rangers raised for the next campaign, and being well convinced of your attachment, I wish, in pursuance of General Amherst's orders, to engage your assistance early in the spring. Should you choose to come out as captain, you shall have a commission; if not, I shall expect Doquipe and Nunipad. You shall choose the ensign and sergeants. The company shall consist of fifty men or more. If the deserters from

Brewer's corps will join you, the general will pardon them. You may employ a clerk, who shall be allowed the usual pay. I wish you success in raising the men, and shall be glad to be joined by you as soon as possible.

Your humble servant,

R. ROGERS.

With letters to Indians, a belt of wampum is sent. The bearer reads the letter, and delivers that and the belt to the sachem, to whom they are directed.

Toward the last of February Sir William Johnson sent Captain Lotridge, with fifty Mohawks, to join Rogers in a scout to Ticonderoga.

On the 3d of March Colonel Haldiman ordered Rogers to reconnoitre the enemy's forts. He marched, with three hundred and fifty-eight men, to Half-way brook, and there encamped. One Indian, being hurt, returned. On the 4th he marched within a mile and a half of Lake George, and halted till evening, that he might pass the enemy undiscovered, should any of them be on the hill. He then marched on until two o'clock in the morning, and halted at the first narrows, whence several frost-bitten men were sent back in charge of a careful sergeant. At eleven, on the night of the 5th, the party reached Sabbath-day Point, almost overcome with cold. At two o'clock the march was resumed, and the landing-place reached at eight o'clock in the forenoon. Here a scout was sent out, who reported two working parties on the east side, but none on the west. This being a suitable opportunity for the engineer to make his observations, Rogers left Captain Williams in command of the regulars and thirty rangers, and proceeded with the engineer and forty-nine rangers, Captain Lotridge and forty-five Indians, to the isthmus which overlooks the fort, where the engineer made his observations. They then returned, leaving five Indians and one ranger to observe what numbers crossed the lake from the east side in the evening, that the party might know how to attack them in the morning. At dark the engineer went again to the intrenchments with Lieutenant Tute and a guard of ten men. He returned without molestation at midnight, having completed his survey. Upon his return Captain Williams and the regulars were ordered back to Sabbath-day Point; they, being distressed with cold, and having no snow-shoes, it appeared imprudent to march them farther. Lieutenant Tute and thirty rangers were sent with them to kindle fires at the point.

At three o'clock Rogers marched with forty rangers, one regular, and Lotridge's Indians to attack the working parties when they crossed the lake early in the morning. He crossed South bay eight miles south of the fort, and at six o'clock bore down opposite to it, within half a mile of the French parties who were cutting wood. A scout of two Indians and two rangers reported that they were forty in number, and at work close upon the lake shore, nearly opposite the fort. Throwing off their blankets, the rangers ran down upon the choppers, took several prisoners, and destroyed most of the party in their retreat. Being discovered by the garrison, the party was pursued by eighty Canadians and Indians, supported by one hundred and fifty regulars, who, in a mile's march, commenced a fire upon their rear. The rangers, halting upon a rising ground, repulsed the enemy before their whole party came up, and resumed their line of march abreast. After proceeding half a mile, their rear was again assailed; but, having gained an advantageous position upon a long ridge, they made a stand on the side opposite to the enemy. The Canadians and Indians came very near, but, receiving a warm fire from the rangers and Mohawks, they broke immediately, were pursued, and entirely routed before their regulars could come up. The party now marched without interruption. In these skirmishes one regular and two rangers were killed, and one Indian wounded. Thirty of the enemy were left dead. At twelve o'clock at night the party reached Sabbath-day Point,*

* Considering that three skirmishes took place in the course of it, this must be considered an extraordinary march on snow-shoes.

fifty miles from the place they left in the morning. Captain Williams was up, and received them with good fires, than which nothing could have been more acceptable, as many of the men had their feet frozen, the weather being intensely cold, and the snow four feet deep. Next morning the whole party marched to Long island, on Lake George, and encamped for the night. During the march several rangers and Indians had leave to hunt on the lake shore, and brought in plenty of venison. Fearing that a party of Indians, who had gone up South bay, might do some mischief before his return, Major Rogers dispatched Lieutenant Tute with the following letter to Colonel Haldiman:

Camp at Sabbath-day Point, 8 o'clock A. M.

Sir—I would inform you that sixty Indians, in two parties, have gone toward Fort Edward and Saratoga, and I fear they will strike a blow before this reaches you. Mr. Brheme, the engineer, has completed his business agreeably to his orders; since which I have taken and destroyed several of the enemy near Ticonderoga, as the bearer will inform. The Mohawks behaved well, and ventured within pistol shot of the fort. The weather is extremely severe, and we are compelled to carry some of our men whose feet are frozen.

Yours, &c.,

R. ROGERS.

N. B. Two-thirds of my detachment have frozen their feet.

[Answer.]

Fort Edward, March 20, 1759.

Dear Sir—I congratulate you on your success, and send twenty-two sleighs to transport your sick. You will also bring as many boards * as you can conveniently. My compliments to Captain Williams and the gentlemen.

Your most obed't serv't,

FRED. HALDIMAN.

* Boards left at south end of Lake George, and wanted at Fort Edward.

P. S. The signal guns * have been fired to give notice to the different posts to be on their guard. Nothing has yet appeared.

At Lake George the party met the sleighs and a detachment of one hundred men, and all returned in safety to Fort Edward, where Rogers received the following letter:

New-York, February 26, 1759.

Sir—Your letter by Mr. Stark was yesterday received. The general approves of raising the Indians, but does not agree to raise any more companies of rangers until the present ones are completed. Your arms have been proved by the artillery, and answer well. They will be sent you as fast as possible. We have chosen one hundred men from each regiment, and selected officers, to act this year as light infantry. They are equipped as lightly as possible, and are much wanted in our service. Brigadier Gage recommends you highly to the general. With him merit will not pass unrewarded, nor will he favor recommendations unless the person deserves promotion. Please return your companies when complete.

Your humble servant,

R. TOWNSHEND.

New-York, February 13, 1759.

Sir—This will be delivered by Captain Jacob Nannawapateonks, who during the last campaign commanded the Stockbridge Indians, who, upon hearing that you had written concerning him, came to offer his services for the ensuing campaign. As you have not mentioned any terms, I refer him to you to receive his proposals. Report them to me, and inform me whether his service is adequate to them. After which I will give an answer.

Your most obed't serv't,

JEFF. AMHERST.

To Major Rogers.

* A party of Indians near Fort Miller, eight miles below, heard these guns, and, supposing they were discovered, retreated.

Before receiving this letter, Rogers had waited on the general at Albany, by whom he was well received, and assured of the rank of major in the line of the army from the date of his commission under General Abercrombie. Returning to Fort Edward, May 15th, he received the melancholy news of the death of Captain Burbank,* who, during his absence, had been cut off with thirty men while on a scout. He was a good officer, and the scout upon which he was sent was needless and ill-advised.

Preparations for the campaign were now hastened in every quarter. Levies from the provinces arrived, the ranger companies were completed, and in June a portion of the army under General Gage advanced to the lake. Rogers was ordered to send Captain Stark, with three companies, to join him. With the other three, Rogers remained under the orders of the general-in-chief, who directed several scouts to be made to the enemy's forts.

June 20. The second division of the army proceeded to the lake, the rangers forming the advanced guard. Here the general fulfilled his promise to Rogers, by declaring publicly, in general orders, his rank as major in the army from the date of his commission as major of rangers. The army lay here collecting its strength, and procuring information of the enemy, until July 21st, when it was again embarked for Ticonderoga, in little more than a year from the time of the memorable repulse before the lines of that fortress.

June 22. The rangers were in front, on the right wing, and were the first troops landed at the north end of Lake George. They were followed by the grenadiers and light infantry, under Colonel Haviland. The rangers marched across the mountains in the isthmus, thence, through a by-path in the woods, to the bridge at the saw-mills; where, finding the bridge uninjured, they crossed to the

* An Indian scalped Captain Burbank, and held up the trophy with great exultation, thinking it to be that of Major Rogers. The prisoners informed him of the mistake, and the Indians appeared to be sorry, saying he was a good man. He had some time previously shown some of them kindness, which Indians never forget.

other side, and took possession of a rising ground. From this they drove a party of the enemy, killed several, took a number of prisoners, and routed the whole party before Colonel Haviland's corps had crossed the bridge. The army took possession of the heights near the saw-mills, where it remained during the night. The enemy kept out a scout of Canadians and Indians, who killed several men, and galled the army severely.

July 23. At an early hour the general put the troops in motion. The rangers were ordered to the front, with directions to proceed across Chestnut plain, the nearest route to Lake Champlain, and endeavor to strike the lake near the edge of the cleared ground, between that and the breastwork; there to await farther orders. The general had by this time prepared a detachment to attack the main breastwork on the hill, which they carried; while two hundred rangers carried a small intrenchment near Lake Champlain, without much loss. From the time when the army came in sight, the enemy kept up a constant fire of cannon from their walls and batteries. The general employed several provincial regiments in transporting cannon and stores across the carrying-place, which service they performed with great expedition.

July 24. This day engineers were employed in raising batteries, with the assistance of a large portion of the troops, the remainder being employed in preparing fascines, until the 26th,* at night. Scouts of rangers were during this interval kept out in the vicinity of Crown Point, by whose means the general received hourly information from that post. Orders were now given to cut

* The brave Colonel Townshend was killed this day by a cannon ball. He was deeply lamented by the general, to whom he acted as deputy adjutant general.

Roger Townshend, fourth son of Charles, Viscount Townshend, was commissioned lieutenant colonel February 1, 1758, and served as adjutant general in the expedition against Louisburg, and deputy adjutant general in the campaign of 1759, with the rank of colonel. He was killed in the trenches at Ticonderoga, by a cannon ball, July 26, 1759. His remains were conveyed to Albany for interment. His spirit and military knowledge entitled him to the esteem of every soldier, and his loss was universally lamented.— *Wilson's Orderly Book.*

away a boom, which the French had thrown across the lake opposite the fort, which prevented the English from passing in boats to cut off the French retreat. To effect this object, two whale-boats and one English flat-boat were conveyed across the land from Lake George to Lake Champlain. In these, after dark, Rogers embarked with sixty rangers, and passed over to the other shore, opposite the enemy's camp; from thence intending to steer along the east shore, and silently saw off the boom, which was composed of large timber logs, fastened together with strong chains. At nine o'clock the party had nearly reached their destination, when the French, who had previously undermined the fortress, sprung their mines, which blew up the fort with a tremendous explosion, and the garrison commenced a retreat in their boats. Rogers and his party availed themselves of this favorable opportunity of attacking them, and drove several boats on shore; so that in the morning ten boats were taken on the east shore, containing a large quantity of baggage, fifty casks of powder, and a quantity of shot and shells; which Rogers reported to the general at ten o'clock next morning.

On the 27th Rogers was ordered with a party to the saw-mills, to waylay flying parties of the enemy who were expected to return that way. There he remained until August 11th, when he received the following order:

You are this night to send a captain, with a suitable proportion of subalterns, and two hundred men, to Crown Point, where they will post themselves in such a manner as not to be surprised; and, if attacked, they are not to retreat, but to maintain their ground until reinforced.

JEFF. AMHERST.

Captain Brewer was detached with this party, and the general, following next morning with the whole army, took possession of Crown Point the same day. Captain Brewer had executed his orders in a most satisfactory manner.

August 12. This evening the encampment was arranged, the rangers' station being in front of the army. The next day the general directed the ground to be cleared, and employed a large portion of the troops in erecting a new fort. Captain Stark, with two hundred rangers, was employed in cutting a road from Crown Point through the wilderness to Number Four.* While the army lay at Crown Point, several scouts were sent out, who brought prisoners from St. John's, and penetrated far into the enemy's back country.

On the 12th of September, the general, being exasperated at the treatment of Captain Kennedy by the St. Francis Indians, to whom he had been sent with a flag of truce and proposals of peace, but who, with his party, had been made prisoners by the Indians, resolved to inflict upon them a signal chastisement, and gave orders as follows:

You are this night to join the detachment of two hundred men which was yesterday ordered out, and proceed to Missisqui bay. From thence you will proceed to attack the enemy's settlements on the south side of the St. Lawrence, in such a manner as shall most effectually disgrace and injure the enemy, and redound to the honor and success of his majesty's arms. Remember the barbarities committed by the enemy's † Indian scoundrels on every occasion where they have had opportunities of showing their infamous cruelties toward his majesty's subjects. Take your revenge, but remember that, although the villains have promiscuously murdered women and children of all ages, it is my order that no women or children should be killed or hurt. When you have performed this service, you will again join the army wherever it may be.

Yours, &c., JEFF. AMHERST.

Camp at Crown Point, September 13, 1759.

To Major Rogers.

* Charlestown, N. H.

† The plan for this expedition was formed on the day previous; but, that all due caution might be observed, it was announced, in public orders, that Rogers would proceed another way, while he had secret orders to proceed to St. Francis.

The account of this expedition is contained in Rogers' official dispatch, and is in substance as follows:

On the evening of the twenty-second day after our departure from Crown Point, we came in sight of the Indian town of St. Francis, which we discovered by climbing a tree at three miles' distance. Here my party, consisting of one hundred and forty-two,* officers included, were ordered to refresh themselves. At eight o'clock Lieutenant Turner, Ensign Avery, and myself reconnoitred the town. We found the Indians engaged in a high frolic,† and saw them execute several dances with great spirit and activity. We returned to our camp at two o'clock A. M., and at three advanced with the whole party within three hundred yards of the village, where the men were lightened of their packs, and formed for action.

Half an hour before sunrise we surprised the village, approaching it in three divisions, on the right, left, and centre; which was effected with so much caution and promptitude on the part of the officers and men that the enemy had no time to recover themselves, or to take arms in their own defence, until they were mostly destroyed. Some few fled to the water; but my people pursued, sunk their canoes, and shot those who attempted to escape by swimming. We then set fire to all the houses except three, reserved for the use of our party.

The fire consumed many Indians who had concealed themselves in their cellars and house-lofts, and would not come out. At seven o'clock in the morning the affair was completely over. We had by that time killed two hundred Indians, and taken twenty women and children prisoners. Fifteen of the latter I suffered to go their own way, and brought home with me two Indian boys and

* Captain Williams of the royal troops, on the fifth day out, accidentally burnt himself with powder, and was obliged to return, taking with him forty men sick or hurt.

† The prisoners afterward informed me that the Indians celebrated a wedding the night before the destruction of their town.

three girls.* Five English captives were also found, and taken into our care.

When the detachment paraded, Captain Ogden was found to be badly wounded, being shot through the body, but still able to perform his duty. Six privates were wounded, and one Stockbridge Indian killed. I ordered the party to take corn out of the reserved houses, for their subsistence home, which was the only provision to be found.† While they were loading themselves, I examined the captives, who reported that a party of three hundred French and Indians were down the river, four miles below us, and that our boats were waylaid. I believed this to be true, as they told the exact number of the boats, and the place where they had been left. They also stated that two hundred French had three days before gone up the river to Wigwam Martinique, supposing that I intended to attack that place. A council of war now concluded that no other course remained for us than to return by Connecticut river to Number Four. The detachment accordingly marched in a body eight days upon that course, and, when provisions became scarce, near Memphremagog lake, it was divided into companies, with proper guides to each, and directed to assemble at the mouth of Ammonoosuc river, as I expected to find provisions there for our relief. Two days after our separation, Ensign Avery, of Fitch's regiment, with his party, fell upon my track, and followed in my rear. The enemy fell upon them, and took seven prisoners, two of whom escaped, and joined me the next morning. Avery and his men soon afterward came up with us, and we proceeded to the Coös intervales, where I left them under the orders of Lieutenant Grant. I then

* These prisoners, when brought to Number Four, claimed Mrs. Johnson as an old acquaintance, she having been with their tribe as a prisoner some time before. One of them was called Sebattis. The bell of the Catholic chapel was also brought away, and a quantity of silver brooches taken from the savages who were slain.

† One ranger, instead of more important plunder, placed in his knapsack a large lump of tallow, which supported him on his way home, while many, who had secured more valuable plunder, perished with hunger.

proceeded with Captain Ogden, and one private, upon a raft, and arrived at this place yesterday. Provisions were in half an hour after dispatched up the river to Mr. Grant, which will reach him this night. Two other canoes, with provisions, have been sent to the mouth of Ammonoosuc river. I shall go up the river to-morrow, to look after my men, and return as soon as possible to Crown Point. Captain Ogden can inform you of other particulars respecting this scout, as he was with me through the whole of the expedition, and behaved nobly.

Your most obedient servant,

R. ROGERS.

Number Four, November 5, 1759.

To General Amherst.

The following additional particulars, stated by Major Rogers, exhibit the daring and hazardous character of this enterprise, and the hardships endured, dangers encountered, and difficulties surmounted, by the brave men by whom it was accomplished. He says:

"I cannot forbear making some remarks upon the difficulties and distresses which attended the expedition, under my command, against St. Francis, situated within three miles of the river St. Lawrence, in the heart of Canada, half way between Montreal and Quebec. While we kept the water, it was found extremely difficult to pass undiscovered by the enemy, who were cruising in great numbers upon the lake, and had prepared certain vessels to decoy English parties on board, to destroy them; but we escaped their designs, and landed at Missisqui bay in ten days. Here I left my boats, and provisions sufficient to carry us back to Crown Point, under the charge of two trusty Indians, who were to remain there until we returned, unless the enemy should discover the boats; in which case they were to follow my track, and bring the intelligence. On the second day after this, they joined me at night, informing me that four hundred French had found my boats, and two hundred were following my track. This report caused us much uneasiness. Should the enemy overtake us, and we obtain an advantage in the encounter, they would be immediately reinforced, while we could expect no assistance, being so far advanced beyond our military posts. Our boats and provisions also being taken, cut off all hope of retreat by the route we came; but, after due deliberation, it was resolved to accomplish our object, and return by Connecticut river.

Lieutenant McMullen was dispatched by land to Crown Point, to desire General Amherst to relieve us with provisions at Ammonoosuc river, at the extremity of the Coös intervales, that being the route by which we should return, if ever. We now determined to outmarch our pursuers, and destroy St. Francis before we were overtaken. We marched nine days through a spruce bog, where the ground was wet and low, a great portion of it being covered with water a foot deep. When we encamped at night, boughs were cut from the trees, and with them a rude kind of hammock constructed to secure us from the water. We uniformly began our march at a little before day-break, and continued it until after dark at night. The tenth day after leaving the bay, brought us to a river, fifteen miles north of St. Francis, which we were compelled to ford against a swift current. The tallest men were put up stream, and holding by each other, the party passed over, with a loss of several guns, which were recovered by diving to the bottom.

We had now good marching ground, and proceeded to destroy the town, as before related, which would probably have been effected, with no other loss than that of the Indian killed in the action, had not our boats been discovered and our retreat that way cut off. This tribe of Indians was notoriously attached to the French, and had for a century past harassed the frontiers of New-England, murdering people of all ages and sexes, and in times of peace, when they had no reason to suspect hostile intentions. They had, within my own knowledge, during six years past, killed and carried away more than six hundred persons. We found six hundred scalps hanging upon poles over the doors of their wigwams.

It is impossible to describe the dejected and miserable condition of the party on arriving at the Coös intervales. After so long a march, over rocky, barren mountains, and through deep swamps,* worn down with hunger and fatigue, we expected to be relieved at the intervales, and assisted in our return.

The officer dispatched to the general reached Crown Point in nine days, and faithfully discharged his commission; upon which the general ordered an officer to Number Four, to proceed from thence, with provisions, up the river to the place I had designated, and there to wait as long as there were any hopes of my return. The officer † remained but two days, and returned, carrying with him all the provisions, about two hours before our arrival. We found a fresh fire burning in his camp, and fired guns to bring him back, which he heard, but would not return, supposing we were an enemy.

In this emergency, I resolved to make the best of my way to Number Four, leaving the remainder of the party, now unable to proceed farther, to obtain such wretched subsistence as the wilderness afforded ‡ until I could relieve them, which I promised to do in ten days.

Captain Ogden, myself, and a captive Indian boy, embarked on a raft of dry pine trees. The current carried us down the stream, in the middle of which we kept our miserable vessel with such paddles as could be split and hewn with small hatchets. On the second day we reached White River falls, and narrowly escaped running over them. The raft went over and was lost; but our remain-

* In one of these swamps a party was led about for three days by a squaw, and finally brought back to their tracks. This she did to afford the Indians an opportunity to overtake them.

† This gentleman was censured for his conduct; but that reproach afforded no consolation to the brave men to whom his negligence caused such distress and anguish; and of whom many actually died of hunger.

‡ Ground-nuts and lily-roots, boiled, will support life.

ing strength enabled us to land, and pass by the falls, at the foot of which Captain Ogden and the ranger killed several red squirrels and a partridge, while I attempted to construct a new raft. Not being able to cut the trees, I burned them down, and burned them off at proper lengths. This was our third day's work after leaving our companions. The next day we floated to Wattoquichie falls, which are about fifty yards in length. Here we landed, and Captain Ogden held the raft by a withe of hazle-bushes, while I went below to swim in, board the raft, and paddle it ashore. This was our only hope of life; for we had not strength to make another raft, should this be lost. I succeeded in securing it, and next morning we floated down to within a short distance of Number Four. Here we found several men cutting timber, who relieved and assisted us to the fort. A canoe was immediately sent up the river with provisions, which reached the men at Coös in four days, being the tenth day after my departure. Two days afterward I went up the river with two canoes, to relieve others of my party who might be coming that way.

I met several parties: viz., Lieutenants Cargill, Campbell and Farrington; also Sergeant Evans, with their respective parties; and proceeding farther, fell in with several who had escaped of Turner's and Dunbar's parties, which, twenty in number, had been overtaken and mostly taken or killed by the enemy. Expresses were sent to Suncook * and Pennacook, † upon Merrimack river, directing that any who should stray that way should be assisted. At Number Four, the following letter was received from the general.

Crown Point, Nov. 8, 1759.

Sir—Captain Ogden has delivered your letter of the 5th, which I have read with great satisfaction. Every step you have taken was well judged, and deserves my approbation. I am sorry Lieutenant * * * * conducted so ill in coming away with the provisions, from the place where I ordered him to wait for you.

* Pembroke, N. H.

† Concord, N. H.

An Indian came in last night, who left some of your men at Otter river. I sent for them, and they have come in. This afternoon came in four Indians, two rangers, a German woman, and three other prisoners. They left four of your party some days since, and supposed they had arrived. I hope the residue may get in safe. The only risk will be in meeting the enemy's hunting parties.

I am, sir, your obed't serv't,

JEFF. AMHERST.

After the party had recruited their strength, such as were able to march started for Crown Point, where they arrived December 1, 1759.

Since leaving the ruins of St. Francis the party had lost three officers: Lieutenant Dunbar of Gage's light infantry, Lieutenant Turner of the rangers, and Lieutenant Jenkins of the provincials, with forty-six sergeants and privates.

The rangers at Crown Point were all dismissed before Roger's return, excepting two companies, commanded by Captains Johnson and Tute. The general had left him orders to continue in that garrison during the winter, with leave to proceed down the country, and wait upon him at New-York. After reporting to the general at that city what intelligence he had obtained respecting the enemy, he was desired, at his leisure, to draw a plan of the march to St. Francis. He returned by way of Albany, which place he left February 6, 1760, with thirteen recruits. On the 13th, while on the way between Ticonderoga and Crown Point, he was attacked by sixty Indians, who killed five of his men, and took four prisoners. With the remaining four he escaped to Crown point, and would have pursued the party; but Colonel Haviland* thought the step

* This officer was the same who sent him out in March, 1758, with a small force, when he knew a superior one lay in wait for him. He was one of those sort of men who manage to escape public censure, let them do what they will. He ought to have been cashiered for his conduct on that occasion. He was one of the many British officers who were meanly jealous of the daring achievements of their brave American comrades, but for whose intrepidity and arduous services, all the British armies, sent to America during the seven years' war, would have effected little toward the conquest of Canada.

would be imprudent, as the garrison was very sickly. His sleigh was taken, containing £1,196, York currency, beside stores and necessaries. Of the money, £800 belonged to the crown, which was allowed him. The remainder, £396, being his own, was lost.

March 31. Captain Tute, with two regular officers and six men, went on a scout, and were all taken prisoners. The sickness of the garrison prevented pursuit. The following letter was received from the general.

New-York, March 1, 1760.

Sir—The command of his majesty, to pursue the war in this country, has determined me to complete the companies of rangers which were on foot last campaign. Captain Waite yesterday informed me that his company could easily be filled up in Massachusetts and Connecticut, and I have given him a warrant for $800, and beating orders.

I have also written to Captain John Stark, in New-Hampshire, and Captain David Brewer, in Massachusetts, inclosing to each beating orders for their respective provinces. I send you a copy of their instructions, which are to send their men to Albany as fast as recruited.

Your humble servant,

JEFF. AMHERST.

To Major Rogers.

[Answer.]

Crown Point, March 15, 1760.

Sir—Since the receipt of yours, I have dispatched Lieutenant McCormick, of Captain William Stark's corps, and Lieutenants Fletcher and Holmes to recruit for my own and Captain Johnson's companies. I have no doubt they will bring in good men to replace those who have been frost bitten, who may be discharged or sent to the hospital. The smallness of our force has prevented any incursions to the French settlements in quest of a prisoner, which may be obtained at any time.

Yours respectfully, R. ROGERS.

March 9. The general wrote to Major Rogers that he had given a company of rangers to Captain Ogden, and to desire some one to be sent to Stockbridge to engage Lieutenant Solomon (Indian) to raise a company of Indians for the ensuing campaign. Mr. Stuart, adjutant of the rangers, was accordingly sent to explain to Solomon the conditions of the service. The Indians agreed to enter the service, but, as many of them were out hunting, they could not be collected at Albany until the 10th of May. In the mean time, the ranger companies at Crown Point were completed.

May 4. Sergeant Beverly, having escaped from Montreal, arrived at Crown Point after seven days' journey. He had lived in the house of Governor Vaudreuil, and reported that, on the tenth of April, the enemy withdrew their troops from Isle aux Noix, excepting a garrison of three hundred, under Monsieur Bonville; that they had already brought away half the cannon and ammunition; that two French frigates, of thirty-six and twenty guns, and several smaller vessels, lay all winter in the St. Lawrence; that all the French troops in Canada had concentrated at Jecortè on the 20th of April, excepting slender garrisons in their forts; all the militia who could be spared from the country, leaving one male to every two females to sow the grain, were also collected at the same place, under General Levi, who intended to retake Quebec; * that ninety-nine men were drowned in their passage to Jecortè; that he saw a private, belonging to our troops, at Quebec, who was taken prisoner April 15th. He stated that the garrison was healthy; that Brigadier General Murray had four thousand troops fit for duty in the city, and an advanced guard of three hundred men at Point Levi, which place the enemy attempted to occupy in February last with a considerable force, and began to fortify a stone church near the point; but that General Murray sent over a detachment of one thousand men, which drove the enemy from their position, with the loss of a captain and thirty

* Quebec had been taken by General Wolfe, in 1759.

French soldiers; that General Murray had another military post, of three hundred men, on the north side of the river, at Laurette, a short distance from the town; that all along the land-ward side of the town was a line of block-houses, under cover of the cannon; that a breastwork of fraziers extended from one to the other of the block-houses; that General Murray had heard that the enemy intended to beat up his quarters, but was not alarmed; that a party from Quebec surprised two of the enemy's guards at Point Trimble, who were all killed or taken, one guard being composed entirely of French grenadiers; that two more English frigates had passed up the river, and two other men-of-war lay near the Isle of Orleans; that the French told him that a fleet of ten sail of men-of-war had been seen at Gaspee bay, and had again put to sea on account of the ice, but did not know whether they were French or English; that the French intended, on the 1st of May, to draw off two thousand men to Isle aux Noix, and as many more to Oswegatchie, and did not intend to attack Quebec unless the French fleet entered the river before the English; that, on the 5th of May, one hundred Indians departed for our forts—the remainder had gone to Jecortè; that the Attawawa and Cold Country Indians would join General Levi in June, ten sachems having been dispatched last fall to solicit aid of those natives from the far north-west; that many deserters from the corps of Royal Americans are at Quebec, in the French service; that they were to be sent, under the charge of Monsieur Boarbier, up the Attawawa river to the colony between the lakes and the Mississippi; that most of the enemy's Indians intend going there; that many of the French who have money intend to secure it by going to New-Orleans; that he saw at Montreal Reynolds and Hill, who were last fall reported to Colonel Haviland as deserters—they were taken near River-head block-house while in quest of cattle; two more rangers will be here in two days with fresh tidings from Montreal, if they can escape; that Lougee, the famous partisan, was drowned in the St. Lawrence a few days after his return with the party which surprised Captain Tute; that the Indians keep a sharp look-out upon the Number Four roads, where they intercept plenty of sheep and cattle on their way to Crown Point. General Murray had hanged several Canadians, who were detected conveying ammunition from Quebec to the enemy; that the two Indian captains, Jacob, are still in Canada; one is with Captain Kennedy on board a vessel, in irons; the other ran away last fall, but returned, having frozen his feet; he is at Montreal."

Soon after this Major Rogers went down Lake Champlain to reconnoitre the Isle aux Noix, the landing-places, &c. He then proceeded to Albany, and gave the general all the information he possessed in regard to the passage into Canada by the Isle aux Noix; as, also, by Oswego and la Gallette.

The general, having learned by express that Quebec was besieged by the French, formed the design of sending Major Rogers, with a force, into Canada, with directions, if the siege continued, to lay waste the country, and, by marching from place to place, to endeavor to draw off the enemy's troops, and protract the siege, until the English vessels should ascend the river. He was to be governed entirely by the motions of the French army. If the siege was raised, he was to retreat; if not, to harass the country, even at the expense of his party. The orders were as follows:

You are to proceed with a detachment of three hundred men: viz., two hundred and seventy-five rangers, with their officers, a subaltern, two sergeants, and twenty-five men from the light infantry regiments, down the lake, under convoy of the brig, and lay up your boats in a safe place upon one of the islands while executing the following orders:

You will send two hundred and fifty men on the west side, in such a manner as to reach St. John's without being discovered by the enemy at Isle aux Noix. You will endeavor to surprise the fort at St. John's, and destroy the vessels, boats, provisions, or whatever else may be there for the use of the troops at Isle aux Noix. You will then proceed to Chamblée, and destroy every magazine you can find in that quarter.

These proceedings will soon be known at Isle aux Noix, and the enemy will endeavor to cut off your retreat; therefore, your safest course will be to cross the river, and return on the east side of the Isle aux Noix. Upon landing on the west side, you will send an officer, with fifty rangers, to Wigwam Martinique, to destroy what he may there find on both sides of the river, and then retreat. You will take such provisions as are necessary, and direct Captain Grant, with his vessels, to wait for your return at such places as you may direct.

Your men should be as lightly equipped as possible. They should be strictly cautioned respecting their conduct, and obedience to their officers. There should be no firing, no unnecessary alarms, and no retreating without order. The men are to stand by each other, and nothing can injure them. Let every man who has a proper musket be furnished with a bayonet. You are not to suffer the Indians* to destroy women or children, nor your men to load themselves with plunder. They shall be rewarded on their return as they deserve.

JEFF. AMHERST.

With these instructions the general delivered him a letter, directed to General Murray at Quebec, with orders to have it conveyed to him as soon as possible. He then returned to Crown Point, and about the 1st of June embarked from thence in four vessels, taking on board their boats and provisions, that the enemy might have no opportunity of discovering their design.

June 3. Lieutenant Holmes, with fifty men, landed at Missisqui bay, with orders to proceed to Wigwam Martinique. A sloop was directed to cruise for him, and on

* The Stockbridge Indians had not arrived, but orders were left for them to follow the track of Rogers.

his return to take him and his party on board, upon his making certain signals. From this place Rogers dispatched Sergeant Beverly, with the general's letter to General Murray, with these instructions:

You will take under your command John Shute, Luxford Goodwin, and Joseph Eastman, and proceed, under the convoy of Lieutenant Holmes, to Missisqui bay, and land in the night; otherwise, you may be discovered by a party from Isle aux Noix. You will then steer a north-easterly course, and proceed with all possible dispatch to Quebec, or to the English army at or near that city, and deliver the letter intrusted to your care to Brigadier Murray, or the officer commanding his majesty's forces in and upon the river St. Lawrence.

You have herewith a plan of the country, that you may know the considerable rivers between Missisqui bay and Quebec. The distances are marked in the plan, as is the road I travelled last fall to St. Francis, which road you will cross several times. The rivers you will know by their descriptions, when you come to them.

The river St. Francis, about midway of your journey, is very still water, and may be easily rafted where you will cross it; lower down it is so rapid that its passage must not be attempted.

The Chaudière river is rapid for some miles above its mouth, and should be well examined before you cross it. After passing this river, lay your course east, leaving Point Levi on the left, and strike the St. Lawrence near the lower end of the Isle of Orleans, as General Murray may possibly be encamped on that or the Isle of Quadoa.

You are directed to look out for the English fleet, and may venture on board the first line-of-battle ship you see, whose commander will convey you to the general, who will pay you fifty pounds, and give farther orders as soon as you have rested from your march.

Major Rogers, with his party, now crossed Lake Champlain to the west shore, and, embarking in boats, on the

4th landed two hundred men twelve miles south of Isle aux Noix. Captain Grant, with his sloops, was directed to cruise down the lake near the fort, to attract the notice of the enemy until Rogers could get into the country. In consequence of the rain, and the risk of spoiling their provisions, he lay with his party, during the whole day of the 5th, concealed in bushes.

In the afternoon of that day several French boats appeared on the lake, continuing as near to our vessels as they could with safety, until after dark. Concluding these boats would watch the vessels all night, Rogers went on board after dark, in a small boat, and ordered them to retire to the Isle of Motte. The enemy, who were out all night, discovered his landing, and sent a force from the island to cut off the party. The scouts counted their number as they crossed from the fort in boats, making it three hundred and fifty men. At eleven o'clock the left of the rangers was briskly attacked. Their right was protected by a bog, which the enemy did not venture over; through which, however, by the edge of the lake, seventy rangers, under Lieutenant Farrington, passed, and fell upon their rear. At the same time they were attacked in front, and immediately broke. They were pursued a mile, where they separated into small parties, and took refuge in a thick cedar swamp. The rain now came on again, and the party was recalled to the boats, where they found that Ensign Wood, of the 17th regiment, had been killed, and Captain Johnson shot through the body, the left arm, and wounded in the head. Of the rangers sixteen were killed and eight wounded; two light infantry men were wounded. Forty of the French fell; their commander, Monsieur la Force was wounded (mortally), with several of his men. Fifty muskets were taken. After the action the party embarked with their killed and wounded, and returned to the Isle of Motte, near which the brig lay. One of the vessels, having on board the corpse of Mr. Wood, and that of Captain Johnson (who died on the passage thither), was dispatched to Crown

Point, with orders to return with provisions. The dead were buried upon a small island, and the party prepared for a second landing.

Being now joined by the Stockbridge Indians, Rogers determined to execute his orders, and, to conceal his motions, left the following orders for Captain Grant:

You will immediately fall down the lake, with your vessels, to Wind-mill Point, and there cruise two or three days, to attract the attention of the enemy from my motions. When I suppose you are near the point, my party will land on the west side, opposite the north end of the Isle of Motte, near the river which enters the bay at that place.

If we are not attacked, we shall return on the east side, and endeavor to join you near Wind-mill Point, or somewhere between that and the Isle of Motte. Our signal will be a smoke, and three guns discharged in succession, at a minute's interval, the signal to be repeated in half an hour.

But, should we be attacked before reaching our destination, in case we have the worst of it, you may expect us to make the above signals on the west side, between the Isle of Motte and the place of our action, on the 6th instant. As the time of our return is uncertain, I advise your not coming south of the Isle of Motte, as a contrary wind may prevent your getting in to my relief. Sergeant Hacket and ten rangers will remain with you during my absence. I advise you not to send parties to the island to take prisoners until the fifth day after my landing, as the loss of a man may be a serious misfortune at this time, and discover our intentions to the enemy. Mr. Holmes will probably return between the 11th and 16th days from his departure from the Missisqui bay; one of the sloops may cruise for him off the bay.

On the 9th of June, at midnight, Rogers landed, with two hundred men, on the west shore, opposite la Motte, and marched with all dispatch for St. John's. On the evening of the 15th they came to the road leading from that place to Montreal. At eleven at night they advanced within four hundred yards of the fort. The enemy was stronger than was expected, with seventeen sentinels so well posted as to render a surprise impossible.

The scout was discovered, and alarm guns fired; upon which the party retired at two o'clock, and proceeded down river to St. d'Étrees. This place was reconnoitred at daybreak. The fort was a stockade, proof against small arms, and containing two large store-houses. The enemy were carting hay into the fort, and the rangers, watching their opportunity, when a cart was entering the gateway, rushed forward from their concealment, and captured the place before the gate could be closed. In the meantime other parties proceeded to the houses near the garrison (fifteen), which were all surprised without firing a gun. In the fort were twenty-four soldiers, and in the houses seventy-eight prisoners—men, women, and children. Several young men escaped to Chamblée.

Ascertaining, from an examination of the prisoners, that Chamblée could not be attacked with success, they burned the fort and village, with a large magazine of hay and provision. They killed all the cattle and horses; and every batteau, canoe, wagon, and every thing which could be of service to the enemy, was destroyed. To the women and children Rogers gave a pass to Montreal, directed to all officers of the several detachments under his command. After this the party continued their march to the east side of Lake Champlain. While passing Missisqui bay, opposite the Isle aux Noix, their advanced guard engaged with that of a detachment of eight hundred French, who were in quest of them; but, as the enemy's main body was a mile behind, their advanced party retreated. The party continued their march to the lake, where a party had been sent forward to repeat the signals, and found the boats waiting, in which they all embarked, thus escaping the enemy, who appeared in full force a few minutes after. Mr. Grant had performed his duty like an able and faithful officer, patiently waiting with his vessels, and securing the retreat of the party.

Several of the prisoners had been at the siege of Quebec, and reported that the French lost five hundred men, and, after bombarding the place twelve days, had retired to "Jack's quarters," where General Levi had left five hundred regulars and four hundred Canadians; that the remainder of his troops were quartered by threes and twos upon the inhabitants from that place to St. John's; that in Montreal one hundred troops were stationed, the inhabitants themselves performing duty; that Chamblée fort contained one hundred and fifty men, workmen included; that the remnant of the Queen's regiment were in the village; that St. John's fort had twelve cannon and three hundred men, including workmen, who were obliged to take up arms at a moment's notice; that three hundred men and one hundred pieces of cannon were stationed at the Isle aux Noix.

On the 21st the twenty-six prisoners, under a guard of fifty men, were dispatched in a vessel to Crown Point, the others of the party remaining to cover Mr. Holmes' retreat. He joined them the same evening, having failed in his enterprise by mistaking a river which falls into the Sorelle for that called Wigwam Martinique, which falls into the St. Lawrence near St. Francis. On the 23d the party reached Crown Point, and encamped on Chimney Point, directly opposite.

The general wrote to Rogers, from Canajoharie, soon after his return, expressing his satisfaction of his conduct in this enterprise. Preparations were made for the army to advance into Canada, and, on the 16th of August, the embarkation was effected in the order following: Six hundred rangers and seventy Indians, in whale-boats, formed the advanced guard, at the distance of half a mile from the main body. Next followed the light infantry and grenadiers in two columns, under Colonel Darby. The right wing was composed of provincials, commanded by Brigadier Ruggles (of Boston), who was second in command. The left was made up of New-Hampshire and Boston troops, under Colonel Thomas. The 17th and 27th regiments formed the centre column under Major Campbell. Colonel Haviland was posted in front of these, between the light infantry and grenadiers. The royal artillery, under Colonel Orde, followed in four rideaux. In this order the troops moved down the lake forty miles the first day, and encamped on the west side. On the 18th, embarking with a fresh south wind, they proceeded within ten miles of the Isle of Motte. The roughness of the water split one of the rangers' boats, by which accident ten were downed.

On the 9th the army encamped on the Isle of Motte. On the 20th they proceeded twenty-two miles farther, and came in sight of the French fort. At ten o'clock A. M. Colonel Darby landed his infantry and grenadiers, the rangers following without opposition, and occupied the ground over against the fort. Batteries were raised the next day, and shells thrown into the place.

On the 25th Colonel Darby proposed to capture the enemy's rideaux and vessels lying at anchor. Two companies of regulars, four of rangers, and the Indians, were selected for the service, under Colonel Darby. Two light howitzers and a six-pounder were silently conveyed through the trees, and brought to bear upon the vessels before the enemy were aware of the design. The first shot from the six-pounder cut the cable of the great rideau, and the wind blew her to the east shore, where the English party were stationed. The other vessels weighed anchor, and steered for St. John's, but grounded in turning a point two miles from the fort. Rogers then led a party down the east shore, and, crossing a river thirty yards wide, arrived opposite the vessels. From thence a portion of his men kept up a fire, while others, armed with tomahawks, swam off and boarded one of them. In the meantime Colonel Darby captured the rideau, had her manned, and secured the other two. Colonel Haviland sent down men to work the vessels, and ordered the party to join the army that night.

At midnight the French evacuated the island, and reached the main land, leaving their sick behind. Next morning Colonel Haviland took possession of the fort.

On the second day after Monsieur Bonville's retreat, Colonel Haviland ordered the rangers to pursue him as far as St. John's, about twenty miles down the lake, and await the arrival of the army, but by no means to approach nearer to Montreal.

At daylight they reached St. John's in boats. The place was on fire, and the enemy had retreated. Two prisoners informed that Monsieur Bonville was that night to encamp half way on the road to Montreal; that he left St. John's at nine o'clock the night before; that many of his troops were sick, and they thought some of them would not reach the place of encampment until late in the afternoon. It was now seven o'clock in the morning, and a portion of the men were directed to fortify the houses standing near the lake shore, while the remainder should pursue Monsieur Bonville. At eight o'clock Rogers left the boats, under the protection of two hundred rangers, while, with four hundred others and the two Indian companies, he pursued the track of the French army, now consisting of fifteen hundred French and one hundred Indians. Rogers followed with such diligence as to overtake their rear guard of two hundred men two miles before they reached their ground of encampment. They were immediately attacked, broken, and pursued to the main body.* The rangers pursued in good order, expecting General Bonville would make a stand. But, instead of this, he pushed forward to the river, where he intended to encamp; which he crossed, and broke down the bridge, thus putting a stop to the pursuit. The enemy encamped within a good breast-work, which had been prepared for their reception. In the pursuit the rangers lessened their numbers, and

* In this attack the rangers fired the last hostile guns for the conquest of Canada. This was the finishing skirmish.

returned in safety. In the evening Colonel Haviland's detachment arrived at St. John's, and next day proceeded down the Sorelle as far as St. d'Estrees, and fortified their camp.

From this place Rogers proceeded, with his rangers, down the Sorelle, to bring the inhabitants under subjection to his Britannic majesty. They entered the settled parts of the country by night, collected all the priests and militia officers, and directed them to assemble all the inhabitants who were willing to surrender their arms, take the oath of allegiance, and keep their possessions. After this he joined Colonel Darby, at Chamblée, where he had brought several pieces of light artillery to reduce the fort; but, as the garrison consisted of but fifty men, they soon after surrendered at discretion.

September 2. The army having nothing farther to perform, and favorable intelligence having been received from Generals Amherst and Murray, Major Rogers, with the rangers, was detached to join the latter, and on the 6th reached Longueville, four miles below Montreal, and next morning reported himself to General Murray, whose camp was directly opposite. General Amherst had at this time arrived, and landed his army within about two miles of the city. Early in the morning General Vaudreuil, the commander-in-chief of all the Canadas, proposed to General Amherst a capitulation. The articles of surrender were signed on the 8th, and on the same evening the English troops took possession of the gates of Montreal. Next morning the light infantry and grenadiers of the whole army, under Colonel Haldiman, with two pieces of cannon and several howitzers, entered the city. Among the trophies here recovered were the colors of Pepperell's and Shirley's regiments, which had been captured at Oswego. Thus, at the end of five campaigns, the whole Canadian territory became subject to the king of Great Britain.

On the 12th of September General Amherst issued the following orders:

By His Excellency, Jeffrey Amherst, Esquire, Major General and Commander-in-chief of His Majesty's Forces in North-America, &c.

To Major Rogers, of His Majesty's Independent Companies of Rangers:

You will, upon receipt of this, proceed with Waite's and Hazen's companies of rangers to Fort William Augustus, taking with you one Joseph Poupao, alias la Fleur, an inhabitant of Detroit, and Lieutenant Brheme, assistant engineer.

From that fort you will continue your voyage by the north shore to Niagara, thence transporting your boats over the carrying-place to Lake Erie. Major Walters, commanding at Niagara, will render you any assistance you may require, and deliver up Monsieur Gamelin, who was made prisoner at the taking of that fortress, to be conducted, with said la Fleur, to their habitations at Detroit; where, upon taking the oath of allegiance to his majesty, whose subjects they have become by the capitulation of the 8th, they are to be protected in the peaceable enjoyment of their property.

You will next proceed to Presque Isle,* and make known your orders to the commander of that post. You will there leave your whale-boats and most of your detachment, proceeding with the remainder to join General Monckton, wherever he may be. Deliver him your dispatches, and obey such orders as he may give you for relieving the garrisons of Detroit, Michilimackinac, and their dependencies; for collecting the arms of the inhabitants, and administering the oath of allegiance. This you will see administered to the said Poupao.

You are to bring away the French troops and arms to such place as General Monckton shall direct. After completing this service, you will march your detachment back to Presque Isle or Niagara, according to the orders you receive from General Monckton, and, leaving your boats in charge of the officer at one of those posts, march your

* Erie, Pennsylvania.

detachment by land to Albany, or wherever I may be, to receive farther orders.

Given under my hand, at head quarters, in the camp at Montreal, 12th September, 1760.

JEFF. AMHERST.

By His Excellency's command—

J. Appy, Sec'y.

An additional order was given him, to be shown only to commanders of the different posts he might touch at. The objects of the expedition were to be kept secret, lest the Indians, through whose country he must pass, should impede his march. The order was as follows:

Major Walters, or the commander at Niagara, will judge whether there is sufficient provision at Presque Isle, and Major Rogers will accordingly take provisions from Niagara or not, as the case may be. The route from Montreal to Fort William Augustus will require eight days' provisions; from that post he will take a sufficient quantity to proceed to Niagara. Major Rogers knows whither he is going, and what provisions he will want. A quantity should also be in store at Presque Isle, for the party General Monckton will send.

JEFF. AMHERST.

Montreal, 12th September, 1760.

September 13, 1760. In pursuance of these orders, Major Rogers and his party embarked at Montreal, in fifteen whale-boats. The detachments consisted of Captains Brewer and Waite, Lieutenant Brheme, of the engineers, Lieutenant Davis, of the royal artillery, and two hundred rangers. At night they encamped at La Chien. Next morning they reached Isle de Prairies, and surveyed the Indian settlements at Cayawaga and Canasedaga.

16th. They reached an island in lake St. Francis, and the next night encamped on the western shore, at the foot of the upper rifts. Next day they ascended the rifts, and passed the night on the north shore, opposite a number of islands.

19th. At evening they reached the Isle de Galettes, and spent the next day in repairing the boats which had been damaged in passing the rapids. Ten sick rangers were sent to Colonel Fitch, at Oswego, to proceed thence to Albany.

21st. At twelve o'clock they left the island, but the wind being unfavorable, they passed Oswegatchie, and encamped three miles above, on the north shore.

22d. The course was continued up the river, and the party halted in the evening, at the narrow passes near the islands. The wind abating, at midnight they embarked, rowed the remainder of the night and the next day, until they reached the ruins of old Fort Frontenac, where a party of Indian hunters from Oswegatchie were encamped. The next day proving stormy, with snow and rain squalls, the engineer took a plan of the old fort, situated at the bottom of a fine safe harbor. Five hundred acres had been cleared around the fort; a few pine trees were still standing, and the situation was pleasant. The soil, though covered with clover, appeared rocky and barren. The Indians were highly pleased with the news of the surrender of Canada, and supplied plenty of venison and wild fowl.

25th. They steered S. two miles, then W. six miles, to the mouth of a river thirty feet wide; thence S. four miles, where the party halted to refresh. In the afternoon they steered for a mountain, bearing S. W., which was reached in the night, and proved to be a steep rock, one hundred feet high. They rowed all night, and breakfasted on shore at eight next morning. They then proceeded, and at eight in the evening were one hundred miles from Frontenac.

27th. This day being windy, the party hunted and killed many deer. The land was poor and rocky, as is generally the case on the north shore of Lake Ontario. The timber is chiefly hemlock and pine.

28th. They steered S. W., leaving on the right a large bay, twenty miles wide, the western side of which terminates in a point, and a small island. Proceeding fifteen miles W. by S., they entered the mouth of a river, called by the Indians the "Grace of Man;" there they encamped, and found fifty Mississaqua Indians fishing for salmon. Upon the first appearance of the boats, the whole party ran down to the shore to testify their joy at the sight of English colors, and fired their muskets until the party landed. They presented the major with a deer, just killed, and split in halves, with the skin on, which is a significant token of their great respect. They pretended to be well pleased with the success of the English.

In the evening they invited the men to fish with them. They went out, and in half an hour filled a bark canoe with salmon. They returned, much pleased with the sport, and the attentions of their tawny companions. Their mode of taking the fish was a curious one: one person held a pine torch, while another struck the fish with a spear. The soil near the river was good, and the country level. The timber was chiefly oak and maple, or the sugar tree.

29th. The party proceeded fifteen miles farther on a W. S. W. course, and came to a river called "the Life of Man." Here twenty Mississaquas were hunting, and paid them compliments similar to those of their brethren. They presented Major Rogers with a young bear, split in halves. The rangers here caught plenty of salmon. The land was level, the soil rich, and of a dark color. The shore of the lake was quite low.

30th. The wind was fair, and, by the aid of sails, they reached Toronto in the evening, having run seventy miles. Many long points, extending into the lake, caused frequent alterations of their course. They passed a bank twenty miles long, behind which was a heavy growth of oak, hickory, maple, poplar, and white wood. The soil was principally clay. A tract of three hundred acres, cleared, surrounded the remains of the old fort of Toronto. Deer were plenty.

A party of Indians, at the mouth of the river, fled to the woods, but returned next morning, expressing great joy at the news of the success over the French. They said that the party could reach Detroit in eight days; that, when the French resided here, the Indians brought furs from Michilimackinac down the river Toronto; that the portage was only twenty miles from that to a river falling into Lake Huron, which was broken by several falls, but none of any consequence; and that there was a carrying-place of fifteen miles, from some westerly part of Lake Erie to a river running through several Indian towns, without any falls, into Lake St. Clair. Toronto appeared an eligible place for a factory, from which the British government might easily settle the north side of Lake Erie.

October 1. They steered south, across the west end of Lake Ontario, and reached the shore four miles from Fort Niagara, where they passed the night, and repaired the boats.

October 2. The party embarked with orders for the boats to be in line; and, if the wind should rise, a red flag was to be hoisted, upon which signal the boats were to close, so as to be enabled to assist each other in case of leaks. By this measure Lieutenant McCormick's boat's crew was saved, with no other loss than the men's knapsacks. They halted next day at Niagara, and were supplied with blankets, coats, shoes, shirts, moccasins, &c. They also received eighty barrels of beef, and exchanged two whale-boats for as many batteaux, which proved leaky.

October 3. In the evening a party proceeded up the Niagara river seven miles, to the falls, with provisions. Next morning they were followed by the whole detachment, who immediately commenced the portage of the baggage and provisions. While they were thus occupied, Messrs. Brheme and Davis took a survey of the great cataract of Niagara, the roaring of which had been heard at several miles distance.

Modern travellers who yearly visit this, one of the grandest creations of nature, can imagine the arduous labors of these hardy rangers in transporting their boats and baggage up the bank of this river, from the foot of the cataract, which is one hundred and fifty feet in height, to ascend which, even at the present time, without a load, by aid of steps and stairs, is a laborious undertaking. The rangers were more than one day engaged in conveying their boats and baggage round the falls. On the fifth of October Rogers, with Lieutenants Brheme, Holmes and eight rangers embarked, in a birch-bark canoe, for Presque Isle, leaving Captain Brewer in command, with orders to follow to the same post. Rogers encamped that night eight miles up the Niagara river, and at noon next day entered the waters of Lake Erie. Leaving a small bay* or creek upon his left, he reached the south shore at sunset, and, thence proceeding west until eight o'clock, drew up his canoe on a sandy beach, forty miles from the last night's encampment.

October 7. The wind being fresh, he made but twenty-eight miles in a south-west course.

October 8. Pursuing a southerly course, he reached Presque Isle in the afternoon. Here the party remained until three o'clock, when the eight rangers were sent back to meet and assist Captain Brewer; while, with three men, in a bark canoe furnished by Colonel Bouquet, commander of the post, Rogers, with Messrs. Bhreme and Holmes, proceeded to French creek, and that night encamped half way on the road to Fort du Bœuf, which they reached at ten o'clock next day. After three hours' rest they passed on to the lower crossings. The land on both sides appeared rich, and covered with large and valuable timber. They passed the night of the 11th at the Mingo Cabins, and on the 12th lodged at Venango. Thence they proceeded down the Alleghany river, and, on the 17th delivered their dispatches to General Monckton, at Pittsburg. The general promised to forward his instructions by Mr. Croghan, and to dispatch Captain Campbell, with a company of Royal Americans, to his support. On

* Now Buffalo harbor.

the 20th Rogers started on his return to Presque Isle, which he reached October 30th. Mr. Brewer had arrived there three days before, having lost several boats and part of the provisions. Captain Campbell arrived next day. The boats were now repaired, and Rogers, having learned that a vessel expected from Niagara, with provisions, had been lost in a gale on the lake, dispatched Captain Brewer, with a drove of forty cattle supplied by Colonel Bouquet, to proceed by land to Detroit. Mr. Waite was sent back to Niagara for more provisions, and directed to cruise along the north shore of Lake Erie, and wait for farther orders about twenty miles east of the strait, between Lake St. Clair and Lake Erie. Captain Brewer was furnished with a bateau to ferry his party over the creeks, two horses, and Captain Monter, with twenty Indians of the Six Nations, Delawares, and Shawanese, to protect him from the hostile tribes of the west. The following order of march was adopted on the reëmbarkment of the party from Presque Isle: "The boats are to row two deep—Major Rogers' and Captain Croghan's boats in front; next Captain Campbell's corps, followed by the rangers—Lieutenant Holmes commanding the rear guard with his own boat; and that of Mr. Waite will hold himself in readiness to assist any boat in distress. Should the wind blow so hard that the boats can not preserve their order, a red flag will be hoisted in the major's boat. The other boats will then steer for the flag, and make their landing as well as may be. Officers and men were advised to pay no attention to the waves of the lake, but, when the surf was high, to ply their oars, and the men at the helms to keep the boats quartering, in which case no injury can happen. Ten of the best steersmen of the rangers will attend Captain Campbell's party. The officers of the boats will hearken to the steersmen in all cases in a storm. If thought best to proceed in the night, a blue flag will be hoisted in the major's boat, which is the signal for the boats to dress. Mr. Brheme is to pay no regard to this order of march, but to steer as is most convenient for making his observations. On landing, the regulars are to encamp in the centre; Lieutenant Holmes and Mr. Croghan, with their men, on the left wing; and Mr. Joquipe with his Mohegans, will constitute a picket, and encamp in front. The *generale* shall be beat, when ordered by the major, as the signal for embarking. No guns are to be fired unless by permission, or in case of distress. No man must leave the lines unless by order. Captain Campbell will parade and review his men as often as he thinks proper. Mr. Croghan will regularly report to the major the intelligence received from the Indians during the day.

November 4. The detachment left Presque Isle, and, proceeding slowly, with bad weather, reached Chogagee river on the 7th, where they met a party of Attawawas returning from Detroit. They were informed of the reduction of the Canadas, and that this party were on their way to Detroit to bring away the French garrison. Rogers offered them a belt, and proposed to them to go with him and witness the result. They retired to hold a council, promising an answer next day. In the evening the calumet or pipe of peace was smoked, all the officers and Indians smoking in turn from the same pipe. The peace being thus concluded, the party went to rest; but, as the sincerity of the Indians was doubted, a strict guard was kept. In the morning the Indians said their young warriors would go, while the old ones would stay and hunt for their families. Rogers gave them a string of wampum, and charged them to send some of their chiefs with the party who drove the cattle on shore, to spread the news of his arrival, and prevent any annoyance from their hunters. Bad weather detained the English party here until the 12th, during which time the Indians held a plentiful market of venison and wild turkeys in their camp. After passing the mouths of several small streams, the party reached a small river a few miles beyond Sandusky, and encamped. From this place a letter was dispatched to the commandant of Detroit, as follows:

Sir—That you may not be alarmed at the approach of English troops, I send this in advance, by Lieutenant Bhreme, to inform you that I have General Amherst's orders to take possession of Detroit and its dependencies, which, according to a capitulation signed on the 8th of September last by the Marquis de Vaudreuil and General Amherst, now belong to his Britannic majesty. I have with me letters from the Marquis de Vaudreuil to you directed, which I will deliver on arriving at or near your fort. I have also a copy of the capitulation.

I am, sir, your obed't serv't,

R. ROGERS.

To Captain Beleter.

The land on the south shore of Lake Erie has a fine appearance. The country is mostly level, and heavily timbered with oak, hickory, maple, beach, and locust; and for plenty and variety of game was at this time not surpassed by any country in the world.

On the 20th of November Rogers followed Mr. Bhreme, proceeding nine miles to a river three hundred feet wide. Here several Huron sachems gave information that four hundred Indian warriors were assembled at the mouth of the strait to oppose his passage, and that Monsieur Beleter had incited them to defend their country; and that themselves were messengers to demand his business, and whether the person sent forward told the truth that all Canada was surrendered to the English. Rogers confirmed the account. He told them that Detroit was to be given up to him, gave them a large belt, and spoke as follows: "Brothers, with this belt I take you by the hand. Go to your people at the strait, and tell them to go home to their towns until I arrive at the fort. There I will send for you, after Monsieur Beleter is sent away, which will be in two days after my arrival. You shall live happily in your own country. Tell your warriors to mind their French fathers no more, for they are all prisoners to the English, who have left them their houses and goods upon their swearing by the Great One, who made the world, to become as Englishmen. They are your brothers, and you must not abuse them. When we meet at Detroit I will convince you that what I say is true."

November 22. The party encamped upon a river twenty yards wide, where fuel was procured with difficulty, the western shore of Lake Erie abounding in swamps. Next day they rowed ten miles to Cedar point. Here several Indians they had seen the day before came to them. They said their warriors had gone up to Monsieur Beleter, who was a strong man, and intended to fight. On the 24th the party proceeded twenty-four miles, and encamped upon a long point. That night sixty Indians came with congratulations, and offered to escort them to Detroit. They reported that Mr. Bhreme and his party were confined, and that Monsieur Beleter had set up a high flag-staff, with a wooden effigy of a man's head at the top of it, and upon that a crow; that the crow meant himself, and the head meant Rogers, whose brains he should pick out. This, they said, had no effect on them, for they told him the reverse would be the true sign. At the mouth of the strait the sachems desired Rogers to call together his officers. He did so, and the 26th was spent in conciliating their savage dispositions to peace and friendship. On the 27th Monsieur Babec brought the following letter:

Sir—I have read your letter, but, having no interpreter, can not fully understand it. Your officer informs me that he was sent to give notice of your arrival to take possession of this post, according to the capitulation of Canada. I beg you will halt at the mouth of the river, and send me Monsieur Vaudreuil's letter, that I may conform to his instructions. I am surprised that no French officer accompanies you, as is usual in such cases.

I have the honor, &c.,

DE BELETER.

To Major Rogers.

Soon after this Captain Barrenger, with a French party, beat a parley on the western shore. Mr. McCormick went over to him, and returned with an officer, bearing the following letter:

Sir—I have already, by Mr. Barrenger, informed you the reasons why I could not answer particularly your letter delivered by your officer on the 22d. I am unacquainted with his reasons for not returning to you. I have sent my Huron interpreter to that nation to stop them, should they be on the road, not knowing whether they are disposed in your favor or my own; and to direct them to behave peaceably; to inform them that I knew my duty to my general, and should conform to his orders. Be not surprised, sir, if you find the inhabitants of this coast upon their guard. They were told you had several Indian nations with you, and had promised them the plunder of the place. I have, therefore, directed the inhabitants to take up arms, which may be for your safety as well as ours; for, should these Indians become insolent, you may not be able to subdue them alone.

I flatter myself, sir, that when this comes to hand, you will send some of your gentlemen with Monsieur Vaudreuil's letter and the capitulation.

I have the honor to be, &c.,

PIGN. BELETER.

To Major Rogers.

November 28. The detachment encamped five miles up the river, having rowed against the wind. On the 29th Captain Campbell, with Messieurs Barrenger and Babec, were dispatched with this letter:

Sir—I acknowledge the receipt of your two letters yesterday. Mr. Bhreme has not yet returned. The inclosed letter from Monsieur Vaudreuil will inform you of the surrender of Canada; of the indulgence granted the inhabitants, and the terms allowed to the troops of his most christian majesty. Captain Campbell will show you the capitulation. I beg you will not detain him, as I have General Amherst's orders immediately to relieve the place. My troops will halt without the town till four o'clock, when I shall expect your answer. Your inhabitants being under arms will not surprise me, as I have as yet seen no others in that condition, excepting savages awaiting my orders. The inhabitants of Detroit shall not be molested, they and you complying with the capitulation. They shall be protected in their estates, and shall not be pillaged by my Indians, nor yours who have joined me.

Yours, &c.,

R. ROGERS.

To Captain De Beleter, Commander of Detroit.

The detachment landed half a mile below the fort, and drew up in front of it in a field of grass. Here Captain Campbell joined them, with a French officer, who, with Captain Beleter's compliments, informed Major Rogers that the garrison was at his command. Lieutenants McCormick and Leslie, with thirty-six Royal Americans, immediately took possession of the fort. The troops of the garrison piled their arms; the French flag was hauled down, and that of the English run up in its place. Upon this about seven hundred Indians, who were looking on at a little distance, gave a shout, exulting in the verification of their prophecy that the crow represented the English instead of the French. They appeared astonished at the submissive salutations of the inhabitants, and expressed great satisfaction at the generosity of the English in not putting them all to death. They declared that in future they would fight for a nation thus favored by the Great Spirit. The commander delivered Major Rogers a plan of the fort, with an inventory of the stores and armament, and before noon of December 1st the militia had been collected, disarmed, and taken the oath of allegiance. Monsieur Beleter and his troops were ordered to Philadelphia, under the charge of Lieutenant Holmes and thirty rangers. Captain Campbell, with the Royal Americans, was ordered to garrison the fort. Captain Waite and Lieutenant Butler were detached, with twenty men, to bring the French garrisons from Forts Miami and Gatanois. A party was directed to remain there, if possible, through the winter, to watch the enemy's motions in Illinois. Mr. McKee, with a French officer, was sent to Shawanese Town, on the Ohio, to bring off the French troops. As provisions grew scarce at Detroit, Captain Brewer, with most of the rangers, was ordered to Niagara, leaving Lieutenant McCormick, with thirty-seven privates, to accompany Major Rogers to Michilimackinac. Rogers concluded a treaty with the several tribes living in the vicinity of Detroit, and departed for Lake Huron.

December 10. He encamped at the north end of Lake St. Clair, and the next evening at the entrance of a considerable river, where a large body of Indians were hunting.

December 12. He came to the entrance of Lake Huron, and met many Indians hunting on both sides of the outlet. He coasted along the west shore for three days, making one hundred miles, when the ice cakes obstructed his farther passage. He consulted the Indians as to the practicability of a journey to Michilimackinac by land. They declared it an impossibility at this season without snow-shoes. Rogers was therefore obliged to return. He was so impeded by the ice, that he did not reach Detroit until the 21st of December.

December 23. Rogers left the command of Detroit to Captain Campbell, and departed for Pittsburg. He marched along the lake shore, and reached Sandusky January 2, 1761. The soil from Detroit is excellent, being well timbered with black and white oak, hickory, locust, maple, sassafras, and white wood. Several immense black walnuts* are also found on the south shore of Lake Erie.

* One of these trees stood, in 1824, near Cataraugus creek, N. Y., which was thirty feet in circumference. The trunk was hollow, and used for a refreshment shop for travellers passing along the road. A section of it was afterward carried down the New-York canal to place in a bar-room at New-York.

Along the west end of Lake Erie Rogers reports that plenty of wild apples were found. He passed through many rich savannahs (or prairies), of many miles' extent, without a tree, and clothed with long jointed grass, nearly six feet high, which, decaying every year, adds fertility to the soil. Sandusky bay is fifteen miles long, and about six miles wide. Here Rogers halted to refresh at a village of Wyandots. The next day he passed through a meadow, saw several wigwams, and halted at a small village of ten wigwams. Here he saw a spring issuing from the side of a small hill, with such force as to rise three feet. He judged that it discharged ten hogsheads in a minute. He continued his march through the prairies, killing plenty of deer and wild turkeys, and encamped in the woods.

January 4. He crossed a river twenty-five yards wide, where were two wigwams. A few yards onward, in a south-east course, he came to another wigwam of Wyandots who were hunting there. From this he proceeded south, and crossed the same river he passed in the morning. Several deer were killed during the day's march.

January 5. He encamped on Muskingum creek, there eight yards wide.

January 6. He travelled fourteen miles farther, and encamped by a fine spring.

January 7. After travelling six miles he came to Muskingum creek, there twenty yards wide; and an Indian town, called the Mingo Cabins, lies about twenty yards from the creek on the east side. Only three Indians were at home, the remainder being out on a hunting party. They had plenty of cows, horses, hogs, &c.

January 8. This day was passed with the Indians, repairing moccasins and preparing provisions.

January 9. The party travelled twelve miles south-east, and encamped on a long meadow, where the Indians were hunting.

January 10. They made eleven miles, and on their march killed three bears and two elks.

January 11. They fell in with a party of Wyandot and Six Nations Indians hunting together.

January 12. They travelled six miles, and in the evening killed several beavers.

January 13. The party travelled six miles north-east, and came to Beaver Town, a village of the Delawares. The town covers a good tract of land, on the west side of the Muskingum, which is joined by a river opposite the town. The latter is thirty yards wide, and the former forty. Their junction forms a fine stream, which flows with a swift current toward the south-west. The Indians have here three thousand acres of land cleared. The warriors number one hundred and eighty. The country from Sandusky to this place is low and rich. No pine timber was noticed, but plenty of white, black, and yellow oak, black and white walnut, cypress, chestnut, and locust. The party rested here until the 16th, and obtained a supply of corn from the Indians.

January 16. They marched nine miles to a small river.

January 19. After passing several creeks, they came to a small river where the Delawares were hunting.

January 20. They reached Beaver creek in sight of the Ohio. Three Indian wigwams were seen on the west side.

January 21. They travelled south-east twenty miles, and encamped with the Indians.

January 25. They reached the Ohio, opposite Fort Pitt. From this post Lieutenant McCormick was ordered to cross the country to Albany, with the rangers, while Major Rogers proceeded by the common road over the mountains to Philadelphia, and thence to New-York, where he reported his proceedings to General Amherst February 14, 1761.

EXTRACTS FROM GENERAL ORDERS IN THE CAMPAIGN OF 1759.

June 12, 1759. "It is the general's orders that no scouting parties or others in the army under his command shall, whatsoever opportunity they have, scalp any women or children belonging to the enemy. They may bring them away if they can; but, if not, they are to leave them unhurted; and he is determined that, if they should murther or scalp any women or children who are subjects of the king of England, he will revenge it by the death of two men of the enemy, whenever he has occasion, for every man, woman, or child murthered by the enemy."

June 22, 1759. "Commanding officers may send their men for greens; but they must go only a short distance from the fort, and never without a covering party. No soldier, except with a party, is to go beyond the outposts of the camp."

June 24. "Effects of late Lieutenant Watts, of late Forbes' regiment, to be sold at auction at the head of the colors of said regiment."

The following extract from general orders regards a field of green peas, in the vicinity of Crown Point, August 5, 1759:

"As there is a field of pease found, they shall be divided amongst the army; and the corps are to send to-morrow two men per company with arms, a sergeant per regiment, and an officer per brigade; each corps and the artillery taking two batteaux, and assembling in the front of the fort at five in the morning. Gage's light infantry sends a captain, two subalterns, and a partie of men in the English boat, with the three-pounder, to cover the batteaux; Lieutenant Willamoze to shew where the pease are; and major of brigade, Skeene, will proportion out the quantity each regiment is to take, taking care that they pluck them properly, and to take none but what is fit to be gathered, and that they do not spoil them in gathering them. They are then to return altogether to camp; and the pease muste be equallie divided amongst the messes."

Similar parties were frequently sent out to obtain spruce for brewing beer for the army. Extract from general orders, August 6, 1759:

"An officer and fifty rangers to assemble at Gage's light infantry at five o'clock to-morrow morning. They will take six batteaux, and proceed two miles down the lake, where they will cut spruce. The officer will take the French prisoner who is on the general's guard, who will shew him where the spruce is; and a man who can talk German to the interpreter. A party of Gage's light infantry will go in the English boat to guard the batteaux. The officer will deliver the spruce under the care of the sergeant's guard at the fort."*

EXTRACTS FROM GENERAL ORDERS TO MAJOR ROGERS.

June 9. "Major Rogers will furnish forty men for a covering party."

June 17. "Major Rogers will take care the ground in front is clear;" meaning the ground where the provincials who were not marksmen were to fire five rounds each for practice, officers of their several regiments attending to see that the men leveled well.

June 20. "Major Rogers, with the rangers, and Major Gladwin, with Gage's light infantry, will form the advanced guard, and are to take great precautions in keeping out flanking parties to the left, as well as to the right."

June 22. "Major Rogers is on all detachments to take rank as major, according to the date of his commission as such, next after majors who have the king's commission, or one from his majesty's commander-in-chief."

June 25. "The three eldest companies of light infantry under Major Holmes, two hundred rangers and Indians under Major Rogers, the whole under the command of Colonel Haviland, to be ready to march when dark."

*Opposition writers for the British press, commenting upon the slow progress of General Amherst, insinuated "that if, instead of wasting so much time in gathering peas and brewing spruce beer, at Crown Point, he had advanced into Canada to coöperate with the expedition of the daring and heroic Wolfe, the campaign of 1759 would have terminated with the capitulation of Canada the same season which witnessed the surrender of Quebec.

July 16, 1759. "Eight of the provincial regiments are to give thirteen men each, and two of the provincial regiments fourteen men, for the ranging service; the men to be told they will be paid for it the difference between the provincial pay and that of the rangers. Commanding officers of those battalions to turn out all volunteers willing to serve in the rangers to-morrow morning at ten o'clock. Major Rogers will attend, and choose the number each regiment is to turn out of such volunteers."

July 18. "The men that have chose to serve with the rangers to join them this afternoon at five o'clock, and follow such orders as they shall receive from Major Rogers."

Ticonderoga, 25 July, 1759. "Sixty of Major Rogers' rangers will march with the commanding officer to the trenches this night, and will be employed at a proper time to alarm the enemy, by firing into their covered way, and keeping their attention from the workmen.

July 27. Major Rogers will send a company of rangers to-morrow morning, with all the boats, to the fort. The companies posted on the lake side from Colonel Haviland's corps will join their corps at reveille beating; after which Major Rogers will put trees across the foot path that has been made by the lake side. Major Rogers will receive his orders from the general. * * * Major Ord will send this night for the two twelve-pounders that are at Major Rogers' camp."

July 28. "The rangers will be posted beyond the saw-mills, on the right, as ordered by Major Rogers."

August 4. "Major Rogers is to send a sufficient party of men, with an officer, to take three batteaux to-morrow morning, very early, to Ticonderoga to apply to Serjeant Airy, who will load them with spruce beer, which they are immediately to bring to camp here."

July 5. "The camp not be alarmed by Major Rogers firing on the other side of the lake."

August 6. "Major Rogers to send a party of men, with an officer, to take two batteaux immediately to Ticonderoga, to apply to Serjeant Airy for spruce beer, which they are to load and bring to camp here without the loss of time." * * *

"Major Rogers will send one captain, two subalterns, and sixty men as a covering party, with some Indians, and an officer with them, to shew the commanding officer of the working party the best wood on the other side of the lake. The covering party must not fire any dropping shots at game."

"A captain and sixty rangers to set out to-morrow morning, at 5 o'clock, with six batteaux; Gage's light infantry will send at the same time the English boat to cover the batteaux, and the English boat to stay out till towards evening. The captain of the rangers will take out the French deserter from the general's guard, and must go to the place that the deserter will shew him; at which place the French have supplied themselves with spruce, and they must bring as much spruce to camp as they can."

August 10. "A detachment of two hundred rangers, and one hundred of Gage's light infantry, and one company of light infantry, and one of grenadiers, to assemble to-morrow, in their whale-boats, as soon as reveille is beat in the front of the fort. Gage's light infantry will be commanded by a captain and three subalterns, and are to take the two boats, with the three-pounders, and one boat, with a two-pounder. The whole must take one day's provision with them. Major Rogers will command the rangers; and the whole detachment is to be commanded by Lieut. Col. Darby, who will receive his orders from the general."

PUNISHMENTS INFLICTED DURING THE CAMPAIGN OF 1759.

	Shot or hanged.	Whipped.
May 29	3	0
June 14	1	5
" 28	0	1
July 13	1	0
" 19	0	7
August 2	2	3
" 8	0	1
" 14	0	2
October 4	1	1
	8	20

Commissary Wilson's Orderly Book.

THOMAS BURNSIDE.

THOMAS BURNSIDE was one of the celebrated corps of rangers whose exploits contributed a very important portion of materials for the history of the "seven years war" in America. If his majesty, Frederic of Prussia, acted during that war, in Europe, the part of general, as he may be considered, for his cousin and ally, George of England, humbler individuals in America were striving to attain the same object—that of humbling the power of France.

Among those individuals was Mr. Burnside. Although reported as wounded in the bloody skirmish near Ticonderoga, January 21, 1757, he volunteered, as an attendant of Lieutenant Stark, to convey the account of it to Fort William Henry, a distance of forty miles, and request sleighs to bring in the wounded.

After the peace of 1763, he settled at Stratford, in Coös county, N. H., and soon afterward that township contained two inhabitants—Mr. Burnside and his neighbor ———. The former, desirous of becoming one of his majesty's justices of the peace, inquired of the facetious Colonel Barr, of Londonderry, how he should proceed to obtain his commission. He advised him to procure a firkin of butter, and a piece of Londonderry linen, both of Scotch Irish manufacture, as presents to Governor Wentworth, and proceed to Portsmouth and make his application in person.

Accordingly, with his presents, he called upon Governor Wentworth, at his seat (Little Harbor), and preferred his request. The latter inquired how many inhabitants the township contained. Burnside replied, "Oh, only me and my neighbor, and we can not live any longer without a justice of the peace."

Amused by this most singular application, the governor inquired who was the most suitable person to be appointed. "Myself," was the reply; "for my neighbor is no more fit for it than the devil is." The commission was granted, and the new justice immediately qualified.

Observing, upon the side-board, several well filled decanters and glasses, Burnside said: "Suppose, when I get home, my neighbor should ask me what your excellency offered me to drink, what shall I tell him?" "Help yourself, Mr. Justice," replied the latter.

After refreshing himself with a glass of brandy and water, Burnside returned to his "White mountain" region, much gratified with his easily acquired official dignity, and with his first visit to the provincial capitol.

The foregoing is one instance of the system of bribery countenanced by and made a source of profit to the royal governors in their appointments and charters. In the grants of townships, the grantees invariably set off a liberal allowance of farm lots, for the governor, his secretary and treasurer, "to them and their heirs forever." The American revolution, however, a convulsion unanticipated and unprecedented in the history of the world, "indefinitely postponed" all these admirable schemes for future family wealth and power. Confiscation settled the account of most of these so easily obtained grants of land.

APPENDIX.

COLONEL PHILIP SKENE.

General Burgoyne could not have selected from his whole army an individual so capable of advising Colonels Baum and Breyman in their "Secret Expedition," as this brave and intelligent Scottish officer. The following notice of him is copied from a note in Commissary Wilson's orderly book:

Philip Skene was the grandson of John Skene, of Halyards, in Fifeshire, Scotland, and a descendant of the famous Sir William Wallace. He entered the army in 1739, in which year he served at Porto Bello,* and in 1740, at the reduction of Carthagena, on the Spanish Main.

He fought at the celebrated battle of Fontenoy, in 1745; in that of Culloden, in the year following, and was present at the battle of Laffeldt, under the Duke of Cumberland.

He came to America in 1756, and on the second of February, 1757, was promoted to a company in the 27th, or Inniskillen regiment of foot, which formed part of the force under Lord Loudoun's command that year. He was next engaged, under the command of Lord Howe, in the unfortunate attack on Ticonderoga, in 1758, on which occasion he was wounded; and on the 31st of July, 1759, appointed Major of Brigade by General Amherst.

In October following he was left in charge of Crown Point, the works of which he had orders to strengthen. His position at that fortress made him familiar with the surrounding country, and, encouraged by General Amherst, he projected a settlement at Wood Creek and South Bay, at the head of Lake Champlain, and in the prosecution of that design settled about thirty families there.

In 1762 he was ordered on the expedition against Martinico and Havana, and was one of the first to enter the breach at the storming of the Moro Castle. On his return to New-York, in 1763, he renewed his efforts to complete his settlement at Wood Creek. He went to England, and obtained a royal order for a considerable tract of land at that place, for which a patent was granted, in March, 1765, which was formed into a township under the name of Skenesborough. His regiment having been ordered to Ireland, Major Skene exchanged into the 10th Foot, in May, 1768, so as to remain in America. He did not continue long in the army, for he sold out in December of the following year, and in 1770 established his residence at Skenesborough, now White Hall, Washington county, New-York.

There he established forges for smelting iron, mills for sawing lumber, and opened a road to Salem and Bennington, which was afterward known as "Skene's road."

*** Porto Bello was captured by the English fleet, commanded by Admiral Vernon. Lawrence Washington, elder brother of General Washington, served on this occasion, as a midshipman of the British Navy. The family estate having descended to him, he called it "Mont-Vernon," in honor of his former commander.**

His plans were interrupted by the Revolution. In June, 1775, he was arrested at Philadelphia, and brought to New-York. Thence he was taken to Hartford. He was allowed to reside on parole at Middletown, Conn., but in May, of the following year, on refusing to renew his parole, was committed to prison. He was finally exchanged in October, 1776, when he was conveyed to the city of New-York, whence he sailed, in the beginning of 1777, for England. He volunteered to accompany Burgoyne the same year, and in August was ordered to attend Lieutenant Colonel Baum in his "Secret Expedition," which met with a disastrous defeat at the hands of General Stark, on the 16th of that month.

In this campaign Colonel Skene had his horse twice shot under him,* and was afterward made prisoner with Burgoyne's army. In 1779 he was attainted by the legislature of New-York.

After the war it was said Colonel Skene came over to this country during Governor Clinton's administration, and tried to recover his property; but, not succeeding, went back to England, where he lived in retirement, and died on the 9th of October, 1810, at an advanced age, at Addersey Lodge, near Stoke, Berks. In the obituary notice he is styled, "formerly Lieut. Governor of Crown Point and Ticonderoga, and Surveyor of His Majesty's woods and forests bordering on Lake Champlain."

MAJOR BENJAMIN WHITCOMB.

EXTRACT FROM AUNBURY'S LETTERS.

"I am most agreeably interrupted in my serious reflections, by a visit from our friend S., who is just arrived from New-York. He was taken prisoner last summer by a notorious fellow of the name of Whitcomb, the same who shot Brigadier General Gordon, the particulars of which I will inform you in my next.

MONTREAL, June 12, 1777.

My Dear Friend—In my last I mentioned to you the name of one Whitcomb, a native of Connecticut, and a great partisan of the Americans, who, after the defeat upon the lakes, offered his services to venture through the woods and bring in prisoner an English officer, for which purpose he stationed himself among the thickest copses that are between La Prairie and St. Johns. The first officer who happened to pass him was Brigadier General Gordon. He was mounted on a spirited horse, and Whitcomb, thinking there was little probability of seizing him, fired at and wounded him in the shoulder. The General rode as fast as he could to camp, which he had but just reached, when, with loss of blood and fatigue, he fell from his horse. Some soldiers took him up and carried him to the hospital, where, after his wound was dressed, he related the circumstances, which were immediately made known to General Carleton.

* He narrowly escaped being captured at Bennington. A soldier of the New-Hampshire line stated that, observing a mounted officer actively engaged in cheering on the troops of Colonel Breyman, he fired at him twice, but only killed his horse; that he then cut the traces of an artillery horse, mounted, and rode off at full speed. He learned afterward that the officer was Colonel Skene.

A party of Indians were sent out to scour the woods and search for Whitcomb, but in vain, as he hastened back to Ticonderoga. General Carleton, however, imagining he might be lurking in the woods, or secreted in the house of some disaffected Canadian, issued a proclamation among the inhabitants, offering a reward of fifty guineas to any one that would bring in Whitcomb, dead or alive, to the camp. A few days after this General Gordon died of his wound, in whose death we sincerely lamented the loss of a brave and experienced officer.

When Whitcomb returned to Ticonderoga and informed the General who commanded there, that, although he could not take an officer, he believed he had mortally wounded one, the General expressed his disapprobation in the highest terms, and was so displeased at the transaction that Whitcomb, in order to effect a reconciliation, offered his service to go again, professing that he would forfeit his life if he did not return with a prisoner.

He accordingly, with two other men, proceeded down Lake Champlain in a canoe to a small creek, where they secreted it, and repaired to the woods, to the same spot where Whitcomb had stationed himself before. The two men lay concealed in the wood, while he skulked about the borders of it.

The regiment of which our friend S—— is Quarter Master, having occasion for some stores from Montreal, he was going from the camp at St. Johns to procure them. He was advised not to go this road, but by way of Chamblee, on account of the late accident; but you know him to be a man of great bravery and personal courage, joined with uncommon strength, and he resolved not to go so many miles out of his way for any Whitcomb whatever. He jocosely remarked that he should be very glad to meet him, as he was sure he should get the reward.

In this, however, he was greatly mistaken, his reward being no other than that of being taken prisoner himself.

Previous to his setting out he took every precaution, having not only loaded his fusee, but charged a brace of pistols. When he came near to the woods I have already described, he was very cautious; but in an instant Whitcomb and the two men he had with him sprang from behind a thick bush, and seized him before he could make the least resistance. They then took from him his fusee and pistols, tied his hands behind him with ropes, and blind-folded him.

It was three days before they reached the canoe that had been concealed, during which time they had but very scanty fare. A few hard biscuits served to allay hunger, while the fruits of the woods were a luxury. When Whitcomb had marched him to such a distance as he thought he could not make his escape, were he at liberty, through fear of losing himself, for the greater ease on his own part, and to facilitate their march, they untied his hands and took the cloth from his eyes. Only picture to yourself what must have been his feelings, at seeing himself in the midst of a thick wood, surrounded by three desperate fellows, and uncertain as to their intentions!

At night, when they had partaken of their scanty pittance, two of them used to sleep, while the other kept watch. The first night he slept, through fatigue. On the second, as you may naturally suppose, from his great anxiety of mind, he could not close his eyes; in the middle of which an opportunity occurred whereby he could have effected his escape, for the man whose watch it was fell fast asleep.

He has since told me that his mind wavered for a length of time, what measures to pursue. He could not bear the idea of putting them to death, though justified by the rules of war. If he escaped from them, they might, in all probability, retake and ill treat him.

The greatest hazard of all, which determined him to abide by his fate, was, that being so many miles in a tract of wood where he could not tell what direction to take, having been blind-folded when he entered it. He might possibly wander up and down until he perished with hunger. In this restless state he remained till day-break, when they resumed their march; and in the evening came to the creek where the canoe was concealed. They then secured him again, put him into the canoe, and proceeded up the lake to Ticonderoga, where they arrived early the next morning.

When they landed he was again blind-folded, that he might not see their works, and thus conducted to the General, whose only motive for endeavoring to get an officer was, either by threats or entreaties, to gain information relative to our army. In this, however, he was greatly disappointed, as he could not obtain the least intelligence from our friend."

In regard to the case of General Gordon, Wilkinson states, pp. 67, 68, 69, 70:

"In this place the reader may not be dissatisfied with a particular narrative of an adventure. * * * * * * I shall now give the details from my own knowledge, and the information of the partisan.

Lieut. Whitcomb, of Warner's regiment, an unlettered child of the woods from the frontier of the Hampshire Grants, with all the little strategy of an Indian, and a dauntless heart, had been selected for the service, and sent into Canada before Gen. Gates' arrival, to take a prisoner for the purpose of intelligence. Being well acquainted with his business, he chose one man only for the companion of his enterprise, who, he informed me, either deserted him, or got lost before he reached the ultimate point of his march.

Proceeding down the west side of Lake Champlain, Whitcomb turned St. Johns on his right, and, approaching Chamblee late in the night, unintentionally crept within the chain of sentinels of a newly formed encampment. He was hailed, and found himself surrounded before he discovered his situation. The ground had not been cleared, and the surface was thickly covered with the sprouts of the scrubby oak, or black jack, little more than knee high. Encircled and closely pressed by the soldiery in quest of him, who, in the dark, were scattered in every direction, his immediate escape became impracticable. In this extremity he prostrated himself among the bushes, and distinctly heard the observations and inquiries of his pursuers respecting him. Turning on his back, with his knife, he cut detached twigs, which he found within his reach, and sticking them carelessly in the ground around him, before day, his person was concealed; and in this *position he continued motionless until the following night*, when he made his escape by crawling on the earth.

He informed me that in the course of the day the soldiery passed and repassed within six feet of him, and an officer very nearly rode over him; but the greatest danger of his being discovered arose from the clearing of the ground, which was pushed within twenty feet of him, the next day, when the retreat called off the fatigue.

Having regained the forest, Whitcomb concealed himself a few days until the alarm he had occasioned subsided. He then ambuscaded the road leading from Chamblee to St. Johns, at a point from whence his eye commanded an extensive view up and down. Here he expected to intercept some unsuspicious passenger.

The hard fortune of Brigadier-General Gordon, of the British army, led him the same morning to take a solitary ride, and his approach was discovered by Whitcomb soon after he had taken his stand. The General was in full uniform; his epaulets rich; he might have a gold watch and money about him, and he appeared to be a great chief.

The time for our partisan's return was at hand, and it was uncertain whether he could make a prisoner; and if he did, it would be difficult to conduct him in. This reasoning was too powerful for Whitcomb's sense of morals and humanity. He determined to disobey his orders and marked his victim.

The road brought Gordon within thirty feet of Whitcomb's ambuscade. He presented, took aim, and covered his object, and kept his sight on him until he got a side view of his back. He then fired, and the ball took effect under the right shoulder blade; but the wound, though mortal, did not produce sudden death, and the General's horse carried him into St. Johns, where he soon after expired. *Thus the assassin missed his spoil!!!*

That Whitcomb believed he was performing a meritorious act, is clearly evinced by his reporting it with exultation; for it would otherwise have been impossible ever to have convicted him of it. In speaking of the adventure, he gave me the preceding detail, and added that he "*lost his object by shooting a little too high, owing to the accidental intervention of a fluttering leaf, in the instant he pulled trigger.*"

This abominable outrage on the customs of war and the laws of humanity, produced a sensation of strong disgust in the army, and men of sensibility and honor did not conceal their abhorrence of its perpetrator. Yet it was impossible, in the temper of the times, to bring him to punishment, without disaffecting the fighting men on that whole frontier.* But if he could not be punished consistently with sound policy, his promotion to a Majority the ensuing winter not only sanctioned the murder but rewarded the murderer. Such are the demoralizing effects of war, and more particularly of a civil war.—*Wilk.*, vol. 1, p. 67.

Wilkinson himself, afterward, thus speaks of this partisan: "Whitcomb returned from Split Rock last night, and confutes the intelligence transmitted you by General ———. He says there is only a schooner in that quarter of the Lake, and she lies off Otter Creek.—*Wilk.*, vol. 1, p. 171.

In regard to this matter, Major Caleb Stark, from whom General Wilkinson received much information for his memoirs, stated that he was present at Headquarters, being then adjutant of a regiment at Mount Independence, when Whitcomb returned and gave an account of his scout. He said that Whitcomb reported the circumstances partly as they are published by Wilkinson; and said that he knew it was a field officer he had fired at, because he had two epaulets; and that two officers rode in his rear, who dismounted and gave him chase.

The American General inquired if he *killed the man* at whom he fired. He said "his gun never had deceived him when aimed at a deer; but as a leaf came in the way of his sight as he fired, he could not be positive; but was sure he struck him, as he saw him quiver about the shoulders."

A flag of truce soon afterward came from the enemy, demanding the delivery up of Whitcomb. But the American General answered, in substance, that if the British employed Indians to waylay, murder, and scalp Americans, they might reasonably expect retaliation. Major Whitcomb was one of the most active and efficient partisans who served under the orders of General Stark, where, in 1778, he commanded the Northern Department, and is mentioned in several of his letters.

General Wilkinson terms him an "unlettered child of the woods." The copy of a letter from Whitcomb, which follows this notice, (the original written in a very plain, legible hand,) indicates that his acquirements were far above those we might expect to find in "an unlettered child of the woods."

We know nothing of his birth or place of residence, or any particulars respecting Major Whitcomb, other than those contained in the above statements.

TO BRIGADIER GENERAL STARK.

BENNINGTON, Sept. 14, 1778.

Dear General:—I forwarded the ammunition from Albany, agreeably to your orders. It has arrived thus far, but by what means I shall be able to transport it to Rutland, I know not, as the Quarter-Master at this place utterly refuses to receipt for said ammunition to him who has charge of the same. I am, therefore, under the disagreeable necessity of delaying my time here, until I can see it forwarded in person.

If such conduct is allowed to pass unnoticed, I see but a poor prospect of prosecuting your orders, on the duty of my office. The tools which I am in immediate want of, for the service of the fort, are still at the shore in this place, and there they must lie, until I receive farther assistance from the Quarter-Master's Department than I now have.

The General's orders for my conduct in this situation will greatly oblige him who is

Your very obedient and very humble servant,

BENJAMIN WHITCOMB.

* General W. here insinuates that the object of the American partisan was plunder. We have no reason to believe that such was the case, except from General W.'s declaration.

REV. THOMAS ALLEN.

Thomas Allen was born at Northampton, Mass., Jan. 7, 1743, and graduated at Harvard College in 1762, being ranked among the first classical scholars of that time. He studied theology under the direction of Mr. Hooker, of Northampton, and was ordained, April 18, 1764, the first minister of Pittsfield, Berkshire County, Massachusetts, which was named in honor of William Pitt, and was then a frontier town, in which a garrison had been kept during the French War. The Indian name was Pontoosuc. At the time of Mr. Allen's settlement, Pittsfield contained but six houses not built of logs. He lived to see it become a wealthy and beautiful town, containing nearly three thousand inhabitants.

He espoused the cause of his country in the Revolution with ardent zeal, and twice went out as a volunteer chaplain. From October 3 until January 23, 1776, he was with the army at White Plains, and in June and July, 1777, at Ticonderoga. After the retreat of the northern army from that post he returned home.

Upon the approach of the enemy under Col. Baum to the vicinity of Bennington, who threatened to desolate the country, he marched with the Pittsfield volunteers to repel the invasion. Prior to the assault of the intrenchments occupied by the refugees, he advanced, and in a voice which they distinctly heard, called upon them to surrender, promising good treatment; but, being fired upon, he rejoined the militia, and was among the foremost who entered the breastwork. His exertions and example contributed to the triumph of August 16, which checked the enemy's progress, and led the way to the capture of Burgoyne.

After the action he secured the horse of a Hessian surgeon, which carried a pair of panniers filled with bottles of wine. The wine he administered to the wounded and weary; but two large, square, glass case bottles he carried home, as trophies of his campaign of four days.

During Shay's Rebellion, Mr. Allen supported the State authorities, and the insurgents, at one period, threatened to seize and convey him as a hostage into the State of New-York. His intrepidity was, however, not to be shaken, nor was he deterred from the performance of his duty to his country. He slept with arms in his bed room, ready to defend himself against the violence of lawless men.

In the political controversy which followed the adoption of the federal constitution, Mr. Allen's principles attached him to the Democratic, or Republican party. Among his parishioners were several who had been tories in the Revolutionary War, who remembered, with no good will, the active zeal of their whig minister. Others were furious politicians, deeply imbued with the malevolent spirit of the times, and intent upon the accomplishment of their object, even by using the weapons of obloquy and outrage.

"During the Presidency of Mr. Jefferson," says the History of Berkshire, "that spirit of political rancor that affected every class of citizens in this country, arraying fathers, brothers, sons and neighbors against each other, entered even the sanctuary of the church. A number of Mr. Allen's church and congregation withdrew, and were incorporated, by the legislature, into a separate parish, in 1808, thus presenting to the world the ridiculous spectacle of a church divided on party politics, and known by the party names of the day."

This division was, however, healed in a few years, though not until after the death of him whose last days were thus embittered, as well as by domestic afflictions, in the loss of his eldest son and daughter.

After the death of his brother Moses, in 1779, he performed a journey to Savannah, on horse back, to remove his widow and infant son from the South, where the war then raged, to the happy security, for the time, of his own home. To bring home to his family an infant child of his daughter, who died in London, in 1799, he encountered the dangers of a voyage across the Atlantic.

He sailed in the ship Argo, Captain Rich. On the voyage, fears were awakened by a vessel of force, which pursued the Argo, and was supposed to be a French ship of war. The idea of a French prison was by no means welcome. In expectation of a fight, Mr. Allen obtained the captain's consent to offer a prayer with the men, and to make an encouraging speech to them before the action. The stranger proved to be a British frigate, and the deliverance was acknowledged in a thanksgiving prayer.

On his arrival in London he was received with great kindness by his friends, Mr. Robert Cowie and Mr. Robert Steele, and was made acquainted with several of the distinguished evangelical ministers of England: with Newton and Hawies, Rowland Hill, Bogue and others, from whom he caught a pious zeal for the promotion of foreign missions, which, on his return, he diffused around him. It appears, from his journal, that he was absent from Pittsfield from July 3d to December 30, 1799.

Among other objects of curiosity which attracted his attention in London, he saw the king, as he passed from St. James to the Parliament house, in a coach drawn by six cream-colored horses, and on this sight recorded the following reflections: "This is he who desolated my country; who ravaged the American coasts; annihilated our trade; burned our towns; plundered our cities; sent forth his Indian allies to scalp our wives and children; starved our youth in his prison ships, and caused the expenditure of a hundred millions of money, and a hundred thousand of precious lives. Instead of being the father of his people, he has been their destroyer. May God forgive him so great guilt. And yet, he is the idol of the people, who think they cannot live without him."

The late gallant Major General E. W. Ripley married a daughter of Mr. Allen, who died, September 11, 1820, at the Bay of St. Louis. Mr. Allen died Sabbath morning, February 11, 1810, in the 68th year of his age and the 47th of his ministry.

This notice has been obtained principally from President Allen's Biographical Dictionary, which contains many interesting particulars respecting this exemplary clergyman, and ever to be honored patriot of the Revolution.

GENERAL MOSES NICHOLS.

[Copied from Farmer's History of Amherst.]

" *May* 23, 1790. General Moses Nichols died at Amherst. He was a native of Reading, Mass. He had served his townsmen in the capacity of delegate to the Convention, which assembled in 1778, for forming a permanent plan or system of government, on certain established principles, and a representative to the General Court three years. Ardently attached to the cause of Liberty, he took a conspicuous part in the Revolution which established our independence.

He was appointed Colonel of the Sixth Regiment of Militia, December 6, 1776, and commanded a regiment under General Stark, in the engagement at Bennington. Beside his military services, he was useful as a physician in this place (Amherst), where he practiced several years.

He was Register of Deeds for the county from 1766 until his death. His duties in this office, as well as in many others of trust and responsibility, it is believed he discharged with fidelity.

General Nichols left nine children: Hannah, Moses, Elizabeth, Eaton, Perkins,* Mary, Pearson, and Charity. Moses is a physician, and resides in Sherbrooke, Lower Canada."

* Some forty-five years ago Perkins Nichols was a well known, enterprising citizen of Boston; also in New-York, in 1825.

FULLNAME AND SUBJECT INDEX

The reader is reminded that General Stark's Correspondence is indexed on pages *v-vii*. In an effort to reduce redundant entries, the indexer has omitted all instances where General Stark's name appears as his signature in the correspondence. His name has been indexed in the correspondence section only when he is mentioned by someone else. The indexer has made a sincere effort to select the most important names and events for this index, without making it cumbersome. Selected subjects have been arranged chronologically to enhance the use of the index.